AUTOMOTIVE HEATING AND AIR CONDITIONING

SEVENTH EDITION

James D. Halderman

Tom Birch

PEARSON

Boston   Columbus   Indianapolis   New York   San Francisco   Hoboken
Amsterdam   Cape Town   Dubai   London   Madrid   Milan   Munich   Paris   Montréal   Toronto
Delhi   Mexico City   São Paulo   Sydney   Hong Kong   Seoul   Singapore   Taipei   Tokyo

Product Manager: Lindsey Prudhomme Gill
Program Manager: Holly Shufeldt
Project Manager: Rex Davidson
Editorial Assistant: Nancy Kesterson
Team Lead Project Manager: JoEllen Gohr
Team Lead Program Manager: Laura Weaver
Director of Marketing: David Gesell
Senior Marketing Coordinator: Stacey Martinez

Senior Marketing Assistant: Les Roberts
Procurement Specialist: Deidra M. Skahill
Media Project Manager: Noelle Chun
Media Project Coordinator: April Cleland
Cover Designer: Cenveo Publisher Services
Creative Director: Andrea Nix
Art Director: Diane Y. Ernsberger
Full-Service Project Management and Composition: Integra Software Services, Ltd.
Printer/Binder: R.R. Donnelley & Sons
Cover Printer: Phoenix Color Corp.

Copyright © 2015 by Pearson Education, Inc. All rights reserved. Manufactured in the United States of America. This publication is protected by Copyright, and permission should be obtained from the publisher prior to any prohibited reproduction, storage in a retrieval system, or transmission in any form or by any means, electronic, mechanical, photocopying, recording, or likewise. To obtain permission(s) to use material from this work, please submit a written request to Pearson Education, Inc., Permissions Department, 221 River Street, Hoboken, New Jersey 07030, or you may fax your request to 201-236-3290.

Many of the designations by manufacturers and sellers to distinguish their products are claimed as trademarks. Where those designations appear in this book, and the publisher was aware of a trademark claim, the designations have been printed in initial caps or all caps.

Library of Congress Cataloging-in-Publication Data

Halderman, James D.
  [Automotive heating and air conditioning]
  Automotive heating and air conditioning/James Halderman, Tom Birch.—Seventh edition.
    pages cm
  Rev. ed. of: Automotive heating and air conditioning/Tom Birch. 2012.
  Includes index.
  ISBN 978-0-13-351499-5 (alk. paper)—ISBN 0-13-351499-4 (alk. paper) 1. Automobiles—Heating and ventilation. 2. Automobiles—Air conditioning. I. Birch, Thomas W. (Thomas Wesley), II. Birch, Thomas W. (Thomas Wesley), Automotive heating and air conditioning. III. Title.
  TL271.B57 2015
  629.2'772—dc23

                                                          2014012799

10 9 8 7 6 5 4 3 2

ISBN 10:   0-13-351499-4
ISBN 13: 978-0-13-351499-5

PREFACE

PROFESSIONAL TECHNICIAN SERIES Part of the Pearson Automotive Professional Technician Series, the seventh edition of *Automotive Heating and Air Conditioning* represents the future of automotive textbooks. The series is a full-color, media-integrated solution for today's students and instructors. The series includes textbooks that cover all eight areas of ASE certification, plus additional titles covering common courses. The series is peer reviewed for technical accuracy.

UPDATES TO THE SEVENTH EDITION Based on comments and suggestions from instructors throughout the country, the following changes have been made to the new seventh edition:

- New full-color design makes it easier to read.
- All new full-color line drawings and photos throughout to help bring the subject to life.
- Many new or extensively updated chapters on heating and air-conditioning systems.
- A new chapter covering A/C compressors and compressor service all in one chapter (Chapter 5).
- A new chapter covering all aspects of automatic temperature control systems added (Chapter 12).
- Another new chapter on hybrid electric vehicle heating and A/C systems (Chapter 13) added.
- All chapters updated with the latest technology.
- New questions at the end of the chapters (both review questions and chapter quizzes).
- More concisely written to make teaching and learning easier.
- Two new appendixes. Sample ASE certification test (Appendix 1) and NATEF correlation chart (Appendix 2).

- Unlike other textbooks, this book is written so that the theory, construction, diagnosis, and service of a particular component or system are presented in one location. There is no need to search the entire book for other references to the same topic.

ASE AND NATEF CORRELATED NATEF certified programs need to demonstrate that they use course material that covers NATEF and ASE tasks. All Professional Technician textbooks have been correlated to the appropriate ASE and NATEF task lists. These correlations can be found in Appendix 2.

A COMPLETE INSTRUCTOR AND STUDENT SUPPLEMENTS PACKAGE All Professional Technician textbooks are accompanied by a full set of instructor and student supplements. Please see page vi for a detailed list of supplements.

A FOCUS ON DIAGNOSIS AND PROBLEM SOLVING The Professional Technician Series has been developed to satisfy the need for a greater emphasis on problem diagnosis. Automotive instructors and service managers agree that students and beginning technicians need more training in diagnostic procedures and skill development. To meet this need and demonstrate how real-world problems are solved, "Real World Fix" features are included throughout and highlight how real-life problems are diagnosed and repaired.

The following pages highlight the unique core features that set the Professional Technician Series book apart from other automotive textbooks.

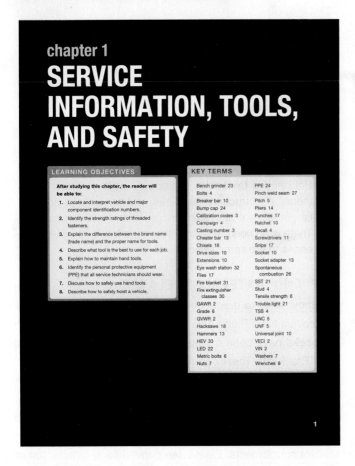

chapter 1
SERVICE INFORMATION, TOOLS, AND SAFETY

LEARNING OBJECTIVES

After studying this chapter, the reader will be able to:

1. Locate and interpret vehicle and major component identification numbers.
2. Identify the strength ratings of threaded fasteners.
3. Explain the difference between the brand name (trade name) and the proper name for tools.
4. Describe what tool is the best to use for each job.
5. Explain how to maintain hand tools.
6. Identify the personal protective equipment (PPE) that all service technicians should wear.
7. Discuss how to safely use hand tools.
8. Describe how to safely hoist a vehicle.

KEY TERMS

Bench grinder 23
Bolts 4
Breaker bar 10
Bump cap 24
Calibration codes 3
Campaign 4
Casting number 3
Cheater bar 13
Chisels 18
Drive sizes 10
Extensions 10
Eye wash station 32
Files 17
Fire blanket 31
Fire extinguisher classes 30
GAWR 2
Grade 6
GVWR 2
Hacksaws 18
Hammers 13
HEV 33
LED 22
Metric bolts 6
Nuts 7

PPE 24
Pinch weld seam 27
Pitch 5
Pliers 14
Punches 17
Ratchet 10
Recall 4
Screwdrivers 11
Snips 17
Socket 10
Socket adapter 13
Spontaneous combustion 26
SST 21
Stud 4
Tensile strength 6
Trouble light 21
TSB 4
UNC 5
UNF 5
Universal joint 10
VECI 2
VIN 2
Washers 7
Wrenches 8

1

LEARNING OBJECTIVES AND KEY TERMS appear at the beginning of each chapter to help students and instructors focus on the most important material in each chapter. The chapter objectives are based on specific ASE and NATEF tasks.

 TECH TIP

It Just Takes a Second

Whenever removing any automotive component, it is wise to screw the bolts back into the holes a couple of threads by hand. This ensures that the right bolt will be used in its original location when the component or part is put back on the vehicle.

TECH TIPS feature real-world advice and "tricks of the trade" from ASE-certified master technicians.

 SAFETY TIP

Shop Cloth Disposal

Always dispose of oily shop cloths in an enclosed container to prevent a fire. ● **SEE FIGURE 1–69.** Whenever oily cloths are thrown together on the floor or workbench, a chemical reaction can occur, which can ignite the cloth even without an open flame. This process of ignition without an open flame is called **spontaneous combustion**.

SAFETY TIPS alert students to possible hazards on the job and how to avoid them.

 REAL WORLD FIX

Cabin Filter Fault

The owner of a 2008 Ford Escape complained that the air-conditioning system was not cooling the inside of the vehicle and there seemed to be no airflow from the dash vents yet the blower motor could be heard running. A quick visual inspection of the cabin air with access under the hood showed that the cabin filter was almost completely blocked with paper, leaves, and debris. The vehicle had almost 80,000 miles on the odometer and the way it looked, the air filter had never been replaced. Most vehicle manufacturers recommend replacement of the cabin air filter about every three years or every 36,000 miles. Replacing the cabin air filter restored proper operation of the A/C system.

REAL WORLD FIXES present students with actual automotive scenarios and show how these common (and sometimes uncommon) problems were diagnosed and repaired.

 FREQUENTLY ASKED QUESTION

How Many Types of Screw Heads Are Used in Automotive Applications?

There are many, including Torx, hex (also called Allen), plus many others used in custom vans and motor homes. ● **SEE FIGURE 1–9.**

FREQUENTLY ASKED QUESTIONS are based on the author's own experience and provide answers to many of the most common questions asked by students and beginning service technicians.

NOTE: Most of these "locking nuts" are grouped together and are commonly referred to as *prevailing torque nuts*. This means that the nut will hold its tightness or torque and not loosen with movement or vibration.

NOTES provide students with additional technical information to give them a greater understanding of a specific task or procedure.

CAUTION: *Never* use hardware store (nongraded) bolts, studs, or nuts on any vehicle steering, suspension, or brake component. Always use the exact size and grade of hardware that is specified and used by the vehicle manufacturer.

CAUTIONS alert students about potential damage to the vehicle that can occur during a specific task or service procedure.

☠ **WARNING**

Do not use incandescent trouble lights around gasoline or other flammable liquids. The liquids can cause the bulb to break and the hot filament can ignite the flammable liquid, which can cause personal injury or even death.

WARNINGS alert students to potential dangers to themselves during a specific task or service procedure.

SUMMARY

1. Bolts, studs, and nuts are commonly used as fasteners in the chassis. The sizes for fractional and metric threads are different and are not interchangeable. The grade is the rating of the strength of a fastener.
2. Whenever a vehicle is raised above the ground, it must be supported at a substantial section of the body or frame.
3. Wrenches are available in open end, box end, and combination open and box end.
4. An adjustable wrench should only be used where the proper size is not available.
5. Line wrenches are also called flare-nut wrenches, fitting wrenches, or tube-nut wrenches and are used to remove fuel or refrigerant lines.
6. Sockets are rotated by a ratchet or breaker bar, also called a flex handle.
7. Torque wrenches measure the amount of torque applied to a fastener.
8. Screwdriver types include straight blade (flat tip) and Phillips.
9. Hammers and mallets come in a variety of sizes and weights.
10. Pliers are a useful tool and are available in many different types, including slip-joint, multigroove, linesman's, diagonal, needle-nose, and locking pliers.
11. Other common hand tools include snap-ring pliers, files, cutters, punches, chisels, and hacksaws.
12. Hybrid electric vehicles should be de-powered if any of the high-voltage components are going to be serviced.

REVIEW QUESTIONS

1. List three precautions that must be taken whenever hoisting (lifting) a vehicle.
2. Describe how to determine the grade of a fastener, including how the markings differ between fractional and metric bolts.
3. List four items that are personal protective equipment (PPE).
4. List the types of fire extinguishers and their usage.
5. Why are wrenches offset 15 degrees?
6. What are the other names for a line wrench?
7. What are the standard automotive drive sizes for sockets?
8. Which type of screwdriver requires the use of a hammer or mallet?
9. What is inside a dead-blow hammer?
10. What type of cutter is available in left and right cutters?

CHAPTER QUIZ

1. The correct location for the pads when hoisting or jacking the vehicle can often be found in the _____.
   a. Service manual
   b. Shop manual
   c. Owner's manual
   d. All of the above
2. For the best working position, the work should be _____.
   a. At neck or head level
   b. At knee or ankle level
   c. Overhead by about 1 foot
   d. At chest of elbow level
3. A high-strength bolt is identified by _____.
   a. A UNC symbol
   b. Lines on the head
   c. Strength letter codes
   d. The coarse threads
4. A fastener that uses threads on both ends is called a _____.
   a. Cap screw
   b. Stud
   c. Machine screw
   d. Crest fastener
5. When working with hand tools, always _____.
   a. Push the wrench—don't pull toward you
   b. Pull a wrench—don't push a wrench away from you
6. The proper term for Channel Locks is _____.
   a. Vise Grips
   b. Crescent wrench
   c. Locking pliers
   d. Multigroove adjustable pliers
7. The proper term for Vise Grips is _____.
   a. Locking pliers
   b. Slip-joint pliers
   c. Side cuts
   d. Multigroove adjustable pliers

THE SUMMARY, REVIEW QUESTIONS, AND CHAPTER QUIZ at the end of each chapter help students review the material presented in the chapter and test themselves to see how much they've learned.

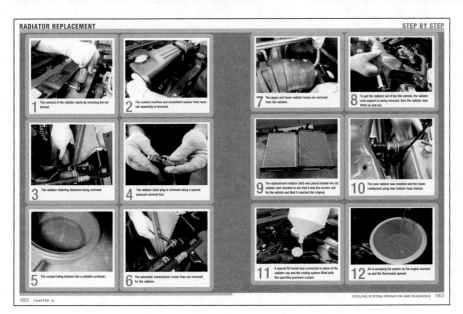

RADIATOR REPLACEMENT   STEP BY STEP

1. The removal of the radiator starts by removing the fan shroud.
2. The coolant overflow and windshield washer fluid reservoir assembly is removed.
3. The radiator retaining fasteners being removed.
4. The radiator drain plug is removed using a special peacock removal tool.
5. The coolant being drained into a suitable container.
6. The automatic transmission cooler lines are removed for the radiator.
7. The upper and lower radiator hoses are removed from the radiator.
8. To get the radiator out of the this vehicle, the radiator core support is being removed, then the radiator was lifted up and out.
9. The replacement radiator (left) was placed beside the old radiator and checked to see that it was the correct unit for the vehicle and that it matched the original.
10. The new radiator was installed and the hoses reattached using new radiator hose clamps.
11. A special fill funnel was connected in place of the radiator cap and the cooling system filled with the specified premixed coolant.
12. Air is escaping the system as the engine warmed up and the thermostat opened.

182 CHAPTER 10   COOLING SYSTEM OPERATION AND DIAGNOSIS 183

STEP-BY-STEP photo sequences show in detail the steps involved in performing a specific task or service procedure.

RESOURCES IN PRINT AND ONLINE
Automotive Heating and Air Conditioning

NAME OF SUPPLEMENT	PRINT	ONLINE	AUDIENCE	DESCRIPTION
Instructor Resource Manual 0133515362		✔	Instructors	NEW! The Ultimate teaching aid: Chapter summaries, key terms, chapter learning objectives, lecture resources, discuss/demonstrate classroom activities, and answers to the in text review and quiz questions.
TestGen 0133515389		✔	Instructors	Test generation software and test bank for the text.
PowerPoint Presentation 0133515397		✔	Instructors	Slides include chapter learning objectives, lecture outline of the test, and graphics from the book.
Image Bank 0133515079		✔	Instructors	All of the images and graphs from the textbook to create customized lecture slides.
NATEF Correlated Task Sheets – for instructors 0133515087		✔	Instructors	Downloadable NATEF task sheets for easy customization and development of unique task sheets.
NATEF Task Sheets – For Students 0133515354	✔		Students	Study activity manual that correlates NATEF Automobile Standards to chapters and pages numbers in the text. Available to students at a discounted price when packaged with the text.
CourseSmart eText 0133515109		✔	Students	An alternative to purchasing the print textbook, students can subscribe to the same content online and save up to 50% off the suggested list price of the print text. Visit **www.coursesmart.com**

All online resources can be downloaded from the Instructor's Resource Center: **www.pearsonhighered.com/irc**

ACKNOWLEDGMENTS

A large number of people and organizations have cooperated in providing the reference material and technical information used in this text. The authors wish to express sincere thanks to the following organizations for their special contributions:

American Honda
Bill Steen, Yuba College
David Brainerd, Santa Barbara City College
Fluke Corporation
Four Seasons
Frank Allison, International Mobile Air Conditioning Association (IMACA), Executive Director
Frederick Peacock, Purdue University
General Motors Corporation
Harold Beck, Yuba City
James Johnson, Four Seasons
Lorie Homolish Apollo America Corporation
Martin Duvic, Louisiana Technical College
Mastercool
Modine Manufacturing
Nartron Corp. /Smart Power Products
Neutronics Inc.
Patrick L. O'Conner, Fedco Automotive Components
Paul De Guiseppi, Mobile Air Conditioning Society (MACS)
Raytek Corp.
Red Dot Corp.
Robert Bassett, The Gates Rubber Company
Robinaire Division, SPX Corporation
Sanden International (USA)
Santech Industries
Simon Oulouhojian, Past President Mobile Air Conditioning Society (MACS)
Society of Automotive Engineers (SAE)
Stant Manufacturing
System Guard
Tom Broxholm, Skyline College
Tony Jewel, Reedley College
Toyota Motor Sales, USA

TECHNICAL AND CONTENT REVIEWERS The following people reviewed the manuscript before production and checked it for technical accuracy and clarity of presentation. Their suggestions and recommendations were included in the final draft of the manuscript. Their input helped make this textbook clear and technically accurate while maintaining the easy-to-read style that has made other books from the same authors so popular.

Tom Broxholm
Skyline College

Ron Chappell
Santa Fe Community College

Curtis Cline
Wharton County Junior College

Matt Dixon
Southern Illinois University

Kenneth P. Dytrt
Pennsylvania College of Technology

Curtis Happe
Richland Community College

Chris Holley
Penn College Professor

Paul Hye
Brookdale Community College

Dr. David Gilbert
Southern Illinois University

Richard Krieger
Michigan Institute of Technology

Russell A. Leonard
Ferris State University

William Milam
Eastfield College

Justin Morgan
Sinclair Community College

Greg Pfahl
Miami-Jacobs Career College

Steve Polley
Pittsburg State University

Jeff Rehkopf
Florida State College

Michael Reimer
South Plains College

Scott Russell
Blue Ridge Community College

Eugene Talley
Southern Illinois University

Chuck Taylor
Sinclair Community College

Omar Trinidad
Southern Illinois University

Ken Welch
Saddleback College

Special thanks to instructional designer **Alexis I. Skriloff James.**

PHOTO SEQUENCES The authors wish to thank Chuck Taylor of Sinclair Community College in Dayton, Ohio, plus Greg Pfahl and James (Mike) Watson who helped with many of the photos. A special thanks to Randal Sedwick, Dick Krieger, Jeff Rehkopf, and Eugene Talley for their detailed and thorough review of the manuscript before publication and to Richard Reaves for all of his help. Most of all, we wish to thank Michelle Halderman for her assistance in all phases of manuscript preparation.

James D. Halderman
Tom Birch

JAMES D. HALDERMAN Jim Halderman brings a world of experience, knowledge, and talent to his work. His automotive service experience includes working as a flat-rate technician, a business owner, and a professor of automotive technology at a leading U.S. community college for more than 20 years.

He has a Bachelor of Science degree from Ohio Northern University and a Master's degree in Education from Miami University in Oxford, Ohio. Jim also holds a U.S. patent for an electronic transmission control device. He is an ASE-certified Master Automotive Technician and Advanced Engine Performance (L1) ASE certified. Jim is the author of many automotive textbooks, all published by Pearson. Jim has presented numerous technical seminars to national audiences, including the California Automotive Teachers (CAT) and the Illinois College Automotive Instructor Association (ICAIA). He is also a member and presenter at the North American Council of Automotive Teachers (NACAT). Jim was also named Regional Teacher of the Year by General Motors Corporation and an outstanding alumnus of Ohio Northern University. Jim and his wife, Michelle, live in Dayton, Ohio. They have two children. You can reach Jim at:

jim@jameshalderman.com

TOM BIRCH Tom Birch started his automotive service career working as a service technician at a Ford dealership. Then, while in the army, he was a wheel vehicle mechanic and worked as a technician on army vehicles when stationed in Europe. He earned his Bachelor's and Master's degrees from Chico State College, now California State University, Chico, and taught in the California school system before going to Yuba College in Northern California. Tom is past president and board member of the California Automotive Teachers (CAT), plus a member and winner of the MVP award of the North American Council of Automotive Teachers (NACAT). He is also a member of the Mobile Air Conditioning Society (MACS), Automotive Service Council California (ASC-CA), and the Society of Automotive Engineers (SAE). Tom is the author of many automotive textbooks, all published by Pearson.

BRIEF CONTENTS

CONTENTS

LEARNING OBJECTIVES

After studying this chapter, the reader will be able to:

1. Locate and interpret vehicle and major component identification numbers.
2. Identify the strength ratings of threaded fasteners.
3. Explain the difference between the brand name (trade name) and the proper name for tools.
4. Describe what tool is the best to use for each job.
5. Explain how to maintain hand tools.
6. Identify the personal protective equipment (PPE) that all service technicians should wear.
7. Discuss how to safely use hand tools.
8. Describe how to safely hoist a vehicle.

KEY TERMS

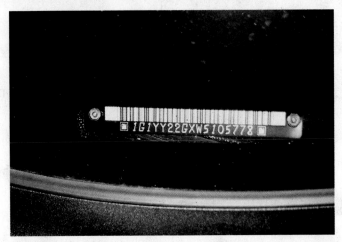

FIGURE 1–1 Typical vehicle identification number (VIN) as viewed through the windshield.

1 = United States	J = Japan	U = Romania
2 = Canada	K = Korea	V = France
3 = Mexico	L = China	W = Germany
4 = United States	M = India	X = Russia
5 = United States	P = Philippines	Y = Sweden
6 = Australia	R = Taiwan	Z = Italy
8 = Argentina	S = England	
9 = Brazil	T = Czechoslovakia	

CHART 1–1

The first number or letter in the VIN identifies the country where the vehicle was made.

A = 1980/2010	L = 1990/2020	Y = 2000/2030
B = 1981/2011	M = 1991/2021	1 = 2001/2031
C = 1982/2012	N = 1992/2022	2 = 2002/2032
D = 1983/2013	P = 1993/2023	3 = 2003/2033
E = 1984/2014	R = 1994/2024	4 = 2004/2034
F = 1985/2015	S = 1995/2025	5 = 2005/2035
G = 1986/2016	T = 1996/2026	6 = 2006/2036
H = 1987/2017	V = 1997/2027	7 = 2007/2037
J = 1988/2018	W = 1998/2028	8 = 2008/2038
K = 1989/2019	X = 1999/2029	9 = 2009/2039

CHART 1–2

The pattern repeats every 30 years for the year of manufacture.

VEHICLE IDENTIFICATION

MAKE, MODEL, AND YEAR   All service works require that the vehicle and its components be properly identified. The most common identifications are make, model, and year of manufacture the vehicle.

Make: e.g., Chevrolet

Model: e.g., Impala

Year: e.g., 2008

VEHICLE IDENTIFICATION NUMBER   It is often difficult to determine the exact year of manufacture of the vehicle. A model may be introduced as the next year's model as soon as January of the previous year. Typically, a new model year starts in September or October of the year prior to the actual new year, but not always. This is why the **vehicle identification number**, usually abbreviated **VIN**, is so important. ● **SEE FIGURE 1–1.**

Since 1981, all vehicle manufacturers have used a VIN that is 17 characters long. Although every vehicle manufacturer assigns various letters or numbers within these 17 characters, there are some constants, including:

- The first number or letter designates the country of origin. ● **SEE CHART 1–1.**
- The fourth or fifth character is the car line/series.
- The sixth character is the body style.
- The seventh character is the restraint system.
- The eighth character is often the engine code. (Some engines cannot be determined by the VIN number.)
- The tenth character represents the year on all vehicles. ● **SEE CHART 1–2.**

VEHICLE SAFETY CERTIFICATION LABEL   A vehicle safety certification label is attached to the left side pillar post on the rearward-facing section of the left front door. This label indicates the month and year of manufacture as well as the **gross vehicle weight rating (GVWR)**, the **gross axle weight rating (GAWR)**, and the vehicle identification number.

VECI LABEL   The **vehicle emissions control information (VECI)** label under the hood of the vehicle shows informative settings and emission hose routing information. ● **SEE FIGURE 1–2.**

The VECI label (sticker) can be located on the bottom side of the hood, the radiator fan shroud, the radiator core support, or on the strut towers. The VECI label usually includes the following information:

- Engine identification
- Emissions standard that the vehicle meets
- Vacuum hose routing diagram

FIGURE 1–2 The vehicle emissions control information (VECI) sticker is placed under the hood.

- Base ignition timing (if adjustable)
- Spark plug type and gap
- Valve lash
- Emission calibration code

CALIBRATION CODES **Calibration codes** are usually located on Powertrain Control Modules (PCMs) or other controllers. Whenever diagnosing an engine operating fault, it is often necessary to use the calibration code to be sure that the vehicle is the subject of a technical service bulletin or other service procedure. ● **SEE FIGURE 1–3.**

CASTING NUMBERS When an engine part such as a block is cast, a number is put into the mold to identify the casting. ● **SEE FIGURE 1–4.** These **casting numbers** can be used to identify the part and check dimensions such as the cubic inch displacement and other information, such as the year of manufacture. Sometimes changes are made to the mold, yet the casting number is not changed. Most often the casting number is the best piece of identifying information that the service technician can use for identifying an engine.

SERVICE INFORMATION

SERVICE MANUALS Service information is used by the service technician to determine specifications and service procedures, and any needed special tools.

Factory and aftermarket service manuals contain specifications and service procedures. While factory service manuals cover just one year and one or more models of the same vehicle, most aftermarket service manufacturers cover

FIGURE 1–3 A typical calibration code sticker on the case of a controller. The information on the sticker is often needed when ordering parts or a replacement controller.

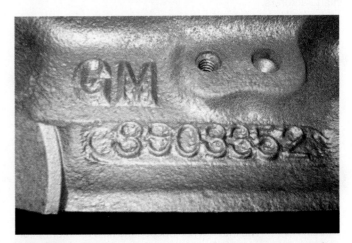

FIGURE 1–4 Casting numbers on major components can be either cast or stamped.

multiple years and/or models in one manual. Included in most service manuals are the following:

- Capacities and recommended specifications for all fluids
- Specifications including engine and routine maintenance items
- Testing procedures
- Service procedures including the use of special tools when needed

ELECTRONIC SERVICE INFORMATION Electronic service information is available mostly by subscription and provides access to an Internet site where service manual–type information is available. ● **SEE FIGURE 1–5.** Most vehicle manufacturers also offer electronic service information to their dealers and to most schools and colleges that offer corporate training programs.

FIGURE 1-5 Electronic service information is available from aftermarket sources such as ALLDATA and Mitchell On Demand, as well as on websites hosted by vehicle manufacturers.

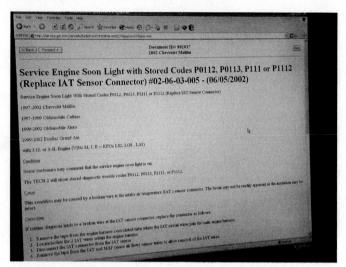

FIGURE 1-6 Technical service bulletins (TSBs) are issued by vehicle manufacturers when a fault occurs that affects many vehicles with the same problem. The TSB then provides the fix for the problem including any parts needed and detailed instructions.

TECHNICAL SERVICE BULLETINS **Technical service bulletins**, often abbreviated **TSBs**, sometimes called *technical service information bulletins (TSIB)*, are issued by the vehicle manufacturer to notify service technicians of a problem and include the necessary corrective action. Technical service bulletins are designed for dealership technicians but are republished by aftermarket companies and made available along with other service information to shops and vehicle repair facilities. ● **SEE FIGURE 1-6**.

INTERNET The Internet has opened the field for information exchange and access to technical advice. One of the most useful websites is the International Automotive Technician's Network at **www.iatn.net**. This is a free site but service technicians must register to join. If a small monthly sponsor fee is paid, the shop or service technician can gain access to the archives, which include thousands of successful repairs in the searchable database.

RECALLS AND CAMPAIGNS A **recall** or **campaign** is issued by a vehicle manufacturer and a notice is sent to all owners in the event of a safety-related fault or concern. While these faults may be repaired by shops, it is generally handled by a local dealer. Items that have created recalls in the past have included potential fuel system leakage problems, exhaust leakage, or electrical malfunctions that could cause a possible fire or the engine to stall. Unlike technical service bulletins whose cost is only covered when the vehicle is within the warranty period, a recall or campaign is always done at no cost to the vehicle owner.

? **FREQUENTLY ASKED QUESTION**

What Should Be Included on a Work Order?

A work order is a legal document that should include the following information:

1. Customer information
2. Identification of the vehicle including the VIN
3. Related service history information
4. The "three Cs":
   • Customer concern (complaint)
   • Cause of the concern
   • Correction or repairs that were required to return the vehicle to proper operation.

THREADED FASTENERS

BOLTS AND THREADS Most of the threaded fasteners used on vehicles are **bolts**. Bolts are called *cap screws* when they are threaded into a casting. Automotive service technicians usually refer to these fasteners as *bolts*, regardless of how they are used. In this chapter, they are called bolts. Sometimes, studs are used for threaded fasteners. A **stud** is a short rod with threads on both ends. Often, a stud will have coarse threads on one end and fine threads on the other end. The end of the stud with coarse threads is screwed into the casting. A nut is used on the opposite end to hold the parts together.

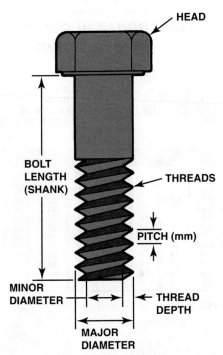

FIGURE 1–7 The dimensions of a typical bolt showing where sizes are measured.

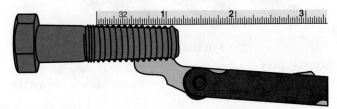

FIGURE 1–8 Thread pitch gauge used to measure the pitch of the thread. This bolt has 13 threads to the inch.

The fastener threads *must* match the threads in the casting or nut. The threads may be measured either in fractions of an inch (called fractional) or in metric units. The size is measured across the outside of the threads, called the *crest* of the thread. ● **SEE FIGURE 1–7.**

FRACTIONAL BOLTS Fractional threads are either coarse or fine. The coarse threads are called **unified national coarse** (**UNC**), and the fine threads are called **unified national fine** (**UNF**). Standard combinations of sizes and number of threads per inch (called **pitch**) are used. Pitch can be measured with a thread pitch gauge as shown in ● **SEE FIGURE 1–8.** Bolts are identified by their diameter and length as measured from below the head, and not by the size of the head or the size of the wrench used to remove or install the bolt.

SIZE	THREADS PER INCH		OUTSIDE DIAMETER INCHES
	NC UNC	NF UNF	
0	..	80	0.0600
1	64	..	0.0730
1	..	72	0.0730
2	56	..	0.0860
2	..	64	0.0860
3	48	..	0.0990
3	..	56	0.0990
4	40	..	0.1120
4	..	48	0.1120
5	40	..	0.1250
5	..	44	0.1250
6	32	..	0.1380
6	..	40	0.1380
8	32	..	0.1640
8	..	36	0.1640
10	24	..	0.1900
10	..	32	0.1900
12	24	..	0.2160
12	..	28	0.2160
1/4	20	..	0.2500
1/4	..	28	0.2500
5/16	18	..	0.3125
5/16	..	24	0.3125
3/8	16	..	0.3750
3/8	..	24	0.3750
7/16	14	..	0.4375
7/16	..	20	0.4375
1/2	13	..	0.5000
1/2	..	20	0.5000
9/16	12	..	0.5625
9/16	..	18	0.5625
5/8	11	..	0.6250
5/8	..	18	0.6250
3/4	10	..	0.7500
3/4	..	16	0.7500
7/8	9	..	0.8750
7/8	..	14	0.8750

CHART 1–3

American standard is one method of sizing fasteners.

Fractional thread sizes are specified by the diameter in fractions of an inch and the number of threads per inch. Typical UNC thread sizes would be 5/16–18 and 1/2–13. Similar UNF thread sizes would be 5/16–24 and 1/2–20. ● **SEE CHART 1–3.**

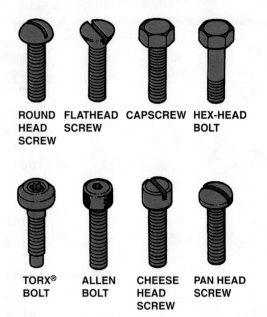

ROUND HEAD SCREW   FLATHEAD SCREW   CAPSCREW   HEX-HEAD BOLT

TORX® BOLT   ALLEN BOLT   CHEESE HEAD SCREW   PAN HEAD SCREW

FIGURE 1–9 Bolts and screws have many different heads which determine what tool is needed.

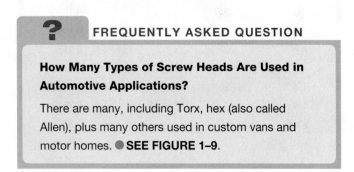

? FREQUENTLY ASKED QUESTION

How Many Types of Screw Heads Are Used in Automotive Applications?

There are many, including Torx, hex (also called Allen), plus many others used in custom vans and motor homes. ● **SEE FIGURE 1–9.**

METRIC BOLTS The size of a **metric bolt** is specified by the letter *M* followed by the diameter in millimeters (mm) across the outside (crest) of the threads. Typical metric sizes would be M8 and M12. Metric threads are specified by the thread diameter followed by X and the distance between the threads measured in millimeters (M8 × 1.5). ● **SEE FIGURE 1–10.**

GRADES OF BOLTS Bolts are made from many different types of steel, and for this reason some are stronger than others. The strength or classification of a bolt is called the **grade**. The bolt heads are marked to indicate their grade strength.

The actual grade of bolts is two more than the number of lines on the bolt head. Metric bolts have a decimal number to indicate the grade. More lines or a higher grade number indicate a stronger bolt. In some cases, nuts and machine screws have similar grade markings. Higher grade bolts usually have threads that are rolled rather than cut, which also makes them stronger. ● **SEE FIGURE 1–11.**

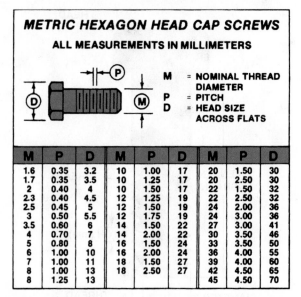

METRIC HEXAGON HEAD CAP SCREWS

ALL MEASUREMENTS IN MILLIMETERS

M = NOMINAL THREAD DIAMETER
P = PITCH
D = HEAD SIZE ACROSS FLATS

M	P	D	M	P	D	M	P	D
1.6	0.35	3.2	10	1.00	17	20	1.50	30
1.7	0.35	3.5	10	1.25	17	20	2.50	30
2	0.40	4	10	1.50	17	22	1.50	32
2.3	0.40	4.5	12	1.25	19	22	2.50	32
2.5	0.45	5	12	1.50	19	24	2.00	36
3	0.50	5.5	12	1.75	19	24	3.00	36
3.5	0.60	6	14	1.50	22	27	3.00	41
4	0.70	7	14	2.00	22	30	3.50	46
5	0.80	8	16	1.50	24	33	3.50	50
6	1.00	10	16	2.00	24	36	4.00	55
7	1.00	11	18	1.50	27	39	4.00	60
8	1.00	13	18	2.50	27	42	4.50	65
8	1.25	13				45	4.50	70

FIGURE 1–10 The metric system specifies fasteners by diameter, length, and pitch.

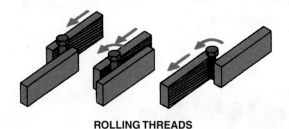

ROLLING THREADS

FIGURE 1–11 Stronger threads are created by cold-rolling a heat-treated bolt blank instead of cutting the threads, using a die.

CAUTION: *Never* use hardware store (nongraded) bolts, studs, or nuts on any vehicle steering, suspension, or brake component. Always use the exact size and grade of hardware that is specified and used by the vehicle manufacturer.

TENSILE STRENGTH OF FASTENERS Graded fasteners have a higher tensile strength than nongraded fasteners. **Tensile strength** is the maximum stress used under tension (lengthwise force) without causing failure of the fastener. Tensile strength is specified in pounds per square inch (psi).

The strength and type of steel used in a bolt is supposed to be indicated by a raised mark on the head of the bolt. The type of mark depends on the standard to which the bolt was manufactured. Most often, bolts used in machinery are made to SAE Standard J429. ● **SEE CHART 1–4** that shows the grade and specified tensile strength.

SAE BOLT DESIGNATIONS

SAE GRADE NO.	SIZE RANGE	TENSILE STRENGTH, PSI	MATERIAL	HEAD MARKING
1	1/4 through 1 1/2	60,000	Low or medium carbon steel	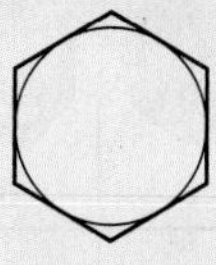
2	1/4 through 3/4	74,000		
	7/8 through 1 1/2	60,000		
5	1/4 through 1	120,000	Medium carbon steel, quenched and tempered	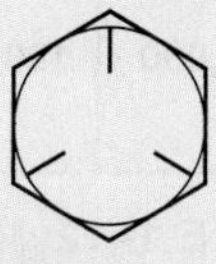
	1 1/8 through 1 1/2	105,000		
5.2	1/4 through 1	120,000	Low carbon martensite steel,* quenched and tempered	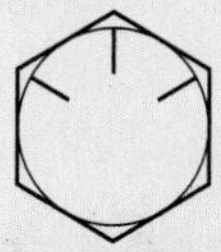
7	1/4 through 1 1/2	133,000	Medium carbon alloy steel, quenched and tempered	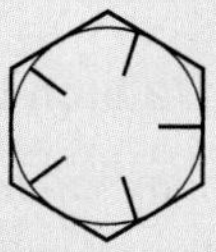
8	1/4 through 1 1/2	150,000	Medium carbon alloy steel, quenched and tempered	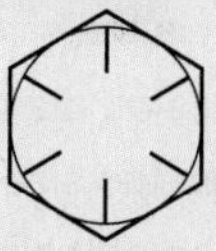
8.2	1/4 through 1	150,000	Low carbon martensite steel,* quenched and tempered	

CHART 1–4

The tensile strength rating system as specified by the Society of Automotive Engineers (SAE).

*Martensite steel is a specific type of steel that can be cooled rapidly, thereby increasing its hardness. It is named after a German metallurgist, Adolf Martens.

Metric bolt tensile strength property class is shown on the head of the bolt as a number, such as 4.6, 8.8, 9.8, and 10.9; the higher the number, the stronger the bolt. ● SEE FIGURE 1–12.

NUTS Nuts are the female part of a threaded fastener. Most nuts used on cap screws have the same hex size as the cap screw head. Some inexpensive nuts use a hex size larger than the cap screw head. Metric nuts are often marked with dimples to show their strength. More dimples indicate stronger nuts. Some nuts and cap screws use interference fit threads to keep them from accidentally loosening. This means that the shape of the nut is slightly distorted or that a section of the threads is deformed. Nuts can also be kept from loosening with a nylon washer fastened in the nut or with a nylon patch or strip on the threads.● SEE FIGURE 1–13.

NOTE: Most of these "locking nuts" are grouped together and are commonly referred to as *prevailing torque nuts*. This means that the nut will hold its tightness or torque and not loosen with movement or vibration. Most prevailing torque nuts should be replaced whenever removed to ensure that the nut will not loosen during service. Always follow the manufacturer's recommendations. Anaerobic sealers, such as Loctite, are used on the threads where the nut or cap screw must be both locked and sealed.

WASHERS Washers are often used under cap screw heads and under nuts. ● SEE FIGURE 1–14. Plain flat washers are used to provide an even clamping load around the fastener. Lock washers are added to prevent accidental loosening. In some accessories, the washers are locked onto the nut to provide easy assembly.

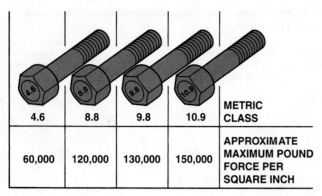

				METRIC CLASS
4.6	8.8	9.8	10.9	
60,000	120,000	130,000	150,000	APPROXIMATE MAXIMUM POUND FORCE PER SQUARE INCH

FIGURE 1–12 Metric bolt (cap screw) grade markings and approximate tensile strength.

HEX NUT   JAM NUT   NYLON LOCK NUT   CASTLE NUT   ACORN NUT

FIGURE 1–13 Nuts come in a variety of styles, including locking (prevailing torque) types, such as the distorted thread and nylon insert type.

FLAT WASHER   LOCK WASHER   STAR WASHER   STAR WASHER

FIGURE 1–14 Washers come in a variety of styles, including flat and serrated used to help prevent a fastener from loosening.

 TECH TIP

A 1/2 Inch Wrench Does Not Fit a 1/2 Inch Bolt

A common mistake made by persons new to the automotive field is to think that the size of a bolt or nut is the size of the head. The size of the bolt or nut (outside diameter of the threads) is usually smaller than the size of the wrench or socket that fits the head of the bolt or nut. Examples are given in the following table:

Wrench Size	Thread Size
7/16 inch	1/4 inch
1/2 inch	5/16 inch
9/16 inch	3/8 inch
5/8 inch	7/16 inch
3/4 inch	1/2 inch
10 mm	6 mm
12 or 13 mm*	8 mm
14 or 17 mm*	10 mm

* European (Système International d'Unités-SI) metric.

 TECH TIP

It Just Takes a Second

Whenever removing any automotive component, it is wise to screw the bolts back into the holes a couple of threads by hand. This ensures that the right bolt will be used in its original location when the component or part is put back on the vehicle. Often, the same diameter of fastener is used on a component, but the length of the bolt may vary. Spending just a couple of seconds to put the bolts and nuts back where they belong when the part is removed can save a lot of time when the part is being reinstalled. Besides making certain that the right fastener is being installed in the right place, this method helps prevent bolts and nuts from getting lost or kicked away. How much time have you wasted looking for that lost bolt or nut?

HAND TOOLS

WRENCHES Wrenches are the most used hand tool by service technicians. **Wrenches** are used to grasp and rotate threaded fasteners. Most wrenches are constructed of forged alloy steel, usually chrome-vanadium steel. ● **SEE FIGURE 1–15.**

After the wrench is formed, it is hardened, and then tempered to reduce brittleness, and then chrome plated. There are several types of wrenches.

OPEN-END WRENCH. An open-end wrench is usually used to loosen or tighten bolts or nuts that do not require a lot of torque. Because of the *open* end, this type of wrench can be easily placed on a bolt or nut with an angle of 15 degrees, which allows the wrench to be flipped over and used again to continue to rotate the fastener. The major disadvantage of an open-end wrench is the lack of torque that can be applied due to the fact that the open jaws of the wrench only contact two flat surfaces of the fastener. An open-end wrench has two different sizes, one at each end. ● **SEE FIGURE 1–16.**

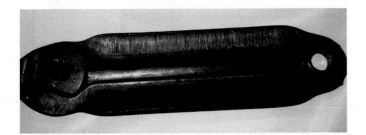

FIGURE 1–15 A wrench after it has been forged but before the flashing, extra material around the wrench, has been removed.

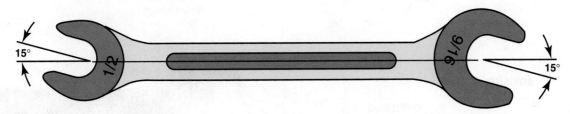

FIGURE 1–16 A typical open-end wrench. The size is different on each end and notice that the head is angled 15 degrees at the end.

BOX-END WRENCH. A *box-end wrench*, also called a *closed-end wrench*, is placed over the top of the fastener and grips the points of the fastener. A box-end wrench is angled 15 degrees to allow it to clear nearby objects.

Therefore, a box-end wrench should be used to loosen or to tighten fasteners because it grasps around the entire head of the fastener. A box-end wrench has two different sizes, one at each end. ● **SEE FIGURE 1–17**.

Most service technicians purchase *combination wrenches*, which have the open end at one end and the same size box end on the other end. ● **SEE FIGURE 1–18**.

A combination wrench allows the technician to loosen or tighten a fastener using the box end of the wrench, turn it around, and use the open end to increase the speed of rotating the fastener.

ADJUSTABLE WRENCH. An *adjustable wrench* is often used where the exact size wrench is not available or when a large nut, such as a wheel spindle nut, needs to be rotated but not tightened. An adjustable wrench should not be used to loosen or tighten fasteners because the torque applied to the wrench can cause the movable jaws to loosen their grip on the fastener, causing it to become rounded. ● **SEE FIGURE 1–19**.

LINE WRENCHES. Line wrenches are also called *flare-nut wrenches*, *fitting wrenches,* or *tube-nut wrenches* and are designed to grip almost all the way around a nut used to retain a fuel or refrigerant line, and yet, be able to be installed over the line. ● **SEE FIGURE 1–20**.

TECH TIP

Hide Those from the Boss

An apprentice technician started working for a shop and put his top tool box on a workbench. Another technician observed that, along with a complete set of good-quality tools, the box contained several adjustable wrenches. The more experienced technician said, "Hide those from the boss." The boss does not want any service technician to use adjustable wrenches. If any adjustable wrench is used on a bolt or nut, the movable jaw often moves or loosens and starts to round the head of the fastener. If the head of the bolt or nut becomes rounded, it becomes that much more difficult to remove.

SAFE USE OF WRENCHES Wrenches should be inspected before use to be sure they are not cracked, bent, or damaged. All wrenches should be cleaned after use before being returned to the tool box. Always use the correct size of wrench for the fastener being loosened or tightened to help prevent the rounding of the flats of the fastener. When attempting to loosen a fastener, pull a wrench—do not push a wrench. If a wrench is pushed, your knuckles can be hurt when forced into another object if the fastener breaks loose or

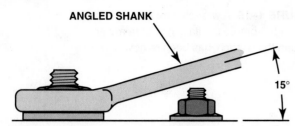

FIGURE 1–17 The end of a box-end wrench is angled 15 degrees to allow clearance for nearby objects or other fasteners.

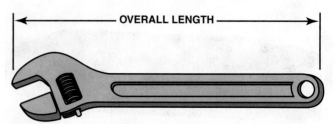

FIGURE 1–19 An adjustable wrench. Adjustable wrenches are sized by the overall length of the wrench and not by how far the jaws open. Common sizes of adjustable wrenches include 8, 10, and 12 inch.

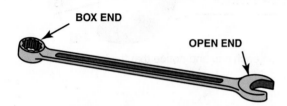

FIGURE 1–18 A combination wrench has an open end at one end and a box end at the other end.

FIGURE 1–20 The end of a typical line wrench, which shows that it is capable of grasping most of the head of the fitting.

if the wrench slips. Always keep wrenches and all hand tools clean to help prevent rust and to allow for a better, firmer grip. Never expose any tool to excessive heat. High temperatures can reduce the strength ("draw the temper") of metal tools.

Never use a hammer on any wrench unless you are using a special "staking face" wrench designed to be used with a hammer. Replace any tools that are damaged or worn.

RATCHETS, SOCKETS, AND EXTENSIONS
A **socket** fits over the fastener and grips the points and/or flats of the bolt or nut. The socket is rotated (driven) using either a long bar called a **breaker bar** (flex handle) or a ratchet. ● SEE **FIGURES 1–21 AND 1–22.**

A **ratchet** is a tool that turns the socket in only one direction and allows the rotating of the ratchet handle back and forth in a narrow space. Socket **extensions** and **universal joints** are also used with sockets to allow access to fasteners in restricted locations.

DRIVE SIZE. Sockets are available in various **drive sizes**, including 1/4, 3/8, and 1/2 inch sizes for most automotive use. ● SEE **FIGURES 1–23 AND 1–24.**

Many heavy-duty truck and/or industrial applications use 3/4 and 1 inch sizes. The drive size is the distance of each side

TECH TIP

Right to Tighten

It is sometimes confusing which way to rotate a wrench or screwdriver, especially when the head of the fastener is pointing away from you. To help visualize while looking at the fastener, say "righty tighty, lefty loosey."

of the square drive. Sockets and ratchets of the same size are designed to work together.

REGULAR AND DEEP WELL. Sockets are available in regular lengths for use in most applications or in a deep well design that allows for access to a fastener that uses a long stud or other similar conditions. ● SEE FIGURE 1–25.

TORQUE WRENCHES
Torque wrenches are socket turning handles that are designed to apply a known amount of force to the fastener. There are two basic types of torque wrenches:

1. **Clicker type.** This type of torque wrench is first set to the specified torque and then it "clicks" when the set torque value has been reached. When force is removed from the

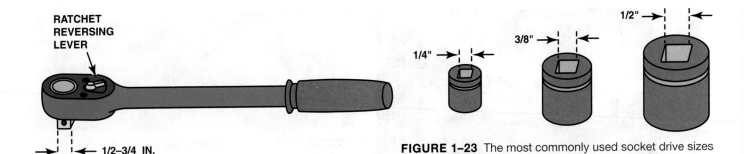

FIGURE 1–21 A typical ratchet used to rotate a socket. A ratchet makes a ratcheting noise when it is being rotated in the opposite direction from loosening or tightening. A knob or lever on the ratchet allows the user to switch directions.

FIGURE 1–23 The most commonly used socket drive sizes include 1/4, 3/8, and 1/2 inch drive.

FIGURE 1–22 A typical flex handle used to rotate a socket, also called a breaker bar because it usually has a longer handle than a ratchet and, therefore, can be used to apply more torque to a fastener than a ratchet.

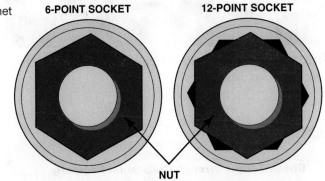

FIGURE 1–24 A 6-point socket fits the head of a bolt or nut on all sides. A 12-point socket can round off the head of a bolt or nut if a lot of force is applied.

torque wrench handle, another click is heard. The setting on a clicker-type torque wrench should be set back to zero after use and checked for proper calibration regularly. ● **SEE FIGURE 1–26.**

2. **Beam-type.** This type of torque wrench is used to measure torque, but instead of presenting the value, the actual torque is displayed on the dial of the wrench as the fastener is being tightened. Beam-type torque wrenches are available in 1/4, 3/8, and 1/2 inch drives and both English and metric units. ● **SEE FIGURE 1–27.**

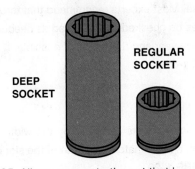

FIGURE 1–25 Allows access to the nut that has a stud plus other locations needing great depth, such as spark plugs.

SAFE USE OF SOCKETS AND RATCHETS Always use the proper size socket that correctly fits the bolt or nut. All sockets and ratchets should be cleaned after use before being placed back into the tool box. Sockets are available in short and deep well designs. Never expose any tool to excessive heat. High temperatures can reduce the strength ("draw the temper") of metal tools.

Never use a hammer on a socket handle unless you are using a special "staking face" wrench designed to be used with a hammer. Replace any tools that are damaged or worn.

Also select the appropriate drive size. For example, for small work, such as on the dash, select a 1/4 inch drive. For most general service work, use a 3/8 inch drive and for suspension and steering and other large fasteners, select a 1/2 inch drive. When loosening a fastener, always pull the ratchet toward you rather than push it outward.

SCREWDRIVERS

STRAIGHT-BLADE SCREWDRIVER. Many smaller fasteners are removed and installed by using a **screwdriver.** Screwdrivers are available in many sizes and tip shapes. The most commonly used screwdriver is called a *straight blade* or *flat tip.*

FIGURE 1–26 Using a clicker-type torque wrench to tighten connecting rod nuts on an engine.

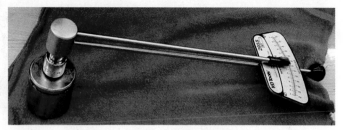

FIGURE 1–27 A beam-type torque wrench that displays the torque reading on the face of the dial. The beam display is read as the beam deflects, which is in proportion to the amount of torque applied to the fastener.

 TECH TIP

Check Torque Wrench Calibration Regularly

Torque wrenches should be checked regularly. For example, Honda has a torque wrench calibration setup at each of its training centers. It is expected that a torque wrench be checked for accuracy before every use. Most experts recommend that torque wrenches be checked and adjusted as needed at least every year and more often if possible. ● SEE FIGURE 1–28.

FIGURE 1–28 Torque wrench calibration checker.

Flat-tip screwdrivers are sized by the width of the blade and this width should match the width of the slot in the screw. ● SEE FIGURE 1–29.

CAUTION: **Do not use a screwdriver as a pry tool or as a chisel. Screwdrivers are hardened steel only at the tip and are not designed to be pounded on or used for prying because they could bend easily. Always use the proper tool for each application.**

PHILLIPS SCREWDRIVER. Another type of commonly used screwdriver is called a Phillips screwdriver, named for Henry F. Phillips, who invented the crosshead screw in 1934. Due to the shape of the crosshead screw and screwdriver, a Phillips screw can be driven with more torque than can be achieved with a slotted screw.

A Phillips head screwdriver is specified by the length of the handle and the size of the point at the tip. A #1 tip has a sharp point, a #2 tip is the most commonly used, and a #3 tip is blunt and is only used for larger sizes of Phillips head fasteners. For example, a #2 × 3 inch Phillips screwdriver would typically measure 6 inch from the tip of the blade to the end of the handle (3 inch long handle and 3 inch long blade) with a #2 tip.

Both straight-blade and Phillips screwdrivers are available with a short blade and handle for access to fasteners with limited room. ● SEE FIGURE 1–30.

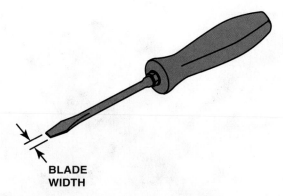

**BLADE
WIDTH**

FIGURE 1–29 A flat-tip (straight-blade) screwdriver. The width of the blade should match the width of the slot in the fastener being loosened or tightened.

FIGURE 1–30 Two stubby screwdrivers that are used to access screws that have limited space above. A straight blade is on top and a #2 Phillips screwdriver is on the bottom.

TECH TIP

Use Socket Adapters with Caution

A **socket adapter** allows the use of one size of socket and another drive size ratchet or breaker bar. Socket adapters are available and can be used for different drive size sockets on a ratchet. Combinations include:

- 1/4 inch drive—3/8 inch sockets
- 3/8 inch drive—1/4 inch sockets
- 3/8 inch drive—1/2 inch sockets
- 1/2 inch drive—3/8 inch sockets

   Using a larger drive ratchet or breaker bar on a smaller size socket can cause the application of too much force to the socket, which could crack or shatter. Using a smaller size drive tool on a larger socket will usually not cause any harm, but would greatly reduce the amount of torque that can be applied to the bolt or nut.

TECH TIP

Avoid Using "Cheater Bars"

Whenever a fastener is difficult to remove, some technicians will insert the handle of a ratchet or a breaker bar into a length of steel pipe sometimes called a **cheater bar**. The extra length of the pipe allows the technician to exert more torque than can be applied using the drive handle alone. However, the extra torque can easily overload the socket and ratchet, causing them to break or shatter, which could cause personal injury.

SAFE USE OF SCREWDRIVERS   Always use the proper type and size screwdriver that matches the fastener. Try to avoid pressing down on a screwdriver because if it slips, the screwdriver tip could go into your hand, causing serious personal injury. All screwdrivers should be cleaned after use. Do not use a screwdriver as a prybar; always use the correct tool for the job.

HAMMERS AND MALLETS   **Hammers** and mallets are used to force objects together or apart. The shape of the back part of the hammer head (called the *peen*) usually determines the name. For example, a ball-peen hammer has a rounded end like a ball and it is used to straighten oil pans and valve covers, using the hammer head, and for shaping metal, using the ball peen. ● **SEE FIGURE 1–33**.

NOTE: A claw hammer has a claw used to remove nails and is not used for automotive service.

   A hammer is usually sized by the weight of the head of the hammer and the length of the handle. For example,

OFFSET SCREWDRIVERS. Offset screwdrivers are used in places where a conventional screwdriver cannot fit. An offset screwdriver is bent at the ends and is used similar to a wrench. Most offset screwdrivers have a straight blade at one end and a Phillips end at the opposite end. ● **SEE FIGURE 1–31**.

IMPACT SCREWDRIVER.   An *impact screwdriver* is used to break loose or tighten a screw. A hammer is used to strike the end after the screwdriver holder is placed in the head of the screw and rotated in the desired direction. The force from the hammer blow does two things: It applies a force downward holding the tip of the screwdriver in the slot and then applies a twisting force to loosen (or tighten) the screw. ● **SEE FIGURE 1–32**.

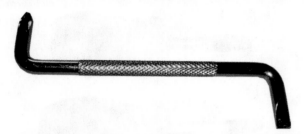

FIGURE 1–31 An offset screwdriver is used to install or remove fasteners that do not have enough space above to use a conventional screwdriver.

 FREQUENTLY ASKED QUESTION

What Is a Torx?

A Torx is a six-pointed star-shaped tip that was developed by Camcar (formerly Textron) to offer higher loosening and tightening torque than is possible with a straight blade (flat tip) or Phillips. Torx is very commonly used in the automotive field for many components. Commonly used Torx sizes from small to large include T15, T20, T25, and T30.

Some Torx fasteners include a round projection in the center requiring that a special version of a Torx bit be used. These are called security Torx bits, which have a hole in the center to be used on these fasteners. External Torx fasteners are also used as engine fasteners and are labeled E instead of T, plus the size, such as E45.

FIGURE 1–32 An impact screwdriver used to remove slotted or Phillips head fasteners that cannot be broken loose using a standard screwdriver.

FIGURE 1–33 A typical ball-peen hammer.

a commonly used ball-peen hammer has an 8 ounce head with an 11 inch handle.

MALLETS. *Mallets* are a type of hammer with a large striking surface, which allows the technician to exert force over a larger area than a hammer, so as not to harm the part or component. Mallets are made from a variety of materials including rubber, plastic, or wood. ● **SEE FIGURE 1–34**.

DEAD-BLOW HAMMER. A shot-filled plastic hammer is called a *dead-blow hammer*. The small lead balls (shot) inside a plastic head prevent the hammer from bouncing off of the object when struck. ● **SEE FIGURE 1–35**.

SAFE USE OF HAMMERS AND MALLETS All mallets and hammers should be cleaned after use and not exposed to extreme temperatures. Never use a hammer or mallet that is

damaged in any way and always use caution to avoid doing damage to the components and the surrounding area. Always follow the hammer manufacturer's recommended procedures and practices.

PLIERS

SLIP-JOINT PLIERS. **Pliers** are capable of holding, twisting, bending, and cutting objects and is an extremely useful classification of tools. The common household type of pliers is called *slip-joint pliers*. There are two different positions where the junction of the handles meets to achieve a wide range of sizes of objects that can be gripped. ● **SEE FIGURE 1–36**.

MULTIGROOVE ADJUSTABLE PLIERS. For gripping larger objects, a set of *multigroove adjustable pliers* is a commonly used tool of choice by many service technicians. Originally designed to remove the various size nuts holding rope seals used in water pumps, the name *water pump pliers* is also used.

FIGURE 1–34 A rubber mallet used to deliver a force to an object without harming the surface.

FIGURE 1–35 A dead-blow hammer that was left outside in freezing weather. The plastic covering was damaged, which destroyed this hammer. The lead shot is encased in the metal housing and then covered.

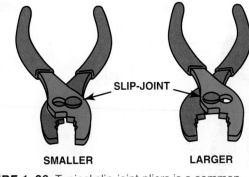

FIGURE 1–36 Typical slip-joint pliers is a common household pliers. The slip joint allows the jaws to be opened to two different settings.

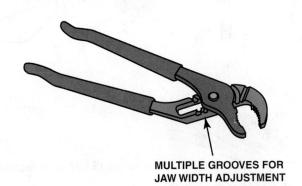

FIGURE 1–37 Multigroove adjustable pliers is known by many names, including the trade name "Channel Locks®."

TECH TIP

Pound with Something Softer

If you must pound on something, be sure to use a tool that is softer than what you are about to pound on to avoid damage. Examples are given in the following table.

The Material Being Pounded	What to Pound with
Steel or cast iron	Brass or aluminum hammer or punch
Aluminum	Plastic or rawhide mallet or plastic-covered dead-blow hammer
Plastic	Rawhide mallet or plastic dead-blow hammer

These types of pliers are commonly called by their trade name *Channel Locks®*. ● **SEE FIGURE 1–37.**

LINESMAN'S PLIERS. *Linesman's pliers* is a hand tool specifically designed for cutting, bending, and twisting wire. While commonly used by construction workers and electricians, linesman's pliers is a very useful tool for the service technician who deals with wiring. The center parts of the jaws are designed to grasp round objects such as pipe or tubing without slipping. ● **SEE FIGURE 1–38.**

DIAGONAL PLIERS. *Diagonal pliers* is designed only to cut. The cutting jaws are set at an angle to make it easier to cut wires. Diagonal pliers are also called *side cuts* or *dikes*. These pliers are constructed of hardened steel and they are used mostly for cutting wire. ● **SEE FIGURE 1–39.**

NEEDLE-NOSE PLIERS. *Needle-nose pliers* are designed to grip small objects or objects in tight locations. Needle-nose pliers

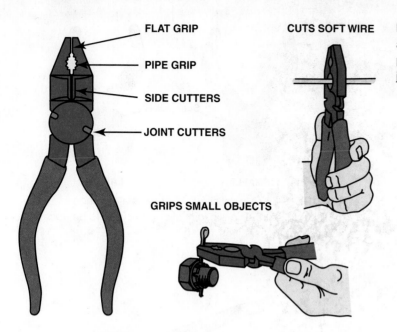

FLAT GRIP

PIPE GRIP

SIDE CUTTERS

JOINT CUTTERS

CUTS SOFT WIRE

GRIPS SMALL OBJECTS

FIGURE 1–38 Linesman's pliers are very useful because it can help perform many automotive service jobs.

CUTTING WIRES CLOSE TO TERMINALS

PULLING OUT AND SPREADING COTTER PIN

FIGURE 1–39 Diagonal-cut pliers is another common tool that has many names.

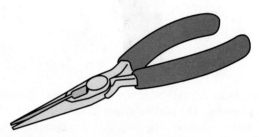

FIGURE 1–40 Needle-nose pliers are used where there is limited access to a wire or pin that needs to be installed or removed.

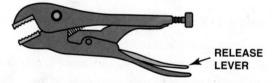

RELEASE LEVER

FIGURE 1–41 Locking pliers are best known by their trade name Vise Grips®.

have long, pointed jaws, which allow the tips to reach into narrow openings or groups of small objects. ● **SEE FIGURE 1–40.**

Most needle-nose pliers have a wire cutter located at the base of the jaws near the pivot. There are several variations of needle nose pliers, including right angle jaws or slightly angled to allow access to certain cramped areas.

LOCKING PLIERS. *Locking pliers* are adjustable pliers that can be locked to hold objects from moving. Most locking pliers also have wire cutters built into the jaws near the pivot point. Locking pliers come in a variety of styles and sizes and are commonly referred to by the trade name *Vise Grips®*. The size is the length of the pliers, not how far the jaws open. ● **SEE FIGURE 1–41.**

SNAP-RING PLIERS. *Snap-ring pliers* is used to remove and install snap-rings. Many snap-ring pliers are designed to be able to remove and install both inward, as well as outward, expanding snap rings. Some snap-ring pliers can be equipped with serrated-tipped jaws for grasping the opening in the snap ring, while others are equipped with points, which are inserted into the holes in the snap ring. ● **SEE FIGURE 1–42.**

SAFE USE OF PLIERS Pliers should not be used to remove any bolt or other fastener. Pliers should only be used when specified for use by the vehicle manufacturer.

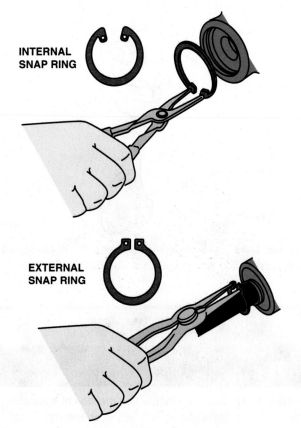

INTERNAL SNAP RING

EXTERNAL SNAP RING

FIGURE 1–42 Snap-ring pliers are also called lock ring pliers and most are designed to remove internal and external snap rings (lock rings).

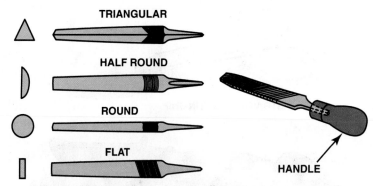

TRIANGULAR

HALF ROUND

ROUND

FLAT

HANDLE

FIGURE 1–43 Files come in many different shapes and sizes. Never use a file without a handle.

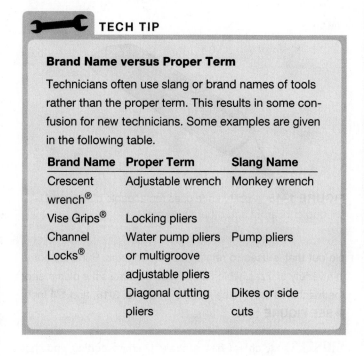

🔧 **TECH TIP**

Brand Name versus Proper Term

Technicians often use slang or brand names of tools rather than the proper term. This results in some confusion for new technicians. Some examples are given in the following table.

Brand Name	Proper Term	Slang Name
Crescent wrench®	Adjustable wrench	Monkey wrench
Vise Grips®	Locking pliers	
Channel Locks®	Water pump pliers or multigroove adjustable pliers	Pump pliers
	Diagonal cutting pliers	Dikes or side cuts

FILES   **Files** are used to smooth metal and are constructed of hardened steel with diagonal rows of teeth. Files are available with a single row of teeth called a *single cut file*, as well as two rows of teeth cut at an opposite angle called a *double cut file*. Files are available in a variety of shapes and sizes from small flat files, half-round files, and triangular files. ● **SEE FIGURE 1–43.**

SAFE USE OF FILES   Always use a file with a handle. Because files cut only when moved forward, a handle must be attached to prevent possible personal injury. After making a forward strike, lift the file and return it to the starting position; avoid dragging the file backward.

SNIPS   Service technicians are often asked to fabricate sheet metal brackets or heat shields and need to use one or more types of cutters available called **snips**. *Tin snips* are the simplest and are designed to make straight cuts in a variety of materials, such as sheet steel, aluminum, or even fabric. A variation of the tin snips is called *aviation tin snips*. There are three designs of aviation snips including one designed to cut straight (called a *straight cut aviation snip*), one

designed to cut left (called an *offset left aviation snip*), and one designed to cut right (called an *offset right aviation snip*). ● **SEE FIGURE 1–44.**

UTILITY KNIFE   A *utility knife* uses a replaceable blade and is used to cut a variety of materials such as carpet, plastic, wood, and paper products, such as cardboard. ● **SEE FIGURE 1–45.**

SAFE USE OF CUTTERS   Whenever using cutters, always wear eye protection or a face shield to guard against the possibility of metal pieces being ejected during the cut. Always follow recommended procedures.

PUNCHES   A **punch** is a small diameter steel rod that has a smaller diameter ground at one end. A punch is used to drive a

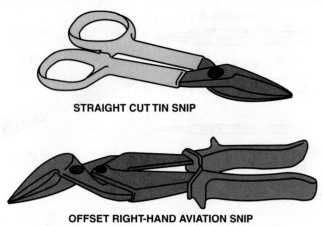

STRAIGHT CUT TIN SNIP

OFFSET RIGHT-HAND AVIATION SNIP

FIGURE 1–44 Tin snips are used to cut thin sheets of metal or carpet.

FIGURE 1–45 A utility knife uses replaceable blades and is used to cut carpet and other materials.

pin out that is used to retain two components. Punches come in a variety of sizes, which are measured across the diameter of the machined end. Sizes include 1/16, 1/8, 3/16, and 1/4 inch. ● **SEE FIGURE 1–46.**

CHISELS   A **chisel** has a straight, sharp cutting end that is used for cutting off rivets or to separate two pieces of an assembly. The most common design of chisel used for automotive service work is called a *cold chisel*.

SAFE USE OF PUNCHES AND CHISELS   Always wear eye protection when using a punch or a chisel because the hardened steel is brittle and parts of the punch could fly off and cause serious personal injury. See the warning stamped on the side of this automotive punch in ● **FIGURE 1–47.**

The tops of punches and chisels can become rounded off from use, which is called "mushroomed." This material must be ground off to help avoid the possibility of the overhanging material being loosened and becoming airborne during use. ● **SEE FIGURE 1–48.**

HACKSAWS   A **hacksaw** is used to cut metals, such as steel, aluminum, brass, or copper. The cutting blade of a hacksaw

PIN

FIGURE 1–46 A punch used to drive pins from assembled components. This type of punch is also called a pin punch.

WEAR SAFETY GOGGLES

FIGURE 1–47 Warning stamped on the side of a punch warning that goggles should be worn when using this tool. Always follow safety warnings.

is replaceable and the sharpness and number of teeth can be varied to meet the needs of the job. Use 14 or 18 teeth per inch (TPI) for cutting plaster or soft metals, such as aluminum and copper. Use 24 or 32 teeth per inch for steel or pipe. Hacksaw blades should be installed with the teeth pointing away from the handle. This means that a hacksaw only cuts while the blade is pushed in the forward direction. ● **SEE FIGURE 1–49.**

SAFE USE OF HACKSAWS   Check that the hacksaw is equipped with the correct blade for the job and that the teeth are pointed away from the handle. When using a hacksaw, move the hacksaw slowly away from you, then lift slightly and return for another cut.

BASIC HAND TOOL LIST

The following is a typical list of hand tools every automotive technician should possess. Specialty tools are not included.

Safety glasses

Tool chest

1/4 inch drive socket set (1/4 to 9/16 inch standard and
    deep sockets; 6 to 15 mm standard and deep sockets)

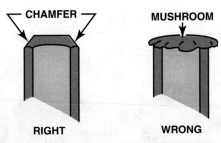

CHAMFER · MUSHROOM

RIGHT · WRONG

FIGURE 1–48 Use a grinder or a file to remove the mushroom material on the end of a punch or chisel.

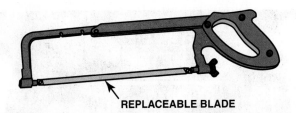

REPLACEABLE BLADE

FIGURE 1–49 A typical hacksaw that is used to cut metal. If cutting sheet metal or thin objects, a blade with more teeth should be used.

1/4 inch drive ratchet

1/4 inch drive 2 inch extension

1/4 inch drive 6 inch extension

1/4 inch drive handle

3/8 inch drive socket set (3/8 to 7/8 inch standard and deep sockets; 10 to 19 mm standard and deep sockets)

3/8 inch drive Torx set (T40, T45, T50, and T55)

3/8 inch drive 13/16 inch plug socket

3/8 inch drive 5/8 inch plug socket

3/8 inch drive ratchet

3/8 inch drive 1 1/2 inch extension

3/8 inch drive 3 inch extension

3/8 inch drive 6 inch extension

3/8 inch drive 18 inch extension

3/8 inch drive universal

1/2 inch drive socket set (1/2 to 1 inch standard and deep sockets)

1/2 inch drive ratchet

1/2 inch drive breaker bar

1/2 inch drive 5 inch extension

1/2 inch drive 10 inch extension

3/8 to 1/4 inch adapter

1/2 to 3/8 inch adapter

3/8 to 1/2 inch adapter

Crowfoot set (fractional inch)

Crowfoot set (metric)

3/8 through 1 inch combination wrench set

10 through 19 mm combination wrench set

1/16 through 1/4 inch hex wrench set

2 through 12 mm hex wrench set

3/8 inch hex socket

13 to 14 mm flare-nut wrench

15 to 17 mm flare-nut wrench

5/16 to 3/8 inch flare-nut wrench

7/16 to 1/2 inch flare-nut wrench

1/2 to 9/16 inch flare-nut wrench

Diagonal pliers

Needle pliers

Adjustable-jaw pliers

Locking pliers

Snap-ring pliers

Stripping or crimping pliers

Ball-peen hammer

Rubber hammer

Dead-blow hammer

Five-piece standard screwdriver set

Four-piece Phillips screwdriver set

#15 Torx screwdriver

#20 Torx screwdriver

Center punch

Pin punches (assorted sizes)

Chisel

Utility knife

Valve core tool

Filter wrench (large filters)

Filter wrench (smaller filters)

Test light

Feeler gauge

Scraper

Pinch bar

Magnet

FIGURE 1–50 A typical beginning technician tool set that includes the basic tools to get started.

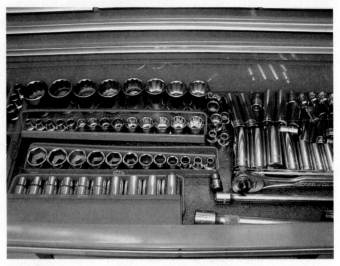

FIGURE 1–51 A typical large tool box, showing just one of many drawers.

 TECH TIP

Need to Borrow a Tool More Than Twice? Buy It!

Most service technicians agree that it is okay for a beginning technician to borrow a tool occasionally. However, if a tool has to be borrowed more than twice, then be sure to purchase it as soon as possible. Also, whenever a tool is borrowed, be sure that you clean the tool and let the technician you borrowed the tool from know that you are returning the tool. These actions will help in any future dealings with other technicians.

TOOL SETS AND ACCESSORIES

A beginning service technician may wish to start with a small set of tools before purchasing an expensive tool set. ● **SEE FIGURES 1–50 AND 1–51.**

ELECTRICAL HAND TOOLS

TEST LIGHT A test light is used to test for electricity. A typical automotive test light consists of a clear plastic screwdriver-like handle that contains a lightbulb. A wire is attached to one terminal of the bulb, which the technician connects to a clean metal part of the vehicle. The other end

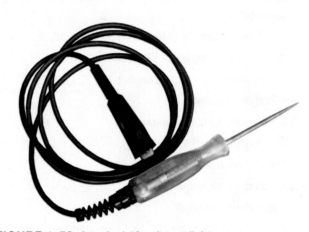

FIGURE 1–52 A typical 12 volt test light.

of the bulb is attached to a point that can be used to test for electricity at a connector or wire. When there is power at the point and a good connection at the other end, the lightbulb lights. ● **SEE FIGURE 1–52.**

SOLDERING GUNS

ELECTRIC SOLDERING GUN. This type of soldering gun is usually powered by 110 volt AC and often has two power settings expressed in watts. A typical electric soldering gun will produce from 85 to 300 watts of heat at the tip, which is more than adequate for soldering.

ELECTRIC SOLDERING PENCIL. This type of soldering iron is less expensive and creates less heat than an electric soldering gun. A typical electric soldering pencil (iron) creates 30 to 60 watts of heat and is suitable for soldering smaller wires and connections.

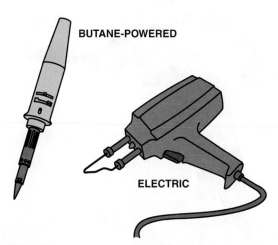

BUTANE-POWERED

ELECTRIC

FIGURE 1–53 Electric and butane-powered soldering guns used to make electrical repairs. Soldering guns are sold by the wattage rating. The higher the wattage, the greater amount of heat created. Most solder guns used for automotive electrical work usually fall within the 60 to 160 watt range.

BUTANE-POWERED SOLDERING IRON. A butane-powered soldering iron is portable and very useful for automotive service work because an electrical cord is not needed. Most butane-powered soldering irons produce about 60 watts of heat, which is enough for most automotive soldering. ● **SEE FIGURE 1–53.**

ELECTRICAL WORK HAND TOOLS
In addition to a soldering iron, most service technicians who do electrical-related work should have the following:

- Wire cutters
- Wire strippers
- Wire crimpers
- Heat gun for heat shrink tubing

DIGITAL METER
A digital meter is a necessary tool for any electrical diagnosis and troubleshooting. A digital multimeter, abbreviated DMM, is usually capable of measuring the following units of electricity:

- DC volts
- AC volts
- Ohms
- Amperes

HAND TOOL MAINTENANCE

Most hand tools are constructed of rust-resistant metals but they can still rust or corrode if not properly maintained. For best results and long tool life, the following steps should be taken:

 FREQUENTLY ASKED QUESTION

What Is an "SST"?

Vehicle manufacturers often specify a **special service tool (SST)** to properly disassemble and assemble components, such as transmissions and other components. These tools are also called special tools and are available from the vehicle manufacturer or their tool supplier, such as Kent-Moore and Miller tools. Many service technicians do not have access to special service tools so they use generic versions that are available from aftermarket sources.

- Clean each tool before placing it back into the tool box.
- Keep tools separated. Moisture on metal tools will start to rust more readily if the tools are in contact with another metal tool.
- Line the drawers of the tool box with a material that will prevent the tools from moving as the drawers are opened and closed. This helps to quickly locate the proper tool and size.
- Release the tension on all "clicker-type" torque wrenches.
- Keep the tool box secure.

TROUBLE LIGHTS

INCANDESCENT *Incandescent lights* use a filament that produces light when electric current flows through the bulb. This was the standard **trouble light**, also called a *work light* for many years until safety issues caused most shops to switch to safer fluorescent or LED lights. If incandescent lightbulbs are used, try to locate bulbs that are rated "rough service," which is designed to withstand shock and vibration more than conventional lightbulbs.

☠ WARNING

Do not use incandescent trouble lights around gasoline or other flammable liquids. The liquids can cause the bulb to break and the hot filament can ignite the flammable liquid, which can cause personal injury or even death.

FIGURE 1–54 A fluorescent trouble light operates cooler and is safer to use in the shop because it is protected against accidental breakage where gasoline or other flammable liquids would happen to come in contact with the light.

FIGURE 1–55 A typical 1/2 inch drive air impact wrench. The direction of rotation can be changed to loosen or tighten a fastener.

FLUORESCENT A trouble light is an essential piece of shop equipment, and for safety, should be fluorescent rather than incandescent. Incandescent lightbulbs can scatter or break if gasoline were to be splashed onto the bulb creating a serious fire hazard. Fluorescent light tubes are not as likely to be broken and are usually protected by a clear plastic enclosure. Trouble lights are usually attached to a retractor, which can hold 20 to 50 feet of electrical cord. ● **SEE FIGURE 1–54.**

LED TROUBLE LIGHT **Light-emitting diode (LED)** trouble lights are excellent to use because they are shock resistant, long lasting, and do not represent a fire hazard. Some trouble lights are battery powered and therefore can be used in places where an attached electrical cord could present problems.

FIGURE 1–56 A typical battery-powered 3/8 inch drive impact wrench.

AIR AND ELECTRICALLY OPERATED TOOLS

IMPACT WRENCH An impact wrench, either air or electrically powered, is a tool that is used to remove and install fasteners. The air-operated 1/2 inch drive impact wrench is the most commonly used unit. ● **SEE FIGURE 1–55.**

Electrically powered impact wrenches commonly include:

- Battery-powered units. ● **SEE FIGURE 1–56.**
- 110 volt AC-powered units. This type of impact is very useful, especially if compressed air is not readily available.

☠ **WARNING**

Always use impact sockets with impact wrenches, and always wear eye protection in case the socket or fastener shatters. Impact sockets are thicker walled and constructed with premium alloy steel. They are hardened with a black oxide finish to help prevent corrosion and distinguish them from regular sockets. ● SEE FIGURE 1–57.

FIGURE 1–57 A black impact socket. Always use an impact-type socket whenever using an impact wrench to avoid the possibility of shattering the socket, which could cause personal injury. If a socket is chrome plated, it is not to be used with an impact wrench.

AIR RATCHET An air ratchet is used to remove and install fasteners that would normally be removed or installed using a ratchet and a socket. ● **SEE FIGURE 1–58.**

DIE GRINDER A die grinder is a commonly used air-powered tool which can also be used to sand or remove gaskets and rust. ● **SEE FIGURE 1–59.**

BENCH- OR PEDESTAL-MOUNTED GRINDER These high-powered grinders can be equipped with a wire brush wheel and/or a stone wheel.

- **Wire brush wheel**—This type is used to clean threads of bolts as well as to remove gaskets from sheet metal engine parts.
- **Stone wheel**—This type is used to grind metal or to remove the mushroom from the top of punches or chisels. ● **SEE FIGURE 1–60.**

Most **bench grinders** are equipped with a grinder wheel (stone) on one end and a wire brush wheel on the other end. A bench grinder is a very useful piece of shop equipment and the wire wheel end can be used for the following:

- Cleaning threads of bolts
- Cleaning gaskets from sheet metal parts, such as steel valve covers

CAUTION: Use a steel wire brush only on steel or iron components. If a steel wire brush is used on aluminum or copper-based metal parts, it can remove metal from the part.

FIGURE 1–58 An air ratchet is a very useful tool that allows fast removal and installation of fasteners, especially in areas that are difficult to reach or do not have room enough to move a hand ratchet or wrench.

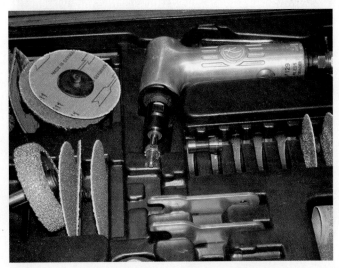

FIGURE 1–59 This typical die grinder surface preparation kit includes the air-operated die grinder as well as a variety of sanding disks for smoothing surfaces or removing rust.

FIGURE 1–60 A typical pedestal grinder with a wire wheel on the left side and a stone wheel on the right side. Even though this machine is equipped with guards, safety glasses or a face shield should always be worn whenever using a grinder or wire wheel.

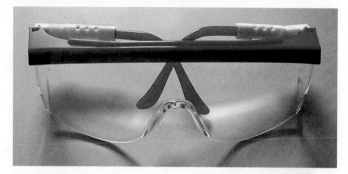

FIGURE 1–61 Safety glasses should be worn at all times when working on or around any vehicle or servicing any components.

☠ **WARNING**

Always wear a face shield when using a wire wheel or a grinder.

The grinding stone end of the bench grinder can be used for the following:

- Sharpening blades and drill bits
- Grinding off the heads of rivets or parts
- Sharpening sheet metal parts for custom fitting

PERSONAL PROTECTIVE EQUIPMENT

Service technicians should wear **personal protective equipment (PPE)** to prevent personal injury. The personal protection devices include the following:

SAFETY GLASSES Wear safety glasses at all times while servicing any vehicle and be sure that they meet standard ANSI Z87.1. ● **SEE FIGURE 1–61.**

STEEL-TOED SAFETY SHOES ● **SEE FIGURE 1–62.** If steel-toed safety shoes are not available, then leather-topped shoes offer more protection than canvas or cloth covered shoes.

BUMP CAP Service technicians working under a vehicle should wear a **bump cap** to protect the head against under-vehicle objects and the pads of the lift. ● **SEE FIGURE 1–63.**

HEARING PROTECTION Hearing protection should be worn if the sound around you requires that you raise your voice (sound level higher than 90 dB). For example, a typical

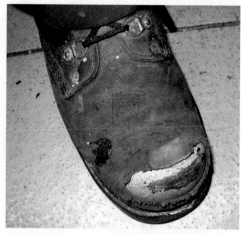

FIGURE 1–62 Steel-toed shoes are a worthwhile investment to help prevent foot injury due to falling objects. Even these well-worn shoes can protect the feet of this service technician.

FIGURE 1–63 One version of a bump cap is a molded plastic insert that is worn inside a regular cloth cap.

lawnmower produces noise at a level of about 110 dB. This means that everyone who uses a lawnmower or other lawn or garden equipment should wear ear protection.

GLOVES Many technicians wear gloves not only to help keep their hands clean but also to help protect their skin from the effects of dirty engine oil and other possibly hazardous materials.

Several types of gloves and their characteristics include:

- **Latex surgical gloves.** These gloves are relatively inexpensive, but tend to stretch, swell, and weaken when exposed to gas, oil, or solvents.
- **Vinyl gloves.** These gloves are also inexpensive and are not affected by gas, oil, or solvents.
- **Polyurethane gloves.** These gloves are more expensive, yet very strong. Even though these gloves are also not affected by gas, oil, or solvents, they do tend to be slippery.

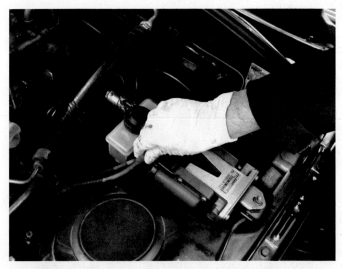

FIGURE 1-64 Protective gloves are available in several sizes and materials.

- **Nitrile gloves.** These gloves are exactly like latex gloves, but are not affected by gas, oil, or solvents, yet they tend to be expensive.
- **Mechanic's gloves.** These gloves are usually made of synthetic leather and spandex and provide thermo protection, as well as protection from dirt and grime.

● **SEE FIGURE 1-64.**

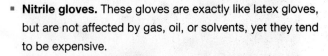

Besides wearing personal safety equipment, there are also many actions that should be performed to keep safe in the shop. These actions include:

- Remove jewelry that may get caught on something or act as a conductor to an exposed electrical circuit. ● **SEE FIGURE 1-65.**
- Take care of your hands. Keep your hands clean by washing with soap and hot water that is at least 110°F (43°C).
- Avoid loose or dangling clothing.
- When lifting any object, get a secure grip with solid footing. Keep the load close to your body to minimize the strain. Lift with your legs and arms, not your back.
- Do not twist your body when carrying a load. Instead, pivot your feet to help prevent strain on the spine.
- Ask for help when moving or lifting heavy objects.

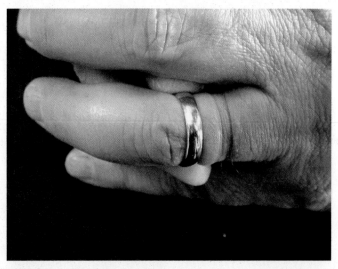

FIGURE 1-65 Remove all jewelry before performing service work on any vehicle.

FIGURE 1-66 Always connect an exhaust hose to the tailpipe of a vehicle to be run inside a building.

- Push a heavy object rather than pull it. (This is opposite to the way you should work with tools—never push a wrench! If you do and a bolt or nut loosens, your entire weight is used to propel your hand(s) forward. This usually results in cuts, bruises, or other painful injury.)
- Always connect an exhaust hose to the tailpipe of any running vehicle to help prevent the buildup of carbon monoxide inside a closed garage space. ● **SEE FIGURE 1-66.**
- When standing, keep objects, parts, and tools with which you are working between chest height and waist height. If seated, work at tasks that are at elbow height.
- Always be sure the hood is securely held open.

FIGURE 1–67 A binder clip being used to keep a fender cover from falling off.

FIGURE 1–68 Covering the interior as soon as the vehicle comes in for service helps improve customer satisfaction.

VEHICLE PROTECTION

FENDER COVERS Whenever working under the hood of any vehicle, be sure to use fender covers. They not only help protect the vehicle from possible damage but they also provide a clean surface to place parts and tools. The major problem with using fender covers is that they tend to move and often fall off the vehicle. To help prevent the fender covers from falling off secure them to a lip of the fender using a *binder clip* available at most office supply stores. ● **SEE FIGURE 1–67.**

INTERIOR PROTECTION Always protect the interior of the vehicle from accidental damage or dirt and grease by covering the seat, steering wheel, and floor with a protective covering. ● **SEE FIGURE 1–68.**

SAFETY LIFTING (HOISTING) A VEHICLE

Many chassis and underbody service procedures require that the vehicle be hoisted or lifted off the ground. The simplest methods involve the use of drive-on ramps or a floor jack and safety (jack) stands, whereas in-ground or surface-mounted lifts provide greater access.

SAFETY TIP

Shop Cloth Disposal

Always dispose of oily shop cloths in an enclosed container to prevent a fire. ● **SEE FIGURE 1–69.** Whenever oily cloths are thrown together on the floor or workbench, a chemical reaction can occur, which can ignite the cloth even without an open flame. This process of ignition without an open flame is called **spontaneous combustion.**

Setting the pads is a critical part of this hoisting procedure. All vehicle service information, including service, shop, and owner's manuals, include recommended locations to be used when hoisting (lifting) a vehicle. Newer vehicles have a triangle decal on the driver's door indicating the recommended lift points. The recommended standards for the lift points and lifting procedures are found in SAE Standard JRP-2184. ● **SEE FIGURE 1–70.**

FIGURE 1–69 All oily shop cloths should be stored in a metal container equipped with a lid to help prevent spontaneous combustion.

LIFT POINT LOCATION SYMBOL

FIGURE 1–70 Most newer vehicles have a triangle symbol indicating the recommended hoisting lift location.

These recommendations typically include the following points:

1. The vehicle should be centered on the lift or hoist so as not to overload one side or put too much force either forward or rearward. ● **SEE FIGURE 1–71.**

2. The pads of the lift should be spread as far apart as possible to provide a stable platform.

3. Each pad should be placed under a portion of the vehicle that is strong and capable of supporting the weight of the vehicle.

   a. Pinch welds at the bottom edge of the body are generally considered to be strong.

CAUTION: Even though **pinch weld seams** are the recommended location for hoisting many vehicles with unitized

(a)

(b)

FIGURE 1–71 (a) Tall safety stands can be used to provide additional support for the vehicle while on the hoist. (b) A block of wood should be used to avoid the possibility of doing damage to components supported by the stand.

bodies (unit-body), care should be taken not to place the pad(s) too far forward or rearward. Incorrect placement of the vehicle on the lift could cause the vehicle to be imbalanced, and the vehicle could fall. This is exactly what happened to the vehicle in ● **FIGURE 1–72.**

   b. Boxed areas of the body are the best places to position the pads on a vehicle without a frame. Be careful to note whether the arms of the lift might come into

FIGURE 1–72 This training vehicle fell from the hoist because the pads were not set correctly. No one was hurt but the vehicle was damaged.

contact with other parts of the vehicle before the pad touches the intended location. Commonly damaged areas include the following:

(1) Rocker panel moldings

(2) Exhaust system (including catalytic converter)

(3) Tires or body panels (● **SEE FIGURES 1–73 AND 1–74.**)

4. The vehicle should be raised about a foot (30 centimeters [cm]) off the floor, then stopped and shaken to check for stability. If the vehicle seems to be stable when checked at a short distance from the floor, continue raising the vehicle and continue to view the vehicle until it has reached the desired height. The hoist should be lowered onto the mechanical locks, and then raised off of the locks before lowering.

CAUTION: Do not look away from the vehicle while it is being raised (or lowered) on a hoist. Often one side or one end of the hoist can stop or fail, resulting in the vehicle being slanted enough to slip or fall, creating physical damage not only to the vehicle and/or hoist but also to the technician or others who may be nearby.

NOTE: Most hoists can be safely placed at any desired height. For ease while working, the area in which you are working should be at chest level. When working on brakes or suspension components, it is not necessary to work on them down near the floor or over your head. Raise the hoist so that the components are at chest level.

5. Before lowering the hoist, the safety latch(es) must be released and the direction of the controls reversed. The speed downward is often adjusted to be as slow as possible for additional safety.

JACKS AND SAFETY STANDS

Floor jacks properly rated for the weight of the vehicle being raised are a common vehicle lifting tool. Floor jacks are portable and relatively inexpensive and must be used with safety (jack) stands. The floor jack is used to raise the vehicle off the ground and safety stands should be placed under the frame on the body of the vehicle. The weight of the vehicle should never be kept on the hydraulic floor jack because a failure of the jack could cause the vehicle to fall. ● **SEE FIGURE 1–75.** The jack is then slowly released to allow the vehicle weight to be supported on the safety stands. If the front or rear of the vehicle is being raised, the opposite end of the vehicle must be blocked.

CAUTION: Safety stands should be rated higher than the weight they support.

DRIVE-ON RAMPS

Ramps are an inexpensive way to raise the front or rear of a vehicle. ● **SEE FIGURE 1–76.** Ramps are easy to store, but they can be dangerous because they can "kick out" when driving the vehicle onto the ramps.

CAUTION: Professional repair shops do not use ramps because they are dangerous to use. Use only with extreme care.

ELECTRICAL CORD SAFETY

Use correctly grounded three-prong sockets and extension cords to operate power tools. Some tools use only two-prong plugs. Make sure these are double insulated and repair or replace any electrical cords that are cut or damaged to prevent the possibility of an electrical shock. When not in use, keep electrical cords off the floor to prevent tripping over them. Tape the cords down if they are placed in high foot traffic areas.

(a)

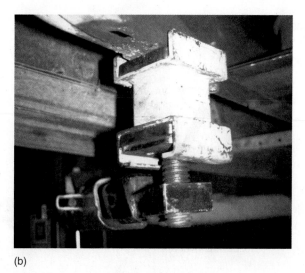
(b)

FIGURE 1–73 (a) An assortment of hoist pad adapters that are often needed to safely hoist many pickup trucks, vans, and sport utility vehicles (SUVs). (b) A view from underneath a Chevrolet pickup truck showing how the pad extensions are used to attach the hoist lifting pad to contact the frame.

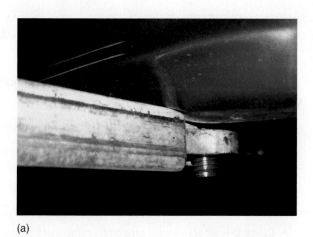
(a)

(b)

FIGURE 1–74 (a) The pad arm is just contacting the rocker panel of the vehicle. (b) The pad arm has dented the rocker panel on this vehicle because the pad was set too far inward underneath the vehicle.

JUMP STARTING AND BATTERY SAFETY

To jump start another vehicle with a dead battery, connect good-quality copper jumper cables as indicated in ● **SEE FIGURE 1–77** or a jump box. The last connection made should always be on the engine block or an engine bracket as far from the battery as possible. It is normal for a spark to be created when the jumper cables finally complete the jumper cable connections, and this spark could cause an explosion of the gases around the battery. Many newer vehicles have special ground connections built away from the battery just for the purpose of jump starting. Check the owner's manual or service information for the exact location.

Batteries contain acid and should be handled with care to avoid tipping them greater than a 45-degree angle. Always remove jewelry when working around a battery to avoid the possibility of electrical shock or burns, which can occur when the metal comes in contact with a 12 volt circuit and ground, such as the body of the vehicle.

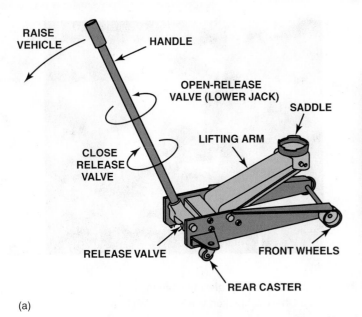

(a)   (b)

FIGURE 1–75 (a) A hydraulic hand-operated floor jack. (b) Whenever a vehicle is raised off the ground, a safety stand should be placed under the frame, axle, or body to support the weight of the vehicle.

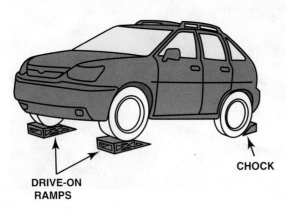

FIGURE 1–76 Drive-on-type ramps are dangerous to use. The wheels on the ground level must be chocked (blocked) to prevent accidental movement down the ramp.

 **SAFETY TIP**

Air Hose Safety

Improper use of an air nozzle can cause blindness or deafness. Compressed air must be reduced to less than 30 psi (206 kPa). ●**SEE FIGURE 1–78.** If an air nozzle is used to dry and clean parts, make sure the airstream is directed away from anyone else in the immediate area. Coil and store air hoses when they are not in use.

FIRE EXTINGUISHERS

There are four **fire extinguisher classes**. Each class should be used on specific fires only:

- **Class A** is designed for use on general combustibles, such as cloth, paper, and wood.
- **Class B** is designed for use on flammable liquids and greases, including gasoline, oil, thinners, and solvents.
- **Class C** is used only on electrical fires.
- **Class D** is effective only on combustible metals such as powdered aluminum, sodium, or magnesium.

The class rating is clearly marked on the side of every fire extinguisher. Many extinguishers are good for multiple types of fires. ●**SEE FIGURE 1–79.**

When using a fire extinguisher, remember the word "PASS."

P = Pull the safety pin.

A = Aim the nozzle of the extinguisher at the base of the fire.

S = Squeeze the lever to actuate the extinguisher.

S = Sweep the nozzle from side-to-side.

● **SEE FIGURE 1–80.**

TYPES OF FIRE EXTINGUISHERS   Types of fire extinguishers include the following:

- **Water.** A water fire extinguisher, usually in a pressurized container, is good to use on Class A fires by reducing

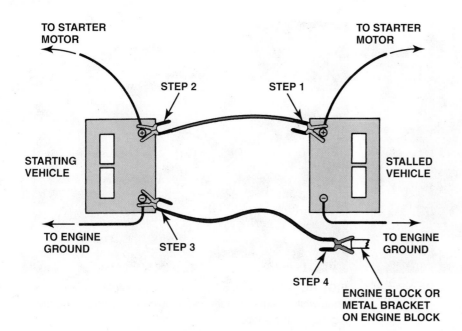

TO STARTER MOTOR

TO STARTER MOTOR

STEP 2

STEP 1

STARTING VEHICLE

STALLED VEHICLE

TO ENGINE GROUND

STEP 3

TO ENGINE GROUND

STEP 4

ENGINE BLOCK OR METAL BRACKET ON ENGINE BLOCK

FIGURE 1–77 Jumper cable usage guide. Follow the same connections if using a portable jump box.

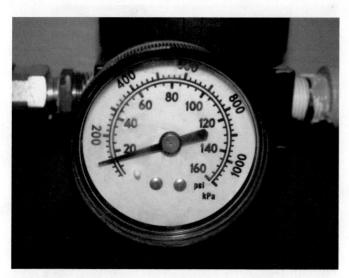

FIGURE 1–78 The air pressure going to the nozzle should be reduced to 30 psi or less to help prevent personal injury.

the temperature to the point where a fire cannot be sustained.

- **Carbon dioxide (CO_2).** A carbon dioxide fire extinguisher is good for almost any type of fire, especially Class B and Class C materials. A CO_2 fire extinguisher works by removing the oxygen from the fire and the cold CO_2 also helps reduce the temperature of the fire.

- **Dry chemical (yellow).** A dry chemical fire extinguisher is good for Class A, B, and C fires. It acts by coating the flammable materials, which eliminates the oxygen from the fire. A dry chemical fire extinguisher tends to be very corrosive and will cause damage to electronic devices.

FIRE BLANKETS

Fire blankets are required to be available in the shop areas. If a person is on fire, a fire blanket should be removed from its storage bag and thrown over and around the victim to smother the fire. ● **SEE FIGURE 1–81** showing a typical fire blanket.

FIRST AID AND EYE WASH STATIONS

All shop areas must be equipped with a first aid kit and an eye wash station centrally located and kept stocked with emergency supplies. ● **SEE FIGURE 1–82.**

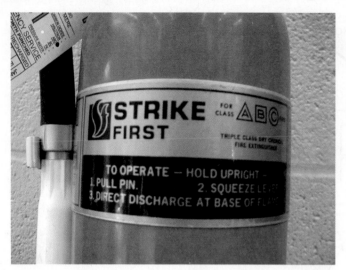

FIGURE 1–79 A typical fire extinguisher designed to be used on type A, B, or C fires.

FIGURE 1–81 A treated wool blanket is kept in an easy-to-open wall-mounted holder and should be placed in a central location in the shop.

FIGURE 1–80 A CO_2 fire extinguisher being used on a fire set in an open drum during a demonstration at a fire training center.

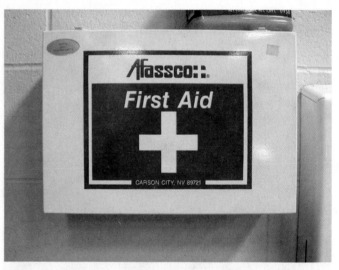

FIGURE 1–82 A first aid box should be centrally located in the shop and kept stocked with the recommended supplies.

FIRST AID KIT   A first aid kit should include:

- Bandages (variety)
- Gauze pads
- Roll gauze
- Iodine swab sticks
- Antibiotic ointment
- Hydrocortisone cream
- Burn gel packets
- Eye wash solution
- Scissors
- Tweezers
- Gloves
- First aid guide

Every shop should have a person trained in first aid. If there is an accident, call for help immediately.

EYE WASH STATION   An **eye wash station** should be centrally located and used whenever any liquid or chemical gets into the eyes. If such an emergency does occur, keep eyes in a constant stream of water and call for professional assistance. ● **SEE FIGURE 1–83.**

FIGURE 1–83 A typical eye wash station. Often a thorough flushing of the eyes with water is the first and often the best treatment in the event of eye contamination.

HYBRID ELECTRIC VEHICLE SAFETY ISSUES

Hybrid electric vehicles (HEVs) use a high-voltage battery pack and an electric motor(s) to help propel the vehicle. ● SEE FIGURE 1–84 for an example of a typical warning label on a hybrid electric vehicle. The gasoline or diesel engine is also equipped with a generator or a combination starter and an integrated starter generator (ISG) or integrated starter alternator (ISA). To safely work around a hybrid electric vehicle, the high-voltage (HV) battery and circuits should be shut off following these steps:

 WARNING

Some vehicle manufacturers specify that insulated rubber *linesman's gloves* be used whenever working around the high-voltage circuits to prevent the danger of electrical shock.

FIGURE 1–84 A warning label on a Honda hybrid warns that a person can be killed due to the high-voltage circuits under the cover.

 SAFETY TIP

Infection Control Precautions

Working on a vehicle can result in personal injury including the possibility of being cut or hurt enough to cause bleeding. Some infections such as hepatitis B, HIV (which can cause acquired immunodeficiency syndrome, or AIDS), and hepatitis C virus are transmitted through blood. These infections are commonly called blood-borne pathogens. Report any injury that involves blood to your supervisor and take the necessary precautions to avoid coming in contact with blood from another person.

STEP 1 Turn off the ignition key (if equipped) and remove the key from the ignition switch. (This will shut off all high-voltage circuits if the relay[s] is [are] working correctly.)

STEP 2 Disconnect the high-voltage circuits.

TOYOTA PRIUS The cutoff switch is located in the trunk. To gain access, remove three clips holding the upper left portion of the trunk side cover. To disconnect the high-voltage system, pull the orange handled plug while wearing insulated rubber linesman's gloves. ● SEE FIGURE 1–85.

FORD ESCAPE/MERCURY MARINER Ford and Mercury specify that the following steps should be included when working with the high-voltage (HV) systems of a hybrid vehicle:

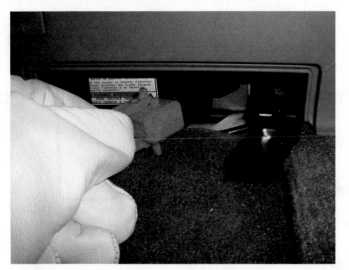

FIGURE 1–85 The high-voltage disconnect switch is in the trunk area on a Toyota Prius. Insulated rubber linesman's gloves should be worn when removing this plug.

FIGURE 1–86 The high-voltage shut-off switch on a Ford Escape hybrid. The switch is located under the carpet at the rear of the vehicle.

- Four orange cones are to be placed at the four corners of the vehicle to create a buffer zone.

- High-voltage insulated gloves are to be worn with an outer leather glove to protect the inner rubber glove from possible damage.

- The service technician should also wear a face shield and a fiberglass hook should be in the area and used to move a technician in the event of electrocution.

The high-voltage shut-off switch is located in the rear of the vehicle under the right side carpet. ● **SEE FIGURE 1–86.**

FIGURE 1–87 The shut-off switch on a GM parallel hybrid truck is green because this system uses 42 volts instead of higher, and possibly fatal, voltages used in other hybrid vehicles.

Rotate the handle to the "service shipping" position, lift it out to disable the high-voltage circuit, and wait five minutes before removing high-voltage cables.

HONDA CIVIC To totally disable the high-voltage system on a Honda Civic, remove the main fuse (labeled number 1) from the driver's side underhood fuse panel. This should be all that is necessary to shut off the high-voltage circuit. If this is not possible, then remove the rear seat cushion and seat back. Remove the metal switch cover labeled "up" and remove the red locking cover. Move the "battery module switch" down to disable the high-voltage system.

CHEVROLET SILVERADO/GMC SIERRA PICKUP TRUCK The high-voltage shut-off switch is located under the rear passenger seat. Remove the cover marked "energy storage box" and turn the green service disconnect switch to the horizontal position to turn off the high-voltage circuits. ● **SEE FIGURE 1–87.**

☠ **WARNING**

Do not touch any orange wiring or component without following the vehicle manufacturer's procedures and wearing the specified personal protective equipment.

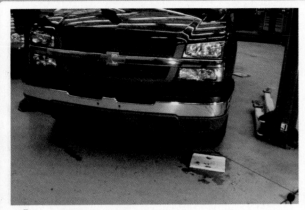

1 The first step in hoisting a vehicle is to properly align the vehicle in the center of the stall.

2 Most vehicles will be correctly positioned when the left front tire is centered on the tire pad.

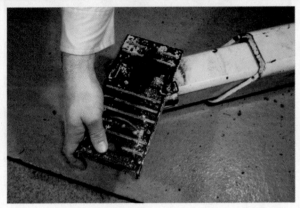

3 The arms can be moved in and out and most pads can be rotated to allow for many different types of vehicle construction.

4 Most lifts are equipped with short pad extensions that are often necessary to use to allow the pad to contact the frame of a vehicle without causing the arm of the lift to hit and damage parts of the body.

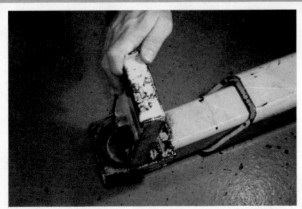

5 Tall pad extensions can also be used to gain access to the frame of a vehicle. This position is needed to safely hoist many pickup trucks, vans, and sport utility vehicles.

6 An additional extension may be necessary to hoist a truck or van equipped with running boards to give the necessary clearance.

CONTINUED ▶

STEP BY STEP

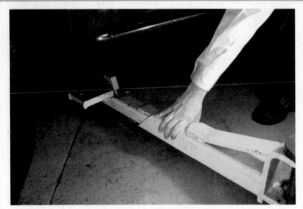

7 Position the pads under the vehicle under the recommended locations.

8 After being sure all pads are correctly positioned, use the electromechanical controls to raise the vehicle.

9 With the vehicle raised one foot (30 cm) off the ground, push down on the vehicle to check to see if it is stable on the pads. If the vehicle rocks, lower the vehicle and reset the pads. The vehicle can be raised to any desired working level. Be sure the safety is engaged before working on or under the vehicle.

10 If raising a vehicle without a frame, place the flat pads under the pinch weld seam to spread the load. If additional clearance is necessary, the pads can be raised as shown.

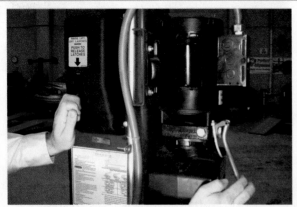

11 When the service work is completed, the hoist should be raised slightly and the safety released before using the hydraulic lever to lower the vehicle.

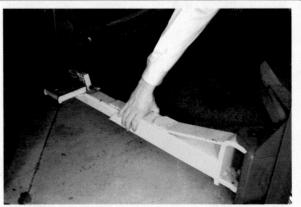

12 After lowering the vehicle, be sure all arms of the lift are moved out of the way before driving the vehicle out of the work stall.

1. Bolts, studs, and nuts are commonly used as fasteners in the chassis. The sizes for fractional and metric threads are different and are not interchangeable. The grade is the rating of the strength of a fastener.

2. Whenever a vehicle is raised above the ground, it must be supported at a substantial section of the body or frame.

3. Wrenches are available in open end, box end, and combination open and box end.

4. An adjustable wrench should only be used where the proper size is not available.

5. Line wrenches are also called flare-nut wrenches, fitting wrenches, or tube-nut wrenches and are used to remove fuel or refrigerant lines.

6. Sockets are rotated by a ratchet or breaker bar, also called a flex handle.

7. Torque wrenches measure the amount of torque applied to a fastener.

8. Screwdriver types include straight blade (flat tip) and Phillips.

9. Hammers and mallets come in a variety of sizes and weights.

10. Pliers are a useful tool and are available in many different types, including slip-joint, multigroove, linesman's, diagonal, needle-nose, and locking pliers.

11. Other common hand tools include snap-ring pliers, files, cutters, punches, chisels, and hacksaws.

12. Hybrid electric vehicles should be de-powered if any of the high-voltage components are going to be serviced.

REVIEW QUESTIONS

1. List three precautions that must be taken whenever hoisting (lifting) a vehicle.

2. Describe how to determine the grade of a fastener, including how the markings differ between fractional and metric bolts.

3. List four items that are personal protective equipment (PPE).

4. List the types of fire extinguishers and their usage.

5. Why are wrenches offset 15 degrees?

6. What are the other names for a line wrench?

7. What are the standard automotive drive sizes for sockets?

8. Which type of screwdriver requires the use of a hammer or mallet?

9. What is inside a dead-blow hammer?

10. What type of cutter is available in left and right cutters?

CHAPTER QUIZ

1. The correct location for the pads when hoisting or jacking the vehicle can often be found in the _____.
   a. Service manual
   b. Shop manual
   c. Owner's manual
   d. All of the above

2. For the best working position, the work should be _____.
   a. At neck or head level
   b. At knee or ankle level
   c. Overhead by about 1 foot
   d. At chest or elbow level

3. A high-strength bolt is identified by _____.
   a. A UNC symbol
   b. Lines on the head
   c. Strength letter codes
   d. The coarse threads

4. A fastener that uses threads on both ends is called a _____.
   a. Cap screw
   b. Stud
   c. Machine screw
   d. Crest fastener

5. When working with hand tools, always _____.
   a. Push the wrench—don't pull toward you
   b. Pull a wrench—don't push a wrench away from you

6. The proper term for Channel Locks is _____.
   a. Vise Grips
   b. Crescent wrench
   c. Locking pliers
   d. Multigroove adjustable pliers

7. The proper term for Vise Grips is _____.
   a. Locking pliers
   b. Slip-joint pliers
   c. Side cuts
   d. Multigroove adjustable pliers

8. Two technicians are discussing torque wrenches. Technician A says that a torque wrench is capable of tightening a fastener with more torque than a conventional breaker bar or ratchet. Technician B says that a torque wrench should be calibrated regularly for the most accurate results. Which technician is correct?
   a. Technician A only
   b. Technician B only
   c. Both Technicians A and B
   d. Neither Technician A nor B

9. What type of screwdriver should be used if there is very limited space above the head of the fastener?
   a. Offset screwdriver
   b. Standard screwdriver
   c. Impact screwdriver
   d. Robertson screwdriver

10. What type of hammer is plastic coated, has a metal casing inside, and is filled with small lead balls?
    a. Dead-blow hammer   c. Sledgehammer
    b. Soft-blow hammer   d. Plastic hammer

chapter 2
ENVIRONMENTAL AND HAZARDOUS MATERIALS

LEARNING OBJECTIVES

After studying this chapter, the reader will be able to:

1. Identify hazardous waste materials in accordance with state and federal regulations and follow proper safety precautions while handling hazardous materials.
2. Define the Occupational Safety and Health Act (OSHA).
3. Explain the term material safety data sheets (MSDS).
4. Define the steps required to safely handle and store automotive chemicals and waste.

KEY TERMS

Aboveground storage tank (AGST) 43
Asbestosis 42
BCI 46
CAA 41
CFR 40
EPA 40
Hazardous waste material 40
HEPA vacuum 42

Mercury 48
MSDS 40
OSHA 40
RCRA 41
Right-to-know laws 40
Solvent 42
Underground storage tank (UST) 43
Used oil 43
WHMIS 40

HAZARDOUS WASTE

DEFINITION OF HAZARDOUS WASTE **Hazardous waste materials** are chemicals, or components, that the shop no longer needs and that pose a danger to the environment and people if they are disposed of in ordinary garbage cans or sewers. However, no material is considered hazardous waste until the shop has finished using it and is ready to dispose of it.

PERSONAL PROTECTIVE EQUIPMENT (PPE) When handling hazardous waste material, one must always wear the proper protective clothing and equipment detailed in the right-to-know laws. This includes respirator equipment. All recommended procedures must be followed accurately. Personal injury may result from improper clothing, equipment, and procedures when handling hazardous materials.

FEDERAL AND STATE LAWS

OCCUPATIONAL SAFETY AND HEALTH ACT The U.S. Congress passed the **Occupational Safety and Health Act (OSHA)** in 1970. This legislation was designed to assist and encourage the citizens of the United States in their efforts to assure:

- Safe and healthful working conditions by providing research, information, education, and training in the field of occupational safety and health.
- Safe and healthful working conditions for working men and women by authorizing enforcement of the standards developed under the act.

Because about 25% of workers are exposed to health and safety hazards on the job, OSHA standards are necessary to monitor, control, and educate workers regarding health and safety in the workplace.

EPA The **Environmental Protection Agency (EPA)** publishes a list of hazardous materials that is included in the **Code of Federal Regulations (CFR)**. The EPA considers waste hazardous if it is included on the EPA list of hazardous materials, or it has one or more of the following characteristics:

- **Reactive**—Any material that reacts violently with water or other chemicals is considered hazardous.
- **Corrosive**—If a material burns the skin, or dissolves metals and other materials, a technician should consider

it hazardous. A pH scale is used, with number 7 indicating neutral. Pure water has a pH of 7. Lower numbers indicate an acidic solution and higher numbers indicate a caustic solution. If a material releases cyanide gas, hydrogen sulfide gas, or similar gases when exposed to low pH acid solutions, it is considered hazardous.

- **Toxic**—Materials are hazardous if they leak one or more of eight different heavy metals in concentrations greater than 100 times the primary drinking water standard.
- **Ignitable**—A liquid is hazardous if it has a flash point below 140°F (60°C), and a solid is hazardous if it ignites spontaneously.
- **Radioactive**—Any substance that emits measurable levels of radiation is radioactive. When individuals bring containers of a highly radioactive substance into the shop environment, qualified personnel with the appropriate equipment must test them.

 **WARNING**

Hazardous waste disposal laws include serious penalties for anyone responsible for breaking these laws.

RIGHT-TO-KNOW LAWS The **right-to-know laws** state that employees have a right to know when the materials they use at work are hazardous. The right-to-know laws started with the Hazard Communication Standard published by the OSHA in 1983. Originally, this document was intended for chemical companies and manufacturers that required employees to handle hazardous materials in their work situation but the federal courts have decided to apply these laws to all companies, including automotive service shops. Under the right-to-know laws, the employer has responsibilities regarding the handling of hazardous materials by their employees. All employees must be trained about the types of hazardous materials they will encounter in the workplace. The employees must be informed about their rights under legislation regarding the handling of hazardous materials.

MATERIAL SAFETY DATA SHEETS. All hazardous materials must be properly labeled, and information about each hazardous material must be posted on **material safety data sheets (MSDS)**, now called simply *safety data sheets (SDS)*, available from the manufacturer. In Canada, MSDS information is called **Workplace Hazardous Materials Information Systems (WHMIS)**.

FIGURE 2–1 Safety data sheets (SDS), formerly known as material safety data sheets (MSDS), should be readily available for use by anyone in the area who may come into contact with hazardous materials.

The employer has a responsibility to place SDS information where they are easily accessible by all employees. The data sheets provide the following information about the hazardous material: chemical name, physical characteristics, protective handling equipment, explosion/fire hazards, incompatible materials, health hazards, medical conditions aggravated by exposure, emergency and first-aid procedures, safe handling, and spill/leak procedures.

The employer also has a responsibility to make sure that all hazardous materials are properly labeled. The label information must include health, fire, and reactivity hazards posed by the material, as well as the protective equipment necessary to handle the material. The manufacturer must supply all warning and precautionary information about hazardous materials. This information must be read and understood by the employee before handling the material. ● **SEE FIGURE 2–1.**

RESOURCE CONSERVATION AND RECOVERY ACT

Federal and state laws control the disposal of hazardous waste materials and every shop employee must be familiar with these laws. Hazardous waste disposal laws include the **Resource Conservation and Recovery Act (RCRA)**. This law states that hazardous material users are responsible for hazardous materials from the time they become a waste until the proper disposal is completed. Many shops hire an independent hazardous waste hauler to dispose of hazardous waste material. The shop owner, or manager, should have a written contract with the hazardous waste hauler. Rather than have hazardous waste material hauled to an approved hazardous

FIGURE 2–2 Tag identifying that the power has been removed and service work is being done.

waste disposal site, a shop may choose to recycle the material in the shop. Therefore, the user must store hazardous waste material properly and safely, and be responsible for the transportation of this material until it arrives at an approved hazardous waste disposal site, where it can be processed according to the law. The RCRA controls the following types of automotive waste:

- Paint and body repair products waste
- Solvents for parts and equipment cleaning
- Batteries and battery acid
- Mild acids used for metal cleaning and preparation
- Waste oil and engine coolants or antifreeze
- Air-conditioning refrigerants and oils
- Engine oil filters

LOCKOUT/TAGOUT According to OSHA Title 29, code of Federal Regulations (CPR), part 1910.147, machinery must be locked out to prevent injury to employees when maintenance or repair work is being performed. Any piece of equipment that should not be used must be tagged and the electrical power disconnected to prevent it from being used. Always read, understand, and follow all safety warning tags. ● **SEE FIGURE 2–2.**

CLEAN AIR ACT Air-conditioning (A/C) systems and refrigerant are regulated by the **Clean Air Act (CAA)**, Title VI, Section 609. Technician certification and service equipment is also regulated. Any technician working on automotive A/C systems must be certified. A/C refrigerants must not be released or vented into the atmosphere, and used refrigerants must be recovered.

ASBESTOS HAZARDS

Friction materials such as brake and clutch linings often contain asbestos. While asbestos has been eliminated from most original equipment friction materials, the automotive service technician cannot know whether or not the vehicle being serviced is or is not equipped with friction materials containing asbestos. It is important that all friction materials be handled as if they do contain asbestos.

Asbestos exposure can cause scar tissue to form in the lungs. This condition is called **asbestosis**. It gradually causes increasing shortness of breath, and the scarring to the lungs is permanent.

Even low exposures to asbestos can cause *mesothelioma*, a type of fatal cancer of the lining of the chest or abdominal cavity. Asbestos exposure can also increase the risk of *lung cancer* as well as cancer of the voice box, stomach, and large intestine. It usually takes 15 to 30 years or more for cancer or asbestos lung scarring to show up after exposure. Scientists call this the *latency period*.

Government agencies recommend that asbestos exposure should be eliminated or controlled to the lowest level possible. These agencies have developed recommendations and standards that the automotive service technician and equipment manufacturer should follow. These U.S. federal agencies include the National Institute for Occupational Safety and Health (NIOSH), Occupational Safety and Health Administration (OSHA), and Environmental Protection Agency (EPA).

ASBESTOS OSHA STANDARDS The Occupational Safety and Health Administration has established three levels of asbestos exposure. Any vehicle service establishment that does either brake or clutch work must limit employee exposure to asbestos to less than 0.2 fibers per cubic centimeter (cc) as determined by an air sample.

If the level of exposure to employees is greater than specified, corrective measures must be performed and a large fine may be imposed.

NOTE: Research has found that worn asbestos fibers such as those from automotive brakes or clutches may not be as hazardous as first believed. Worn asbestos fibers do not have sharp flared ends that can latch onto tissue, but rather are worn down to a dust form that resembles talc. Grinding or sawing operations on unworn brake shoes or clutch discs *will*, however, contain *harmful* asbestos fibers. To limit health damage, always use proper handling procedures while working around any component that may contain asbestos.

FIGURE 2–3 All brakes should be moistened with water or solvent to help prevent brake dust from becoming airborne.

ASBESTOS EPA REGULATIONS The federal Environmental Protection Agency has established procedures for the removal and disposal of asbestos. The EPA procedures require that products containing asbestos be "wetted" to prevent the asbestos fibers from becoming airborne. According to the EPA, asbestos-containing materials can be disposed of as regular waste. Only when asbestos becomes airborne is it considered to be hazardous.

ASBESTOS HANDLING GUIDELINES The air in the shop area can be tested by a testing laboratory, but this can be expensive. Tests have determined that asbestos levels can easily be kept below the recommended levels by using a liquid, like water, or a special vacuum.

NOTE: Even though asbestos is being removed from brake and clutch lining materials, the service technician cannot tell whether or not the old brake pads, shoes, or clutch discs contain asbestos. Therefore, to be safe, the technician should assume that all brake pads, shoes, or clutch discs contain asbestos.

HEPA VACUUM. A special **high-efficiency particulate air (HEPA) vacuum** system has been proven to be effective in keeping asbestos exposure levels below 0.1 fiber per cubic centimeter.

SOLVENT SPRAY. Many technicians use an aerosol can of brake cleaning solvent to wet the brake dust and prevent it from becoming airborne. A **solvent** is a liquid that is used to dissolve dirt, grime, or solid particles. Commercial brake cleaners are available that use a concentrated cleaner that is mixed with water. ● **SEE FIGURE 2–3**. The waste liquid is filtered, and when dry, the filter can be disposed of as solid waste.

WARNING

Never use compressed air to blow brake dust. The fine talclike brake dust can create a health hazard even if asbestos is not present or is present in dust rather than fiber form.

DISPOSAL OF BRAKE DUST AND BRAKE SHOES. The hazard of asbestos occurs when asbestos fibers are airborne. Once the asbestos has been wetted down, it is then considered to be solid waste, rather than hazardous waste. Old brake shoes and pads should be enclosed, preferably in a plastic bag, to help prevent any of the brake material from becoming airborne. *Always follow current federal and local laws concerning disposal of all waste.*

USED BRAKE FLUID

Most brake fluid is made from polyglycol, is water soluble, and can be considered hazardous if it has absorbed metals from the brake system.

STORAGE AND DISPOSAL OF BRAKE FLUID

- Collect brake fluid in a container clearly marked to indicate that it is designated for that purpose.
- If the waste brake fluid is hazardous, be sure to manage it appropriately and use only an authorized waste receiver for its disposal.
- If the waste brake fluid is nonhazardous (such as old, but unused), determine from your local solid waste collection provider what should be done for its proper disposal.
- Do not mix brake fluid with used engine oil.
- Do not pour brake fluid down drains or onto the ground.
- Recycle brake fluid through a registered recycler.

USED OIL

Used oil is any petroleum-based or synthetic oil that has been used. During normal use, impurities such as dirt, metal scrapings, water, or chemicals can get mixed in with the oil. Eventually, this used oil must be replaced with virgin or re-refined oil. The EPA's used oil management standards include a three-pronged approach to determine if a substance meets the definition of *used oil*. To meet the EPA's definition of used oil, a substance must meet each of the following three criteria.

- **Origin.** The first criterion for identifying used oil is based on the oil's origin. Used oil must have been refined from crude oil or made from synthetic materials. Animal and vegetable oils are excluded from the EPA's definition of used oil.
- **Use.** The second criterion is based on whether and how the oil is used. Oils used as lubricants, hydraulic fluids, heat transfer fluids, and for other similar purposes are considered used oil. The EPA's definition also excludes products used as cleaning agents, as well as certain petroleum-derived products like antifreeze and kerosene.
- **Contaminants.** The third criterion is based on whether or not the oil is contaminated with either physical or chemical impurities. In other words, to meet the EPA's definition, used oil must become contaminated as a result of being used. This aspect of the EPA's definition includes residues and contaminants generated from handling, storing, and processing used oil.

NOTE: The release of only one gallon of used oil (a typical oil change) can make a million gallons of fresh water undrinkable.

If used oil is dumped down the drain and enters a sewage treatment plant, concentrations as small as 50 to 100 PPM (parts per million) in the waste water can foul sewage treatment processes. Never mix a listed hazardous waste, gasoline, waste water, halogenated solvent, antifreeze, or an unknown waste material with used oil. Adding any of these substances will cause the used oil to become contaminated, which classifies it as hazardous waste.

STORAGE AND DISPOSAL OF USED OIL Once oil has been used, it can be collected, recycled, and used over and over again. An estimated 380 million gallons of used oil are recycled each year. Recycled used oil can sometimes be used again for the same job or can take on a completely different task. For example, used engine oil can be re-refined and sold at some discount stores as engine oil or processed for furnace fuel oil. After collecting used oil in an appropriate container such as a 55-gallon steel drum, the material must be disposed of in one of two ways:

- Shipped offsite for recycling
- Burned in an onsite or offsite EPA-approved heater for energy recovery

Used oil must be stored in compliance with an existing **underground storage tank (UST)** or an **aboveground**

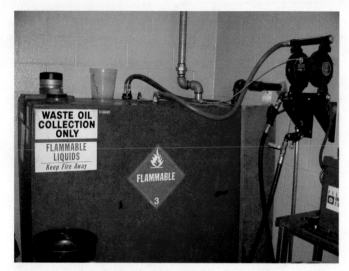

FIGURE 2–4 A typical aboveground oil storage tank.

storage tank (AGST) standard, or kept in separate containers.
● SEE FIGURE 2–4. Containers are portable receptacles, such as a 55-gallon steel drum.

KEEP USED OIL STORAGE DRUMS IN GOOD CONDITION. This means that they should be covered, secured from vandals, properly labeled, and maintained in compliance with local fire codes. Frequent inspections for leaks, corrosion, and spillage are an essential part of container maintenance.

NEVER STORE USED OIL IN ANYTHING OTHER THAN TANKS AND STORAGE CONTAINERS. Used oil may also be stored in units that are permitted to store regulated hazardous waste.

USED OIL FILTER DISPOSAL REGULATIONS. Used oil filters contain used engine oil that may be hazardous. Before an oil filter is placed into the trash or sent to be recycled, it must be drained using one of the following hot-draining methods approved by the EPA.

- Puncture the filter antidrainback valve or filter dome end and hot-drain for at least 12 hours
- Hot-drain and crushing
- Dismantling and hot draining
- Any other hot-draining method, which will remove all the used oil from the filter

After the oil has been drained from the oil filter, the filter housing can be disposed of in any of the following ways:

- Sent for recycling
- Picked up by a service contract company
- Disposed of in regular trash

SOLVENTS

The major sources of chemical danger are liquid and aerosol brake cleaning fluids that contain chlorinated hydrocarbon solvents. Several other chemicals that do not deplete the ozone, such as heptane, hexane, and xylene, are now being used in nonchlorinated brake cleaning solvents. Some manufacturers are also producing solvents they describe as environmentally responsible, which are biodegradable and noncarcinogenic (non-cancer-causing).

There is no specific standard for physical contact with chlorinated hydrocarbon solvents or the chemicals replacing them. All contact should be avoided whenever possible. The law requires an employer to provide appropriate protective equipment and ensure proper work practices by an employee handling these chemicals.

 SAFETY TIP

Hand Safety

Service technicians should wash their hands with soap and water after handling engine oil, differential oil, or transmission fluids or wear protective rubber gloves. Another safety tip is that the service technician should not wear watches, rings, or other jewelry that could come in contact with electrical or moving parts of a vehicle. ● SEE FIGURE 2–5.

EFFECTS OF CHEMICAL POISONING The effects of exposure to chlorinated hydrocarbon and other types of solvents can take many forms. Short-term exposure at low levels can cause symptoms such as:

- Headache
- Nausea
- Drowsiness
- Dizziness
- Lack of coordination
- Unconsciousness

It may also cause irritation of the eyes, nose, and throat, and flushing of the face and neck. Short-term exposure to higher concentrations can cause liver damage with symptoms such as yellow jaundice or dark urine. Liver damage may not become evident until several weeks after the exposure.

FIGURE 2–5 Washing hands and removing jewelry are two important safety habits all service technicians should practice.

 FREQUENTLY ASKED QUESTION

How Can You Tell If a Solvent Is Hazardous?

If a solvent or any of the ingredients of a product contains "fluor" or "chlor," then it is likely to be hazardous. Check the instructions on the label for proper use and disposal procedures.

HAZARDOUS SOLVENTS AND REGULATORY STATUS

Most solvents are classified as hazardous wastes. Other characteristics of solvents include the following:

- Solvents with flash points below 140 degrees F (60 degrees C) are considered flammable and, like gasoline, are federally regulated by the Department of Transportation (DOT).
- Solvents and oils with flash points above 60°C are considered combustible and, like engine oil, are also regulated by the DOT. All flammable items must be stored in a fireproof container. ● SEE FIGURE 2–6.

It is the responsibility of the repair shop to determine if its spent solvent is hazardous waste. Solvent reclaimers are available that clean and restore the solvent so it lasts indefinitely.

USED SOLVENTS Used or spent solvents are liquid materials that have been generated as waste and may contain xylene, methanol, ethyl ether, and methyl isobutyl ketone (MIBK). These materials must be stored in OSHA-approved safety containers with the lids or caps closed tightly. Additional requirements include the following:

FIGURE 2–6 Typical fireproof storage cabinet used to store flammable materials such as solvents, paint or gasoline cans.

- Containers should be clearly labeled "Hazardous Waste" and the date the material was first placed into the storage receptacle should be noted.
- Labeling is not required for solvents being used in a parts washer.
- Used solvents will not be counted toward a facility's monthly output of hazardous waste if the vendor under contract removes the material.
- Used solvents may be disposed of by recycling with a local vendor, like SafetyKleen®, to have the used solvent removed according to specific terms in the vendor agreement.
- Use aqueous-based (nonsolvent) cleaning systems to help avoid the problems associated with chemical solvents. ● SEE FIGURE 2–7.

COOLANT DISPOSAL

Coolant is a mixture of antifreeze and water. New antifreeze is not considered to be hazardous even though it can cause death if ingested. Used antifreeze may be hazardous due to dissolved metals from the engine and other components of the cooling system. These metals can include iron, steel, aluminum, copper, brass, and lead (from older radiators and

FIGURE 2–7 Using a water-based cleaning system helps reduce the hazards from using strong chemicals.

FIGURE 2–8 Used antifreeze coolant should be kept separate and stored in a leakproof container until it can be recycled or disposed of according to federal, state, and local laws. Note that the storage barrel is placed inside another container to catch any coolant that may spill out of the inside barrel.

heater cores). Coolant should be disposed of in one of the following ways:

- Coolant should be recycled either onsite or offsite.
- Used coolant should be stored in a sealed and labeled container. ● **SEE FIGURE 2–8**.
- Used coolant can often be disposed of into municipal sewers with a permit. Check with local authorities and obtain a permit before discharging used coolant into sanitary sewers.

LEAD-ACID BATTERY WASTE

About 70 million spent lead-acid batteries are generated each year in the United States alone. Lead is classified as a toxic metal, and the acid used in lead-acid batteries is highly corrosive. The vast majority (95% to 98%) of these batteries are recycled through lead reclamation operations and secondary lead smelters for use in the manufacture of new batteries.

BATTERY DISPOSAL Used lead-acid batteries must be reclaimed or recycled in order to be exempt from hazardous waste regulations. Leaking batteries must be stored and transported as hazardous waste. Some states have more strict regulations, which require special handling procedures and

transportation. According to the **Battery Council International (BCI)**, battery laws usually include the following rules:

1. Lead-acid battery disposal is prohibited in landfills or incinerators. Batteries are required to be delivered to a battery retailer, wholesaler, recycling center, or lead smelter.

2. All retailers of automotive batteries are required to post a sign that displays the universal recycling symbol and indicates the retailer's specific requirements for accepting used batteries.

3. Battery electrolyte contains sulfuric acid, which is a very corrosive substance capable of causing serious personal injury, such as skin burns and eye damage. In addition, the battery plates contain lead, which is highly poisonous. For this reason, disposing of batteries improperly can cause environmental contamination and lead to severe health problems.

BATTERY HANDLING AND STORAGE Batteries, whether new or used, should be kept indoors if possible. The storage location should be an area specifically designated for battery storage and must be well ventilated (to the outside). If outdoor storage is the only alternative, a sheltered and secured area with acid-resistant secondary containment is strongly recommended. It is also advisable that acid-resistant secondary containment be used for indoor storage. In addition, batteries should be placed on acid-resistant pallets and never stacked.

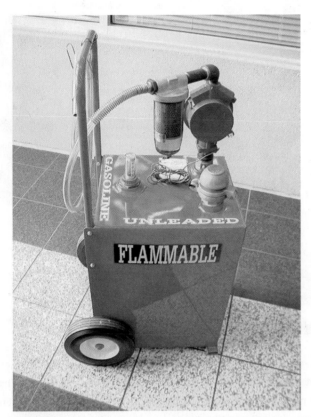

FIGURE 2–9 This red gasoline container holds about 30 gallons of gasoline and is used to fill vehicles used for training.

FUEL SAFETY AND STORAGE

Gasoline is a very explosive liquid. The expanding vapors that come from gasoline are extremely dangerous. These vapors are present even in cold temperatures. Vapors formed in gasoline tanks on many vehicles are controlled, but vapors from gasoline storage may escape from the can, resulting in a hazardous situation. Therefore, place gasoline storage containers in a well-ventilated space. Although diesel fuel is not as volatile as gasoline, the same basic rules apply to diesel fuel and gasoline storage. These rules include the following:

1. Use storage cans that have a flash-arresting screen at the outlet. These screens prevent external ignition sources from igniting the gasoline within the can when someone pours the gasoline or diesel fuel.

2. Use only a red approved gasoline container to allow for proper hazardous substance identification. ● **SEE FIGURE 2–9.**

3. Do not fill gasoline containers completely full. Always leave the level of gasoline at least one inch from the top of the container. This action allows expansion of the gasoline at higher temperatures. If gasoline containers are completely full, the gasoline will expand when the temperature increases. This expansion forces gasoline from the can and creates a dangerous spill. If gasoline or diesel fuel containers must be stored, place them in a designated storage locker or facility.

4. Never leave gasoline containers open, except while filling or pouring gasoline from the container.

5. Never use gasoline as a cleaning agent.

6. Always connect a ground strap to containers when filling or transferring fuel or other flammable products from one container to another to prevent static electricity that could result in explosion and fire. These ground wires prevent the buildup of a static electric charge, which could result in a spark and disastrous explosion.

AIRBAG HANDLING

Airbag modules are pyrotechnic devices that can be ignited if exposed to an electrical charge or if the body of the vehicle is subjected to a shock. Airbag safety should include the following precautions:

1. Disarm the airbag(s) if you will be working in the area where a discharged bag could make contact with any part of your body. Consult service information for the exact procedure to follow for the vehicle being serviced. The usual procedure is to deploy the airbag using a 12 volt power supply, such as a jump start box, using long wires to connect to the module to ensure a safe deployment.

2. Do not expose an airbag to extreme heat or fire.

3. Always carry an airbag pointing away from your body.

4. Place an airbag module facing upward.

5. Always follow the manufacturer's recommended procedure for airbag disposal or recycling, including the proper packaging to use during shipment.

6. Wear protective gloves if handling a deployed airbag.

7. Always wash your hands or body well if exposed to a deployed airbag. The chemicals involved can cause skin irritation and possible rash development.

FIGURE 2–10 Air-conditioning refrigerant oil must be kept separated from other oils because it contains traces of refrigerant and must be treated as hazardous waste.

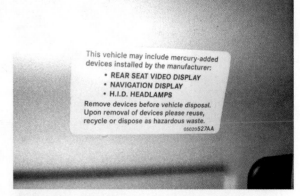

FIGURE 2–11 Placard near driver's door, including what devices in the vehicle contain mercury.

AIR-CONDITIONING REFRIGERANT OIL DISPOSAL

Air-conditioning refrigerant oil contains dissolved refrigerant and is therefore considered to be hazardous waste. This oil must be kept separated from other waste oil or the entire amount of oil must be treated as hazardous. Used refrigerant oil must be sent to a licensed hazardous waste disposal company for recycling or disposal. ● SEE FIGURE 2–10.

WASTE CHART All automotive service facilities create some waste and while most of it is handled properly, it is important that all hazardous and nonhazardous waste be accounted for and properly disposed. ● SEE CHART 2–1 for a list of typical wastes generated at automotive shops, plus a checklist for keeping track of how these wastes are handled.

USED TIRE DISPOSAL

Used tires are an environmental concern because of several reasons, including the following:

1. In a landfill, they tend to "float" up through the other trash and rise to the surface.

2. The inside of tires traps and holds rainwater, which is a breeding ground for mosquitoes. Mosquito-borne diseases include encephalitis and dengue fever.

3. Used tires present a fire hazard and, when burned, create a large amount of black smoke that contaminates the air.

Used tires should be disposed of in one of the following ways:

1. Used tires can be reused until the end of their useful life.

2. Tires can be retreaded.

3. Tires can be recycled or shredded for use in asphalt.

4. Tires that have been removed from the wheels can be sent to a landfill (most landfill operators will shred the tires because it is illegal in many states to landfill whole tires).

5. Tires can be burned in cement kilns or other power plants where the smoke can be controlled.

6. A registered scrap tire handler should be used to transport tires for disposal or recycling.

TECH TIP

Remove Components that Contain Mercury

Some vehicles have a placard near the driver's side door that lists the components that contain the heavy metal, mercury. **Mercury** can be absorbed through the skin and is a heavy metal that once absorbed by the body does not leave. ● SEE FIGURE 2–11.

These components should be removed from the vehicle before the rest of the body is sent to be recycled to help prevent releasing mercury into the environment.

WASTE STREAM	TYPICAL CATEGORY IF NOT MIXED WITH OTHER HAZARDOUS WASTE	IF DISPOSED IN LANDFILL AND NOT MIXED WITH A HAZARDOUS WASTE	IF RECYCLED
Used oil	Used oil	Hazardous waste	Used oil
Used oil filters	Nonhazardous solid waste, if completely drained	Nonhazardous solid waste, if completely drained	Used oil, if not drained
Used transmission fluid	Used oil	Hazardous waste	Used oil
Used brake fluid	Used oil	Hazardous waste	Used oil
Used antifreeze	Depends on characterization	Depends on characterization	Depends on characterization
Used solvents	Hazardous waste	Hazardous waste	Hazardous waste
Used citric solvents	Nonhazardous solid waste	Nonhazardous solid waste	Hazardous waste
Lead-acid automotive batteries	Not a solid waste if returned to supplier	Hazardous waste	Hazardous waste
Shop rags used for oil	Used oil	Depends on used oil characterization	Used oil
Shop rags used for solvent or gasoline spills	Hazardous waste	Hazardous waste	Hazardous waste
Oil spill absorbent material	Used oil	Depends on used oil characterization	Used oil
Spill material for solvent and gasoline	Hazardous waste	Hazardous waste	Hazardous waste
Catalytic converter	Not a solid waste if returned to supplier	Nonhazardous solid waste	Nonhazardous solid waste
Spilled or unused fuels	Hazardous waste	Hazardous waste	Hazardous waste
Spilled or unusable paints and thinners	Hazardous waste	Hazardous waste	Hazardous waste
Used tires	Nonhazardous solid waste	Nonhazardous solid waste	Nonhazardous solid waste

CHART 2–1

Typical wastes generated at auto repair shops and typical category (hazardous or nonhazardous) by disposal method.

 TECH TIP

What Every Technician Should Know

OSHA has adopted new hazardous chemical labeling requirements making it agree with global labeling standards established by the United Nations. As a result, workers will have better information available on the safe handling and use of hazardous chemicals, allowing them to avoid injuries and possible illnesses related to exposures to hazardous chemicals. ● **SEE FIGURE 2–12.**

Health Hazard	Flame	Exclamation Mark
• Carcinogen • Mutagenicity • Reproductive Toxicity • Respiratory Sensitizer • Target Organ Toxicity • Aspiration Toxicity	• Flammables • Pyrophorics • Self-Heating • Emits Flammable Gas • Self-Reactives • Organic Peroxides	• Irritant (Skin and Eye) • Skin Sensitizer • Acute Toxicity • Narcotic Effects • Respiratory Tract Irritant • Hazardous to Ozone Layer (Non-Mandatory)
Gas Cylinder	Corrosion	Exploding Bomb
• Gases Under Pressure	• Skin Corrosion/Burns • Eye Damage • Corrosive to Metals	• Explosives • Self-Reactives • Organic Peroxides
Flame Over Circle	Environment (Non-mandatory)	Skull and Crossbones
• Oxidizers	• Aquatic Toxicity	• Acute Toxicity (fatal or toxic)

FIGURE 2–12 The OSHA global hazardous materials labels.

SUMMARY

1. Hazardous materials include common automotive chemicals, liquids, and lubricants, especially those whose ingredients contain *chlor* or *fluor* in their name.

2. Right-to-know laws require that all workers have access to material safety data sheets (MSDS).

3. Asbestos fibers should be avoided and removed according to current laws and regulations.

4. Used engine oil contains metals worn from parts and should be handled and disposed of properly.

5. Solvents represent a serious health risk and should be avoided as much as possible.

6. Coolant should be disposed of properly or recycled.

7. Batteries are considered to be hazardous waste and should be discarded to a recycling facility.

REVIEW QUESTIONS

1. List five common automotive chemicals or products that may be considered hazardous.

2. Describe the labels used to identify flammables and explosive materials used by OSHA.

1. Hazardous materials include all of the following **except** _____.
   - **a.** Engine oil
   - **b.** Asbestos
   - **c.** Water
   - **d.** Brake cleaner

2. To determine if a product or substance being used is hazardous, consult _____.
   - **a.** A dictionary
   - **b.** SDS (MSDS)
   - **c.** SAE standards
   - **d.** EPA guidelines

3. Exposure to asbestos dust can cause what condition?
   - **a.** Asbestosis
   - **b.** Mesothelioma
   - **c.** Lung cancer
   - **d.** All of the above

4. Wetted asbestos dust is considered to be _____.
   - **a.** Solid waste
   - **b.** Hazardous waste
   - **c.** Toxic
   - **d.** Poisonous

5. An oil filter should be hot drained for how long before disposing of the filter?
   - **a.** 30 to 60 minutes
   - **b.** 4 hours
   - **c.** 8 hours
   - **d.** 12 hours

6. Used engine oil should be disposed of by all **except** the following methods.
   - **a.** Disposed of in regular trash
   - **b.** Shipped offsite for recycling
   - **c.** Burned onsite in a waste oil-approved heater
   - **d.** Burned offsite in a waste oil-approved heater

7. All of the following are the proper ways to dispose of a drained oil filter **except** _____.
   - **a.** Sent for recycling
   - **b.** Picked up by a service contract company
   - **c.** Disposed of in regular trash
   - **d.** Considered to be hazardous waste and disposed of accordingly

8. Which act or organization regulates air-conditioning refrigerant?
   - **a.** Clean Air Act (CAA)
   - **b.** MSDS
   - **c.** WHMIS
   - **d.** Code of Federal Regulations (CFR)

9. Gasoline should be stored in approved containers that include what color(s)?
   - **a.** A red container with yellow lettering
   - **b.** A red container
   - **c.** A yellow container
   - **d.** A yellow container with red lettering

10. What automotive devices may contain mercury?
    - **a.** Rear seat video displays
    - **b.** Navigation displays
    - **c.** HID headlights
    - **d.** All of the above

chapter 3
HEATING AND AIR-CONDITIONING PRINCIPLES

LEARNING OBJECTIVES

After studying this chapter, the reader should be able to:

1. Prepare for the ASE Heating and Air Conditioning (A7) certification test content area "A" (A/C System Service, Diagnosis and Repair).
2. Discuss the changes of states of matter.
3. Discuss the effect of heat and temperature on matter.
4. Discuss the two types of humidity.
5. Explain heating and cooling load.
6. Explain the three ways in which heat flows.
7. Describe the air-conditioning process.
8. Explain the purpose of an HVAC system.

KEY TERMS

Absolute humidity 55
British thermal unit (BTU) 53
Cabin filter 61
Calorie 53
Cooling load 56
Comfort zone 54
Evaporative cooling 57
Heat 53
Heater core 56
Heating load 56
Heating, ventilation, and air conditioning (HVAC) 53
Latent heat 54
Mechanical refrigeration 57
Relative humidity (RH) 55
Temperature 53

FIGURE 3–1 Water is a substance that can be found naturally in solid, liquid, and vapor states.

? FREQUENTLY ASKED QUESTION

Why Is Liquid Sprayed from a Can Cold?

If a pressurized can of liquid is sprayed continuously, the can becomes cold, and so does the liquid being sprayed. The can becomes cold because the pressure in the can is reduced while spraying, allowing the liquid propellant inside the can to boil and absorb heat. The propellant vapor is further cooled as it decompresses when it hits the open air. Rapid decompression results in a rapid temperature drop.

INTRODUCTION

PURPOSE AND FUNCTION The **heating, ventilation, and air-conditioning (HVAC)** system of an automobile is designed to provide comfort for the driver and passengers. It is intended to maintain in-vehicle temperature and humidity within a range that is comfortable for the people inside and provide fresh, clean air. The air-conditioning system transfers the heat from inside the vehicle and moves it to the outside of the vehicle. The heater is needed in cold climates to prevent freezing or death.

PRINCIPLES INVOLVED On earth, matter is found in one of three different phases or states:

1. Solid
2. Liquid
3. Vapor (gas)

The state depends upon the nature of the substance, the temperature, and the pressure or force exerted on it. Water occurs naturally in all three states: solid ice, liquid water, and water vapor, depending upon the temperature and pressure. ● **SEE FIGURE 3–1.**

CHANGES OF STATE A solid is a substance that cannot be compressed and has strong resistance to flow. The molecules of a solid attract each other strongly, and resist changes in volume and shape.

- A substance is solid at any temperature below its melting point. Melting point is a characteristic of the substance, and is related to the temperature at which a solid turns to liquid. For water, the melting point is 32°F (0°C), which

means that changes can be observed between liquid water and ice under normal weather conditions.

- A liquid is a substance that cannot be compressed. A substance in a liquid state has a fixed volume, but no definite shape.
- The boiling point is the temperature at which a liquid substance turns to vapor. For water at normal sea level conditions, the boiling point is 212°F (100°C). A vapor is a substance that can be easily compressed, has no resistance to flow, and no fixed volume. Since a vapor flows, it is considered a fluid just like liquids are.

A vapor condenses to liquid if the temperature falls below the vaporizing temperature. Again, the difference is simply whether heat is being added or taken away. Boiling point and condensation point temperatures are not fixed because they vary with pressure.

HEAT AND TEMPERATURE Molecules in a substance tend to vibrate rapidly in all directions, and this disorganized energy is called heat. The intensity of vibration depends on how much kinetic energy, or energy of motion, the atom or molecule contains. Heat and temperature are not the same.

- **Temperature** is the measure of the level of energy. Temperature is measured in degrees.
- **Heat** is measured in the metric unit called **calorie** and expresses the amount of heat needed to raise the temperature of one gram of water one degree Celsius. Heat is also measured in **British Thermal Units (BTU)**. One BTU is the heat required to raise the temperature of one pound of water 1°F at sea level. One BTU equals 252 calories.

1 GRAM WATER + 540 CALORIES = 1 GRAM VAPOR
1 POUND WATER + 970 BTUs = 1 POUND VAPOR

FIGURE 3–2 The extra heat required to change a standard amount of water at its boiling point to vapor is called latent heat of vaporization.

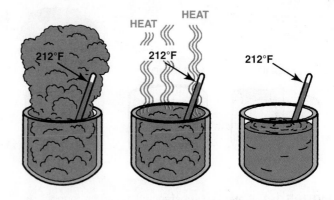

1 GRAM OF VAPOR – 540 CALORIES = 1 GRAM WATER
1 POUND OF VAPOR – 970 BTUs = 1 POUND WATER

FIGURE 3–3 The latent heat of vaporization that water vapor stores is released when the vapor condenses to a liquid. The temperature stays the same.

SENSIBLE HEAT Sensible heat makes sense because it can be felt and measured on a thermometer. If there is 1 lb. of water at 40°F and 1 BTU of heat is added to it, the temperature will increase to 41°F. Adding another BTU of heat will increase the temperature to 42°F and adding another 170 BTU (212–42) will increase the temperature to 212°F, the boiling point.

LATENT HEAT **Latent heat** is the "extra" heat that is needed to transform a substance from one state to another. Imagine that a solid or a liquid is being heated on a stove. When the solid reaches its melting point, or the liquid reaches its boiling point, their temperatures stop rising. The solid begins to melt, and the liquid begins to boil. This occurs without any sensible change in temperature, even though heat is still being applied from the burner. The water in the container on the stove boils at a temperature of 212°F (100°C) at sea level, for as long as any liquid water remains. As heat is further added to the water, heat will be used in changing the state of the liquid to a vapor. This extra, hidden amount of energy necessary to change the state of a substance is called latent heat. ● **SEE FIGURES 3–2 AND 3–3.**

Latent heat is important in the operation of an air-conditioning system because the cooling effect is derived from changing the state of liquid refrigerant to vapor. The liquid refrigerant absorbs the latent heat of vaporization, making the air cooler. The cooler air is then blown into the passenger compartment.

TEMPERATURE, VOLUME, AND PRESSURE OF A VAPOR Unlike a solid, vapor has no fixed volume. Increasing the temperature of a vapor, while keeping the volume confined in the same space, increases the pressure. This happens as the vibrating vapor molecules collide more and more energetically with the walls of the container. Conversely, decreasing the temperature decreases the pressure. This relationship between temperature and pressure in vapor is why a can of nonflammable refrigerant can explode when heated by a flame—the pressure buildup inside the can will eventually exceed the can's ability to contain the pressure. Increasing the pressure by compressing vapor increases the temperature. Decreasing the pressure by permitting the vapor to expand decreases the temperature.

HEAT INTENSITY Intensity of heat is important to us because if it is too cold, humans feel uncomfortable and is measured in degrees. Extremely cold temperatures can cause frostbite and hypothermia. The other end of the scale can also be uncomfortable and may cause heat stress and dehydration. Humans have a temperature **comfort zone** somewhere between 68°F and 78°F (20°C and 26°C). This comfort zone varies among individuals. ● **SEE FIGURE 3–4.**

RULES OF HEAT TRANSFER Heating and air conditioning must follow the basic rules of heat transfer. An understanding of these rules helps greatly in understanding the systems.

- Heat always flows from hot to cold. (From higher level of energy to lower level of energy.) ● **SEE FIGURE 3–5.**
- To warm a person or item, heat must be added.
- To cool a person or item, heat must be removed.
- A large amount of heat is absorbed when a liquid changes state to vapor.

TEMPERATURE COMPARISON

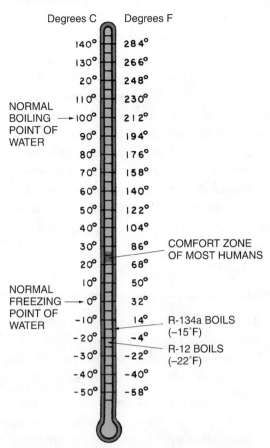

FIGURE 3–4 Heat intensity is measured using a thermometer. The two common measuring scales, Celsius and Fahrenheit, are shown here. This thermometer is also marked with water freezing and boiling and refrigerant boiling temperatures.

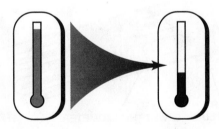

HOT TRAVELS TO COLD UNTIL THE TEMPERATURES EQUAL.

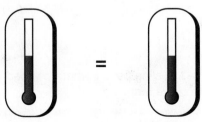

FIGURE 3–5 Heat travels from higher temperature (higher energy level), to lower temperature (lower energy level).

 **TECH TIP**

Quick and Easy Temperature Conversion

Temperature in service information and on scan tools are often expressed in degrees Celsius, which is often confusing to those used to temperature expressed in Fahrenheit degrees. A quick and easy way to get an *approximate* conversion is to take the degrees in Celsius, double it, and add 25.

For example,

Celsius × 2 + 25 = approximate Fahrenheit degrees:

$0°C × 2 = 0 + 25 = 25°F$ (actual = 32°F)
$10°C × 2 = 20 + 25 = 45°F$ (actual = 50°F)
$15°C × 2 = 30 + 25 = 55°F$ (actual = 59°F)
$20°C × 2 = 40 + 25 = 65°F$ (actual = 68°F)
$25°C × 2 = 50 + 25 = 75°F$ (actual = 77°F)
$30°C × 2 = 60 + 25 = 85°F$ (actual = 86°F)
$35°C × 2 = 70 + 25 = 95°F$ (actual = 95°F)
$40°C × 2 = 80 + 25 = 105°F$ (actual = 104°F)
$45°C × 2 = 90 + 25 = 115°F$ (actual = 113°F)
$50°C × 2 = 100 + 25 = 125°F$ (actual = 122°F)

The simplest way to convert between the Fahrenheit and Celsius scales accurately is to use a conversion chart or use an app on a smart phone.

- A large amount of heat is released when a vapor changes state to a liquid.

- Compressing a gas concentrates the heat and increases the temperature.

HUMIDITY Humidity refers to water vapor present in the air. The level of humidity depends upon the amount of water vapor present and the temperature of the air. The amount of water vapor in the air tends to be higher near lakes or the ocean, because more water is available to evaporate from their surfaces. In desert areas with little open water, the amount of water vapor in the air tends to be low.

- **Absolute humidity** is the mass of water vapor in a given volume of air.

- **Relative humidity (RH)** is the percentage of how much moisture is present in the air compared to how much moisture the air is capable of holding at that temperature.

Relative humidity is commonly measured with a *hygrometer* or a *psychrometer*. A hygrometer depends on a sensitive

FIGURE 3–6 A combination meter that measures and displays both the temperature and the humidity is useful to use when working on air-conditioning systems.

element that expands and contracts, based on the humidity. Hygrometers typically resemble a clock, with the scale reading from 0% to 100% relative humidity. ● **SEE FIGURE 3–6.**

HEATING AND COOLING LOAD

HEATING LOAD **Heating load** is the term used when additional heat is needed. The actual load is the number of BTUs or calories of heat energy that must be added. In a home or office, burning fuel is the usual way to generate heat using coal, gas, or oil as a fuel. In most vehicles, the heat is provided by the heated coolant from the engine cooling system. This coolant is typically at a temperature of 190°F to 205°F (88°C to 98°C) when the engine reaches its normal operating temperature. ● **SEE FIGURE 3–8.**

In most vehicles, heated coolant is circulated through a heat exchanger, called a **heater core**. Air is circulated through the heater core, where it absorbs heat. Then it is blown into the passenger compartment, where the heat travels on to warm the car interior and occupants. The air from the blower motor moves the heat from the heater core to the passengers.

COOLING WITH ICE One way to move heat, called **cooling load**, is with a block of ice. A substantial amount of

What Is a Sling Pyschrometer?

A psychrometer is a measuring instrument used to measure relative humidity. It uses two thermometers, one of which has the bulb covered in a cotton wick soaked in distilled water from a built in reservoir. The wick keeps the bulb of the "wet thermometer" wet so that it can be cooled by evaporation. Sling psychrometers are spun round in the air a certain number of times. Water evaporates from the cotton wick at a rate inversely proportional to the relative humidity of the air.

• Faster if the humidity is low
• Slower if the humidity is high.

The "dry thermometer" measures the air temperature.

• The higher the relative humidity, the closer the readings of the two thermometers.
• The lower the humidity, the greater the difference in temperature of the two thermometers.

The different temperatures indicated by the wet and dry thermometers are compared to values given in a chart, which gives the relative humidity. While a sling psychrometer is still used, most technicians use an electronic instrument to measure relative humidity. ● **SEE FIGURE 3–7**.

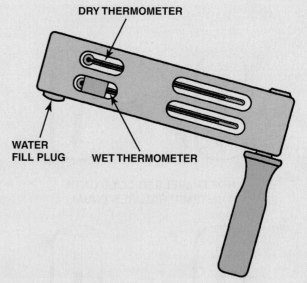

FIGURE 3–7 A sling psychrometer is used to measure relative humidity.

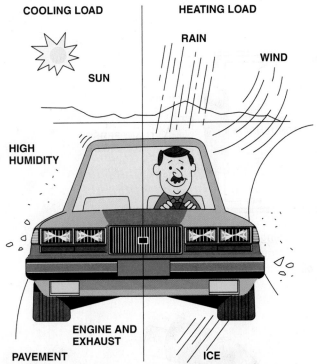

FIGURE 3–8 Winter presents a heat load where heat must be added for comfort (right). Summer presents a cooling load.

latent heat is required to change the state of the solid ice into a liquid:

- 144 BTU per lb. (80 calories per gram).
- A 50-lb. block of ice represents 50 × 144, or 7,200 BTU, of cooling power when it changes from 50 lb. of solid at 32°F to 50 lb. of liquid at 32°F.

In the early days of air conditioning, the term *ton* was commonly used. A ton of air conditioning was the amount of heat it took to melt a ton of ice: 2,000 × 144, or 288,000 BTU. **SEE FIGURE 3–9.**

EVAPORATIVE COOLING A method of cooling that works well in areas of low humidity is evaporation of water, commonly called **evaporative cooling**. If water is spread thinly over the extremely large area of a meshed cooler pad and air is blown across it, the water evaporates. For every pound of water that evaporates, 970 BTU (540 calories per gram) of heat is absorbed. This is the latent heat of evaporation, just as when it is boiled. This is a natural process and uses only the energy required by the blower to circulate the air through the cooler pads and on to the space to be

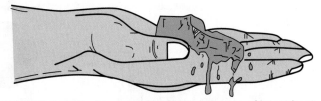

FIGURE 3–9 Ice has a cooling effect because of latent heat of fusion which means that it absorbs heat as it melts.

FIGURE 3–10 At one time, evaporative coolers were used to cool car interiors. Air forced through a water-wetted mesh produces evaporation and a cooling effect.

cooled. Disadvantages of evaporative coolers, often called "swamp coolers" includes:

- increases the relative humidly
- not effective in areas of high humidity because the water does not evaporate rapidly enough to be efficient.

At one time, window-mounted evaporative coolers were used in cars. They were not very popular because they were unattractive and worked well only in dry areas. ● **SEE FIGURE 3–10.**

MECHANICAL COOLING A third way to handle a cooling load is by the use of **mechanical refrigeration**, which is called air conditioning. This system also uses evaporation of a liquid and the large amount of heat required for evaporation. The refrigerant boils so that it changes from liquid to gas, but it is condensed back to gas using an engine or electrically powered compressor to move the refrigerant and to increase its pressure in the system. ● **SEE FIGURE 3–11.**

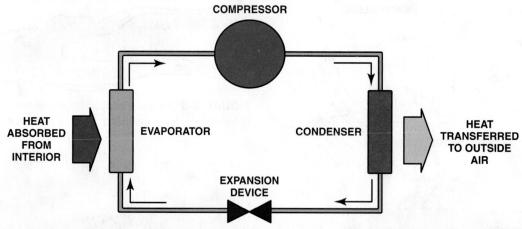

FIGURE 3–11 Heat, from in-vehicle cabin air, causes the refrigerant to boil in the evaporator (left). The compressor increases the pressure and moves refrigerant vapor to the condenser, where the heat is transferred to ambient air. This also causes the vapor to return to liquid form.

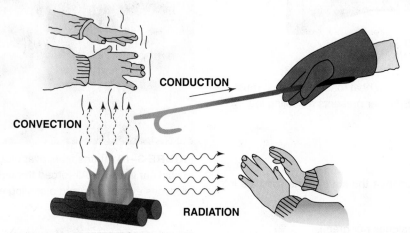

FIGURE 3–12 Heat can be moved from the source by convection, conduction, or radiation.

HEAT MOVEMENT

Heat can travel through one or more of three paths as it moves from hot to cold:

1. conduction
2. convection
3. radiation. ● **SEE FIGURE 3–12.**

CONDUCTION The simplest heat movement method is conduction, by which heat travels through a medium such as a solid or liquid, moving from one molecule of the material to the next. For example, if one end of wire is heated, the heat will travel through the material itself and will be transferred through to the other end of the wire. Some materials (most of the metals) are good heat conductors. Copper and aluminum are among the best of the commonly used metals, so most

heat exchangers (radiators, evaporators, and condensers) use copper or aluminum.

- Some materials, such as wood, are poor heat conductors.
- Some materials, such as Styrofoam, conduct heat so poorly that they are called insulators. Most good insulators incorporate a lot of air or gaseous material in their structure because air is a poor conductor of heat.

CONVECTION Convection is a process of transferring heat by moving the heated medium, usually air or a liquid. An example of convection is the engine cooling system. Coolant is heated in the water jackets next to the cylinders and combustion chambers. Then the coolant is pumped to the radiator, where the heat is transferred to the air traveling through the radiator. Convection also occurs in the interior of the vehicle when air is circulated past the driver and passengers

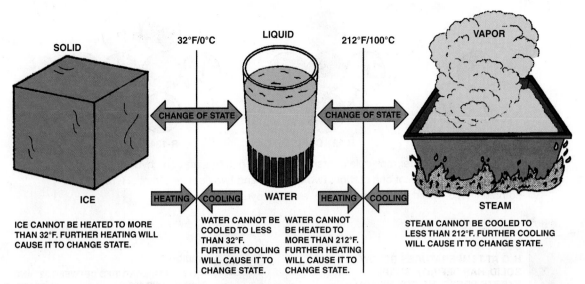

SOLID   32°F/0°C   LIQUID   212°F/100°C   VAPOR

CHANGE OF STATE   CHANGE OF STATE

ICE   HEATING   COOLING   WATER   HEATING   COOLING   STEAM

ICE CANNOT BE HEATED TO MORE THAN 32°F. FURTHER HEATING WILL CAUSE IT TO CHANGE STATE.

WATER CANNOT BE COOLED TO LESS THAN 32°F. FURTHER COOLING WILL CAUSE IT TO CHANGE STATE.

WATER CANNOT BE HEATED TO MORE THAN 212°F. FURTHER HEATING WILL CAUSE IT TO CHANGE STATE.

STEAM CANNOT BE COOLED TO LESS THAN 212°F. FURTHER COOLING WILL CAUSE IT TO CHANGE STATE.

FIGURE 3–13 Matter can change state by adding or removing heat.

to pick up heat and moved to the evaporator, where the heat is transferred to the evaporator fins. The evaporator fins are cooler, so heat is transferred easily.

RADIATION   Heat can travel through heat rays and pass from one location to another without warming the air through which it passes. The best example of this is the heat from the sun, which passes through cold space and warms our planet and everything it shines on. Radiant heat can pass from any warmer object through air to any cooler object. It is affected by the color and texture of the heat emitter, where the heat leaves, and the collector, where the heat is absorbed. Dark, rough surfaces make better heat emitters and collectors than light-colored, smooth surfaces.

NOTE: At one time, California Highway Patrol cars were painted all black. Painting the tops white benefited the patrol officers by lowering the in-vehicle temperature significantly.

AIR-CONDITIONING PROCESS

CHANGING THE STATE OF THE REFRIGERANT   The air-conditioning process works using a fluid, called *refrigerant,* which continuously changes state from liquid to gas and back to liquid.

Most states of matter can be changed from one state to another by adding or removing heat. ● **SEE FIGURE 3–13.**

Molecules are the building blocks for all things that can be seen or felt. Molecules are combinations of atoms, which

are in turn made up of electrons, neutrons, and protons. The protons are in the center, or nucleus, of the atom and the electrons travel in an orbit around them. There are about 100 basic elements or atoms, each having a different atomic number, that combine with other elements to make the many, varied molecules. The atomic number of an element is based on the number of electrons and protons in that element. The periodic table of elements seen in most chemistry laboratories shows the relationship of these elements.

Water molecules, for example, are called H_2O. This is a combination of a single oxygen atom and two hydrogen atoms. Hydrogen has an atomic number of 1 (1 proton and 1 electron), and oxygen has an atomic number of 8 (8 electrons and 8 protons). ● **SEE FIGURE 3–14.** The three states of water are well known and include:

1. Solid ice

2. Liquid water

3. Vapor (gaseous).

SOLID   Solid matter has a definite shape and substance. Solids exert pressure in only one direction, and that is downward because of gravity. For example, ice is the solid form of water, and will hold its shape, and is cold. Water is normally a solid at temperatures below 32°F (0°C), which is the normal freezing point. The electrons in the molecule's atoms are still orbiting around the protons, but the movement has been slowed because much of the heat energy has been removed. ● **SEE FIGURE 3–15.**

LIQUID   Adding heat to most solids causes them to reach their melting point. It is the same material, but heat energy has broken the molecular bond and the matter becomes fluid. Fluid

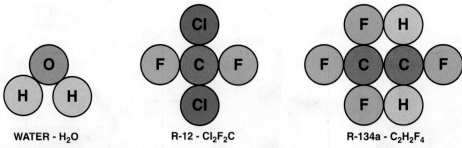

WATER - H₂O   R-12 - Cl₂F₂C   R-134a - C₂H₂F₄

FIGURE 3–14 A water molecule contains two oxygen atoms and one hydrogen atom. R-12 is a combination of one carbon, two chlorine, and two fluorine atoms. R-134a is a combination of two carbon, four fluorine, and two hydrogen atoms.

SOLID:
H_2O AT TEMPERATURES BELOW 32°F, 0°C: SOLID, HAS DEFINITE SHAPE EXERTS PRESSURE DOWNWARD

ICE

FIGURE 3–15 Ice is a solid form of water with a low temperature and slow molecular action.

LIQUID:
H_2O AT TEMPERATURES BETWEEN 32° AND 212°F (0° AND 100°C): LIQUID/FLUID, TAKES SHAPE OF CONTAINER EXERTS PRESSURE DOWNWARD AND TO SIDES

WATER

FIGURE 3–16 Water is warmer than ice and can flow to take the shape of any container.

has no shape and it takes the shape of its container. Liquids can flow through a pipe or hose and can be pumped such as by the air-conditioning compressor.

Water is normally a liquid between 32°F and 212°F (0°C and 100°C). The molecules are same as ice, but heat energy has increased the movement of the electrons. ● **SEE FIGURE 3–16**.

GAS When heat is added to most liquids, it produces gas as the liquids boil. It is the same material, but the heat energy has broken the molecular bonds still further so that the molecules have no shape at all and have expanded so much that they have very little weight. A gas molecule exerts pressure in every direction. Gases can also be pumped through hoses and pipes, making them easy to move through the air-conditioning (A/C) system.

At temperatures above 212°F (100°C), water normally boils to become a gas, called *steam*. Again, the molecules are the same as water or ice, but heat energy has greatly increased molecular movement. ● **SEE FIGURE 3–17**.

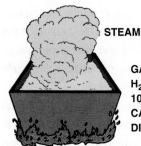

STEAM

GAS:
H_2O AT TEMPERATURES ABOVE 212°F, 100°C: GAS HAS NO SHAPE CAN EXERT PRESSURE IN ALL DIRECTIONS

FIGURE 3–17 Adding heat to water produces steam, the gas state, with a much freer molecular action.

the vehicle, the number of passengers, and the amount of glass area, to name only a few variables. The internal body temperature of humans is about 98.6°F (37°C), which seems odd when our most comfortable temperature is 68°F to 78°F (20°C to 26°C). This means that in the summer heat must be continually given off to be comfortable, but in the winter suitable clothing is needed to maintain warmth. Body comfort is also affected by radiant heat. In the winter, the sun warms the body. Solar engineers are working on ways to control this heat flow as the amount of glass area of a vehicle increases.

The velocity of air past our bodies is another factor in human comfort. Air movement is an important part of heating and air-conditioning systems.

PURPOSE OF AN HVAC SYSTEM

CONTROL OF TEMPERATURE The goal in heating and air conditioning is to maintain a comfortable in-vehicle temperature and humidity. This is affected by the size of

CONTROL OF HUMIDITY Humid cold air feels much colder than dry air at the same temperature.

- Humid hot air slows down our natural body cooling system (evaporation of perspiration), so it can make a day feel much hotter.
- Air that is too dry also tends to make people feel uncomfortable.
- As with temperature, a range of humidity that most people feel comfortable in a relative humidly of about 45% to 55%.

As the air-conditioning system operates, it dehumidifies (removes moisture) from the air. Water vapor condenses on the cold evaporator fins just as it would on a glass holding a cold drink. This condensed water then drops off the evaporator and runs out the drain at the bottom of the evaporator case. In-vehicle humidity is reduced to about 40% to 45% on even the most humid days if the A/C is operated long enough. A good example of this dehumidification process occurs when a vehicle's A/C is operated on cold days when the windows are fogged up. It usually takes only a short time to dry the air and remove the fog from the windows. ● SEE FIGURE 3–18.

CLEANLINESS A side effect of air conditioning is the cleaning of the air coming into the car as it passes through the cooling ductwork. The act of cooling and dehumidifying air at the A/C evaporator causes water droplets to form on

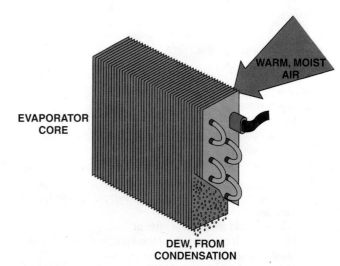

FIGURE 3–18 When air comes into contact with the cold evaporator, excess moisture forms dew. This condensed moisture leaves the car through the evaporator drain.

the evaporator fins. Dust and other contaminants in the air that come into contact with these droplets become trapped and are flushed out of the system as the water drops drain from the evaporator. Most recent vehicles use a **cabin filter** in the A/C and heating systems to clean the air by trapping dust and pollen particles before they enter the passenger compartment.

SUMMARY

1. Heat is moved into or out of the passenger compartment to obtain a good comfort level.
2. Heat intensity is measured using the Fahrenheit or Celsius scales, and heat quantity is measured using calories and BTU.
3. The comfort zone of most humans is between 68°F and 78°F (20°C and 26°C) and 45% to 50% humidity.
4. A/C systems reduce humidity by removing moisture (water) from the air.
5. HVAC systems clean air because particles are caught by moisture on the evaporator and by filters.

REVIEW QUESTIONS

1. What does the abbreviation "HVAC" stand for?
2. What are the three states of matter?
3. What is the difference between heat and temperature?
4. How is relative humidity measured?
5. How does heat move?

CHAPTER QUIZ

1. The three different phases or states of matter include_____.
   a. Solid, water, and steam
   b. Ice, liquid, and gas
   c. Solid, liquid, and gas
   d. Liquid, water, and steam

2. An air-conditioning system cools the interior of the vehicle by_____.
   a. Moving the heat from inside the vehicle to outside the vehicle
   b. Blowing cold air into the interior
   c. Moving heat from inside of the vehicle to the engine cooling system
   d. Using the engine to move air

3. Twenty degrees Celsius is about how many degrees Fahrenheit?
   a. 25
   b. 45
   c. 65
   d. 85

4. Heat intensity is measured in _____.
   a. BTUs
   b. Degrees
   c. RH
   d. Calories

5. A psychrometer measures_____.
   a. Temperature
   b. Relative humidity
   c. Amount of heat
   d. Radiation

6. A BTU is a measure of _____.
   a. Temperature
   b. Relative humidity
   c. Amount of heat
   d. Radiation

7. Heat transferred through the air is called_____.
   a. Radiation
   b. Insulation
   c. Convection
   d. Conduction

8. Air-conditioning process works through a fluid, called a _____ that continuously changes state from liquid to gas and back to liquid.
   a. Element
   b. Conductor
   c. Insulator
   d. Refrigerant

9. Humans prefer temperatures that are between _____ and _____.
   a. 55°F; 65°F
   b. 60°F; 70°F
   c. 68°F; 78°F
   d. 76°F; 86°F

10. Humans prefer relative humidity that is between _____ and _____.
    a. 10%; 20%
    b. 20%; 30%
    c. 30%; 40%
    d. 45%; 55%

chapter 4
THE REFRIGERATION CYCLE

LEARNING OBJECTIVES

After studying this chapter, the reader should be able to:

1. Prepare for the ASE Heating and Air Conditioning (A7) certification test content area "A" (A/C System Service, Diagnosis and Repair).
2. Explain how the A/C system works.
3. Identify the low and high side of an A/C system.
4. Explain the purpose and function of evaporators in an A/C system.
5. Explain the purpose and function of thermal expansion valves and orifice tube systems.
6. Explain the purpose and function of condensers.

KEY TERMS

Compressor 64
Condenser 64
Evaporator 64
Flooded 68
High side 65
Liquid line 65
Low side 65
Orifice tube (OT) 66
Overcharge 71
Pressure sensor 73
Pressure switch 72

Receiver–drier 69
Refrigeration cycle 64
Starved 68
Sub-cooling 70
Suction line 72
Superheat 72
Thermal expansion valve (TXV) 66
Thermistor 72
Undercharge 71

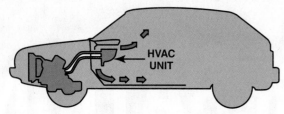

FIGURE 4–1 Air is circulated through the A/C and heating system and the vehicle to either add or remove heat.

BASIC PRINCIPLES

Automotive A/C systems operate on the principle of moving heat from inside to outside of the vehicle. Heat travels from a higher temperature (higher energy level) to a lower temperature (lower energy level).

- The flow of a refrigerant through the system is called the **refrigeration cycle** and is used to cool the interior of the vehicle.

- The heating system transfers heat from the engine's cooling system to the passenger compartment. ● **SEE FIGURE 4–1**.

REFRIGERANT MOVEMENT
All automotive air-conditioning systems are closed and sealed. A refrigerant is circulated through the system by a **compressor** that is usually powered by the engine through an accessory drive belt. Older systems used CFC-12 as a refrigerant, commonly referred to as *R-12* or by its DuPont trade name of *Freon*. Starting in the early 1990s, most vehicle manufacturers now use HFC-134a (R-134a)- a refrigerant that is less harmful to the atmosphere. The basic principle of the refrigeration cycle is that as a liquid changes into a gas, heat is absorbed. The heat that is absorbed by an automotive air-conditioning system is the heat from inside the vehicle.

HOW THE A/C SYSTEM WORKS
The air-conditioning (A/C) system works as follows:

1. High-pressure liquid refrigerant flows through an expansion device, which controls the amount of refrigerant that is allowed to pass through.

2. When the high-pressure liquid passes through the expansion device, the pressure drops. This causes the liquid refrigerant to evaporate in a small radiator-type unit called the **evaporator**. When the refrigerant evaporates, it absorbs heat when changing from a liquid to a gas. As

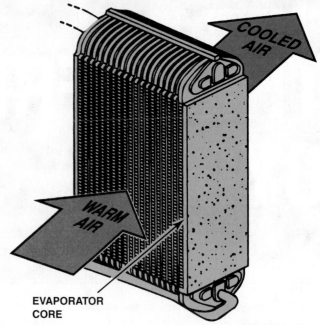

EVAPORATOR CORE

FIGURE 4–2 The evaporator removes heat from the air that enters a vehicle by transferring it to the vaporizing refrigerant.

the heat is absorbed by the refrigerant, the evaporator becomes cold. ● **SEE FIGURE 4–2**.

3. After the refrigerant has evaporated into a *low-pressure gas* in the evaporator, it flows into the engine-driven compressor. The compressor compresses the low-pressure refrigerant gas into a high-temperature, high-pressure gas and forces it through the system. ● **SEE FIGURE 4–3**.

4. This high-pressure gas flows into the condenser located in front of the cooling system radiator. The **condenser** looks like another radiator, and its purpose and function is to remove heat from the high-pressure gas. In the condenser, the high-pressure gas changes (condenses) to form a high-pressure liquid as the heat from the refrigerant is released to the air. ● **SEE FIGURE 4–4**.

5. The high-pressure liquid then flows to the expansion device, which controls the amount of refrigerant that is allowed to pass through and meters the flow into the evaporator. When the high pressure of the liquid passes through the expansion device, the pressure drops and causes the refrigerant to vaporize, starting the cycle all over again.

6. Air is blown through the evaporator by the blower motor. The air is cooled as heat is removed from the air and transferred to the refrigerant in the evaporator. This cooled air is then directed inside the passenger compartment through vents.

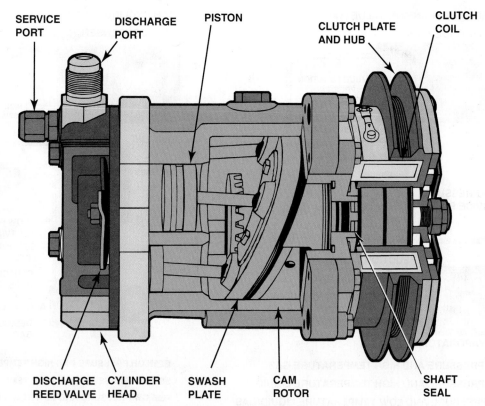

FIGURE 4–3 The compressor provides the mechanical force needed to pressurize the refrigerant.

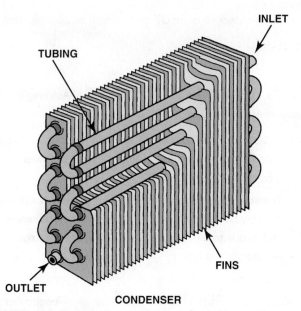

FIGURE 4–4 The condenser changes the refrigerant vapor into a liquid by transferring heat from the refrigerant to the air stream that flows between the condenser fins.

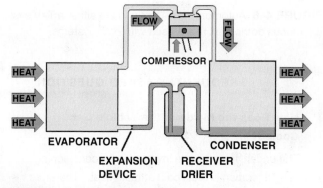

FIGURE 4–5 Refrigerant changes state to a vapor as it absorbs heat in the low side and into a liquid as it loses heat in the high side.

HIGH- AND LOW-SIDE IDENTIFICATION A/C systems can be divided into two parts:

1. **Low side**—it has low pressure and temperature. The low side begins at the expansion device and ends at the compressor. The refrigerant boils or evaporates in the low side.

2. **High side**—it has higher pressures and temperatures. The high side begins at the compressor and ends at the expansion device. The refrigerant condenses in the high side. The high side line is often called the **liquid line**.
● SEE FIGURE 4–5.

In an operating system, the low and high sides can be identified by:

▪ **Pressure**—A pressure gauge shows low pressure in the low side and high pressure in the high side.

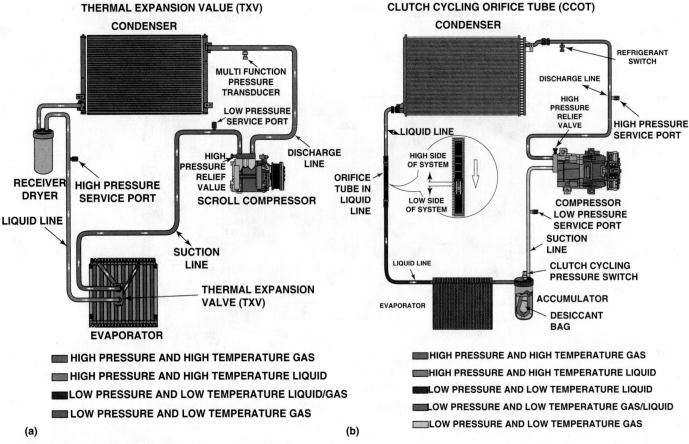

THERMAL EXPANSION VALUE (TXV)
CONDENSER

MULTI FUNCTION
PRESSURE
TRANSDUCER

LOW PRESSURE
SERVICE PORT

DISCHARGE
LINE

HIGH
PRESSURE
RELIEF
VALUE

SCROLL COMPRESSOR

RECEIVER
DRYER

HIGH PRESSURE
SERVICE PORT

LIQUID LINE

SUCTION
LINE

THERMAL EXPANSION
VALVE (TXV)

EVAPORATOR

■ HIGH PRESSURE AND HIGH TEMPERATURE GAS
■ HIGH PRESSURE AND HIGH TEMPERATURE LIQUID
■ LOW PRESSURE AND LOW TEMPERATURE LIQUID/GAS
■ LOW PRESSURE AND LOW TEMPERATURE GAS

(a)

CLUTCH CYCLING ORIFICE TUBE (CCOT)
CONDENSER

REFRIGERANT
SWITCH

DISCHARGE LINE

HIGH
PRESSURE
RELIEF
VALVE

HIGH PRESSURE
SERVICE PORT

LIQUID LINE

HIGH SIDE
OF SYSTEM

ORIFICE
TUBE IN
LIQUID
LINE

LOW SIDE
OF SYSTEM

COMPRESSOR
LOW PRESSURE
SERVICE PORT

SUCTION
LINE

CLUTCH CYCLING
PRESSURE SWITCH

LIQUID LINE

EVAPORATOR

ACCUMULATOR

DESICCANT
BAG

■ HIGH PRESSURE AND HIGH TEMPERATURE GAS
■ HIGH PRESSURE AND HIGH TEMPERATURE LIQUID
■ LOW PRESSURE AND LOW TEMPERATURE LIQUID
■ LOW PRESSURE AND LOW TEMPERATURE GAS/LIQUID
■ LOW PRESSURE AND LOW TEMPERATURE GAS

(b)

FIGURE 4–6 Automotive A/C systems are either a TXV system with a receiver–drier (a) or an OT system with an accumulator. (b) Various compressors are used with both systems.

 FREQUENTLY ASKED QUESTION

How Does the Inside of the Vehicle Get Cooled?

The underlying principle involved in air conditioning or refrigeration is that "cold attracts heat." Therefore, a cool evaporator attracts the hot air inside the vehicle. Heat always travels toward cold and when the hot air passes through the cold evaporator, the heat is absorbed by the cold evaporator, which lowers the temperature of the air. The cooled air is then forced into the passenger compartment by the blower through the air-conditioning vents.

■ **Sight**—On high-humidity days, the cold low-side tubing often collects water droplets and may even frost.

■ **Temperature**—The low side is cool to cold, and the high side is hot.

■ **Tubing size**—Low-side tubes and hoses are larger (vapor), and high-side tubes and hoses are smaller (liquid).

TYPES OF EXPANSION DEVICES Automotive A/C systems are of two types:

■ **Orifice tube (OT)** systems—Orifice tube systems are also called *cycling clutch orifice tube (CCOT)* and *fixed orifice tube (FOT)* systems.

■ **Thermal expansion valve (TXV)** systems. TXV systems are now being used by most vehicle manufacturers mainly due to the reduction in the amount of refrigerant required in this type of system. ● SEE FIGURE 4–6.

LOW-SIDE OPERATION The low side begins at the refrigerant expansion or flow metering device, either a TXV or an OT, which produces a pressure drop. The low side ends at the compressor, which increases the pressure. When the A/C system is in full operation, the goal of most systems is to maintain an evaporator temperature just above the freezing point of water, 32°F (0°C). This temperature produces the greatest heat exchange without ice formation on the evaporator fins (evaporator icing reduces the heat transfer). ● SEE FIGURE 4–7.

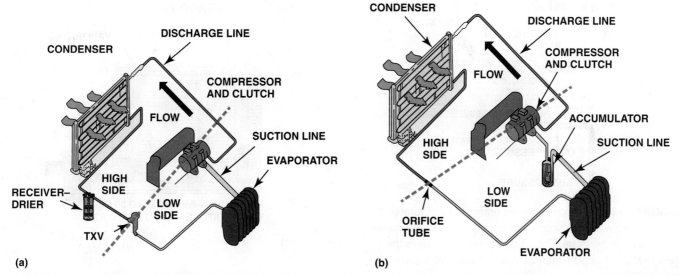

FIGURE 4–7 (a) The low side begins at the TXV or OT and includes the evaporator and suction line to the compressor. (b) The OT system includes an accumulator. The area above the red line represents high pressure and high temperature. The area below the red line represents lower temperature and lower pressures.

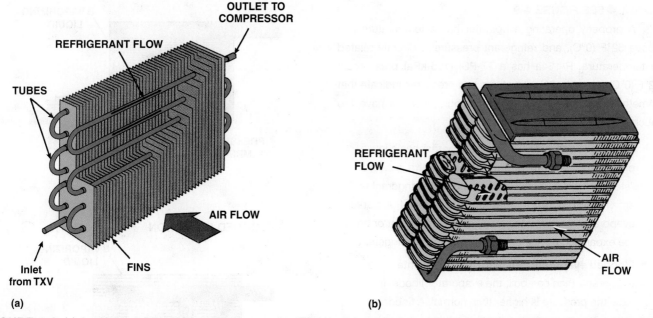

FIGURE 4–8 (a) A tube-and-fin and (b) a plate evaporator. Each type has a large contact area for heat to leave the air and enter the refrigerant.

EVAPORATORS

PURPOSE AND FUNCTION The evaporator is the heat exchanger and absorbs heat from the passenger compartment. The refrigerant enters the evaporator as a liquid spray or mist, leaving an area of a few hundred pounds per square inch (PSI) and passing through a small orifice into an area of about 30 PSI. Like most heat exchangers, a well-designed evaporator has a large amount of surface area in contact with the refrigerant and the air from the passenger compartment. The heat from the air causes the refrigerant to boil and turn into vapor and the cooler air is returned to the passenger compartment. ● SEE **FIGURE 4–8**.

The cold temperature in the evaporator is produced by boiling the refrigerant. Refrigerants have very low boiling points, well below 0°F (–18°C); when the liquid boils, it absorbs a large amount of heat, called the *latent heat of vaporization*. To produce cooling, liquid refrigerant must enter and boil inside the evaporator. The amount of heat an evaporator absorbs is

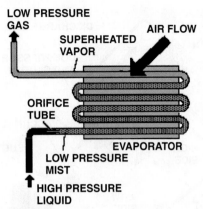

LOW PRESSURE
GAS

SUPERHEATED
VAPOR

AIR FLOW

ORIFICE
TUBE

EVAPORATOR

LOW PRESSURE
MIST

HIGH PRESSURE
LIQUID

FIGURE 4–9 As liquid refrigerant enters the evaporator, the boiling point will try to drop to as low as 32°F (0°C) because of the drop in pressure. The cold temperature causes the refrigerant to absorb heat from the air circulated through the evaporator.

directly related to the amount of liquid refrigerant that boils inside it. ● **SEE FIGURE 4–9**.

A properly operating evaporator has a temperature just above 32°F (0°C), and refrigerant pressure is directly related to temperature. R-134a has a 27-PSI (186-kPa) pressure at 32°F (0°C). Abnormal temperatures and pressures indicate that something is wrong, such as the evaporator might have too much or too little refrigerant.

- **Starved evaporator**—An evaporator that has a low pressure but a temperature that is too warm is called "starved," which means that not enough refrigerant is entering to produce the desired cooling effect. A starved evaporator is usually the result of a restriction at or before the expansion device or an undercharge of refrigerant.

- **Flooded evaporator**—If more refrigerant enters the evaporator than can boil, the evaporator floods. In this case the pressure is higher than normal. A flooded evaporator is usually the result of having too much refrigerant in the system. ● **SEE FIGURE 4–10**.

THERMAL EXPANSION VALVES

TERMINOLOGY A thermal expansion valve (TXV) is a variable valve that changes the size of the valve opening in response to the cooling load of the evaporator. A TXV is controlled by evaporator temperature and pressure so that

NORMAL OPERATION

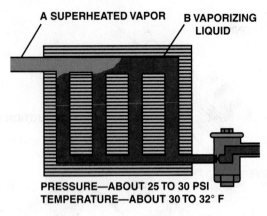

A SUPERHEATED VAPOR   B VAPORIZING LIQUID

PRESSURE—ABOUT 25 TO 30 PSI
TEMPERATURE—ABOUT 30 TO 32° F

(a)

STARVED CONDITION

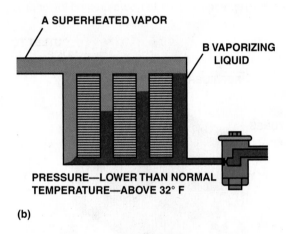

A SUPERHEATED VAPOR   B VAPORIZING LIQUID

PRESSURE—LOWER THAN NORMAL
TEMPERATURE—ABOVE 32° F

(b)

FLOODED CONDITION

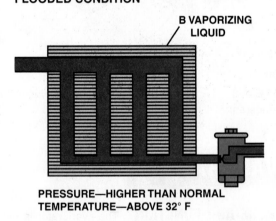

B VAPORIZING LIQUID

PRESSURE—HIGHER THAN NORMAL
TEMPERATURE—ABOVE 32° F

(c)

FIGURE 4–10 (a) If proper amount of refrigerant enters the evaporator, it has a slight superheat as it leaves. (b) A starved condition, in which not enough refrigerant enters the evaporator, does not produce as much cooling. (c) If too much refrigerant enters, the evaporator floods because the refrigerant will not at all boil.

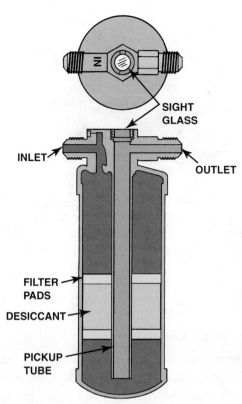

FIGURE 4–11 Expansion-valve systems store excess refrigerant in a receiver–drier, which is located in the high-side liquid section of the system.

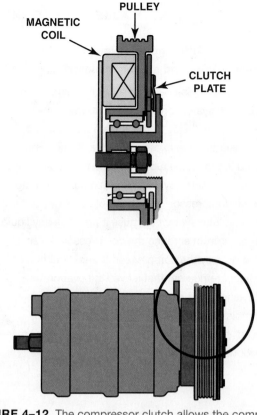

FIGURE 4–12 The compressor clutch allows the compressor to cycle off and on to control evaporator temperature and to shut the system off.

it opens to flow as much refrigerant as possible when a lot of cooling is needed and all of the refrigerant must boil in the evaporator. Most TXVs are calibrated so that the outlet temperature is a few degrees above the inlet pressure and temperature. When there is a lower cooling load, the TXV must reduce the flow.

RECEIVER–DRIER

A **receiver–drier** is used in the high side of a TXV system. It contains a desiccant to remove moisture and provides a storage chamber for liquid refrigerant. Most receiver–driers also contain a filter to trap debris that might plug the TXV.

NOTE: Older receiver–driers have a sight glass in the outlet line so the refrigerant flow can be checked to see if it is all liquid or contains bubbles. A receiver–drier should be about half full of liquid, so vapor bubbles are an indication of an undercharge. A sight glass is not used in most R-134a systems because the refrigerant has a cloudy appearance in a properly charged system. ● SEE FIGURE 4–11.

ORIFICE TUBE SYSTEMS

PURPOSE AND FUNCTION An orifice tube is a restriction in the liquid line that forces the refrigerant to expand as it passes through the small opening (orifice). When the refrigerant expands, the temperature of the refrigerant drops and starts to evaporate in the evaporator. There are two basic designs of orifice tube system, including:

1. A cycling clutch (CC) system that disengages the compressor and shuts the system off when the evaporator temperature or pressure drops below freezing point. Most A/C compressors are driven by a belt from the engine through an electromagnetic clutch. ● SEE FIGURE 4–12.

2. A variable displacement compressor that is used to control evaporator pressure and temperature by controlling the amount of refrigerant passing through the orifice tube.

What is the Difference Between a Receiver–Drier and an Accumulator?

A receiver–drier is used with a thermal expansion valve (TXV) system and is located in the high-pressure (liquid) side of the system between the condenser and the expansion valve. An accumulator is used in the orifice tube system and is located in the low side of the system between the evaporator and the compressor. The accumulator is needed in an orifice tube system because it prevents any liquid refrigerant from entering the compressor, which would destroy the compressor. It traps and holds any liquid refrigerant that leaves the evaporator. Both assemblies contain a desiccant to remove any moisture that may be in the system to help prevent possible acid formation, which can decrease component life. ● SEE FIGURE 4–13.

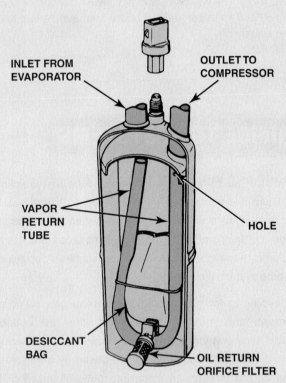

FIGURE 4–13 Expansion-valve systems store excess refrigerant in a receiver–drier, which is located in the high-side liquid section of the system, whereas orifice tube systems store excess refrigerant in an accumulator (shown here) located in the low-side vapor section of the system.

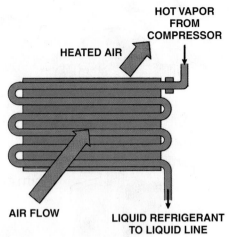

FIGURE 4–14 A condenser is a heat exchanger that transfers heat from the refrigerant to the air flowing through it.

What Is Sub-Cooling?

The term **sub-cooling** refers to a liquid existing at a temperature below its normal condensation temperature. The condenser removes heat and changes a high-pressure vapor into a high-pressure liquid. As the superheated (high-pressure) gas is pushed into the condenser, the temperature is reduced. The refrigerant does not start to change state until the temperature reaches what is called its *saturated pressure-temperature*. At saturation pressure-temperature point, the change of state becomes latent heat (invisible or hidden heat). The temperatures of the liquid and the vapor will stay the same until the temperature of the refrigerant starts to drop. Temperature of the refrigerant will start to drop once 98% to 99% of the refrigerant becomes liquid.

CONDENSERS

PURPOSE AND FUNCTION The condenser, like the evaporator, is a heat exchanger. Low-pressure refrigerant vapor is compressed by the compressor into a high-temperature, high-pressure vapor. This vapor then passes into the condenser where air passing over the condenser cools the refrigerant and causes it to condense into a high-temperature liquid. The refrigerant enters the top of the condenser as a hot vapor and leaves from the bottom as a cooler liquid. ● SEE FIGURE 4–14.

REFRIGERANT CHARGE LEVEL

PRINCIPLES For an A/C system to work properly, there should be a constant flow of liquid refrigerant through the TXV or OT. While operating, the following occurs:

- The evaporator contains a refrigerant mist in the first two-thirds to three-fourths of its volume, with vapor in the remaining portion.
- The condenser contains a condensing vapor in the upper portion, with liquid in the bottom passages.
- The line connecting the condenser to the expansion device is filled with liquid.
- The accumulator is about half full of liquid so that liquid refrigerant does not enter the compressor.

Most recent A/C systems have improved efficiency and reduced the size of some components so they can operate with smaller charge volumes. At one time, the refrigerant capacity of many domestic systems was in the 3-lb. to 4-lb. (1.4 kg to 1.8 kg) range. However, recently most systems hold 1.0 lb. to 2.5 lb. (0.5 kg to 1.1 kg) of refrigerant. Some of the new systems, such as the Toyota Yaris, have a capacity of less than a pound (0.43 kg). With this reduced volume, an accurate charge amount is more critical.

- **Undercharge**—If the volume of liquid drops so that vapor bubbles pass through the TXV or OT, the system is **undercharged** and its cooling effectiveness is reduced.
- **Overcharge**—If an excessive amount of refrigerant is put into a system then the excess volume partially fills the condenser as a liquid and reduces its effective volume. This is called an **overcharge** and causes abnormally high pressures, especially in the high side, and poor cooling at the evaporator. ● **SEE FIGURE 4–15.**

EVAPORATOR ICING CONTROLS

PURPOSE AND FUNCTION Most A/C systems operate at maximum capacity when it is necessary to cool the vehicle. Compressor size (displacement) and the sizes of the evaporator and condenser determine cooling power and are designed to cool the vehicle and its passengers on a hot day. Vehicle

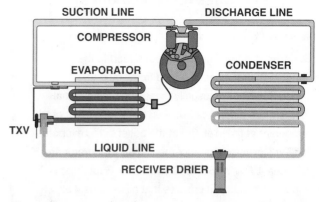

PROPER CHARGE

(a)

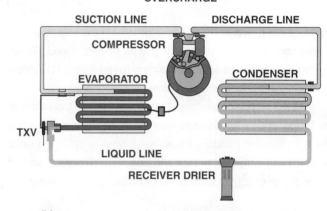

OVERCHARGE

(b)

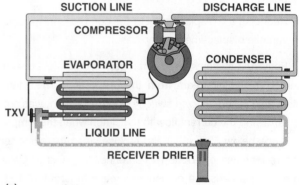

UNDERCHARGE

(c)

FIGURE 4–15 (a) A properly charged system has the condenser filled with condensing vapor and some liquid, a liquid line filled with liquid, a receiver–drier about half full of liquid, and an evaporator with vaporizing liquid. (b) An overcharge with too much liquid causes liquid to partially fill the condenser. (c) An undercharge has vapor in the liquid line and a starved evaporator.

size and glass area, compressor displacement and operating speed, number of passengers, ambient temperature, and vehicle speed are all design parameters that are considered during the initial design of the A/C and heating systems. Some

? FREQUENTLY ASKED QUESTION

What Is "Superheat"?

Superheat is the amount of heat added to the refrigerant after it has changed from liquid to vapor. Superheat is usually measured as the actual temperature difference between the boiling point of the refrigerant at the inlet and at the outlet of the evaporator. Typical values for superheat in an evaporator are between 4°F and 16°F (3°C and 10°C). Superheat is important because it ensures that all (or almost all) of the refrigerant vaporizes before leaving the evaporator.

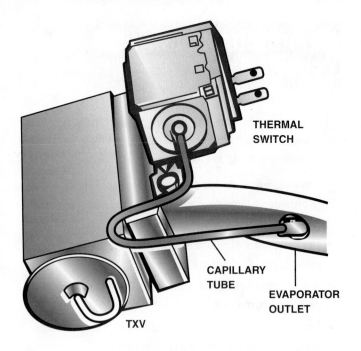

(a)

systems are designed to cool a vehicle with the engine at idle speed and the compressor running at its slowest speed. Newer systems are made as small as practical to reduce HVAC system size and vehicle weight for improved fuel economy.

As the vehicle cools down, the cooling load on the evaporator drops, and its temperature also drops. As mentioned earlier, the minimum temperature for an evaporator is 32°F, the point at which water freezes and ice and frost form. There are several ways of preventing evaporator icing, including the following:

- Cycling the compressor clutch
- Controlling evaporator pressure so it does not drop below 30 PSI
- Reducing the displacement of the compressor by using a variable displacement compressor.

Early A/C systems used a temperature-controlled switch mounted in the airstream from the evaporator. This thermal switch, also called an *icing switch* or *defrost switch*, was set to open and stop the current flow to the clutch when the temperature drops below 32°F (0°C) and reclose when there is a temperature increase of about 10 Fahrenheit degrees (6 Celsius degrees). This causes a pressure increase of about 10 PSI to 20 PSI that, in turn, produces sufficient temperature rise to melt any frost or ice on the fins.

THERMISTOR Some newer systems use a **thermistor**, which is a solid-state device that changes its electrical resistance in inverse relationship to its temperature. When the temperature increases, the resistance of the thermistor decreases. It is used as an input to an electronic control module (ECM) to provide the actual evaporator temperature control.

PRESSURE SWITCHES Many orifice tube systems use a two-wire **pressure switch** mounted in the accumulator or the

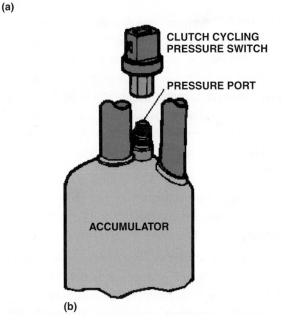

(b)

FIGURE 4–16 (a) Most TXV systems use a thermal switch to cycle the compressor out when the evaporator gets too cold. (b) Most orifice tube systems use a pressure switch to cycle the compressor out when the low-side pressure drops too low.

suction line to the compressor. The evaporator temperature and pressure are closely linked and they drop together. As the *cutout pressure switch* senses the pressure dropping below a certain point (about 30 PSI), it opens to stop the compressor. The pressure switch recloses when the pressure increases, with the *cut-in pressure* being about 42 PSI to 49 PSI, depending on the vehicle. With either of these systems, if ice and frost start to form because the evaporator gets too cold, the ice and frost melt during the off part of the cycle. ● **SEE FIGURE 4–16.**

Most recent vehicles use a **pressure sensor** in place of a pressure switch. The resistance of the sensor changes in direct relation to the pressure. It is an input to a PCM/ECM used for compressor clutch, cooling fan, and idle-speed control as well as low-pressure and high-pressure protection. ● SEE FIGURE 4–17.

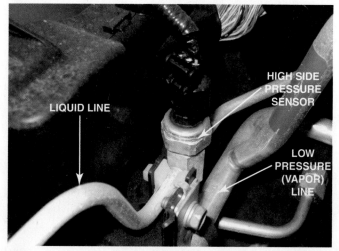

FIGURE 4–17 A typical three-wire pressure sensor used on the high side (vapor) line. The three wires are the voltage supply (usually 5 volts), ground, and signal wire.

SUMMARY

1. Automotive A/C systems operate on the principle of moving heat from inside to outside of the vehicle.

2. All automotive air-conditioning systems are closed and sealed. A refrigerant is circulated through the system by a compressor that is usually powered by the engine through an accessory drive belt.

3. The liquid refrigerant evaporates in a small radiator-type unit called the evaporator.

4. After the refrigerant has evaporated into a low-pressure gas in the evaporator, the refrigerant flows into the engine-driven compressor.

5. From the compressor, high-pressure gas flows into the condenser located in front of the cooling system radiator.

6. Automotive A/C systems are either orifice tube (OT) systems or thermal expansion valve (TXV) systems.

7. A receiver–drier is used with a TXV system and is located in the high pressure (liquid) side of the system.

8. An accumulator is used in orifice tube system and is located in the low side of the system between the evaporator and the compressor.

REVIEW QUESTIONS

1. How does the air conditioning cool the inside of the vehicle?

2. What are the major components of the refrigeration cycle?

3. How does the refrigeration system work?

4. What is the difference between a pressure switch and a pressure sensor?

CHAPTER QUIZ

1. Heat travels from_____.
   a. Hot to cooler
   b. Cold to warmer
   c. Either from hot to cool or the other way depending on the weather
   d. From outside the vehicle to inside the vehicle

2. The refrigerant is circulated through the system by a_____.
   a. Condenser
   b. Evaporator
   c. Compressor
   d. Thermal expansion valve or orifice tube

3. When the refrigerant evaporates, it absorbs heat when it changes from liquid to gas. In which unit does this occur?
   a. Condenser
   b. Evaporator
   c. Compressor
   d. Thermal expansion valve or orifice tube

4. Which unit contains a desiccant to remove moisture from the system?
   a. Receiver–drier
   b. Accumulator
   c. Evaporator
   d. Both a and b

5. The low side of the refrigeration cycle means _____.
   a. It has low pressure and temperature
   b. It begins at the compressor and ends at the expansion device
   c. That the refrigerant condenses
   d. It is called the liquid line

6. The high side of the refrigeration cycle means it_____.
   a. Has low pressure and temperature
   b. Begins at the expansion device and ends at the compressor
   c. Has higher pressures and temperatures
   d. The refrigerant boils or evaporates

7. A _____ is a variable valve that changes the size of the valve opening in response to the cooling load of the evaporator.
   a. Orifice tube
   b. Compressor
   c. Thermal expansion valve (TXV)
   d. Receiver–drier

8. Pressures are controlled in an orifice tube (OT) system by _____.
   a. Using a variable valve
   b. Cycling an electromagnetic compressor clutch on and off as needed.
   c. Using a variable displacement compressor
   d. Either b or c

9. Which condition can cause the air-conditioning system to produce less-than normal cooling?
   a. Overcharged with refrigerant
   b. Undercharged with refrigerant
   c. Either under- or overcharged
   d. Superheat condition

10. The condenser_____
   a. Is a heat exchanger
   b. Is a device where air passing over it cools the refrigerant and causes it to change into a high-temperature liquid.
   c. Transfers heat from the refrigerant to the air flowing
   d. All of the above

chapter 5
AIR-CONDITIONING COMPRESSORS AND SERVICE

LEARNING OBJECTIVES

After studying this chapter, the reader should be able to:

1. Prepare for ASE Heating and Air Conditioning (A7) certification test content area "B" (Refrigeration System Component Diagnosis and Repair).

2. State the different types of A/C compressors.

3. Discuss the parts and operation of compressor clutches.

4. Discuss compressor valves and switches.

5. Explain A/C compressor diagnosis and service.

KEY TERMS

Damper drive 83	Reed valves 76
Discharge stroke 76	Scroll compressor 80
Drive plate 82	Seal cartridge 87
Inline filters 84	Seal seat 87
Lip seal 87	Suction stroke 76
Mufflers 84	Vane compressor 79

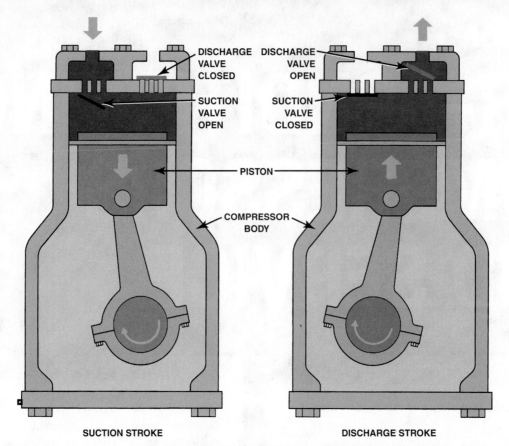

| DISCHARGE VALVE CLOSED | DISCHARGE VALVE OPEN |
| SUCTION VALVE OPEN | SUCTION VALVE CLOSED |

PISTON

COMPRESSOR BODY

SUCTION STROKE **DISCHARGE STROKE**

FIGURE 5–1 In a piston compressor, when moving downward, the piston creates a drop in pressure inside the cylinder. The resulting difference in pressure allows the suction valve to open. Refrigerant then flows into the cylinder. When the piston moves upward on discharge stroke, the pressure closes the intake valve and forces the refrigerant out the discharge valve.

COMPRESSORS

PURPOSE AND FUNCTION The air-conditioning compressor can be thought of as a pump that circulates refrigerant. It has to work against the restriction of the thermal expansion valve (TXV) or orifice tube (OT). The pressure must be increased to the point where refrigerant temperature is above ambient air temperature and there is enough heat transfer at the condenser to get rid of all the heat absorbed in the evaporator. Most A/C compressors are driven by a belt and pulley from the engine.

TYPES OF A/C COMPRESSORS There are many types of A/C compressors used on vehicles, including the following:

- **Piston compressors**—Most older automotive compressors used a crankshaft, similar to a small gasoline engine, and a reciprocating-piston type. Newer piston compressors use a swash or wobble plate.
- **Vane compressors**—Vane compressor has vanes that contact the rotor housing at each end, and they slide to make a seal at each end as the rotor turns.

- **Scroll compressors**—Scroll compressors require rather complex machining to achieve constant sealing between the fixed and movable scrolls.

PISTON COMPRESSORS

PISTON COMPRESSOR OPERATION A piston compressor moves the pistons up and down in a cylinder to produce pumping action and controls the refrigerant flow with two sets of **reed valves**.

- The downward or **suction stroke** of the piston causes the refrigerant to flow from the compressor suction cavity to push the suction reed open and fill the cylinder. The suction cavity is connected to the evaporator so it contains refrigerant vapor at evaporator pressure.
- An upward stroke, or **discharge stroke**, of the piston generates pressure to force the refrigerant through the discharge reed into the discharge chamber and on to the condenser. The discharge pressure becomes high-side pressure. ● **SEE FIGURE 5–1.**

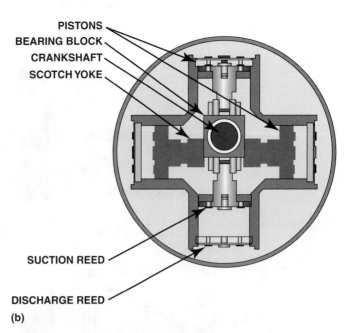

PISTONS
BEARING BLOCK
CRANKSHAFT
SCOTCH YOKE

SUCTION REED

DISCHARGE REED

(a)

(b)

FIGURE 5–2 (a) An R-4 compressor. (b) This unit has two pairs of pistons that are driven by a Scotch yoke.

Piston compressors have some disadvantages; chief among them is the high inertial loads that result from moving a piston at a rather high speed, bringing it to a stop, moving it at a high speed in the opposite direction, bringing it to a stop, and so on. This movement produces vibrations and severe stress on moving parts.

RADIAL-TYPE PISTON COMPRESSORS These compressors use two double pistons that are mounted over a bearing block. The crankshaft moves the bearing block in a circular orbit that moves the pistons through their strokes. The GM R-4 compressor is the most common. ● **SEE FIGURE 5–2.**

COAXIAL SWASH-PLATE COMPRESSORS Coaxial swash-plate compressors drive the pistons through a swash plate, which is attached to the driveshaft. The swash plate is mounted at an angle so it will wobble and cause the reciprocating action of the pistons.

- The swash plate revolves with the shaft with each piston having a pair of bearings that can pivot as the swash plate slides through them.

- The pistons are double ended so that each end can pump, and the pistons are arranged parallel to and around the driveshaft. This is called a *coaxial* arrangement.

- One driveshaft revolution causes each piston end to move through a complete pumping cycle. The most

common arrangement is three double pistons making a 6-cylinder compressor and a 10-cylinder using five pistons. ● **SEE FIGURE 5–3.**

A swash-plate compressor must have passages to transfer refrigerant between the suction and discharge chambers at each end of the compressor. The suction crossover passage is usually designed so that it can provide lubrication to internal moving parts.

General Motors uses the following compressor designations:

- Delco Air: DA
- Harrison: H
- Harrison Radiator: HA
- Harrison Redesigned: HR
- High Efficiency: HE
- Truck: HT
- Upgraded HT: HU

Nippondenso also manufactures 6-cylinder and 10-cylinder coaxial compressors. This design is used as OEM equipment by the Chrysler Corporation, the Ford Motor Company, and other vehicle manufacturers around the world. Denso coaxial compressors, like those of other manufacturers, use a four-part aluminum body with two cylinder assemblies, rear head, and front head sealed by O-rings. Either a single-key drive or a splined drive is used between the clutch drive plate and the compressor shaft.

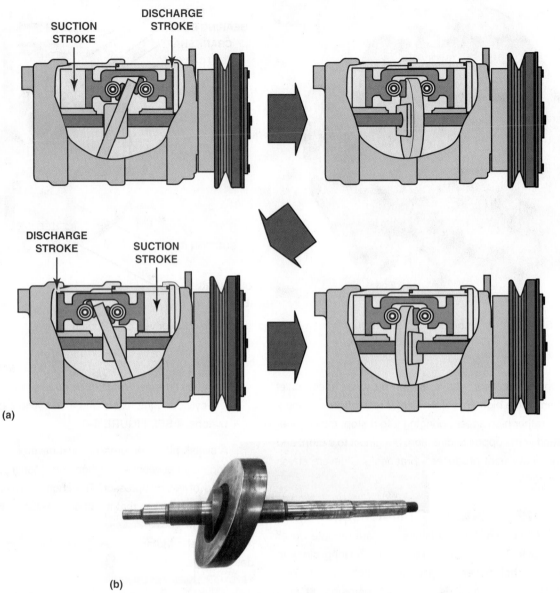

FIGURE 5–3 (a) One of the double pistons of a swash-plate compressor as it move through a pumping cycle. (b) A compressor shaft with the swash plate.

Several other Japanese manufacturers have produced 6-cylinder and 10-cylinder swash-plate compressors. These manufacturers include:

- Calsonic
- Hitachi
- Mitsubishi
- Nihon Radiator
- Seltec
- Zexel (formerly Diesel Kiki)

COAXIAL WOBBLE-PLATE COMPRESSORS Wobble-plate compressors drive the pistons through an angle plate that looks somewhat like a swash plate, but the wobble plate does not rotate and drives single pistons through piston rods. Wobble-plate compressors commonly use five or seven cylinders. ● **SEE FIGURE 5–4.**

VARIABLE DISPLACEMENT WOBBLE-PLATE COMPRESSORS A variable displacement compressor provides smooth operation with no clutch cycling, a constant 32°F (0°C) evaporator, and the most efficiency. Changing the compressor displacement is the major control for preventing evaporator icing.

- This design includes a large compressor that can pump enough refrigerant to meet high cooling loads, and it

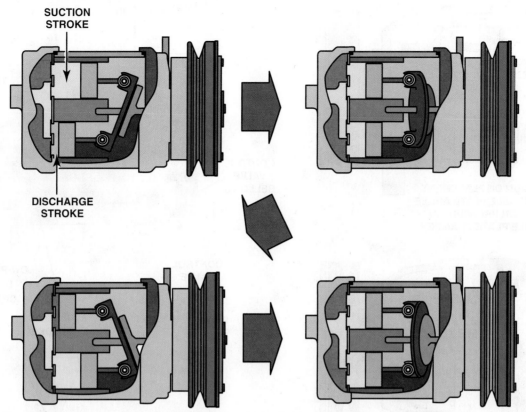

FIGURE 5–4 Two of the pistons of a wobble-plate compressor as they move through a pumping cycle.

reduces the displacement and pumping capacity of the compressor to match the needs of the evaporator as the evaporator cools.

- When there is a low cooling load at the evaporator, the wobble plate is moved to a less angled position. Some designs can reduce wobble-plate angle to 1% or 2% of the maximum stroke angle. This feature makes the compressor more efficient by reducing the drive load when it is not needed and also eliminates the need to cycle the compressor off and on. ● **SEE FIGURE 5–5**.

Wobble-plate angle is determined by the relative pressure at each end of the piston, and the angle is controlled by changing the pressure in the crankcase.

- When cooling load calls for high output and maximum displacement, crankcase pressure is kept low, and the wobble plate is at its maximum angle. The control valve bleeds crankcase pressure into the compressor suction cavity to lower the pressure.

- When cooling demand lessens, the control valve closes the bleed to the suction cavity and opens a passage between the discharge cavity and the crankcase, raising the pressure. Increasing crankcase pressure

raises the pressure on the bottom side of the pistons and causes the wobble plate to move to low angle, reducing displacement. A typical variable compressor has a displacement of 0.6 cu. inch to 9.2 cu. inch (10 cc to 151 cc). When maximum cooling is needed, the displacement is 9.2 cu. inch, and this can drop to as low as 0.6 cu. inch as needed to keep the evaporator pressure above the freezing point or at the pressure to produce the desired outlet air temperature. Compressor displacement is adjusted by changing the pressure inside the crank/piston chamber using a pressure or electronically controlled valve. ● **SEE FIGURE 5–6**.

VANE COMPRESSORS

CONSTRUCTION The vanes of these compressors are mounted in a rotor that runs inside a round, eccentric, or a somewhat elliptical, chamber. The vanes slide in and out of the rotor as their outer end follows the shape of the chamber. Compressors with a round, eccentric chamber have one

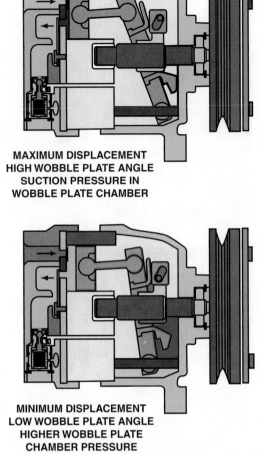

MAXIMUM DISPLACEMENT
HIGH WOBBLE PLATE ANGLE
SUCTION PRESSURE IN
WOBBLE PLATE CHAMBER

MINIMUM DISPLACEMENT
LOW WOBBLE PLATE ANGLE
HIGHER WOBBLE PLATE
CHAMBER PRESSURE

FIGURE 5–5 A variable displacement compressor can change the angle of the wobble plate and piston stroke. This angle is changed by a control valve that senses evaporator pressure, which in turn changes wobble chamber pressure.

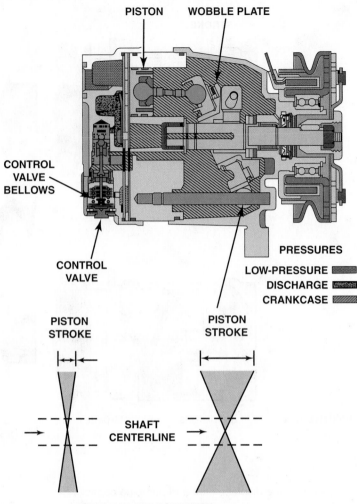

WOBBLE PLATE POSITIONS

AT MINIMUM
DISPLACEMENT

AT MAXIMUM
DISPLACEMENT

FIGURE 5–6 When the evaporator cools and low-side pressure drops, the piston stroke of a variable displacement compressor is reduced so that compressor output matches the cooling load.

pumping action per vane per revolution. Compressors with an elliptical housing have two pumping actions per vane per revolution. This type of compressor is sometimes called *balanced* because there is a pressure chamber on each side of the rotor.

OPERATION As the rotor turns, in one or two areas, the chamber behind the vane increases in size. This area has a port connected to the suction cavity. The following vane traps the refrigerant and forms a chamber as it passes by the suction port. The trapped refrigerant is carried around to the discharge port. In this location, the chamber size gets smaller which increases the gas pressure and forces it into the high side. Vane compressors have the advantage of being very compact and vibration free. ● **SEE FIGURE 5–7.**

SCROLL COMPRESSORS

CONSTRUCTION Scroll compressors use two major components:

1. **Fixed scroll**—The fixed scroll is attached to the compressor housing.

2. **Movable scroll**—The movable scroll is mounted over an eccentric bushing and counterweight on the crankshaft. It does not rotate, but it moves in an orbit relative to the stationary scroll and as a result is also called an *orbiting piston compressor*.

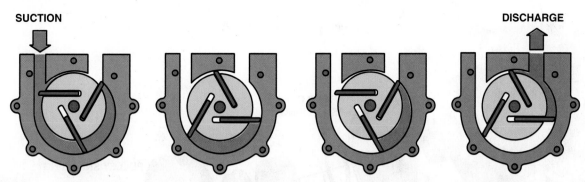

FIGURE 5-7 As the rotor turns in a counterclockwise direction, the vanes move in and out to follow the contour of the housing. This action forms chambers that get larger at the suction ports and smaller at the discharge ports. Evaporator pressure fills the chambers as they get larger, and the reducing size forces the refrigerant into the high side.

Both scrolls have a spiral shape that forms one side of the pumping chamber.

OPERATION   As the scroll orbits, it forms a pumping chamber that is open at the outer end. This chamber is moved to the center by the scroll's action as the pressure is increased. Two or three chambers are present at the same time. The outer ends of the scrolls are open to the suction port, and the inner ends connect to the discharge port. ● **SEE FIGURE 5-8**.

ADVANTAGES   A scroll compressor has the advantage of having very smooth operation and low-engagement torque that allows the use of a small clutch. A scroll compressor can also be driven at higher revolutions per minute (RPM) than other designs, so that a smaller drive pulley is used. This compressor design is also much more efficient than the other compressor styles when it is operated at the design speed, which is an advantage for vehicles that tend to run most of the time at cruising speed.

DISADVANTAGES   The one disadvantage of a scroll compressor is that it is more expensive to manufacture and therefore costs more than a piston-type compressor.

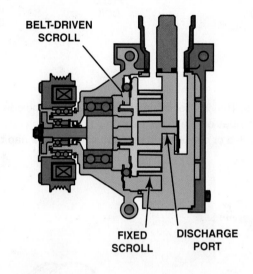

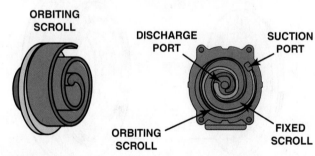

FIGURE 5-8 As the orbital scroll moves, it forms pumping chambers/gas pockets that start at the suction port and forces the refrigerant to the discharge port at the center.

COMPRESSOR CLUTCHES

PURPOSE AND FUNCTION   Electromagnetic clutches allow the compressor to be turned on and off. The clutch uses a coil of wire where a magnetic field is generated when electrical current flows through it. The magnetic field pulls the drive plate against the rotating pulley to drive the compressor.

PARTS AND OPERATION   Magnetic clutches include:

1. The clutch coil and pulley are both mounted on an extension from the front of the compressor housing. The pulley and its bearing are mounted on an extension of the front head. This placement allows the side load of the drive belt to be absorbed by the pulley bearing and compressor housing. It also allows easier servicing of individual clutch parts.

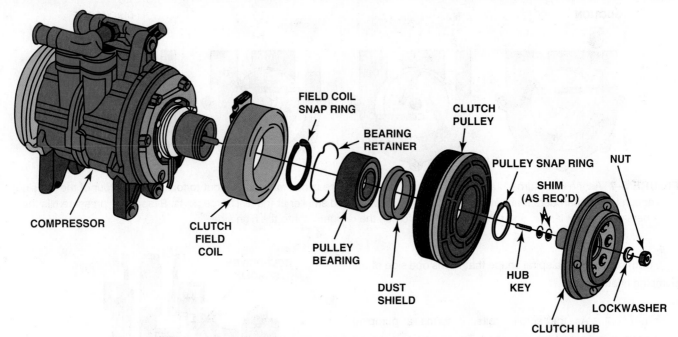

FIGURE 5–9 The electromagnetic clutch assembly includes the clutch field coil, where the magnetic field is created; the clutch pulley, which rides on the pulley bearing; and the clutch hub, which is attached to the input shaft of the compressor. The small shims are added or deleted as needed to adjust the air gap between the clutch hub and the clutch pulley.

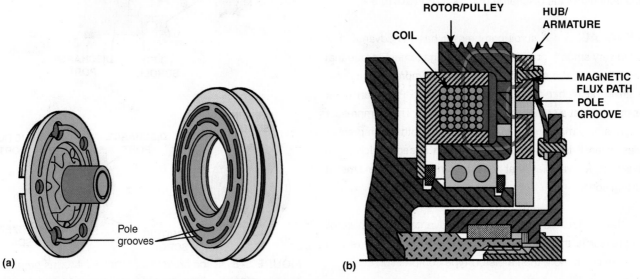

FIGURE 5–10 The magnetic flux path is from the coil and through the metal of the rotor and clutch hub. When it meets a pole groove, it travels from the hub to the rotor or vice versa, which increases the clutch holding power.

2. The **drive plate** is attached to the compressor shaft. The drive plate is also called an a *clutch pulley,* and the pulley is also called a *rotor*. ● **SEE FIGURE 5–9**.

Some design factors used to increase holding power include the following:

- The number of *flux poles*, which are the slots in the face of the clutch armature (the greater the number of slots, the stronger the magnetic hold). ● **SEE FIGURE 5–10**.

- The diameter of the rotor and armature (the larger the diameter, the greater the holding power).

- The use of copper or aluminum in the clutch coil winding (copper produces about 20% greater torque capacity).

- The current draw of the coil (the lower the resistance of the coil, the greater the current draw and the stronger the magnetic field that is created).

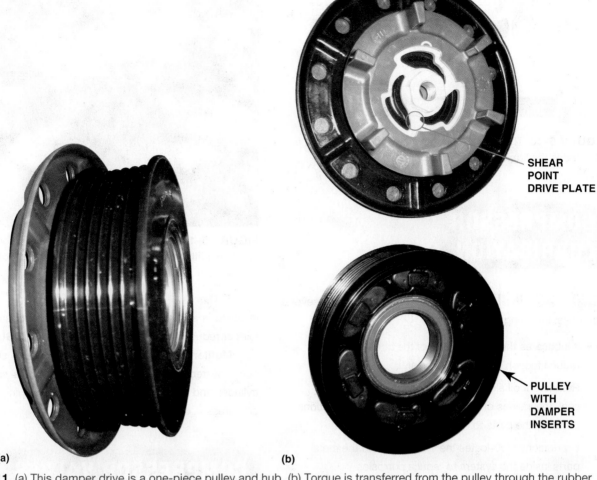

SHEAR
POINT
DRIVE PLATE

PULLEY
WITH
DAMPER
INSERTS

(a)

(b)

FIGURE 5–11 (a) This damper drive is a one-piece pulley and hub. (b) Torque is transferred from the pulley through the rubber damper inserts (bottom), and the drive plate uses torque-limiting fingers that will shear if the compressor should seize (top).

DAMPER DRIVES Many recent vehicles use a clutchless **damper drive**, electronic-controlled, variable displacement compressor. The pulley always drives the compressor through a rubber portion that dampens rotating engine pulsations.

One variable displacement compressor that uses a damper drive is electronically controlled to go to minimum displacement of 2% output when A/C is not used. This displacement requires very little power and is enough to circulate oil through the moving parts. The pulley drive plate includes a metal or rubber shear portion that can break to protect the drive belt in case the compressor should fail and lock up. ● **SEE FIGURE 5–11**.

Damper drives cannot be cycled for evaporator temperature control. The compressor displacement control valve responds to electrical signals from the control module, and

FIGURE 5–12 This tag on the service port indicates a damper-drive compressor that can be damaged if the engine is run without refrigerant in the system.

this controls evaporator temperature to deliver the desired outlet temperature and prevent evaporator freeze-up. ● **SEE FIGURE 5–12**.

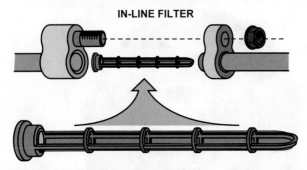

IN-LINE FILTER

FIGURE 5–13 This filter, about the size of an orifice tube, is installed in the liquid line by the vehicle manufacturer.

COMPRESSOR LUBRICATION

NEED FOR LUBRICATION Refrigerant oil serves several purposes, including the following:

- It lubricates the moving parts of the compressor to reduce friction and prevents wear.
- Refrigerant oil also helps *seal* the compressor shaft seal, the insides of the hoses, and various connections between the parts to reduce refrigerant leakage.
- In addition, it lubricates the TXV and coats the metal parts inside the system to reduce corrosion.

HOW OIL IS CIRCULATED With R-12, oil was miscible (could be mixed) in the refrigerant and the refrigerant carried the oil. The refrigerant oil used in R-134a system does not mix with the refrigerant but instead moves through the system simply with the movement of the refrigerant. If the system has the proper refrigerant charge and the proper amount of oil in the system, then the compressor is lubricated. A loss of refrigerant will also mean a loss of lubricating oil and subsequent compressor failure.

FILTERS AND MUFFLERS

PURPOSE AND FUNCTION Inline filters are available from aftermarket sources for installation in the liquid line between the condenser and the OT or TXV and are designed to filter the refrigerant to stop debris from plugging the expansion device.

General Motors is installing inline filters, called a *refrigerant or expansion valve filter*, in the liquid line on selected models. This filter is about the same size and shape as an orifice tube,

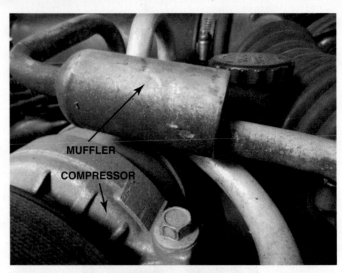

MUFFLER

COMPRESSOR

FIGURE 5–14 A muffler is a simple expansion or pulsation chamber with baffles inside the unit to help smooth compressor pressure pulses.

installed in a connector in the liquid line, and is secured by a joint or reduced/dimpled line section. ● **SEE FIGURE 5–13**.

Mufflers are installed in the discharge or suction line of some systems. These mufflers are usually a simple baffled cylinder and are used to dampen the pumping noise of the compressor. ● **SEE FIGURE 5–14**.

COMPRESSOR VALVES AND SWITCHES

PRESSURE RELIEF VALVES Excessive high-side pressure can produce compressor damage and a potential safety hazard if the system should rupture. Compressors are controlled and protected with several different types of pressure relief valves. Many early systems contain a *high-pressure relief* or *release valve,* or release valve which was mounted on the compressor or at some location in the high side.

- R-12 relief valves are set to release pressure at 440 PSI to 550 PSI (3,000 kPa to 3,800 kPa).
- R-134a valves are a little higher at 500 PSI to 600 PSI (3,450 kPa to 4,130 kPa).
- A relief valve is spring-loaded so excessive pressure will open the valve, and as soon as the excess pressure is released, the valve will reclose. ● **SEE FIGURE 5–15**.

NOTE: Newer systems are designed to release the clutch and shut the system off if pressures get too high to avoid venting refrigerant into the atmosphere.

FIGURE 5-15 A high-pressure relief valve contains a strong spring that keeps the valve closed unless high-side pressure (from the left) forces it open. The valve then closes when the pressure drops.

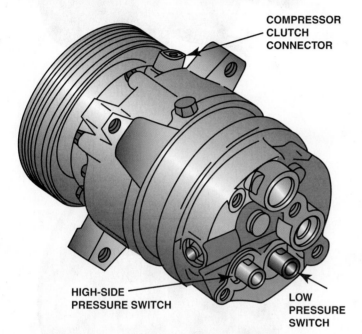

FIGURE 5-16 Check service information for the exact purpose and function of each of the switches located on the compressor because they can vary according to make, model, and year of manufacture of vehicle and can also vary as to what compressor is used.

SWITCHES ON THE COMPRESSOR

Many compressors contain one or more of the following:

- A low-pressure switch
- A high-pressure switch
- A low- and/or high-pressure sensor

Switches can be connected to ports, leading to either the suction or discharge cavities in the compressor. These switches are usually used in circuits either to protect the compressor or system from damage or as sensors for the engine control module. ● SEE FIGURE 5-16.

COMPRESSOR CONTROL SWITCHES

Various electrical switches are used in A/C systems to prevent

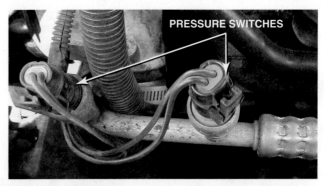

FIGURE 5-17 Typical air-conditioning pressure switches. Check service information to determine the purpose and function of each switch for the vehicle being inspected.

evaporator icing, protect the compressor, and control fan motors. Control switches can be located anywhere in the system, including at the following positions:

- Compressor discharge
- Compressor suction cavities
- Receiver–drier
- Accumulator. ● SEE FIGURE 5-17.

COMPRESSOR SPEED SENSOR

Some vehicles use an A/C compressor speed (RPM) sensor so the ECM will know if the compressor is running, and by comparing the compressor and engine speed signals, the ECM can determine if the compressor clutch is slipping excessively. This system is often called a *belt lock* or *belt protection system.* It prevents a locked-up compressor from destroying the engine drive belt, which, in turn, can cause engine overheating or loss of power steering. If the ECM detects an excessive speed difference for more than a few seconds, it will turn the compressor off. Check service information for the vehicle being serviced to determine if the compressor has a speed (RPM) sensor and if so, where it is located and how to check it for proper operation.

A/C COMPRESSOR DIAGNOSIS AND SERVICE

COMPRESSOR CLUTCH DIAGNOSIS

A faulty compressor or compressor clutch is indicated if the following conditions are observed:

- The high- and low-side pressures are too close, within 50 PSI (345 kPa).

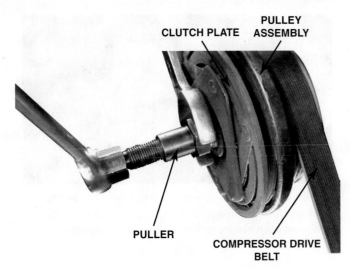

FIGURE 5–18 After removing the retaining nut from the A/C compressor shaft, a special puller is used to remove the compressor clutch plate (hub).

- It cannot produce a high-side pressure of 350 PSI (2,400 kPa) or greater. This test usually requires disconnecting the fan(s) or blocking condenser airflow.
- There is visible damage to the compressor, clutch, or pulley.
- The compressor shaft rotates freely with no resistance.
- Shaft rotation is rough or harsh.
- There is free play when shaft rotation is reversed.
- The clutch has too much or too little air gap.
- The clutch does not apply or release.
- The pulley rotation is rough or with too much free play.

COMPRESSOR CLUTCH REPLACEMENT Most A/C compressor clutches are three-part assemblies with a separate drive hub (armature), rotor pulley, and coil. To remove a clutch assembly, check service information for the exact procedure to follow. Most specified procedures include the following steps:

STEP 1 Remove the locknut or bolt from the compressor shaft. A clutch hub wrench is often required to keep the hub from turning. Some compressors do not use a locknut.

STEP 2 Use the correct tool to pull the hub from the compressor shaft. ● **SEE FIGURE 5–18**.

STEP 3 A special puller is required on most compressors but the rotor pulley can be slid off some compressors, such as the Nippondenso compressors. ● **SEE FIGURE 5–19**.

To reinstall a clutch assembly, perform the following steps:

STEP 1 Install the coil, making sure that the anti-rotation pins and holes are aligned and the wire connector is in the

FIGURE 5–19 (a) The pulley assembly is removed using a special puller on this Dodge truck. (b) The pulley assembly includes the bearing which may or may not be a replaceable part, depending on the compressor.

correct position. The coil must be pressed in place on some compressors.

STEP 2 Install the coil retaining ring.

STEP 3 Install the rotor pulley and replace the retainer ring. Some retainer rings have a beveled face and this side must face away from the pulley. Test this installation by rotating the rotor pulley and it must rotate freely, with no interference.

FIGURE 5–20 Air gap of the clutch is adjusted on some A/C compressors by using thin metal washers called shims. Adding a shim increases the gap and deleting a shim decreases the gap.

FIGURE 5–21 On some compressors, the air gap is adjusted by pressing the plate to the correct position.

STEP 4 On some compressors, install the adjusting shims onto the shaft, install the drive key, and align and install the hub. ● **SEE FIGURE 5–20.**

On many GM compressors, the hub must be pulled onto the shaft. It should be pulled on just far enough to get the correct air gap. ● **SEE FIGURE 5–21.**

STEP 5 If used, install the shaft locknut or bolt and tighten it to the correct torque.

STEP 6 Check the clutch air gap at three locations around the clutch. The clearance should be within specifications at all three points. If it is too wide or too narrow, readjust the air gap. If it is too wide at one point and too narrow at another, replace the hub.

COMPRESSOR SHAFT SEAL REPLACEMENT Every compressor has a seal that keeps refrigerant from escaping through the opening where the pulley driveshaft enters. ● **SEE FIGURE 5–22.**

Many compressors use a rotating **seal cartridge** attached to the shaft and a stationary **seal seat** attached to the front of the compressor housing. The compressor has one or two flats on the shaft so that the seal cartridge is positively driven.

A gasket or rubber O-ring is used so that the seal seat makes a gas-tight seal at the housing, and the seat has an extremely smooth sealing face. The carbon-material sealing member is spring loaded so that its smooth face makes tight contact with the seal seat. The cartridge also uses a rubber O-ring or molded rubber unit to seal the carbon to the driveshaft. Another important part of the seal is the compressor oil,

FIGURE 5–22 The shaft seal must keep refrigerant from escaping out the front of the compressor. Most compressors have an oil flow routed to them to reduce wear and improve the sealing action.

which lubricates the surfaces and forms the final seal between the sealing surfaces. ● **SEE FIGURE 5–23.**

A ceramic material has replaced cast iron for the seal seat in some compressors. Ceramic is not affected by water or acids, which can cause rust, corrosion, or etching of the iron seats. Ceramic seats are easy to identify because they are white instead of gray.

Recent compressor designs use a **lip seal**. The lip of the seal is made from Teflon and rides against a perfectly smooth portion of the driveshaft. Some shaft seals use double seating lips. The outer shell of the seal fits into a recess in the compressor housing and is sealed using a rubber O-ring. Gas pressure in the compressor ensures a tight fit between the seal lip and the shaft. ● **SEE FIGURE 5–24.**

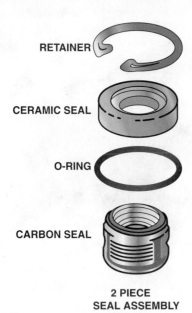

RETAINER

CERAMIC SEAL

O-RING

CARBON SEAL

2 PIECE
SEAL ASSEMBLY

FIGURE 5–23 Many compressors use a two-piece seal with a rotating carbon seal and a stationary seal.

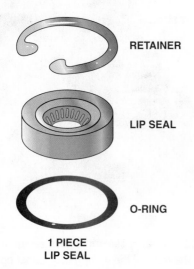

RETAINER

LIP SEAL

O-RING

1 PIECE
LIP SEAL

FIGURE 5–24 Some newer compressors use a stationary lip seal that seals against the rotating shaft.

With most compressors, the shaft seal is removed from the front of the compressor after the clutch plate has been removed. Seals should not be reused and new seal parts should always be installed. Special tools are required for most seal replacements. These tools are designed to grip the seal cartridge or seat so they can be quickly pulled out or slid back into the proper position. Always follow the specified procedure found in service information.

COMPRESSOR DRIVE BELT SERVICE Engine drive belts should be checked periodically for damage and proper tension. If a belt shows excessive wear, severe glazing, rubber breakdown, or frayed cords, it should be replaced. The automatic tensioner on some vehicles includes a belt stretch

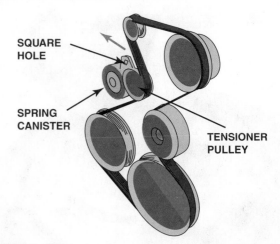

SQUARE
HOLE

SPRING
CANISTER

TENSIONER
PULLEY

FIGURE 5–25 Moving the automatic tensioner outward allows the serpentine belt to be removed from the pulleys.

 TECH TIP

Quick and Easy Belt Noise Test

With the engine running at idle speed, use a spray bottle and squirt some water on the belt and listen for a noise change. If the noise increases, there is a belt tension problem. If the noise decreases but then returns, there is a belt alignment problem.

indicator. If belt stretch of more than 1% is indicated, the belt should be replaced.

Belt slippage is caused by either a worn tensioner or worn belt. A belt that is too tight causes an excessively high load on the bearings of the components driven by the belt. Traditionally, belt tension is checked by pushing the center of the belt inward and then pulling it outward while noticing how much the belt is able to be deflected. Most manufacturers use a total movement of 0.5 inch as a maximum distance. Most manufacturers recommend using a belt tension gauge that is hooked onto the belt and uses a scale to show tension.

To remove and replace a drive belt using an automatic tensioner, perform the following steps:

STEP 1 Note the routing of the belt as per the under hood decal or in-service information.

STEP 2 Relieve the belt tensioner and slip the belt off the pulleys. A wrench can be used for this procedure on most tensioners. ● **SEE FIGURE 5–25.**

STEP 3 Remove the belt, and with the belt off, spin the pulleys to make sure that they are clean, not worn, and rotate freely.

What Is a Stretch Belt?

Starting in 2007, some vehicles use a stretch-fit, multi-rib belt without a tensioner. The elastic nature of the belt allows it to be stretched to install it over the pulleys, and the stretch provides the tension to keep it from slipping. A special tool or strap is required to install a stretch belt, and some manufacturers advise to cut the belt to remove it.
● **SEE FIGURE 5–26.**

Cut the old belt to remove it. Place the new belt in position on the pulley that is hardest to get to. If the second pulley has holes through it:

- Install the belt onto the pulley, and secure it to the pulley using a zip tie.
- Rotate the engine by hand far enough so the pulley rotates and pulls the belt into position.
- Cut the zip tie.

If the second pulley does not have holes, a special tool will be required:

- Place the special tool into position on the second pulley.
- Start the belt onto the pulley.
- Rotate the engine by hand far enough so the pulley rotates and pulls the belt into position.
- Remove the special tool.

STRETCH-FIT BELT

FIGURE 5–26 A stretch-fit belt is identified by the lack of an idler or method of adjusting belt tension.

STEP 4 Install the belt on some pulleys, rotate the tensioner, slide the belt into the proper position, and release the tensioner.

STEP 5 Check to ensure proper belt placement on each pulley. Start the engine and check for proper belt operation.

BELT TENSIONER SERVICE The tensioner is designed to keep the belt tight enough so it does not slip but not so tight that the belt or bearings in the driven components will fail early. It must also dampen the tensioner arm to stop excess motion/bouncing and align the pulley to the belt. Tensioners can fail, and at least one source recommends installing a new tensioner when the belt is replaced.

To check belt tensioner operation, perform the following steps:

STEP 1 With the engine running at idle speed, observe any tensioner movement, and there should be a rather gentle motion. If it appears to bounce back and forth a large amount, the dampener portion is probably worn out.

STEP 2 Stop the engine and move the tensioner through its travel. It should move smoothly against the spring pressure with no catches or free portions.

STEP 3 With the pulley unloaded, check for free play or rough bearing operation. Next, spin the bearing and it should rotate smoothly for two or three revolutions. Also, check for excess arm motion at the pivot bushing.

REPLACEMENT COMPRESSORS

IDENTIFY THE UNIT Replacement compressors are available as new or rebuilt units, and proper identification is made from the vehicle make, model, and engine size. Then, if needed, proper identification is made by the old compressor make and model. At times, a failed compressor is replaced with a different compressor make and model if the mounting points, clutch diameter and belt position, and line fittings are the same.
● **SEE FIGURE 5–27.**

OIL CHARGE Having proper amount of oil in the system during compressor replacement is an important factor. Too much oil in a system can reduce system performance, and too little oil can cause early compressor failure. Many compressors are equipped with *shipping oil* that is not intended for long-term lubrication. Be sure to read the information that usually comes with the new compressor and follow the directions. Most manufacturers recommend draining all the oil from the old compressor and measuring the amount drained. ● **SEE FIGURE 5–28.**

FIGURE 5–27 The decal on this compressor identifies the type (SDB709) and the serial number. Note also that it uses a seven-groove, multi-V clutch, four mounting bolts, and vertical-pad service ports at the side.

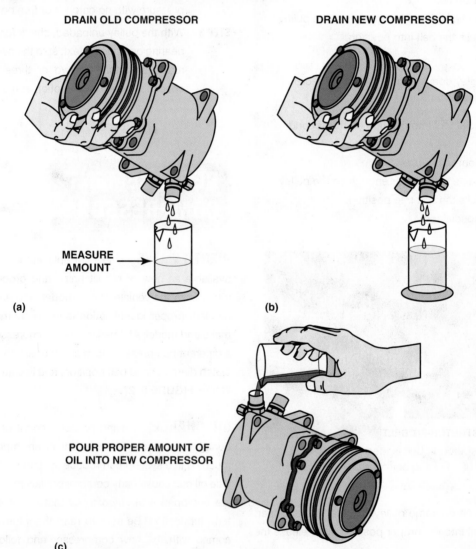

DRAIN OLD COMPRESSOR

DRAIN NEW COMPRESSOR

MEASURE AMOUNT →

(a)

(b)

POUR PROPER AMOUNT OF OIL INTO NEW COMPRESSOR

(c)

FIGURE 5–28 (a) The oil should be drained from the old compressor (top left); rotate the compressor shaft and the compressor to help the draining. (b) Drain the oil from the new compressor (top right). (c) Pour the same amount of oil drained from the old compressor or the amount specified by the compressor manufacturer of the proper oil into the new compressor (lower).

If the amount is within certain limits, such as 3 oz. to 5 oz., the same amount of new oil is then added to the new compressor. Always follow the manufacturer's recommendations or processes. A typical example includes:

- If the amount drained was below 3 oz., then 3 oz. of new oil is added.
- If the amount drained is more than 5 oz., then 5 oz. of new oil is added.

Replacing a compressor usually includes the following steps:

STEP 1 Adjust the oil level in the compressor as instructed by the vehicle or compressor manufacturer.

STEP 2 Install the compressor on the engine and replace the mounting bolts.

STEP 3 Install the drive belt, adjust the belt tension, and tighten all mounting bolts to the correct torque.

STEP 4 Using new gaskets or O-rings, connect the discharge and suction lines. Then evacuate, charge, and check for leaks at all fittings.

SUMMARY

1. Various compressor types and models are used with vehicle A/C systems.
2. Compressor models can use a variety of clutch and pulley designs.
3. Some variable displacement compressors use a damper pulley in place of a clutch.
4. Compressors are lubricated by oil that is circulated by the refrigerant.

REVIEW QUESTIONS

1. What type compressors are used in air-conditioning systems?
2. How does a coaxial swash-plate compressors work?
3. What is the difference between a vane compressor and a radial compressor?
4. How does an electromagnetic compressor clutch work?
5. How is the air gap of a compressor clutch adjusted?

CHAPTER QUIZ

1. In a piston-type compressor, the pistons are driven by a _____.
   a. Crankshaft
   b. Swash plate
   c. Wobble plate
   d. All of the above depending on the compressor

2. Most piston compressors use what type of valves?
   a. Poppet
   b. Reed
   c. Sliding
   d. On-off gate-type valve

3. The basic designs of A/C compressors include _____, _____, and _____?
   a. Piston, vane, and scroll
   b. Radial, piston, and vane
   c. Balanced, piston, and scroll
   d. Fixed scroll, moveable scroll, and piston

4. Two technicians are discussing variable displacement piston compressors. Technician A says that the wobble plate is moved to the high-angle position for maximum output when the cooling load is high. Technician B says that the wobble-plate angle is controlled by the pressure in the crankcase of the compressor. Which technician is correct?
   a. Technician A only
   b. Technician B only
   c. Both technicians A and B
   d. Neither A nor B

5. Wobble-plate compressors commonly use how many cylinders?
   a. Two
   b. Three
   c. Four
   d. Five or seven

6. A clutchless damper drive is used with what type of A/C compressor?
   a. Electronic-controlled, variable displacement compressor
   b. Scroll compressor
   c. Vane-type compressor
   d. Orbiting piston compressor

7. How is the A/C compressor lubricated in an R-134a system?
   a. Uses a sump to hold 3 oz. to 5 oz. of refrigerant oil
   b. The refrigerant oil mixes with the refrigerant
   c. The oil moves through the system simply with the movement of the refrigerant
   d. Most compressors are a sealed unit with their own oil

8. Switches located on the compressor itself may include_____.
   a. A low-pressure switch
   b. High-pressure switch
   c. Low- and/or high-pressure sensor
   d. Any or all of the above

9. A compressor speed (belt lock) sensor is used by the HVAC ECM to_____.
   a. Prevent a locked-up compressor from destroying the engine drive belt
   b. Determine if the compressor is running, and by comparing the compressor and engine speed signals
   c. Vary the displacement of the compressor based on compressor speed
   d. Both a and b

10. A stretch-type A/C compressor belt is removed using_____.
   a. A special tool
   b. A knife (cut it)
   c. By removing the compressor
   d. By removing the tensioner

chapter 6
REFRIGERANTS AND REFRIGERANT OILS

LEARNING OBJECTIVES

After studying this chapter, the reader should be able to:

1. Prepare for the ASE Heating and Air Conditioning (A7) certification test content area "B" (Refrigeration System Component Diagnosis and Repair).

2. Discuss the depletion of the ozone layer and the resulting issues of global warming.

3. Explain the impact of legislative laws on automotive A/C systems.

4. Discuss identifying refrigerants and proper storage container.

5. State the changes considered for future refrigerants.

6. Explain refrigerant safety precautions.

7. Discuss the different types and viscosities of refrigerant oils.

KEY TERMS

Clean Air Act 96
Environmental Protection
 Agency (EPA) 96
Global warming 96
Global warming potential
 (GWP) 96
Greenhouse effect 96
Greenhouse gases
 (GHGs) 96
Hygroscopic 101
Ozone 95

Ozone depletion
 potential (ODP) 95
Section 609 96
Significant new
 alternatives policy
 (SNAP) 97
Stratosphere 94
Total environmental
 warming impact
 (TEWI) 97

FIGURE 6–1 Large 30 pound containers of R-134a are light blue for easy identification.

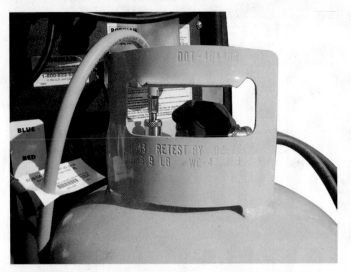

FIGURE 6–2 The stamped text at the top of this container reads "DOT-4BA400."

REFRIGERANTS

DEFINITION Refrigerants are colorless and odorless compounds. Usually, the only way to know that they are present in a container is how the container feels when it is picked up or shaken. On manifold gauge sets equipped with a sight glass, bubbles can be seen in the clear liquid as it passes by the glass.

Refrigerants are commonly available in several sizes of containers including:

- Small cans of 12 oz. to 14 oz. (400 g)—at one time, this was 15 oz. of R-12 and 1 oz. of can for a total of 1 lb and

- Larger drums or canisters of 15 lb. or 30 lb. (6.8 kg or 13.6 kg). Small containers of R-12 can be purchased only by certified technicians; however, there are no national restrictions on purchase of R-134a.

Refrigerant containers are color coded:

- R-12 containers are white
- R-22 containers are green
- R-134a containers are light blue. ● **SEE FIGURE 6–1.**

Refrigerant containers are usually disposable. These containers should be evacuated into a recovery unit, marked

TECH TIP

Think of a Propane Tank

An effective way of telling how much propane there is in the container used in the barbecue grill is by pouring hot water over the container. The heat will warm the top of the container, cause some of the liquid to boil, and increase container pressure, and if felt along the container, the liquid will cool the lower part. The liquid fills the container to the point of temperature change. This same procedure can be used to estimate the level of refrigerant in the container.

empty, and properly disposed of when they are emptied. The storage containers for recycled refrigerant must be approved by the DOT and carry the proper marking to show this. ● **SEE FIGURE 6–2.**

ENVIRONMENTAL ISSUES

TERMINOLOGY Planet Earth is unique in many ways. It has an atmosphere that contains a percentage of oxygen high enough to allow mammals, including humans, to live in it. This atmosphere extends outward from Earth for about 31 miles (50 km). The upper layer of the atmosphere is called the **stratosphere**, and it begins about 7 miles to 10 miles (11 km to 16 km) up and extends to the outer limits. A layer

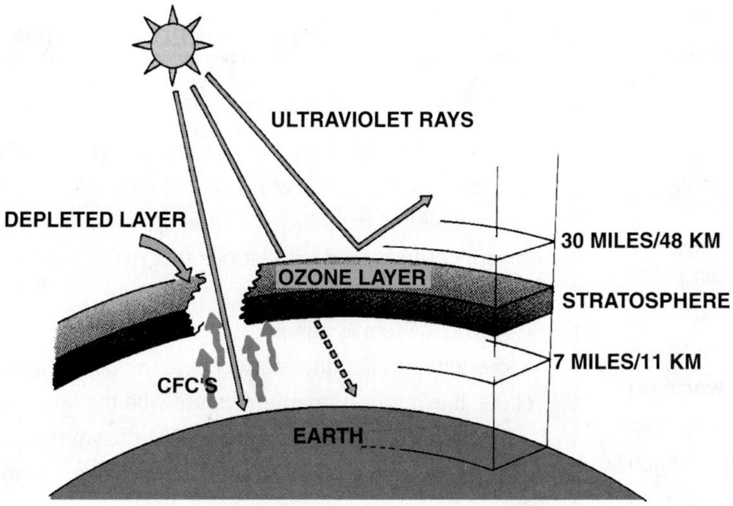

FIGURE 6–3 Depletion of the ozone layer allows more ultraviolet radiation from the sun to reach Earth's surface.

ULTRAVIOLET RAYS

DEPLETED LAYER

OZONE LAYER

30 MILES/48 KM

STRATOSPHERE

7 MILES/11 KM

CFC'S

EARTH

HOW OZONE IS DESTROYED

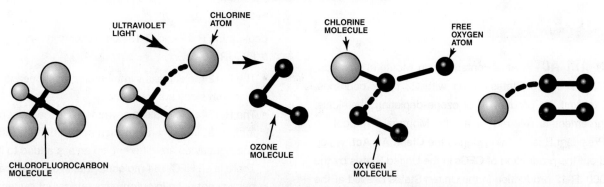

ULTRAVIOLET LIGHT

CHLORINE ATOM

CHLORINE MOLECULE

FREE OXYGEN ATOM

CHLOROFLUOROCARBON MOLECULE

OZONE MOLECULE

OXYGEN MOLECULE

IN THE UPPER ATMOSPHERE ULTRAVIOLET LIGHT BREAKS OFF A CHLORINE ATOM FROM A CHLOROFLUOROCARBON MOLECULE.

THE CHLORINE ATTACKS AN OZONE MOLECULE, BREAKING IT APART. AN ORDINARY OXYGEN MOLECULE AND A MOLECULE OF CHLORINE MONOXIDE ARE FORMED.

A FREE OXYGEN ATOM BREAKS UP THE CHLORINE MONOXIDE. THE CHLORINE IS THEN FREE TO REPEAT THE PROCESS.

FIGURE 6–4 Chlorofluorocarbon molecules break apart in the atmosphere.

of **ozone** (O_3) extends around the Earth in the stratosphere. ● **SEE FIGURE 6–3**.

The ozone layer is important to us because it blocks the ultraviolet wavelengths of light generated by the sun. Ultraviolet rays can be very harmful to our way of life. In humans, an excess of these rays can cause an increase in skin cancer and cataract of the eyes, as well as damage to our immune system. These same problems can affect many animals. Ultraviolet rays can also damage plants and vegetables. This damage probably also extends to plankton and larvae in the sea, the base of the food chain for sea animals.

In the late 1900s, it was determined that the ozone layer is getting much thinner, and large holes are being created in it (mostly near the South Pole). The ozone layer is not providing the same protection from ultraviolet (UV) rays as it once did. It has been determined that

1. The breakup or depletion of the ozone layer is caused by human-made chemical pollution.

2. One of the major ozone-depleting chemicals is chlorine.

3. One of the major sources of chlorine in the atmosphere is R-12.

OZONE DEPLETION A chlorine atom from a *chlorinated fluorocarbon (CFC)* such as R-12 can travel into the stratosphere if it escapes or is released. There, under the effects of ice clouds and sunlight, it can combine with one of the oxygen atoms of an ozone molecule to form chlorine monoxide and an ordinary oxygen molecule, O_2. This destroys that ozone molecule. The chlorine can then break away and attack other ozone molecules. It is believed that 1 chlorine atom can destroy 10,000 to 100,000 ozone molecules. ● **SEE FIGURE 6–4**.

- CFCs do the most damage and have an **ozone depletion potential (ODP)** of 1.

- Hydrochlorofluorocarbon (HCFC), such as R-22, have an ODP around 0.01–0.1, so they have a lesser effect on the ozone layer.

- Since HFCs, such as R-134a, contain no chlorine and have an ODP of 0 (zero), they have no detrimental effect on the ozone layer.

GLOBAL WARMING AND GREENHOUSE GASES

Another area of concern is a layer of gases that is causing a **greenhouse effect**. This gas layer traps heat at the Earth's surface and lower atmosphere, and it is increasing the temperature of our living area. This is called **global warming**. CFC and hydrocarbon (HC) gases such as butane and propane are considered **greenhouse gases (GHGs)**. **Global warming potential (GWP)** compares the ability of different gases to trap heat, and this is based on the heat-absorbing ability of each gas. The lower the GWP number, the lower the global warming potential.

LEGISLATION

CLEAN AIR ACT   At a conference in Montreal, Canada, in 1987, the United States, along with 22 other countries, agreed to limit the production of ozone-depleting chemicals. This agreement is referred to as the Montreal Protocol. In 1990, President Bush (senior) signed the **Clean Air Act**, which phased out the production of CFCs in the United States by the year 2000. R-12 production in the United States ceased at the end of 1995.

SECTION 609   **Section 609** is a portion of the Clean Air Act that places certain requirements on the *mobile vehicle air conditioning (MVAC)* service field. Important portions of this section require the following:

Effective January 1, 1992

- Technicians who repair or service automotive A/C systems shall be properly trained and certified and use approved refrigerant recovery and recycling equipment.

- Recovery and recycling equipment must be properly approved.

- Each shop that performs A/C service on motor vehicles shall certify to the **Environmental Protection Agency (EPA)** that it is using approved recycling equipment and that only properly trained and certified technicians are using this equipment.

Effective November 15, 1992

- Sales of small containers of R-12 (less than 20 lb) are restricted to certified technicians.

FREQUENTLY ASKED QUESTION

How Are Refrigerants Named?

The procedure for determining the refrigerant number is rather tedious and is of no value to the refrigerant technician. It is included in this text to reduce some misconceptions and wild stories that have passed through the industry.

The system is based on the number of carbon, hydrogen, and fluorine atoms in the refrigerant molecule. It is a four-character system with the letter "a" added to indicate a nonsymmetrical or asymmetrical molecule. The most common method of numbering system is:

C (MINUS 1), H (PLUS 1), and F.
R-12 has 1 C ($1-1=0$), O H ($0+1=1$), and 2 F (2), to get 012, or 12.

Look at the R-12 and R-134a molecules in
● **FIGURE 6–5**.

- The R-12 molecule is symmetrical, which means that both sides are the same.

- The R-134a molecule is asymmetrical (the reason for the "a" in the name), which means that the left and right sides are different, so an *a* is added to it. There is an HFC-134 molecule that is symmetrical, but it is not used in automotive refrigerant systems. Letters further down the alphabet indicate greater changes in the molecule.

Technically, the name should be CFC-12, HFC-134a, or HCFC-22 to indicate that the refrigerant is a chlorofluorocarbon, hydrofluorocarbon, or hydrochlorofluorocarbon. The chemical name for CFC-12, dichlorodifluoromethane, indicates that the molecule has two (di) chlorine atoms and two fluorine atoms, and the suffix methane indicates there is one carbon atom. The prefixes, di = 2, tri = 3, tetra = 4, penta = 5, and so on indicate the number of atoms. With carbon-based molecules, single-C molecules are methanes, double-C molecules are ethanes, three-C molecules are propanes, and so on. HFC-134a, tetrafluoroethane, has four (tetra) F atoms, two H (not mentioned in the name), and the suffix ethane, meaning there are two carbon atoms.

This explanation is not complete because chemists use other designations to show bonds within the molecule and different number combinations for blend refrigerants. This numbering system is based on the carbon chain that the molecule is built around. In this system, HFC-134a is 1, 1, 1, 2 tetrafluoroethane.

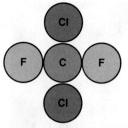

R-12 - Cl₂F₂C **R-134a - C₂H₂F₄**

FIGURE 6–5 R-12 is a combination of one carbon, two chlorine, and two fluorine atoms. R-134a is a combination of two carbon and four fluorine atoms.

Effective November 14, 1994

- MVAC technicians must be certified to purchase EPA-acceptable blend refrigerants.

Effective January 29, 1998

- Equipment used to recover or recycle R-134a must meet SAE standards.
- MVAC service technicians must be certified to handle non-ozone-depleting refrigerants (including R-134a).

Under the Montreal Protocol, phaseout of HCFC began in 2004 (a 35% reduction). This reduction began in 2003 in the United States. Manufacture of HCFC-22 was stopped in 2010 in the United States and other developed countries.

EUROPEAN R-134A PHASE-OUT The concern about climate change has caused the European Community to try to reduce greenhouse gas (GHG) emissions. Part of this legislation is to require that refrigerants must have a GWP of less than 150. Some refrigerants and their GWP include the following:

- R-134a has a GWP of 1,300 (a rather high potential contributor for climate change).
- R-1234yf has a GWP of 4. ● **SEE FIGURE 6–6.**
- R-744—Carbon dioxide (CO_2) has a GWP of 1

This rule was originally to take effect in 2011, with R-134a banned from new vehicle HVAC systems.

KYOTO PROTOCOL There is still a major concern about the global warming effect from escaping refrigerants. Representatives from many nations met in Kyoto, Japan, in 1997 and established the Kyoto Protocol to address these concerns. The **Total Environmental Warming Impact (TEWI)** index was developed, which rates the impact of various refrigerants along with the energy required to perform the cooling operation. In the future, it is hoped that each nation will reduce its negative impact on the environment to zero in order

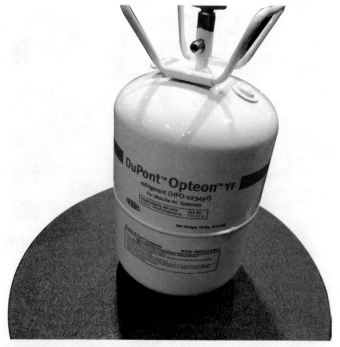

FIGURE 6–6 R-1234yf refrigerant is sold in white containers with a red stripe.

to reduce global change to zero. All factors concerning energy use and emissions will be considered. The United States has not signed the Kyoto Protocol.

ALTERNATE REFRIGERANTS

SNAP PROGRAM Section 612 of the 1990 Clean Air Act established the **Significant New Alternatives Policy (SNAP)** program to determine acceptable replacements for Class I and Class II chemicals. Class I chemicals include CFCs, and Class II chemicals are HCFCs. SNAP is administered by the EPA and identifies refrigerants that are acceptable from their ozone-depleting potential, global warming potential, flammability, and toxicity characteristics. Alternate refrigerants are not tested on their refrigeration quality, but only on their human health and environmental risks.

R-134a is the only alternate product for an R-12 system that has addressed the SAE retrofit documents (SAE J1657, SAE J1658, SAE J1659, and SAE J1662). These standards are designed to ensure long-term, trouble-free operation of the A/C system. An alternate refrigerant can only be used under the following conditions:

- Each refrigerant must have its own unique set of fittings, and all ports not converted must be permanently disabled.

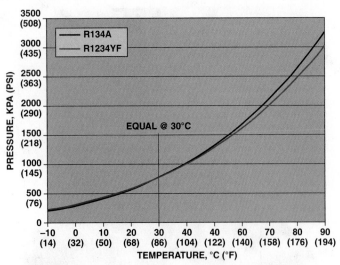

FIGURE 6–7 R-134a and R-1234yf have similar operating pressures.

FIGURE 6–8 The label on a Toyota Fuel Cell Hybrid Vehicle (FCHV) showing that CO_2 (R744) is being used as the refrigerant.

- Each refrigerant must have a label with a unique color that specifies pertinent information.

- All original refrigerants must be removed before charging with the new refrigerant.

- With blends that contain HCFC-22, hoses must be replaced with less permeable barrier hoses.

- With systems that include a high-pressure release device, a high-pressure shutoff switch must be installed.

- Blends containing HCFC-22 will be phased out in the near future.

COUNTERFEIT AND BOOTLEG REFRIGERANTS With the high cost and limited availability of R-12, a refrigerant buyer has to be careful about where it is purchased from. Refrigerant is being illegally imported, and some of it is contaminated. There are stories of counterfeit refrigerant being sold in containers marked the same as those of a reputable, domestic manufacturer. Other stories tell of containers that contain nothing but water with air pressure. Refrigerant should be purchased only from a known source that handles reputable products.

FUTURE REFRIGERANTS

TEWI In order to meet the requirements of **Total Environment Warming Impact (TEWI)**, several possible changes are being considered as a new refrigerant:

- R-1234yf

- R-744—Carbon dioxide (CO_2)

R-1234yf has operating characteristics that are very similar to R-134a, with a much lower GWP and an ODP of zero. ● SEE FIGURE 6–7.

There is concern about possible cross-contamination with either R-134a or an HC:

- As little as 5% of R-134a can increase the pressure in a recovery cylinder high enough to cause an "air purge" and this can empty the entire cylinder in the attempt to bleed off air.

- As little as 2% HC with 2% air will increase flammability to greater-than-limits established by the refrigerant manufacturers.

A carbon dioxide (CO_2) system (R744) is similar to the present-day systems, but it requires extremely high pressure, 7 to 10 times that of an R-134a system. This pressure puts a large added load on the compressor, heat exchanger, and refrigerant lines. The extremely high pressure requires more power from the engine to operate the compressor and this extra energy causes reduced fuel economy. At this time, a CO_2 system is up to 40% less efficient than an R-134a system and can cost about 30% more to produce. ● SEE FIGURE 6–8.

SECONDARY LOOP SYSTEMS Systems that use potentially hazardous refrigerants will probably use a secondary loop. The CO_2 or HC portion of the system will be entirely under the hood. A heat exchanger will provide a very cold fluid to connect with a liquid-to-air heat exchanger that will replace the evaporator. These systems might also use refrigerant-leak-sensing devices and a method of venting/dumping the refrigerant into one of the fender wells to prevent a buildup of refrigerant in the passenger area. ● SEE FIGURE 6–9.

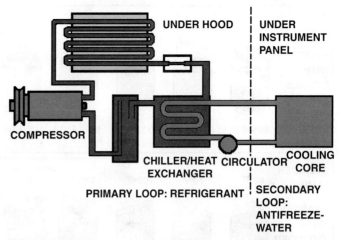

FREQUENTLY ASKED QUESTION

Will R-134a Systems be Required to be Retrofitted to R-1234yf?

No. Currently there is no mandate to retrofit existing systems with R-1234yf. If a vehicle came from the factory with R-1234yf, then this refrigerant, of course, should be used when servicing the vehicle and will require a special machine. R-134a is and will be the primary refrigerant for most vehicles and there is no need or legal requirement to replace it with any other refrigerant at this time.

REFRIGERANT SAFETY PRECAUTIONS

POTENTIAL HAZARDS Refrigerants should be handled only by trained and certified technicians because of potential safety hazards:

- Physiological reaction
- Asphyxiation (this means that the refrigerant does not contain oxygen, so it cannot sustain life if breathed)
- Frostbite and blindness
- Poisoning
- Combustion
- Explosion of storage containers

PRECAUTIONS Precautions when working with refrigerants include:

- Wear safety goggles or a clear face shield and protective clothing (gloves) when working with refrigerants. If refrigerant splashes into your eyes, blindness can occur. If refrigerant splashes into your eyes or onto your skin, do not rub that body part but instead flush it with cool, clean water to restore the temperature. Place sterile gauze over the eye to keep it clean and get professional medical attention immediately.
- Always be in a well-ventilated shop area when working with refrigerants and avoid small, enclosed areas. Refrigerants do not contain oxygen and are heavier than air. If they are released into a confined area, they fill the lower space, forcing air and its oxygen upward. Any humans or animals that breathe refrigerants can

FIGURE 6–9 A secondary loop A/C system keeps the potentially dangerous or flammable refrigerant out of the passenger compartment by using a chiller/heat exchanger to cool an antifreeze and water mixture. This fluid then transfers heat from the cooling core in the air distribution section to the chiller.

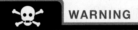

WARNING

The wise technician should use caution when working around chemicals and avoid breathing fumes and vapors, as well as avoid skin contact.

be asphyxiated, and lack of oxygen can cause loss of consciousness or death. In case of accidental release of refrigerant into the atmosphere move immediately to an area with adequate ventilation.

- If liquid refrigerant is splashed onto the skin or into the eyes of a human or animal, it immediately boils and absorbs heat from the body part it is in direct contact with. The temperature of the area is reduced to the low boiling point of the refrigerant, which is cold enough to freeze that body part.
- If a CFC such as R-12 or R-22 comes into contact with a flame or heated metal, a poisonous gas similar to phosgene is formed. This can occur while using a flame-type leak detector, if refrigerant is drawn into a running engine, or even if it is drawn through burning tobacco. An indication that a poisonous gas is forming is a bitter taste.
- Several flammable refrigerants have been marketed, and even though they have been banned and are illegal, they still show up. A mixture of more than 2% hydrocarbon (butane, isobutane, or propane) is considered flammable and about 4 oz. in a vehicle interior can become an explosive mixture. R-134a can become combustible at higher pressures if mixed with air. Air should not be used

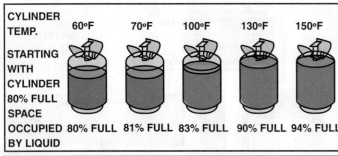

CYLINDER TEMP.	60°F	70°F	100°F	130°F	150°F
STARTING WITH CYLINDER 80% FULL SPACE OCCUPIED BY LIQUID	80% FULL	81% FULL	83% FULL	90% FULL	94% FULL

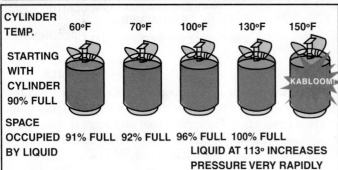

CYLINDER TEMP.	60°F	70°F	100°F	130°F	150°F
STARTING WITH CYLINDER 90% FULL SPACE OCCUPIED BY LIQUID	91% FULL	92% FULL	96% FULL	100% FULL LIQUID AT 113° INCREASES PRESSURE VERY RAPIDLY	KABLOOM

FIGURE 6–10 When recovering refrigerant, the container should be filled to a maximum of about 80%.

to flush an R-134a system because of the remote chance of a fire or explosion.

- When refrigerant containers are filled, room is left for expansion and the container is marked with its critical temperature, the maximum that it should be subjected to. Refrigerant containers are designed to contain the refrigerant under pressures encountered in normal working and storage conditions. Container pressure is about the same as the vapor pressure for that refrigerant up to a certain temperature point, which is where the liquid has expanded to fill the entire container. Beyond this point, any further expansion of the liquid generates very high hydraulic pressures that will rupture the container. The chance of container rupture is generally low unless the container is overfilled or overheated. ● SEE FIGURE 6–10.

REFRIGERANT OILS

PURPOSE AND FUNCTION Refrigerant oil serves several purposes, the most important being to *lubricate* the moving parts of the compressor to reduce friction and prevent wear. Refrigerant oil also helps *seal* the compressor shaft seal, the insides of the hoses, and various connections between the parts to reduce refrigerant leakage. In addition, it lubricates

? FREQUENTLY ASKED QUESTION

What Is an HC Refrigerant?

A hydrocarbon (HC) refrigerant is butane/propane blend that is very flammable. It can be used and will function in present-day A/C systems, but it is too dangerous to use. At the present time, the EPA and 19 states have banned flammable refrigerants. A leak or rupture in the evaporator could easily result in a vehicle explosion. Some hydrocarbon refrigerants are sold to do-it-yourselfers (DIY) and while it can work in either an R-12 or an R-134a system, it would contaminate the system and make future repairs of the system much more difficult. ● SEE FIGURE 6–11.

FIGURE 6–11 A container of refrigerant, which is a replacement for R-12 or R-134a and contains R-134a but also butane, a flammable gas.

the TXV and coats the metal parts inside the system to reduce corrosion.

The oil used in a system must be completely compatible with all the materials in the system.

TYPES OF REFRIGERANT OILS There are three types of refrigerant oils:

1. **Mineral oil** is used in R-12 systems.
2. **PAG (polyalkylene glycol)** oils are used in most R-134a systems. ● SEE FIGURE 6–12.

FIGURE 6–12 PAG oil is the type of refrigerant oil specified for use in most R-134a systems and the "150" is the viscosity.

3. **POE (polyol ester)** (ester) oils are used in a few R-134a systems, and either ester or PAG oils are used in R-12 systems retrofitted to R-134a.

PAG and POE are synthetic, human-made oils. Neither PAG nor POE is soluble in R-134a, but they are easily moved by the refrigerant flow so they travel through the entire A/C system.

Most compressor remanufacturers consider PAG oil a better lubricant than ester oil. There are over 30 varieties of refrigerant oils. whose use depends on the requirements of a particular compressor or system. Piston, scroll, and vane compressors often require a different oil viscosity because of the different operating characteristics and use internal pressures to circulate the oil.

Compressors normally contain a certain amount of oil (often just 2 oz to 8 oz). The oil level can only be checked by removing the compressor and draining all of the oil, then measuring how much oil came out. This is normally done when a compressor is replaced or when major service is performed on the system.

VISCOSITY OF REFRIGERANT OILS Viscosity is a measurement of how thick the oil is and how easily it flows. The oil must be thick enough so that moving parts float on an oil film. Oil must also be fluid enough to flow into the tiny spaces between parts. Compressor manufacturers normally specify the oil type and their viscosity for each type of compressor. The viscosity is determined by the International Standards Organization (ISO) viscosities and is measured at 40°C. Refrigerant oils are commonly available in several viscosities, including:

FIGURE 6–13 This under hood decal gives a Mercedes-Benz part number (A 001 989 08 03) instead of the type and viscosity of refrigerant oil. Service information was needed to determine that it was PAG 46.

- **46**—Called low viscosity—typically used in Ford vehicles
- **100**—Called medium to high viscosity—typically used in Chrysler vehicles
- **150**—Called ultra-high viscosity—typically used in General Motors vehicles

CAUTION: Always check the under hood decal or service information for the exact oil and viscosity to use. ● SEE FIGURE 6–13.

HYGROSCOPIC It is important to keep oil containers closed so that the oil does not absorb water from the atmosphere. A mineral oil can absorb about 0.005% water by weight. PAG or ester oil is very **hygroscopic**, which means that it can absorb moisture directly from the air up to about 2% to 6%. Some synthetic oils undergo hydrolysis if exposed to too much water and revert back to their original components: acid and alcohol.

OIL FLOW IN THE SYSTEM When a system operates, oil is either absorbed or pushed by the refrigerant and moves through the system. It does not stay in any particular component, but a certain amount of oil can be expected in each component. Oil can also move while a system is shut off because of temperature changes of its various parts.

1. Refrigerants escaping into the atmosphere can have detrimental effects on the ozone layer and also increase climate change and global warming.
2. The Clean Air Act places requirements for technicians to follow when servicing mobile A/C systems.
3. The SNAP rule limits which refrigerants can be used in a system.
4. Safety precautions should be followed when handling refrigerants.
5. Refrigerant oils are available in different viscosities and the specified oil must be used when servicing an air-conditioning system.

REVIEW QUESTIONS

1. What do the colors of the containers mean?
2. How can a refrigerant cause the breakup or depletion of the ozone layer?
3. What does the Clean Air Act mandate when it comes to servicing air-conditioning systems?
4. What is a SNAP refrigerant?
5. What precautions are necessary when working with refrigerants?
6. What does hygroscopic mean when referring to refrigerant oils?

CHAPTER QUIZ

1. R-134a is in what color container?
   a. Red
   b. Light blue
   c. White
   d. Green

2. Where is the ozone layer?
   a. Near ground level
   b. In the stratosphere
   c. In the clouds
   d. Between the ground and the clouds

3. The lower the GWP number, the _____.
   a. Lower the global warming potential
   b. Higher the global warming potential
   c. Closer it is to the ground
   d. The more poisonous

4. What section of the Clean Air Act concerns work on air-conditioning systems in vehicles?
   a. 847
   b. 609
   c. 777
   d. 103a

5. Which refrigerant has the lowest Global warming potential (GWP)?
   a. R-744
   b. R-134a
   c. R-1234yf
   d. R-12

6. What is true about a SNAP refrigerant?
   a. Requires unique set of fittings, and all ports not converted must be permanently disabled.
   b. Each refrigerant must have a label with a unique color that specifies pertinent information.
   c. All original refrigerants must be removed before charging with the new refrigerant.
   d. All of the above

7. The letter "a" in R-134a means _____?
   a. Automatic
   b. Automotive
   c. Asymmetrical
   d. Atmosphere

8. Precautions when working with refrigerants include_____.
   a. Wear safety goggles or a clear face shield and protective clothing (gloves) when working with refrigerants
   b. Always be in a well-ventilated shop area when working with refrigerants and avoid small, enclosed areas
   c. When refrigerant containers are filled, reserve room is left for expansion and the container is marked with its critical temperature
   d. All of the above

9. What type of refrigerant oil is used in R-134a systems?
   a. POE
   b. PAG
   c. Mineral
   d. Either a or b depending on the vehicle

10. Why is it important to keep refrigerant oil containers closed?
    a. To keep dirt out
    b. To keep it from evaporating
    c. To keep it from absorbing moisture from the air
    d. It can leak out by traveling upward through an open container

chapter 7

A/C SYSTEM COMPONENTS, OPERATION, AND SERVICE

LEARNING OBJECTIVES

After studying this chapter, the reader will be able to:

1. Prepare for the ASE Heating and Air Conditioning (A7) certification test content area "B" (Refrigeration Component Diagnosis and Repair).

2. Discuss the purpose and function of compressors and condensers.

3. Describe the operation of thermal expansion valves.

4. Explain the construction and operation of orifice tubes.

5. Explain the purpose and function of evaporators and accumulators.

6. Discuss the use of lines and hoses in refrigeration.

7. Describe electrical switches and evaporator temperature controls used in A/C systems. Explain component replacement procedures.

KEY TERMS

Barrier hoses 114
Captive O-ring 116
Discharge line 114
H-block 107
Liquid line 114

Sight glass 114
Suction line 114
Thermistor 119
Transducer 119

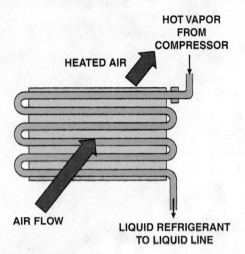

FIGURE 7–1 A condenser is a heat exchanger that transfers heat from the refrigerant to the air flowing through it.

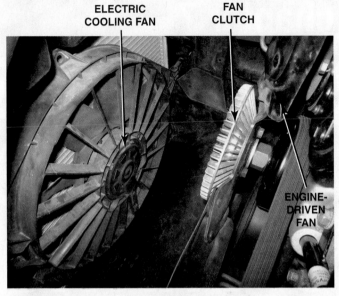

FIGURE 7–2 Two fans, one engine driven and one electric, are used on this rear-wheel-drive Dodge truck.

BACKGROUND

EARLY AIR CONDITIONING Automotive air-conditioning components have been evolving steadily since the introduction of air conditioning (A/C) in vehicles in 1940. Air conditioning in the early days was a very expensive option available only in luxury cars. Today, A/C is standard in many different models and uses many different types of systems.

COMPRESSORS

PURPOSE AND FUNCTION The compressor is the pump in the system that circulates the refrigerant. The pressure must be increased until the refrigerant temperature is above ambient air temperature so the condenser can get rid of all the heat absorbed in the evaporator. See Chapter 5 for details on compressors.

CONDENSERS

PURPOSE AND FUNCTION The condenser is a heat exchanger that is used to get rid of the heat removed from the passenger compartment. The condenser cools the hot refrigerant vapors, which while passing through the condensing tubes condense into high pressure liquid. The condenser of most vehicles is mounted in front of the radiator into which warm air is forced through when the vehicle is moving forward. ● SEE FIGURE 7–1.

On most vehicles, the condenser is part of a *cooling module* that can combine the following:

- Condenser
- Radiator
- Automatic transmission fluid cooler
- Power steering pump oil coolers
- An intercooler for engine intake air on turbocharged engines

Air flow through the condenser is increased by the use of a cooling fan.

- Many rear-wheel-drive (RWD) vehicles use a fan driven by a fan clutch mounted on the water pump. Some RWD vehicles use both an engine-driven fan with fan clutch and an electric fan. ● SEE FIGURE 7–2.
- Front-wheel-drive (FWD) vehicles normally use an electric motor to drive the fan(s).

This motor is controlled by relays that are controlled by the powertrain control module (PCM) using temperature information from the engine coolant temperature (ECT) sensor.

CONDENSER CONSTRUCTION Automotive condensers are heat exchangers that are made in several designs, including the following:

- Older *tube-and-fin* condensers are merely a tube bent back and forth into a *serpentine shape* with fins attached. After the tubes are pressed through the fins, return bends or manifolds are used to connect the tubes to give the desired flow pattern.

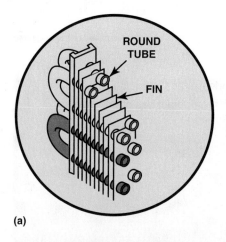

(a)

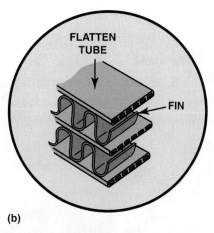

(b)

FIGURE 7–3 (a) A tube-and-fin condenser is made up of a series of fins with the round tubes passing through them. (b) An extruded tube condenser uses flat tubes with the fins attached between them. Flat tube condensers can use either parallel or serpentine flow.

FIGURE 7–4 Notice the size of the passages in a condenser cross section compared to the point of a pencil. The passages are the small holes running vertically and the pencil is pointing to the aluminum fins that are used to transfer the heat from the passages to the air.

- Newer condensers use a *flattened tube* with fins between the tubes. The tubing is formed in either *serpentine* or *parallel-flow* arrangement. ● **SEE FIGURE 7–3.**

- Many condensers use a flattened, extruded aluminum tube that is divided into small refrigerant passages, 13–16 passages in a tube that is 0.875 inch (24 mm) wide. ● **SEE FIGURE 7–4.**

- The numerous fins provide the large amount of contact area needed with the airstream. Newer flat-tube, parallel-flow condensers are more efficient and transfer heat much better and therefore allows for a smaller and lighter component.

- Condensers can be constructed using either a parallel flow or serpentine flow design. ● **SEE FIGURE 7–5.**

As the gas condenses to a liquid, the volume is reduced because a gas has about 1,000 times the volume of the same liquid. As the latent heat of condensation is transferred to the airstream, the refrigerant vapor transforms into a liquid state. ● **SEE FIGURE 7–6.**

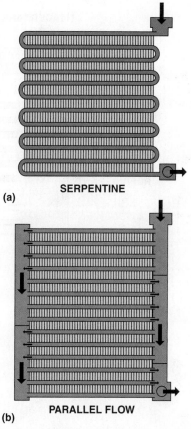

(a)

SERPENTINE

(b)

PARALLEL FLOW

FIGURE 7–5 (a) The refrigerant follows a winding path through a serpentine condenser. (b) The refrigerant follows a back-and-forth path through a parallel-flow condenser.

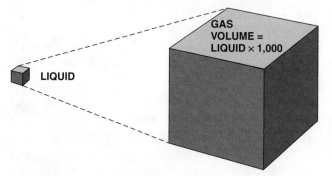

GAS VOLUME = LIQUID × 1,000

LIQUID

FIGURE 7–6 The volume of gas that enters a condenser is about 1,000 times the volume of liquid leaving it.

Why Is Sub-cooling Necessary in Some Condensers?

Condenser sub-cooling makes sure that there is a liquid seal at the bottom of the condenser so the liquid line or receiver will not have any vapors. Some vehicles use a second condenser to make sure that the refrigerant has condensed into liquid before it exits. These secondary condensers can be called as:

- *Dual condenser*
- *Secondary condenser*
- *Sub-condenser*
- *Modulator.* ● SEE FIGURE 7–7.

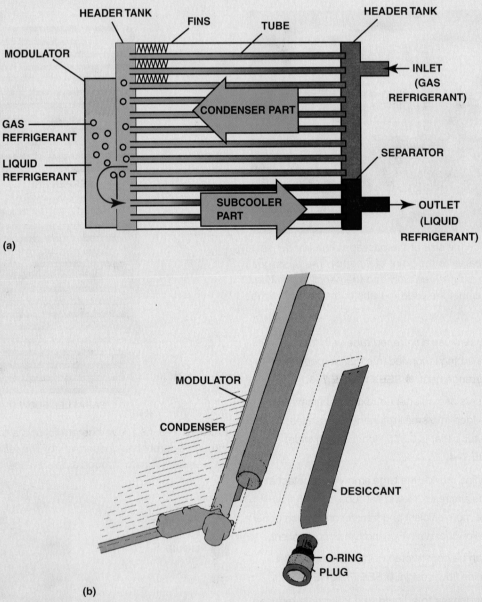

FIGURE 7–7 (a) A dual condenser is a condenser where the refrigerant flows from the condenser portion through the modulator portion and then through the sub-cooling part. (b) The modulator is built as part of the condenser and often includes a removable plug that allows desiccant replacement.

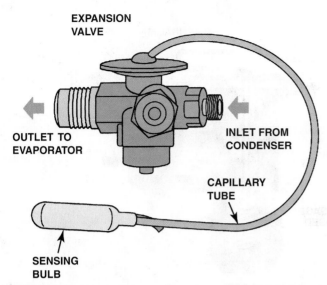

EXPANSION
VALVE

OUTLET TO
EVAPORATOR

INLET FROM
CONDENSER

CAPILLARY
TUBE

SENSING
BULB

FIGURE 7–8 A typical expansion valve uses an inlet and outlet attachment for the evaporator, and a temperature-sensing bulb that is attached to the evaporator outlet tube.

THERMAL EXPANSION VALVES

PURPOSE AND FUNCTION A thermal expansion valve (TXV) senses both temperature and pressure and controls the flow of refrigerant into the evaporator. ● **SEE FIGURE 7–8.**

ADVANTAGES The advantages of a TXV system over an orifice tube system include:

1. The TXV can maintain a low superheat to ensure that the majority of the evaporator surface is being used, resulting in higher efficiency.

2. Requires a smaller refrigerant charge.

DISADVANTAGES The disadvantages of a TXV system over an orifice tube system include:

1. The system costs more to produce

2. There are more moving parts

CONSTRUCTION AND OPERATION In most TXV systems, the evaporator outlet is connected to the compressor inlet by the suction line with an internal diameter (ID) of about 5/8 inch or 3/4 inch (16 mm or 19 mm). The key to the operation of the expansion valve is the variable orifice. In these systems, the outlet from the high-pressure side to the low-pressure side is a variable-diameter hole. A pintle valve is a ball-and-seat

valve used to increase or decrease the size of the opening. The expansion valve uses the pintle valve to control how rapidly refrigerant enters the evaporator. The expansion valve controls the refrigerant flow in response to the temperature of the evaporator outlet, measured by the remotely mounted sensing bulb and capillary tube.

- At room temperature, a TXV is open because the gas pressure in the capillary tube exerts a rather high pressure, greater than the spring pressure.

- As the system cools, the temperature of the sensing bulb and capillary tube drops, and the pressure on the diaphragm drops with it.

- When the pressure at the diaphragm drops below the spring pressure, the valve closes.

- If an excess amount of refrigerant enters the evaporator, high refrigerant pressure can act through the balance passage to close the TXV. ● **SEE FIGURE 7–9.**

INTERNALLY AND EXTERNALLY BALANCED TXVS
There is also a passage that allows evaporator pressure to act on the both sides of the diaphragm in opposition to thermal bulb pressure.

- In an *internally balanced* TXV, this passage is open to evaporator inlet pressure.

- In an *externally balanced* TXV, this passage connects to a length of small tubing that connects to the evaporator tailpipe. Externally balanced valves are used on some larger evaporators to give better response. ● **SEE FIGURE 7–10.**

TYPES OF TXVS Thermal expansion valves come in many types. Most of the early valves threaded onto the evaporator inlet, and the liquid line threaded onto the valve. The thermal bulb, or end of the capillary tube, was clamped onto the evaporator tailpipe or inserted into a well in it. The thermal bulb has to be clamped tightly and should be well insulated so that it can transmit an accurate temperature signal. If used, the external equalizer line is threaded onto a fitting on the tailpipe. Most TXVs have a small, very fine screen at their inlet. This screen traps debris that can plug the valve, and it can be removed for cleaning or installing a replacement.

H-BLOCKS The thermal expansion block valve is another type of TXV. It is called an **H-block o**r an *H-valve.* The H-block design uses four passages and controls the refrigerant flow using opposing pressures. These valves are connected with both the liquid and suction lines and the evaporator inlet and

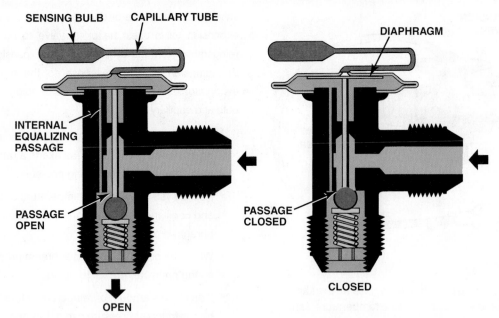

SENSING BULB   CAPILLARY TUBE

DIAPHRAGM

INTERNAL
EQUALIZING
PASSAGE

PASSAGE
OPEN

PASSAGE
CLOSED

OPEN

CLOSED

FIGURE 7–9 Pressure from the capillary tube pushes on the spring-loaded diaphragm to open the expansion valve. As the pressure in the capillary tube contracts, the reduced pressure on the diaphragm allows the valve to close.

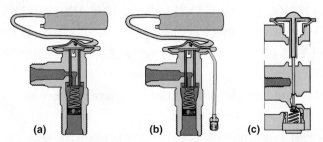

(a)   (b)   (c)

FIGURE 7–10 (a) An internal equalized TXV has two large connectors for the liquid line and evaporator. (b) An external equalized TXV has an additional smaller line to connect to the evaporator outlet. (c) Block-type TXV has four openings that connect to the evaporator, liquid line, and suction line.

outlet. Some block valves use threaded fittings, and some are bolted between manifolds and are sealed using O-rings. ● SEE **FIGURE 7–12**.

ORIFICE TUBE SYSTEMS

TERMINOLOGY   An orifice tube (OT), also called an *expansion tube,* is a fixed-diameter orifice that the refrigerant must flow through. The diameter varies between systems and is about 1/16 inch (0.065 inch or 1.6 mm). ● SEE FIGURE 7–13.

ADVANTAGES   The advantages of an orifice tube system over a TXV system include:

1. An orifice tube system is much simpler and cheaper to produce than a TXV system.

2. In an orifice tube system, the only moving part in the system is the A/C compressor.

DISADVANTAGES   The disadvantages of an orifice tube system over a TXV system include:

1. An orifice tube system cannot respond to evaporator temperature. At times of low cooling loads, the orifice tube allows too much refrigerant to flow and floods the evaporator with liquid.

2. Another disadvantage is that an orifice tube system requires more refrigerant than a TXV system.

CONSTRUCTION AND OPERATION   Most orifice tubes are a thin brass tube that is a couple of inches long and has a plastic filter screen around it. This tube is sized to flow the proper amount of refrigerant into the evaporator for maximum cooling loads. Some orifice tubes use a filter made up of many small plastic beads in place of the screen. The orifice tube floods the evaporator during light cooling loads, so a low-side accumulator is always used with an orifice. The flow through an orifice tube is also affected by pressure, and excessive high-side pressure can cause evaporator pressure and temperature to become too high.

ORIFICE TUBE SIZES   Manufacturers color-code orifice tubes to identify the car make and model for which a tube is made. There are at least eight different sizes of orifice tubes that have similar appearance, but the size ranges from 0.047 inch to 0.072 inch (1.19 mm to 1.8 mm). An R-134a system uses a larger orifice tube than a similar R-12 system.

How Is the Compressor Kept Lubricated?

The expansion valve opens and closes to control the refrigerant flow in response to the temperature of the evaporator outlet. To make sure that the compressor receives the oil it needs for lubrication when the valve is closed, a slot is cut in the ball seat inside the expansion valve to permit a small amount of refrigerant and oil to pass through to the evaporator and then to the compressor. ● SEE FIGURE 7–11.

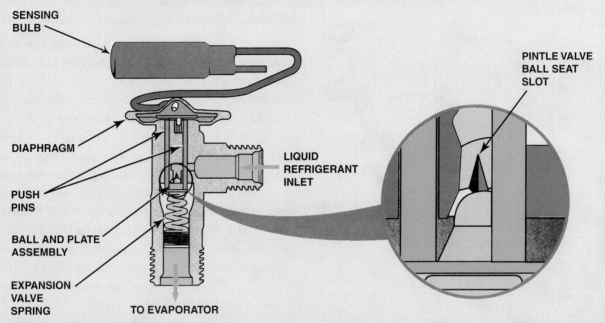

FIGURE 7–11 A slot cut in the ball seat inside the expansion valve permits refrigerant and oil to pass through at all times, even when the valve is closed.

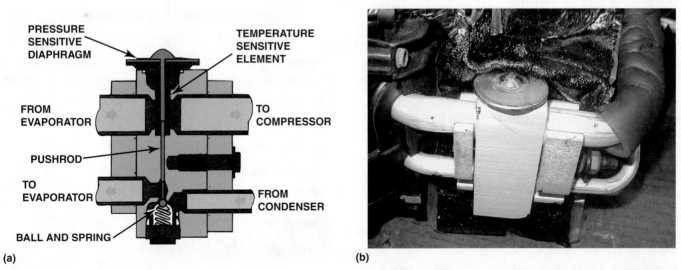

FIGURE 7–12 (a) An H-valve (H-block) combines the temperature sensing and pressure-regulating functions into a single assembly. (b) An H-valve as used on a Chrysler minivan.

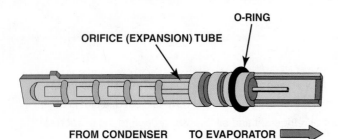

FIGURE 7–13 A typical orifice tube. The refrigerant flow is from the left toward the right.

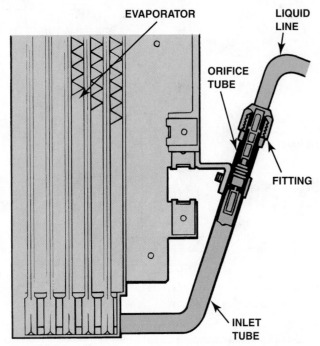

FIGURE 7–14 The orifice tube is usually located at the inlet tube to the evaporator.

ORIFICE TUBE LOCATION
Some orifice tubes are placed into the evaporator inlet tube. An O-ring was fitted around it to stop refrigerant from flowing past the outside of the orifice tube. Several small indentations, or dimples, were put in the tubing wall to keep the orifice tube from moving too far into the evaporator. ● SEE FIGURE 7–14.

Many newer vehicles place the orifice tube in the liquid line farther away from the evaporator, close to the condenser outlet. This is done because of complaints of hissing noises that occur after the vehicle is shut off and high-side pressure bleeds down through the orifice tube.

VARIABLE ORIFICE VALVES (VOVS)
Most orifice tubes have a fixed-size orifice that is sized for the proper refrigerant flow to produce maximum A/C performance during 50-MPH to 60-MPH (80 km/h to 100 km/h) operation. At lower engine speeds, the orifice size is too large. The orifice size should produce the high-side pressure for proper condenser

 **TECH TIP**

How to Locate the Orifice Tube
In an operating system, the orifice tube position can be located by finding the point where the liquid line changes temperature from hot to cold. If the system is not operating, the dimples in the line show the orifice tube location.

action and the pressure drop into the low side to produce proper evaporator pressure and temperature. Vehicles that spend considerable time idling commonly have poor A/C performance and experience short compressor life.

One type uses a variable orifice valve (VOV) that senses temperature to change the size of the orifice. A bimetal coil spring senses the temperature of the liquid refrigerant, and when the temperature increases, the spring moves the variable port to a closed position. This increases the restriction at the VOV and reduces the flow to the evaporator. ● SEE FIGURE 7–15.

A VOV is similar to a fixed orifice tube but contains an internal valve. Installation of the VOV is simply a matter of removing the orifice tube and installing the VOV. Always follow the instructions for the variable orifice valve if installing it in place of a fixed orifice tube.

ELECTRONIC ORIFICE TUBE
Some General Motor's vehicles use an electronic orifice tube. It uses a solenoid to change orifice diameter.

- It has an orifice diameter of 0.062 inch (1.6 mm) when the solenoid is off (de-energized).
- This increases to 0.080 inch (2.0 mm) when the solenoid is on (energized).

The solenoid is controlled by an ECM, or electronic control module, that uses primarily three inputs, including:

1. Vehicle speed (VS) sensor
2. Engine RPM
3. High-side pressure

Energizing the solenoid increases the orifice size to reduce high-side pressure. ● SEE FIGURE 7–16.

EVAPORATORS

PURPOSE AND FUNCTION
An evaporator, sometimes called the *evaporator core*, is a heat exchanger. The purpose and function of the evaporator is to remove heat from the air

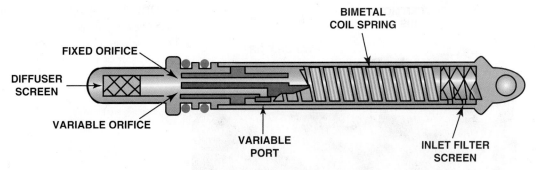

FIGURE 7–15 A VOV uses a bimetal coil spring to sense the temperature of the refrigerant. A higher temperature will cause the coil to expand and partially close the variable port to increase the restriction.

FIGURE 7–16 An electronic orifice tube has a solenoid so it can change orifice size.

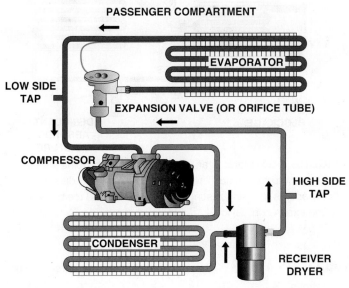

FIGURE 7–17 The evaporator is part of the low pressure side of the refrigeration cycle and is used to transfer the heat from inside the vehicle to the refrigerant flowing through the internal tubes.

being forced through it to cool the inside of the vehicle. ● **SEE FIGURE 7–17**.

CONSTRUCTION Most evaporators are a series of plates sandwiched together to form both the refrigerant and air passages. ● **SEE FIGURE 7–18**.

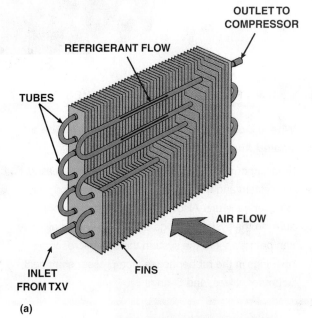

(a)

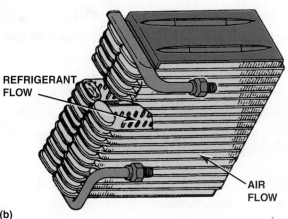

(b)

FIGURE 7–18 (a) An older design tube-and-fin evaporator. (b) A plate evaporator. Each type has a large contact area for heat to leave the air and enter the refrigerant.

Evaporators are normally made from aluminum because it has good thermal properties and is lightweight. Evaporators have at least two line connections:

1. The smaller inlet line (liquid line) connects to the TXV or orifice tube.

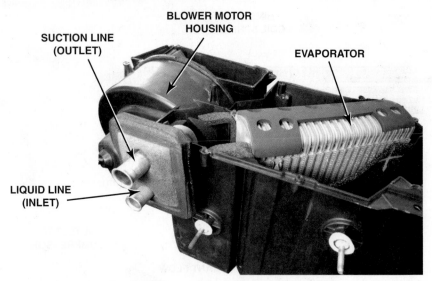

SUCTION LINE (OUTLET)

BLOWER MOTOR HOUSING

EVAPORATOR

LIQUID LINE (INLET)

FIGURE 7–19 An evaporator in the HVAC case showing the liquid line inlet tube from the TXV or orifice tube and suction outlet line to the compressor or accumulator.

? **FREQUENTLY ASKED QUESTION**

Where Does the Moisture Come from Inside a Sealed Air-conditioning System?

Small amounts of moisture may remain after sealing the system and the desiccant is there to absorb this left over moisture. Also, during operation, the pressures in the system change and moisture and air can be drawn into the system through microscopic openings in the rubber hoses, compressor shaft seal, Schrader valves, and O-rings.

2. The larger outlet line connects to the suction line and to the compressor or accumulator on orifice tube systems. ● **SEE FIGURE 7–19.**

RECEIVER–DRIERS AND ACCUMULATORS

PURPOSE AND FUNCTION The purpose of refrigerant storage is to compensate for volume changes due to temperature change or refrigerant loss. Desiccant is needed to remove moisture or water, which can cause rusting or corrosion.

DESICCANT The desiccant is a chemical drying agent called "molecular sieve" and its job is to remove all traces of water vapor from a system. Water can mix with refrigerant to form acids, which cause rust and corrosion of metal parts. Water can also freeze and form ice at the TXV or OT, which can block the flow of refrigerant into the evaporator. ● **SEE FIGURE 7–20.**

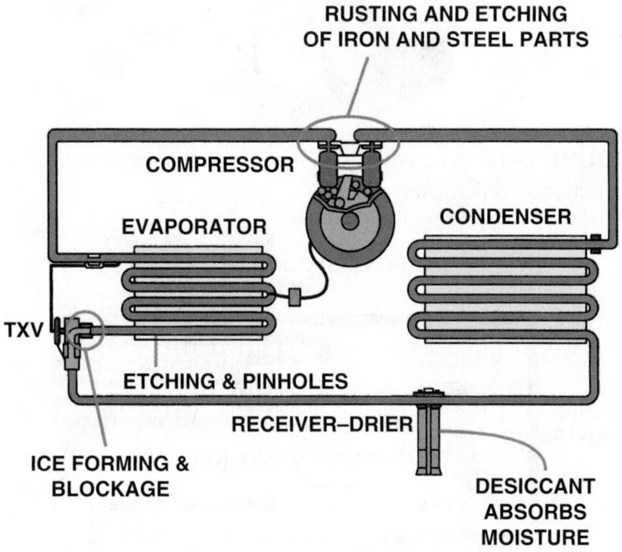

RUSTING AND ETCHING OF IRON AND STEEL PARTS

COMPRESSOR

EVAPORATOR

CONDENSER

TXV

ETCHING & PINHOLES

RECEIVER–DRIER

ICE FORMING & BLOCKAGE

DESICCANT ABSORBS MOISTURE

FIGURE 7–20 Water in an A/C system can combine with the refrigerant to form acid. These acids can etch and dissolve components, causing rusting of metal parts, and ice blockage at the expansion device.

ACCUMULATORS The accumulator serves three major functions.

1. Prevents liquid refrigerant from passing to the compressor
2. Holds the desiccant, which helps remove moisture from the system
3. Holds a reserve of refrigerant

An accumulator is a container that holds about 1 quart (1 L) or less in volume. The inlet line from the evaporator enters near the top of the accumulator and then drops downward to the bottom, and then exits the accumulator at the top. This routing of the outlet tube separates the refrigerant vapor at the top

? FREQUENTLY ASKED QUESTIONS

Are All Desiccants the Same?

No. Desiccant is usually contained in a cloth bag inside the accumulator or receiver–drier. A desiccant variety referred to as XH-5 has commonly been used with R-12 in automotive systems. XH-5 has the ability to absorb about 1% of its weight in water, but this chemical suffers damage when it absorbs fluorine from R-134a, and it begins to decompose when it comes into contact with R-134a and PAG oil. Other desiccant types (XH-7 and XH-9) are compatible with R-134a and PAG. The receiver–drier or accumulator used in an R-134a system should use XH-7 or XH-9 desiccant. All new accumulators and receiver–driers contain either XH-7 or XH-9 desiccant. An accumulator or receiver–drier should contain the desiccant type and amount to suit the A/C system that it is designed for and is therefore required to be replaced when retrofitting a system from R-12 to R-134a.

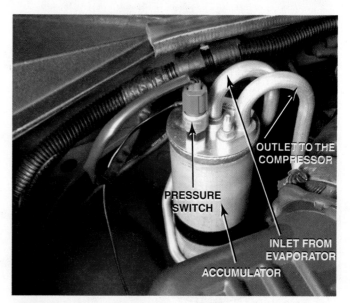

FIGURE 7–22 This accumulator has an accumulator tube that connects the evaporator outlet and a suction line that connects to the compressor inlet.

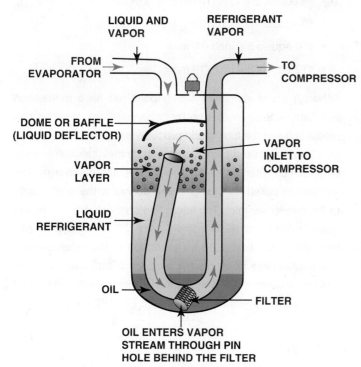

FIGURE 7–21 Accumulators are designed so that vapors from the top move to the compressor. They contain desiccant to absorb water from the refrigerant and many include a fitting for low-side pressure and the clutch cycling switch.

from the liquid at the bottom so that only vapor will leave the accumulator. A small opening for oil bleed is at the lowermost point and this opening usually has a filter so debris will not

block it. A small amount of liquid refrigerant and oil also leaves through the bleed hole. The oil ensures that the compressor is lubricated. ● **SEE FIGURE 7–21.**

The accumulator of some R-134a systems has an insulating jacket to help reduce the heat absorption and lower the air temperature at the discharge ducts. The accumulator or receiver–drier is normally replaced if a system has been opened to the atmosphere for a period of time because the desiccant is probably saturated with moisture. It is also standard practice to replace the accumulator or receiver–drier whenever major service work is done on a system, especially if the compressor is replaced.

The accumulator inlet on many vehicles is connected directly to the evaporator, whereas on other vehicles it is mounted separately with a metal tube or rubber hose to connect it to the evaporator. The outlet of the accumulator is connected to the compressor inlet through the flexible suction line. ● **SEE FIGURE 7–22.**

RECEIVER–DRIER The receiver–drier is used with TXV systems and is normally found in the high-side liquid line, somewhere between the condenser and the TXV.

The receiver–drier inlet dumps incoming refrigerant into the container so that the refrigerant passes through a filter pad and the desiccant. The outlet, often called a *pickup tube*, begins near the bottom and usually exits at the top. A fine-mesh filter screen is used at the inner opening to stop debris from passing out of the receiver–drier and on to the TXV. The receiver–drier is usually about half full of liquid refrigerant. ● **SEE FIGURE 7–23.**

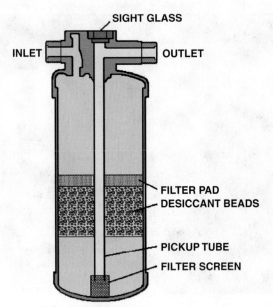

FIGURE 7-23 A cutaway view of a receiver-drier showing the filter pads and desiccant.

SIGHT GLASS   A receiver-drier can contain a sight glass, pressure release plug or valve, or switch. The **sight glass** allows observation of the refrigerant flow as it leaves the receiver-drier. The flow of R-12 should be invisible because R-12 is clear, and the oil is dissolved in the liquid refrigerant. Bubbles or foam in the sight glass can indicate abnormal operation. R-134a would appear cloudy in a sight glass, so sight glasses are not commonly used in R-134a systems. The pressure relief switch is used to sense high-side pressure. It can be used to prevent compressor operation if the pressure is either too low or too high.

LINES AND HOSES

PURPOSE AND FUNCTION   The various system components must be interconnected so that refrigerant can circulate through the system. The components are connected using hoses and tubing (also called pipes).

HOSE CONSTRUCTION   Both flexible rubber and rigid metal tubing are used to link the components. The connections to the compressor must be flexible to allow for engine and compressor movement. ●**SEE FIGURE 7-24.**

- Early R-12 hoses were made from rubber with one or two layers of braided reinforcing material. Over time refrigerants could permeate most of these flexible hose materials

and slowly escape from the system. This design hose worked with R-12, but R-134a (smaller molecule) would permeate (leak through) R-12 hoses.

- Refrigerant hoses designed for R-134a are made with one or two nonpermeable inner layers with internal reinforcement and an outer layer for protection. The nonpermeable nylon layer forms a leak-proof barrier commonly called **barrier hoses**. The materials for the various layers are developed to keep refrigerant loss to a minimum.

METAL LINES   Metal tubing (usually aluminum) is used in many systems to connect stationary components, such as a condenser, to the receiver-drier or OT.

- Metal tubing is sized by its outside diameter (OD).
- Pipe and hose are sized by the inside diameter (ID) and these sizes are often nominal (approximate) sizes.

A number sizing is often used for refrigerant hose and fittings, with the most popular sizes being #4, #6, #8, #10, and #12—

- #4 equals 1/4 inch (6 mm)
- #6 equals 3/8 inch (10 mm)
- #8 equals 1/2 inch (13 mm)
- #10 equals 5/8 inch (16 mm)
- #12 equals 3/4 inch (19 mm)

Although metal aluminum tubing does not have permeation problems, corrosion caused by battery spillage or water can create holes in the tubing and produce leakage.

The lines in a system are named for their function or what they contain. Starting at the compressor, the **discharge line**, sometimes called the *hot gas line,* connects the compressor to the condenser inlet. The **liquid line** connects the condenser outlet to the receiver-drier and TXV or OT. A TXV system can have two liquid lines, one on each side of the receiver-drier. The **suction line** connects the evaporator outlet to the accumulator or compressor and has the largest diameter because it transfers a low-pressure vapor. ●**SEE FIGURE 7-25.**

HOSE SIZES

- The suction line has an ID of 1/2 inch or 5/8 inch (12.7 mm to 15.9 mm) (a #10 or #12 hose). The liquid line has the smallest diameter, usually an ID of 5/16 inch (7.9 mm) (#6 hose).
- The discharge line has an ID of 13/32 inch or 1/2 inch (10.3 mm or 12.7 mm) (#8 hose). Metric sizes are also used. ●**SEE FIGURE 7-26.**

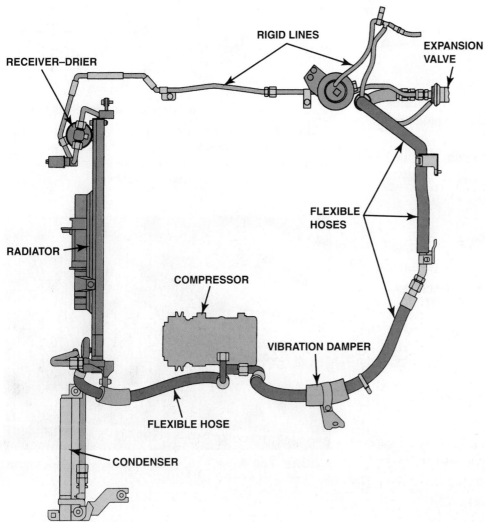

RECEIVER–DRIER

RIGID LINES

EXPANSION VALVE

FLEXIBLE HOSES

RADIATOR

COMPRESSOR

VIBRATION DAMPER

FLEXIBLE HOSE

CONDENSER

FIGURE 7–24 Rigid lines and flexible hoses are used throughout the air-conditioning system. The line to and from the compressor must be flexible because it is attached to the engine, which moves on its mounts during normal vehicle operation.

Parts shown are not in their normal position and some parts are missing, but it does show the locations of the rigid and flexible refrigerant lines.

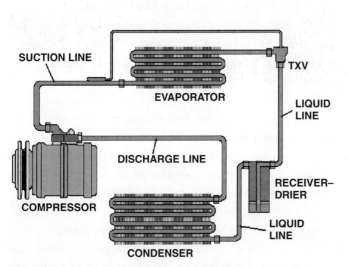

SUCTION LINE

EVAPORATOR

TXV

LIQUID LINE

DISCHARGE LINE

RECEIVER– DRIER

LIQUID LINE

COMPRESSOR

CONDENSER

FIGURE 7–25 The three major hoses/lines are the discharge, liquid, and suction lines. A system can have two liquid lines.

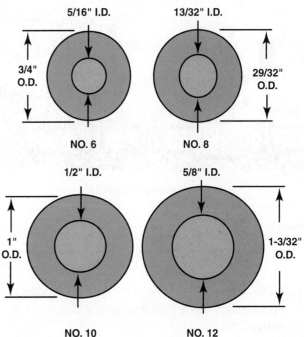

5/16" I.D.

13/32" I.D.

3/4" O.D.

29/32" O.D.

NO. 6

NO. 8

1/2" I.D.

5/8" I.D.

1" O.D.

1-3/32" O.D.

NO. 10

NO. 12

FIGURE 7–26 Most systems use three of these four refrigerant hose sizes. Metal tubing is sized by its outside diameter (OD) and hoses are sized by the inside diameter (ID).

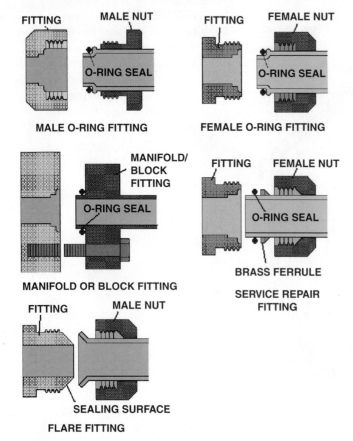

MALE O-RING FITTING

FEMALE O-RING FITTING

MANIFOLD OR BLOCK FITTING

SERVICE REPAIR FITTING

FLARE FITTING

FIGURE 7–27 Various fittings are used to seal the refrigerant line connections. The service fitting is used for metal line repairs or to insert an inline filter.

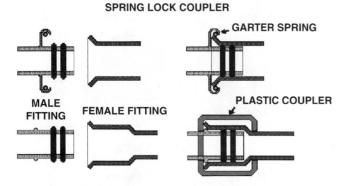

SPRING LOCK COUPLER

QUICK-CONNECT COUPLER

FIGURE 7–28 Spring-lock and quick-connect couplers are merely pushed together, and a garter spring or plastic cage holds them coupled.

CONNECTIONS The lines and hoses are connected to the major components using fittings of several different styles. ● SEE FIGURE 7–27.

These fittings allow the lines to be disconnected and are designed to keep refrigerant leakage to a minimum. Most new fittings use an O-ring seal that can be replaced during service.

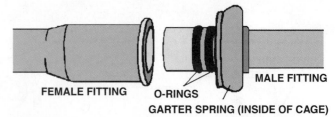

FIGURE 7–29 A spring-lock fitting is a type of quick disconnect fitting that is sealed by two O-rings and held together by a garter spring. A special tool is required to expand the garter spring to release the fitting.

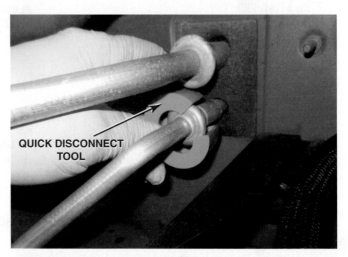

FIGURE 7–30 A quick disconnect tool being used to remove the connections at the evaporator.

A variety of quick-connect couplers are used to hold two lines together and seal the joint between them. Some of these are held together by one of at least two styles of plastic couplers. One style was held together using a garter spring and was called a *spring-lock fitting*. ● SEE FIGURE 7–28.

Spring-lock fittings are connected by pushing one line over the other until the garter spring moves into position. A special tool is inserted into the fitting to expand the garter spring and release the fitting. ● SEE FIGURE 7–29.

A spring-lock fitting is a type of quick-disconnect fitting. The female portion of this fitting has a flare-like ridge at the end and is gripped by a garter spring when connected. One or two O-rings form the seal between the two fitting parts. These O-rings must be resilient enough to compensate for slight movement between the two parts. ● SEE FIGURE 7–30.

O-RINGS O-ring fittings squeeze a rubber O-ring between the two parts being connected to make the seal. In most cases, the O-ring is slid over the end of the metal tube and is located by a raised metal ring or bead. Some manufacturers use a **captive O-ring**, also called *captured O-ring*, which locates the

FIGURE 7–31 Having an assortment of O-rings makes it easier for the service technician to be able to use the correct ones during a repair.

O-ring more positively in a shallow groove. Captive O-rings use a larger-diameter cross section than standard O-rings. Some designs use two O-rings for a better seal.

O-rings made from Buna or nitrile is commonly used in R-12 systems, but these materials are not compatible with R-134a. High-grade neoprene O-rings (HSN or HNBR), often tinted blue or green, are used in R-134a systems. There is no color standard for O-rings but most manufacturers use the following color designations:

- Black indicates nitrile or neoprene.
- Blue indicates neoprene or nitrile.
- Green indicates HNBR and are generally used in R-134a systems. ● **SEE FIGURE 7–31.**

ELECTRICAL SWITCHES AND EVAPORATOR TEMPERATURE CONTROLS

CONTROL SWITCHES Various electrical switches are used in A/C systems to prevent evaporator icing, protect the compressor, and control fan motor. Control switches can be located anywhere in the system, such as at the

- compressor discharge
- suction cavities

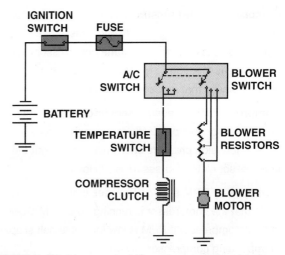

FIGURE 7–32 Many early A/C systems used a simple electrical circuit.

- receiver–drier
- accumulator

Some recent systems use a variable displacement compressor to prevent icing. A valve that senses evaporator pressure is used in the compressor, and compressor displacement is reduced in response to that pressure.

At one time, the A/C electrical circuit was rather simple.

- A typical circuit connects the evaporator blower motor and compressor clutch at one master switch.
- The power to the compressor clutch passes through a temperature switch that opens the circuit to cycle the clutch when the evaporator gets too cold.
- The power to the blower motor passes through a speed control switch so that the blower speed can be changed. ● **FIGURE 7–32.**

Today various switches, sensors, and relays are used. A sensor is usually an input to an electronic control module (ECM) or body control module (BCM). Many sensors provide a variable signal, so the ECM/BCM will know the actual temperature or pressure at a given point. A relay is essentially a magnetic switch that is controlled by another switch. A relay is used to control a greater amount of current than a switch can handle. Relays also allow computer control modules to control electrical circuits. Any one A/C system will have some of these, but not all of the following, depending on the type of system and manufacturer:

- **A/C clutch relay.** Controls current to compressor clutch and is used to turn the compressor on or off
- **Ambient sensor or switch.** Senses outside temperature and is designed to prevent compressor operation when ambient temperature is below a certain point, about 35°F to 40°F (2°C to 4°C)

- **Compressor high-pressure sensor or switch.** Mounted in compressor discharge cavity and senses high-side pressure and is used to cut out the compressor clutch if pressure is too high or too low, or provides a signal to another device that pressure is too high

- **Compressor low-pressure sensor or switch.** Mounted in compressor suction cavity, this switch or sensor detects low-side pressure and is used to cut out the compressor clutch if pressure is too low

- **Compressor RPM sensor.** Provides input to the ECM/BCM that the compressor is running. The ECM/BCM will cut out compressor if RPM is low (possible belt slippage or impending compressor lockup)

- **Compressor superheat sensor or switch.** Function is similar to compressor low-pressure switch

- **Compressor high-temperature switch.** Mounted on the compressor and shuts off the compressor if the temperature of the compressor gets too hot

- **Power Steering Compressor cutoff switch.** Mounted at power steering gear, this switch senses pressure in that system and is used to stop the compressor when the pressure in the power steering rises to a high level which increases the load on the engine. The A/C compressor clutch is then disengaged to help remove some of the load from the engine so it does not stall

- **Engine coolant temperature (ECT).** Mounted near the engine thermostat and senses engine temperature for ECM/BCM and is also used to turn on cooling fan(s)

- **Evaporator pressure sensor.** Provides input to the ECM/BCM as to the operating pressure in the evaporator

- **Evaporator temperature sensor.** Mounted at the evaporator, it senses temperature and is used to cycle compressor clutch to prevent icing

- **High-pressure cutout switch.** Mounted at receiver–drier or liquid line, it senses high-side pressure and is used to cut out the compressor clutch if high-side pressure is too high

- **High-temperature cutoff sensor or switch.** Mounted at the condenser outlet, this switch or sensor measures condenser temperature and is used to cut out the compressor clutch if the temperature is too high

- **Low-pressure cutout sensor or switch.** Mounted in receiver–drier or liquid line, it senses low pressure and is used to cut out the compressor clutch with low refrigerant charge.

- **Master switch.** Mounted at control head, this switch is can be operated by the driver to turn the system on or off

- **Pressure cycling switch.** Mounted at accumulator, it senses low pressure and cycles the compressor clutch to prevent evaporator icing

- **Thermostatic cycling switch.** Mounted at evaporator, it senses air temperature and cycles the compressor clutch to prevent evaporator icing

- **Trinary pressure switch.** Mounted at receiver–drier, this switch senses high-side pressure and cuts out compressor clutch if pressure is too high or too low. It can also be used to control radiator shutters or fan motor

- **Blower relay.** Can be used to turn blower on or off and provide high blower speed

- **Clutch cutoff relay.** Can be used to interrupt compressor clutch

- **Condenser fan relay.** Used to turn condenser fan motor on or off

- **Radiator fan relay.** Used to turn radiator fan motor on or off

THERMOSTATIC CYCLING SWITCH Evaporator temperature in a cycling clutch system is sometimes controlled by either a thermostatic (thermal) switch or pressure switch. A bellows switch uses a capillary tube inserted into the evaporator fins. As with a TXV, the gas pressure in the capillary tube is exerted on the bellows. In a thermal switch, the bellows acts on a set of contact points.

- A warm evaporator produces a higher bellows pressure, which keeps the points closed.

- A cold evaporator reduces the pressure, which causes the points to open.

A bimetal switch has a contact arm that is laminated from two metals with very different thermal expansion rates.

- When the switch is warm, the metals expand to close the contact points.

- When the switch cools, the metals in the arm contract to open the contacts.

Both of these, switch styles are calibrated so they are closed at temperatures above 32°F (0°C) and open at temperatures below 32°F (0°C). When the switch opens, the compressor clutch is turned off. This causes the evaporator to begin warming, and after a few degrees of temperature increase, the

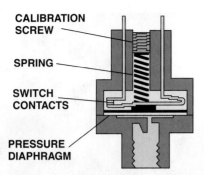

CALIBRATION SCREW

SPRING

SWITCH CONTACTS

PRESSURE DIAPHRAGM

FIGURE 7–33 A pressure switch is either on or off. The contacts are closed by gas pressure on the diaphragm; they are opened by the spring.

switch closes to cycle the compressor in again. Recent systems use thermistors to sense temperature instead of thermostatic cycling switches.

PRESSURE CYCLING SWITCHES A pressure cycling switch is mounted to sense low-side pressure, usually on the accumulator. Ice begins to form when evaporator pressure drops below 30 PSI in an R-12 system or slightly less in an R-134a system.

- When evaporator pressure is above 30 PSI, the switch contacts close so the compressor will operate.
- When the pressure drops below 30 PSI, the switch opens and cycles the compressor out.
- After the compressor stops, evaporator pressure will increase and after an increase of about 10 PSI to 20 PSI, the pressure switch contacts close to cycle the compressor in again. This switch also prevents the compressor from operating if the pressure is too low from a refrigerant loss. ●**SEE FIGURE 7–33**.

LOW-PRESSURE SWITCH Many systems include a low-pressure switch, located in a low-pressure line or the accumulator to prevent compressor operation if there is loss of refrigerant. Damage will occur if the compressor is operated without the refrigerant or the oil through which the refrigerant circulates.

THERMISTORS AND TRANSDUCERS Recent systems use solid-state sensors that do not use switch contacts. The most common sensors are thermistors and transducers and these provide a variable output instead of just being on or off like a switch.

- A **thermistor** is commonly used to sense temperatures. It is basically an electrical resistor that changes resistance in inverse relationship to its temperature. Most

? **FREQUENTLY ASKED QUESTION**

What Do STV, POA and EPR Valves Do?

Some older systems used a valve to control evaporator pressure to prevent icing. These valves include the following:

- Suction throttling valves (STVs),
- Pilot-operated absolutes (POAs)
- Evaporator pressure regulators (EPRs)

Some import vehicles used an EPR valve through the late 1990s. These valves were mounted at the evaporator outlet, the compressor inlet, or somewhere between. Most of them sense evaporator pressure and when the pressure starts to drop below a certain point, the valve closes down to restrict refrigerant flow to the compressor. A system that uses a suction throttling valve maintains an almost constant evaporator temperature of 32°F (0°C) without cycling the clutch. ●**SEE FIGURE 7–34**.

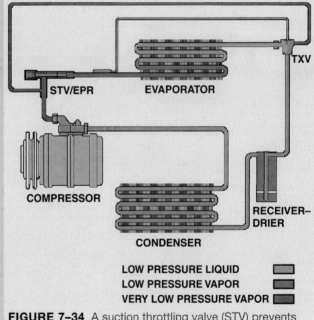

TXV

STV/EPR   EVAPORATOR

COMPRESSOR

RECEIVER–DRIER

CONDENSER

LOW PRESSURE LIQUID
LOW PRESSURE VAPOR
VERY LOW PRESSURE VAPOR

FIGURE 7–34 A suction throttling valve (STV) prevents evaporator pressure from dropping below 30 PSI, and this keeps ice from forming on the evaporator.

automotive thermistors are of the negative temperature coefficient (NTC) type. The resistance will increase as the temperature drops and vice versa.

- A **transducer** senses pressure and changes a variable pressure signal into a variable electrical signal.

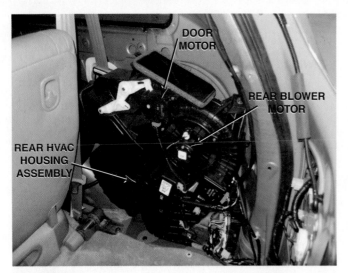

FIGURE 7–35 The rear HVAC module assembly used on a Honda Odyssey minivan.

A transducer can let the ECM/BCM know the actual pressure in the low- and/or high side of the system. Sensors provide an electrical signal to a control module that, in turn, controls compressor clutch or condenser fan operation.

REAR A/C SYSTEMS

PARTS AND OPERATION Some larger vehicles (vans and small buses) have dual heat and A/C assemblies, with the rear unit mounted in a rear side panel or in the roof. The rear A/C unit consists of an evaporator and a TXV that operates in parallel flow with the front unit. ● **SEE FIGURE 7–35.**

Tee fittings are placed in the liquid and suction lines so that refrigerant can flow through both units, with the flow through the rear unit dependent on the cooling load. Many dual systems use an orifice tube to control the refrigerant flow into the front evaporator and a TXV with the rear evaporator. The rear evaporator is normally mounted in an assembly that includes a blower, heater core, and doors to control the air temperature and where the air returns to the passenger compartment.

CAUTION: The rear TXV shuts off the flow through the rear evaporator when the rear system is shut off, but a potential problem is created. A TXV does not ensure a complete shutoff, and refrigerant can leak through the valve. Because the blower is shut off, the evaporator will chill, and liquid refrigerant can puddle in this portion of the suction line. The puddle can flow down the suction

FIGURE 7–36 The line to the condenser from the compressor includes a flange mount with an O-ring. This line is being replaced with a new original equipment line as a result an accident, which caused the line to be kinked.

line and slug the compressor, causing a knock and possible damage. To help prevent this from occurring, ask the customer to operate the rear air-conditioning unit regularly. Some systems use a solenoid valve to stop any flow through the rear system.

COMPONENT REPLACEMENT PROCEDURES

FITTING REPAIR If the fitting is tight and still leaks, it must be taken apart and inspected for damage and a new O-ring must be installed. Torque specifications for the various line fittings are provided by the vehicle manufacturer. Always use two wrenches when servicing fittings.

LINE REPLACEMENT A faulty hose or metal line is often repaired by replacing it with a new or repaired line. This normally involves disconnecting each end of the line at a fitting. Some hoses, like the suction and discharge, are combined with another line, making a double connection at the compressor, condenser, or evaporator. A manifold-type connector sealed with a pair of O-rings is commonly used at these connections. Some aftermarket suppliers can custom make hoses with fittings. ● **SEE FIGURE 7–36.**

Can a Refrigerant Hose Be Repaired?

Sometimes. A hose can sometimes be repaired by replacing one of the ends or by cutting out a damaged section and splicing it back together. Most OEM hoses are connected to the line fitting with a captive, *beadlock ferrule* so the hose is gripped by both the line connector and the ferrule.

• New service fittings with a captive metal ferrule and a new clamping method have been developed to allow field repair and makeup of barrier hoses. These fittings are commonly called *bubble-style crimp*. ● **SEE FIGURE 7–37.**

• The most common fitting styles are female and male O-rings (determined by the nut threads), female and male flares, male insert fittings, and spring-lock styles. These fittings are usually available for the four common hose sizes and in straight, 45° bend, and 90° bend shapes.

If repairing a line or hose, always follow the instructions that came with the repair kit to be sure of a proper and leak-free repair.

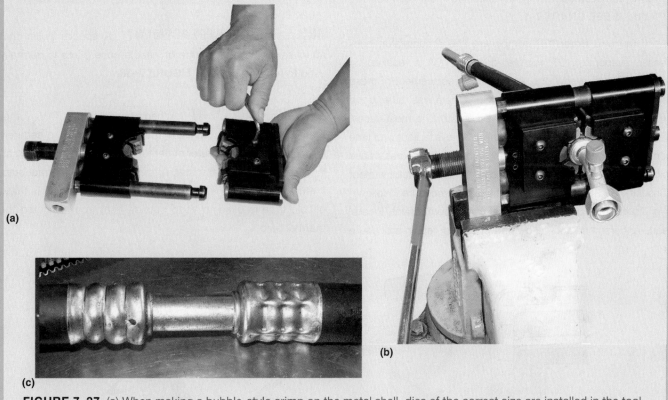

(a)

(b)

(c)

FIGURE 7–37 (a) When making a bubble-style crimp on the metal shell, dies of the correct size are installed in the tool. (b) The shell is crimped by tightening the tool drive bolt. (c) A finished crimp.

A/C COMPONENT REPLACEMENT Inside-out failure is caused by acids inside of the system, and the accumulator or receiver–drier must be replaced and the refrigerant recycled to remove these acids.

• When the compressor, evaporator, or TXV is replaced, the receiver–drier or accumulator should also be replaced. These failures were possibly caused by system contamination. This contamination will probably have loaded the desiccant capacity with moisture.

▪ It is good practice to keep the plastic caps in place on the new components until just before installation to keep as much moisture out of the system as possible.

▪ Removal of an accumulator, condenser, evaporator, or receiver–drier also removes a certain amount of oil from

Component	Fluid OZ.	CC
Accumulator	2	60
Condenser	1	30
Evaporator	2	60
Each hose	0.3	10
Receiver–drier	0.5	15

CHART 7–1

When an A/C component is removed, a certain amount of oil is also removed. These are typical amounts. Check service information for the exact amount to add to each component if it is replaced.

the system, and new oil should be added to the new part. The actual amount is usually specified in service information. ●**SEE CHART 7–1.**

If faulty, a major A/C component (the accumulator, condenser, evaporator, OT, receiver–drier, or TXV) is repaired by replacing it with a new one. At one time, replacement of these components was relatively easy because there was rather good access, except when working with evaporators. In most cases, getting the evaporator case out of the vehicle is tedious and time consuming, sometimes requiring the vehicle or evaporator case to be cut. Many technicians will not change an evaporator without consulting service information for the exact procedure to follow.

To remove and replace a major A/C component, locate, read, understand, and follow the specified repair procedure found in service information, which usually includes the following steps:

STEP 1 Recover the refrigerant from the system.

STEP 2 Disconnect and cap the refrigerant lines to the component.

STEP 3 Disconnect any mounting brackets and wires connected to the component and remove it.

STEP 4 Install the new part and attach any mounting brackets and wires.

STEP 5 Remove the line caps, pour the proper amount of the correct refrigerant oil into the component or line, and connect the refrigerant lines.

STEP 6 Evacuate and recharge the system and test for leaks.

ORIFICE TUBE REPLACEMENT A special puller that attaches to the orifice tube or needle-nose pliers is normally used to remove it. ●**SEE FIGURE 7–38.**

TXV REPLACEMENT When replacing a TXV (other than a H-block-type TXV), the thermal bulb must be securely attached to the evaporator outlet tube. This area must be clean to ensure good heat transfer. After attaching the thermal bulb, it must be wrapped with insulating refrigerant tape. This thick, pliable tape is used to keep outside heat from reaching the thermal bulb.

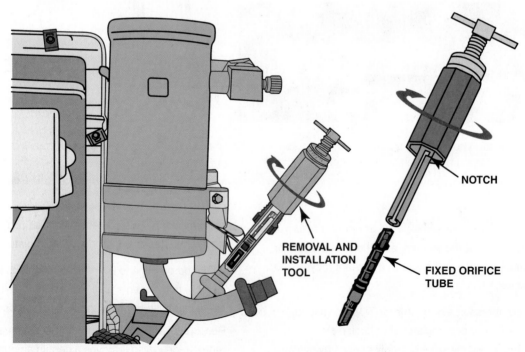

NOTCH

REMOVAL AND INSTALLATION TOOL

FIXED ORIFICE TUBE

FIGURE 7–38 Needle-nose pliers can sometimes be used to remove an orifice tube, but it requires this special tool in most cases.

TECH TIP

Because It Fits, Does Not Mean It Is Correct!

Many air-conditioning systems use orifice tubes that look similar if not identical. They are usually color coded for identification. Always use the recommended orifice tube for the vehicle you are servicing. Some examples of the various colors and sizes available include:

Make, Color, Orifice Size (Inches)

> Chrysler, purple, 0.0605
> Ford, red, 0.0605
> Ford, orange, 0.0560
> Ford, brown, 0.0470
> Ford, green, 0.0505
> GM, yellow, 0.0605. ● **SEE FIGURE 7–39.**

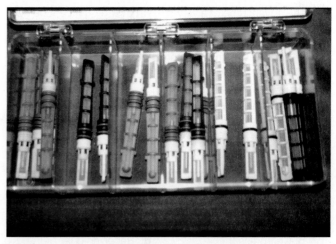

FIGURE 7–39 An assortment of orifice tubes in a plastic case with each size and color listed for easy access.

SUMMARY

1. The major condenser types are round or flat tube and serpentine or parallel flow.
2. TXVs are used with receiver–driers that are located in the high side.
3. Orifice tubes divide the high side from the low side and are used with accumulators located in the low side.
4. Various line fitting types are used to connect the components.
5. Various switches, sensors, and controls are used to control compressor, blower, and fan operation.

REVIEW QUESTIONS

1. What components are often included as part of a cooling module?
2. Why is sub-cooling necessary in some condensers?
3. What are the advantages and disadvantages of a thermal expansion valve system?
4. What are the advantages and disadvantages of an orifice tube system?
5. What is the difference between an accumulator and a receiver–drier?
6. Why does refrigerant oil need to be added to a new component such as a condenser?
7. What is the difference between a switch and a sensor?

CHAPTER QUIZ

1. A cooling module usually includes what components?
   a. Radiator
   b. Automatic transmission fluid cooler
   c. A/C condenser
   d. All of the above

2. As the latent heat of condensation is transferred to the airstream in the condenser, the refrigerant changes into_____.
   a. Liquid   c. Gas
   b. Vapor   d. Solid

3. The advantages of a TXV system over an orifice tube system include_____.
   a. Simpler and cheaper to produce
   c. Requires a smaller refrigerant charge
   b. Fewer moving parts
   d. All of the above

4. The advantages of an orifice tube system over a TXV system include_____.
   a. Simpler and cheaper to produce
   b. Requires a smaller refrigerant charge
   c. More moving parts
   d. All of the above

5. The orifice tube is usually located at the inlet tube to the_____.
   a. Condenser
   b. Compressor
   c. Evaporator
   d. Receiver–drier

6. Two technicians are discussing A/C systems. Technician A says that the TXV system uses a receiver–drier mounted in the suction line. Technician B says that the orifice tube system uses an accumulator in the suction line. Which technician is correct?
   a. Technician A only
   b. Technician B only
   c. Both Technicians A and B
   d. Neither Technician A nor B

7. The liquid line_____.
   a. Connects the condenser to the receiver–drier and TXV or OT
   b. Is smaller than the suction line
   c. Is larger in diameter than the suction line
   d. Both a and b

8. O-rings used in R-134a systems are usually _____.
   a. Green
   b. Black
   c. Red
   d. Orange

9. Various electrical switches used in A/C systems_____.
   a. Prevent evaporator icing
   b. Protect the compressor
   c. Control fan motors
   d. All of the above

10. Rear air-conditioning systems use_____.
    a. An orifice tube to control the refrigerant flow into the front evaporator and a TXV with the rear evaporator
    b. An orifice tube to control the refrigerant flow into the front evaporator and the rear evaporator
    c. A TXV to control the refrigerant flow into the front evaporator and an orifice tube with the rear evaporator
    d. A TXV to control the refrigerant flow into the front evaporator and the rear evaporator

AIR MANAGEMENT SYSTEM

LEARNING OBJECTIVES

After studying this chapter, the reader should be able to:

1. Prepare for the ASE Heating and Air Conditioning (A7) certification test content area "B" (Refrigeration System Component Diagnosis and Repair).

2. Discuss the different components of an air management system.

3. Explain airflow control and air temperature control in an A/C system.

4. Discuss plenum and control doors.

5. Explain nonelectrical and electronic HVAC controls.

KEY TERMS

Air doors 126
Air inlet 126
Air management system 126
Cabin filter 129
Dual-zone 132
Inside air 126

Mode door 126
Outside air 126
Plenum 130
Recirculation 126
Temperature-blend door 126
Vacuum actuator 132

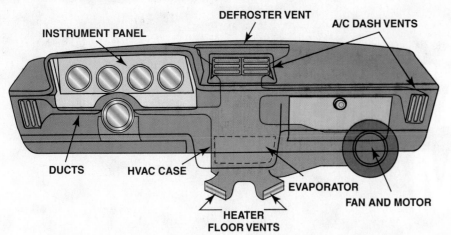

FIGURE 8-1 The HVAC airflow is directed toward the windshield, dash or floor vents, or combinations depending on the system settings.

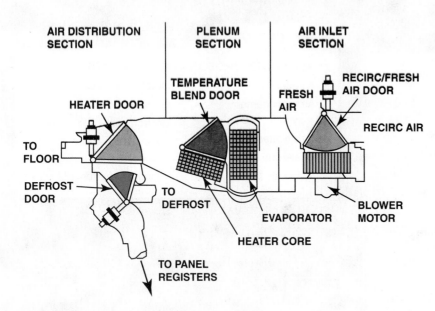

FIGURE 8-2 The three major portions of the A/C and heat system are air inlet, plenum, and air distribution. The shaded portions show the paths of the four control doors.

INTRODUCTION

TERMINOLOGY A system that contains the HVAC plenum, ducts, and **air doors** is called the **air management system**, or *air distribution system,* and controls the airflow to the passenger compartment. ●**SEE FIGURE 8-1.**

Air flows into the case that contains the evaporator and heater core from two possible inlets:

1. **Outside air**, often called *fresh air*

2. **Inside air**, usually called **recirculation**.

Proper temperature control to enhance passenger comfort during heating should maintain an air temperature in the footwell about 7°F to 14°F (4°C to 8°C) above the temperature around the upper body. This is done by directing the heated airflow to the floor. During A/C operation, the upper body should be cooler, so the airflow is directed to the instrument panel registers. Airflow is usually controlled by three or more doors,

which are called *flap doors* or valves by some manufacturers. The three doors include:

- **Air inlet** door is used to select outside or inside air inlet

- **Temperature-Blend door** is used to adjust air temperature

- **Mode door** is used to select air discharge location ●**SEE FIGURE 8-2.**

The use of these components allows the system to provide airflow under the following conditions:

1. Fresh outside air or recirculated air

2. Air conditioning

3. Defrost

4. Heat.

HEAT For heat position, the following can be done:

- Temperature set to the desired setting

- Air intake—select outside air for faster heating

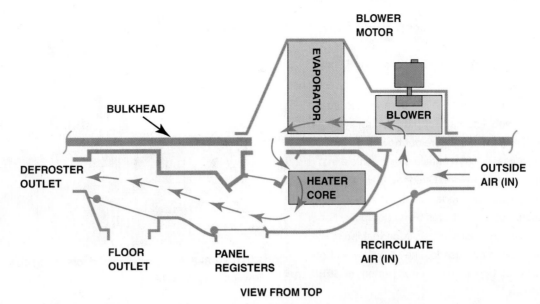

VIEW FROM TOP

FIGURE 8–3 In the defog or defrost mode position, the air is directed through the evaporator to remove the moisture from the air before being sent through the heater core to warm the air.

- Air conditioning set to off
- Set airflow to floor
- Fan speed to desired speed

AIR CONDITIONING For air conditioning position, the following can be done:

- Temperature set to the desired setting
- Air intake—set to outside air or recirculation under high humidity conditions.
- Airflow—select dash vents (also called panel vents)
- Air conditioning set to on
- Fan speed set to desired speed

VENTILATION For ventilation position, the following can be done:

- Temperature set to desired temperature
- Air intake—select outside air
- Airflow—set to dash (panel) vents
- Air conditioning set to off
- Fan speed set to desired speed

DEFOGGING OR DEFROSTING THE INSIDE OF THE WINDSHIELD For defogging or defrosting position, the following can be done:

- Temperature set to high temperature
- Air intake set to outside air
- Airflow set to windshield (defrost)
- Fan speed set to desired speed. ● **SEE FIGURE 8–3.**

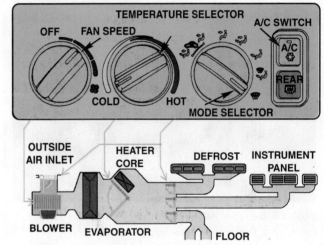

FIGURE 8–4 Most HVAC control heads include a control for turning things on and setting the mode of operation, a control for adjusting the temperature, and a control for the fan speed.

HVAC CONTROL HEAD The HVAC control head or panel is mounted in the instrument panel cluster or console. The control head includes the following controls:

- System on and off
- Outside or recirculated air
- Mode position (floor, vent, or defrost)
- Temperature desired
- Blower speed

The control head is connected to various parts through electrical connections, vacuum connections, mechanical cables, or a combination of these. ● **SEE FIGURE 8–4.**

What Does the Snowflake Button on the Dash Do?

Some people, such as those who drive vehicles that are equipped with automatic climate control systems, sometimes find it hard to figure out how to engage the A/C compressor on a rental car or a vehicle that they have not driven before. Often the driver will turn the fan to high and the mode selector to the dash vent position, but no cool air is being delivered. For the compressor to function, the button that looks like a snowflake has to be pushed. The snowflake button is actually the air conditioning on/off button. ● **SEE FIGURE 8–5.**

FIGURE 8–5 The A/C compressor is turned on or off by depressing the "snow flake" button on the dash.

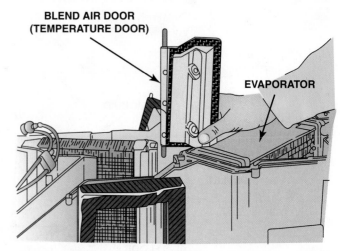

FIGURE 8–6 Many air control doors swing on their upper and lower pivots, in red.

directions of the airflow and the discharge air temperature are controlled by swinging, sliding, or rotating doors.

TYPES OF DOORS Most systems use a flap door that swings about 45° to 90°. Swinging doors are very simple and require little maintenance. ● **SEE FIGURE 8–6.**

Another design uses a *rotary door*. This pan-shaped door has openings at the side and edge, and the door rotates about 100° to one of four different positions. Each position directs airflow to the desired outlet(s).

The space under the instrument panel is very crowded, and some vehicles use a smaller HVAC case using a *sliding mode door* also called a *rolling door*. Some of these door designs roll up, similar to a window shade, and unroll to block a passage. ● **SEE FIGURE 8–7.**

AIR TEMPERATURE CONTROL

TEMPERATURE CONTROL USING AIRFLOW Most HVAC systems are considered *reheat* systems in that the incoming air is chilled as it passes through the evaporator. The air is then heated as part or all of the flow passes through the heater core so it reaches the desired in-vehicle temperature. ● **SEE FIGURE 8–8.**

TEMPERATURE CONTROL USING A VARIABLE COMPRESSOR There is an increasing trend to use an electronically controlled variable displacement compressor with an air temperature sensor after the evaporator. Compressor displacement is adjusted to cool the evaporator just

AIRFLOW CONTROL

OPERATION The amount or volume of HVAC air is controlled by blower speed. A multispeed blower is used to force air through the ductwork when the vehicle is moving at low speeds or to increase the airflow at any speed. At highway speeds, most systems have a natural airflow from ram air pressure created by the forward movement of the vehicle. This is the pressure generated at the base of the windshield by the speed of the vehicle. This airflow is improved in some vehicles by outlet registers placed in low-pressure areas toward the rear of the vehicle. Higher speeds move more air. The inlet and outlet

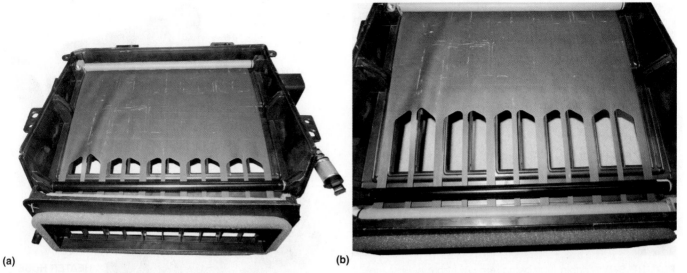

FIGURE 8–7 (a) A typical rolling-door type HVAC door that is shown almost fully closed. (b) The same door shown about half open.

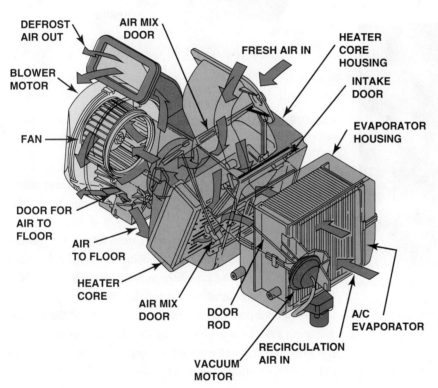

DEFROST
AIR OUT

AIR MIX
DOOR

FRESH AIR IN

HEATER
CORE
HOUSING

BLOWER
MOTOR

INTAKE
DOOR

EVAPORATOR
HOUSING

FAN

DOOR FOR
AIR TO
FLOOR

AIR
TO FLOOR

HEATER
CORE

AIR MIX
DOOR

DOOR
ROD

A/C
EVAPORATOR

VACUUM
MOTOR

RECIRCULATION
AIR IN

FIGURE 8–8 The blower motor forces air to flow through the A/C evaporator to remove moisture from the air before it is sent through the heater core where the air is heated before being directed to the defrost and floor vents.

enough to cool the air to the desired temperature. Cooling the incoming air no more than necessary will reduce compressor load on the engine and should improve fuel economy.

AIR FILTRATION

TERMINOLOGY Most HVAC systems include a **cabin filter** to remove small dust or pollen particles from the incoming airstream. This filter is also called a/an

- *HVAC air filter*
- *Interior ventilation filter*
- *Micron filter*
- *Particulate filter*
- *Pollen filter*

These filters require periodic replacement. If they are not serviced properly, they will cause an airflow reduction when plugged. ● **SEE FIGURE 8–9.**

FIGURE 8–9 A cabin filter being removed from behind the glove compartment. The dark color is part of the filter and is activated charcoal used to help remove odors.

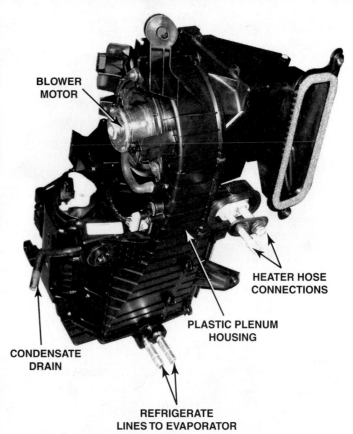

BLOWER MOTOR

HEATER HOSE CONNECTIONS

PLASTIC PLENUM HOUSING

CONDENSATE DRAIN

REFRIGERATE LINES TO EVAPORATOR

FIGURE 8–10 A typical HVAC housing that often has to be removed from the vehicle as an assembly to get access to the heater core and evaporator.

FIGURE 8–11 The air inlet to the HVAC system is usually at the base of the windshield and covered with a plastic screen (grille) to help keep debris such as leaves from entering the system.

and direct airflow, reduce noise, keep outside water and debris from entering, and isolate engine fumes and noises. ● **SEE FIGURE 8–10.**

Air can enter the duct system from either the plenum chamber in front of the vehicle's windshield (outside air) or from the *recirc* (short for *recirculation*) or return register (inside air). The return register is often positioned below the right end of the instrument panel. (The right and left sides of the vehicle are always described as seen by the driver.) The outside air plenum often includes a screen to keep leaves and other large debris from entering with the air. ● **SEE FIGURE 8–11.**

CASES AND DUCTS

CONSTRUCTION The evaporator and heater housing is molded from reinforced plastic and contains the following components:

- Evaporator
- Heater core
- Blower motor
- Most of the air control doors

The housing, called a **plenum**, is connected to the air inlets and outlets using formed plastic. These parts are required to contain

PLENUM AND CONTROL DOORS

AIR INLET CONTROL DOOR The **air inlet control** door is also called

- *Fresh air door*
- *Recirculation door*
- *Outside air door*

Keep the Air Screen Clean

The outside air inlet screen must be kept in good condition to prevent debris and small animals from entering the HVAC case. Leaves and pine needles can enter, decay, and mold. Mice have been known to enter and build nests and/or die. Any of these conditions can create a bad smell and are very difficult to clean.

This door is normally positioned so it allows airflow from one source while it shuts off the other. It can be positioned to allow

- Fresh air to enter while shutting off the recirculation opening
- Air to return or recirculate from inside the vehicle while shutting off fresh air
- A mix of fresh air and return air.

In many newer vehicles, the door is set to the fresh air position in all function lever positions except off, max heat, and max A/C. Max A/C and max heat settings position the door to recirculate in-vehicle air.

NOTE: In some vehicles, the recirculation door blocks most of the outside air and allows 80% of the air to be recirculated from the passenger compartment. About 20% of the air entering the passenger compartment is outside air to help keep the air in the passenger compartment fresh and keep the CO_2 levels low.

TEMPERATURE-BLEND DOOR Most systems position the evaporator so all air must pass through it. This allows removal of moisture by the evaporator's cold temperature. Many systems operate the A/C when defrost is selected to dry the air. The heater core is placed downstream so that air can be routed either through or around it using one or two doors to control this airflow. The door used to control interior temperature is called the temperature-blend door. Some other names for this door include:

- *Air-mix door*
- *Temperature door*
- *Blend door*
- *Diverter door*
- *Bypass door.* ● **SEE FIGURE 8–12.**

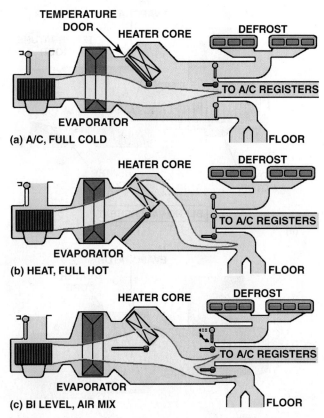

FIGURE 8–12 (a) The temperature and mode doors swing to direct all of the cool air past the heater core, (b) through the core to become hot, (c) or to blend hot and cool air.

The temperature-blend door is connected to the temperature knob or lever at the control head using a mechanical cable or an electric actuator. When the temperature lever is set to the coldest setting, the temperature-blend door routes all air so it bypasses the heater core. This causes the air entering the passenger compartment to be the coldest, coming straight from the evaporator. When the temperature lever is set to the hottest setting, the temperature-blend door routes all air through the heater core, and heated air goes to the passenger compartment. Setting the control lever to somewhere between cold and hot will mix or *temper* cold and hot air, allowing the driver to adjust the temperature to whatever is desired.

In the past in some vehicles, the evaporator was placed or stacked right next to the heater core. These systems controlled the air temperature by regulating the amount of reheat at the heater core. ● **SEE FIGURE 8–13.**

AIR DISTRIBUTION AND OUTLETS Air from the plenum can flow into one or two of three outlet paths:

1. The A/C registers (vents) in the face of the instrument panel
2. The defroster registers at the base of the windshield
3. The heater outlets at the floor under the instrument panel.

AIR MANAGEMENT SYSTEM   131

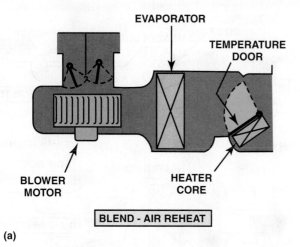

FIGURE 8–13 (a) In a blend-air system, all of the air is cooled. Then some of it is reheated and blended with the cool air to get the right temperature. (b) In a reheat system, all of the air is cooled and then reheated to the correct temperature.

Most vehicles include two ducts under the front seats or in the center console to transfer air to the rear seat area. Most vehicles also direct airflow to the side windows to defog the side windows. ● **SEE FIGURE 8–14.**

Airflow to these ducts is controlled by one or more mode doors controlled by the function lever or buttons. Mode doors are also called *function*, *floor-defrost*, and *panel-defrost* doors. Mode/function control sets the doors as follows:

- **A/C:** in-dash registers with outside air inlet
- **Max A/C:** in-dash registers with recirculation
- **Heat:** floor level with outside air inlet
- **Max Heat:** floor level with recirculation
- **Bi-level:** both in-dash and floor discharge
- **Defrost:** windshield registers

In many systems, a small amount of air is directed to the defroster ducts when in the heat mode, and while in defrost mode, a small amount of air goes to the floor level.

DUAL-ZONE AIR DISTRIBUTION **Dual-zone** air distribution allows the driver and passenger to select different temperature settings. The temperature choices can be as much as 30°F (16°C) different. Dual-zone systems split the duct and airflow past the heater core and use two air mix valves or doors with each air mix valve/temperature door controlled by a separate actuator.

NONELECTRICAL HVAC CONTROLS

CABLE-OPERATED SYSTEMS Mechanical systems are the least expensive. Most early control heads used purely mechanical operation for the doors, and one or more cables connected the function lever to the air inlet and mode doors. The temperature lever was also connected to the temperature-blend door by another cable. These mechanical levers were rather simple and usually trouble free, but they had some disadvantages. They tended to bind and could require a good deal of effort to operate.

VACUUM-OPERATED SYSTEMS Many vehicles use **vacuum actuators**, sometimes called *vacuum motors*, to operate the air inlet and mode doors. ● **SEE FIGURE 8–15.**

The doors are controlled by a vacuum valve that is operated by the control head. Vacuum controls operate more easily than cables, and vacuum hoses are much easier to route through congested areas than cables. ● **SEE FIGURE 8–16.**

ELECTRONIC HVAC CONTROLS

OVERVIEW Most recent vehicles use electrical function switches at the HVAC control head. These are often called *electromechanical controls*. These switches operate a group of solenoid valves that control the vacuum flow to the vacuum motors or use an electric actuator (motor) to operate

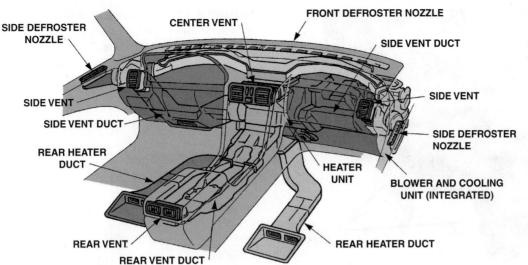

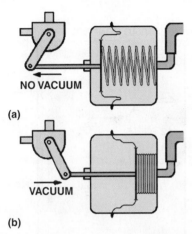

FIGURE 8–15 (a) With no vacuum signal, the spring extends the actuator shaft to place the door in a certain position. (b) A vacuum signal pulls the shaft inward and moves the door to the other position.

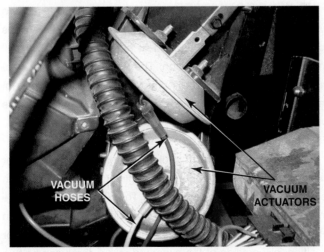

FIGURE 8–16 Many older vehicles used vacuum actuators to move the HVAC doors. When vacuum actuators operate, they alter the air–fuel mixture in the engine. Because vacuum controls affect engine operation and therefore emissions, recent vehicles use electric control systems.

TECH TIP

Defrost All the Time? Check the Vacuum

A common problem with older vehicles that use vacuum actuators involves airflow from the defroster ducts even though the selector lever is in other positions. The defrost setting is the default position in the event of a failure with the vacuum supply. The defrost position is used because it is the *safest* position. For safety, the windshield must remain free from frost. Heat is also supplied to the passenger compartments not only through defrost ducts but also through the heater vents at floor level. If the airflow is mostly directed to the windshield, check under the hood for a broken, disconnected, or missing vacuum hose. Check the vacuum reserve container for cracks or rust (if metal) that could prevent the container from holding vacuum. Check all vacuum hose connections at the intake manifold and trace each carefully, inspecting for cracks, splits, or softened areas that may indicate a problem.

NOTE: This problem of incorrect airflow inside the vehicle often occurs after another service procedure has been performed, such as air filter or cabin filter replacement. The movement of the technician's body and arms can cause a hose to be pulled loose or a vacuum fitting to break without the service technician being aware that anything wrong has occurred.

FIGURE 8–17 Three compact, electric actuators/ servomotors operate the doors in this part of the HVAC case.

ELECTRIC
ACTUATORS

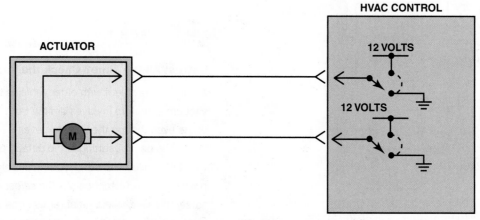

FIGURE 8–18 A two-wire HVAC electronic actuator where the direction of rotation is controlled by the HVAC control head or module, which changes the direction of rotation by changing the polarity of the power and ground connection at the motor.

the air distribution and temperature-blend doors. ● **SEE FIGURE 8–17.**

TWO-WIRE ACTUATORS

A typical two-wire actuator rotates when electric impulses are sent to the brushes by the HVAC control head. The direction of rotation, and therefore the movement of the HVAC door position, is changed by changing the wire that is pulsed with power and the other brush is then connected to ground. ● **SEE FIGURE 8–18.**

THREE-WIRE ACTUATORS

A typical three-wire actuator uses a power, ground, and an input signal wire from the HVAC control module. There is a module (logic chip) inside the motor assembly that receives a 0–5 volt signal from the HVAC control module. When the actuator gets a 0-volt signal from the control module, it rotates in one direction and when it receives a 5-volt signal it rotates in the opposite direction. If the motor receives a 2.5 volt signal, the motor stops rotating. ● **SEE FIGURE 8–19.**

FIVE-WIRE ACTUATORS

A five-wire actuator uses two wires to power the motor (power and ground) and three wires for a potentiometer that is used to signal the HVAC control module of the motor's location. The potentiometer may be a separate gear-driven part attached to the motor or a part of the printed circuit board where a slider moves across resistive paint to create the potentiometer signal voltage. ● **SEE FIGURE 8–20.**

Most HVAC control modules convert the potentiometer signal voltage to a binary number ranging from 0 to 255, which is often seen on a scan tool display. The HVAC control module monitors the feedback signal to determine the actual location of the door and to determine if the door is stuck. If the motor position falls outside of the expected range, there can be two things that can occur, depending on the vehicle.

1. The controller, usually the HVAC control module, will drive the motor until it reaches its desired location. This action

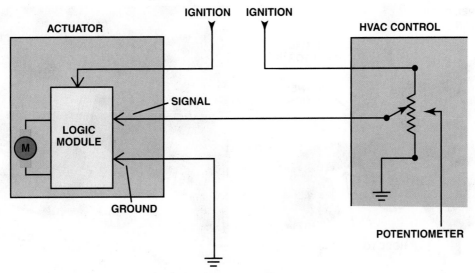

FIGURE 8–19 Three-wire actuators include a logic chip inside the motor assembly. The HVAC control module then sends a 0 volt to 5 volt signal to the motor assembly to control the direction of rotation.

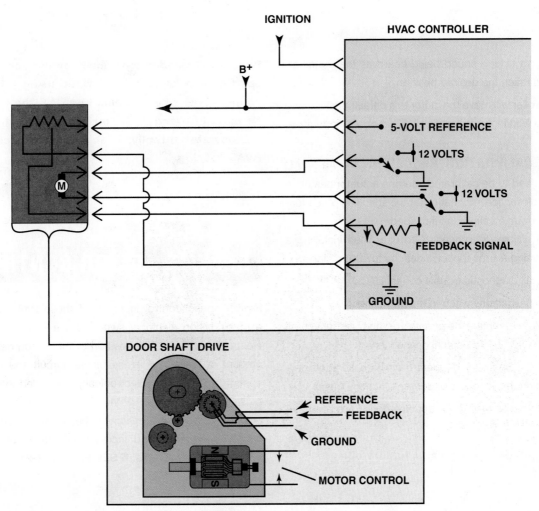

FIGURE 8–20 A typical five-wire HVAC actuator showing the two wires used to power the motor and the three wires used for the motor position potentiometer.

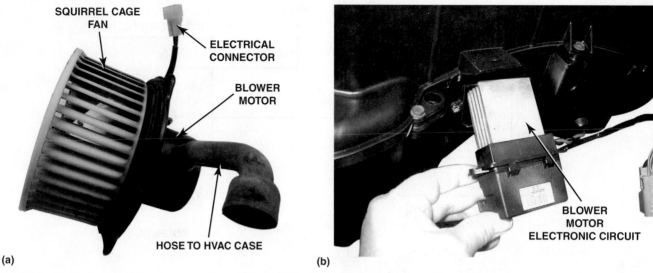

FIGURE 8–21 (a) A typical blower motor assembly with a squirrel-cage fan attached. The hose to the HVAC case is used to bring clean cabin air, instead of dirty outside air, to cool the motor. (b) Blower motor speed is controlled through an electronic circuit (shown) or through a resistor pack.

can result a ticking sound being heard as the motor attempts to reach the desired position.

2. The controller will move the motor to a default position and then stop working, making the HVAC controls inoperative.

ACTUATOR CALIBRATION PROCEDURES An HVAC
actuator may need to be calibrated after the actuator has been replaced. Check service information for the specified procedure to follow to perform a calibration if needed.

A typical calibration procedure to use when installing a new actuator using a scan tool includes the following steps:

STEP 1 Clear all diagnostic trouble codes (DTCs)

STEP 2 Turn the ignition switch to the off position

STEP 3 Install the replacement actuator and reconnect all mechanical and electrical connections

STEP 4 Start the engine and select motor recalibration program on the scan tool under the functions menu

STEP 5 Verify that no diagnostic trouble codes have been set.

CAUTION: Do not operate an actuator prior to installation to "test it" because many actuators operate until they are stopped mechanically by the door being fully open or fully closed. If operated using a battery and jumper wires without being installed, the actuator can be moved beyond its normal range of motion and will not operate correctly, if at all, when placed into the HVAC housing.

BLOWER MOTOR CONTROL

Blower speed control in many of these systems is through a multiposition electrical switch and a group of resistors or electronic controls. The position of the switch determines the amount of resistance in the blower circuit and therefore the speed of the motor. Electronically controlled systems use a pulse-width-modulated (PWM) voltage supply to control the blower motor, which switches the motor off and on, up to 40,000 times per second. Increasing the length of the "on time" produces higher speeds. ● **SEE FIGURE 8–21**.

1. Air flows into the case that contains the evaporator and heater core from two possible inlets:
   - Outside air, often called fresh air
   - Inside air, usually called recirculation air.
2. The HVAC case contains a blower, A/C evaporator, the heater core, and doors to control the air temperature and flow.
3. The control head allows the driver to change blower speed, adjust the temperature, turn A/C on or off, and direct the airflow.

4. Control heads transfer motion to the HVAC case through cables, vacuum control, or electronics and electric motors.
5. Most HVAC systems include a filter to remove particles and odors from the air.

REVIEW QUESTIONS

1. What do the three main HVAC doors do?
2. In the heating mode, why is heat directed toward the floor?
3. Where is the air directed when the control panel is set to defog/defrost position?
4. How does a "reheat" system work and why?
5. Where does the air enter the vehicle when outside air is selected?

CHAPTER QUIZ

1. "Outside air" is also called_____ air.
   - a. Recirculation
   - b. Fresh
   - c. Plenum
   - d. Mode

2. The _____door is used to select air discharge location such as floor, vent, or defrost.
   - a. Mode
   - b. Recirculation
   - c. Fresh air
   - d. Any of the above

3. What does the snowflake button on the dash do?
   - a. Selects defrost
   - b. Selects defog
   - c. Turns on the A/C compressor
   - d. Selects fresh outside air

4. The ram air that enters the vehicle from the outside enters the HVAC system from _____.
   - a. Beside the headlight
   - b. Behind the grille
   - c. The side vents
   - d. The base of the windshield

5. Most systems use a flap door that swings about _____degrees.
   - a. 10 to 25
   - b. 25 to 40
   - c. 45 to 90
   - d. 90 to 120

6. The air inlet control door is also called_____.
   - a. Fresh air door
   - b. Recirculation door
   - c. Outside air door
   - d. Any of the above

7. The door used to control interior temperature is called the _____door.
   - a. Temperature-blend
   - b. Recirculation
   - c. Outside (fresh) air
   - d. Mode

8. A five-wire actuator uses two wires to power the motor (power and ground) and three wires for _____.
   - a. Direction control
   - b. A feedback potentiometer
   - c. Static electricity protection
   - d. Redundant control

9. What is a "reheat" system?
   - a. A system that uses two heater cores.
   - b. A system that cools the air through the evaporator then heats the air though airflow though the heater core.
   - c. A system that uses both engine coolant and an electronic heater to heat the air.
   - d. Any of the above depending on the make and model of vehicle.

10. Most recent HVAC actuators are recalibrated after re-placement by_____.
    - a. Using a battery and jumper wires
    - b. Using a scan tool or allow it to self-learn after being installed
    - c. Turning the ignition switch to the off position
    - d. None of the above

chapter 9

HVAC ELECTRICITY AND ELECTRONICS

LEARNING OBJECTIVES

After studying this chapter, the reader should be able to:

1. Prepare for the Heating and Air Conditioning (A7) ASE certification test content area "D" (Operating Systems and Related Controls Diagnosis and Repair).
2. Explain the characteristics of electricity.
3. Differentiate between conductors, insulators, and semiconductors.
4. Explain the units of electrical measurement.
5. List the parts of a complete circuit.
6. Discuss the types of electrical circuit faults.
7. Explain how to detect and measure electrical voltage, current, and resistance using digital meters.
8. Discuss wire repair.
9. Discuss the purpose of terminals, connectors, relays, and switches.
10. Discuss networks and network classifications.

KEY TERMS

Ammeter 150
Ampere 141
Conductors 140
Connector 152
Conventional
    theory 141
Crimp-and-seal
    connectors 154
Digital multimeter
    (DMM) 148
Digital volt-ohm-meter
    (DVOM) 148
Electricity 139
Electron theory 141
High resistance 146

Insulators 140
Node 157
Ohmmeter 149
Ohms 142
Open circuit 144
Relay 155
Schematic 143
Short-to-ground 144
Short-to-voltage 144
Semiconductor 141
Terminal 152
Volt 142
Voltmeter 148

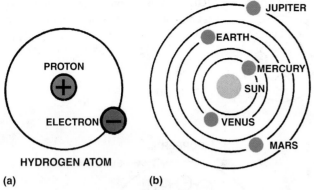

FIGURE 9–1 In an atom (a), electrons orbit protons in the nucleus just as planets orbit the sun in our solar system (b).

INTRODUCTION

The electrical system is one of the most important systems in a vehicle today. Every year more and more vehicle components and systems use electricity.

Electricity may be difficult for some people to learn for the following reasons.

- It cannot be seen.
- Only the results of electricity can be seen.
- It has to be detected and measured.

ELECTRICITY

BACKGROUND Our universe is composed of matter, which is anything that has mass and occupies space. All matter is made from slightly over 100 individual components called elements. The smallest particle that an element can be broken into and still retain the properties of that element is known as an atom. ● SEE FIGURE 9–1.

DEFINITION Electricity is the movement of electrons from one atom to another. The dense center of each atom is called the nucleus. The nucleus contains

- Protons, which have a positive charge
- Neutrons, which are electrically neutral (have no charge)

Electrons, which have a negative charge, orbit the nucleus. Each atom contains an equal number of electrons and protons.

NOTE: As an example of the relative sizes of the parts of an atom, consider that if an atom were magnified so that the nucleus were the size of the period at the end of this sentence, the whole atom would be bigger than a house.

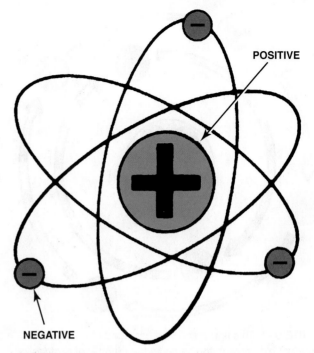

FIGURE 9–2 The nucleus of an atom has a positive (+) charge and the surrounding electrons have a negative (–) charge.

POSITIVE AND NEGATIVE CHARGES The parts of an atom have different charges. The orbiting electrons are negatively charged, while the protons are positively charged. Positive charges are indicated by the "plus" sign (+), and negative charges by the "minus" sign (–). ● SEE FIGURE 9–2.

These same + and – signs are used to identify parts of an electrical circuit. Neutrons have no charge at all. They are neutral. In a normal or balanced atom, the number of negative particles equals the number of positive particles. That is, there are as many electrons as there are protons. ● SEE FIGURE 9–3.

MAGNETS AND ELECTRICAL CHARGE An ordinary magnet has two ends, or poles. One end is called the south pole, and the other is called the north pole. If two magnets are brought close to each other with like poles together (south to south or north to north), the magnets will push each other apart, because like poles repel each other. If the opposite poles of the magnets are brought close to each other, south to north, the magnets will snap together, because unlike poles attract each other. The positive and negative charges within an atom are like the north and south poles of a magnet. Charges that are alike will repel each other, similar to the poles of a magnet. ● SEE FIGURE 9–4.

That is why the negative electrons continue to orbit around the positive protons. They are attracted and held by the opposite charge of the protons. The electrons keep moving in orbit because they repel each other.

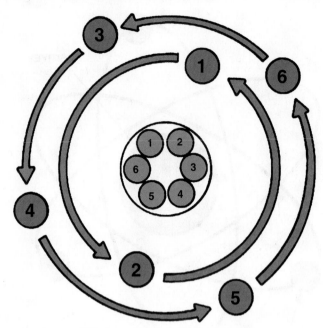

FIGURE 9–3 This figure shows a balanced atom. The number of electrons is the same as the number of protons in the nucleus.

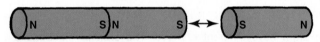

FIGURE 9–4 Unlike charges attract and like charges repel.

ELECTRON ORBITS
Electrons orbit around the nucleus in rings and the outermost ring is called the "valence ring." Whether a material is a conductor or an insulator strictly depends on how many electrons are in the outer ring.

CONDUCTORS
Conductors are materials with fewer than four electrons in their atom's outer orbit. ● SEE FIGURE 9–5.

Copper is an excellent conductor because it has only one electron in its outer orbit. This orbit is far enough away from the nucleus of the copper atom that the pull or force holding the outermost electron in orbit is relatively weak. ● SEE FIGURE 9–6.

Copper is the conductor most used in vehicles because the price of copper is reasonable compared to the relative cost of other conductors with similar properties. Examples of commonly used conductors include:

- Silver
- Copper
- Gold
- Aluminum
- Steel
- Cast iron

CONDUCTORS

FIGURE 9–5 A conductor is any element that has one to three electrons in its outer orbit.

COPPER

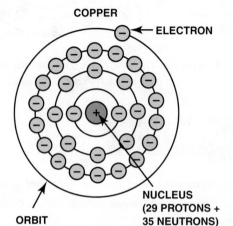

FIGURE 9–6 Copper is an excellent conductor of electricity because it has just one electron in its outer orbit, making it easy to be knocked out of its orbit and flow to other nearby atoms. This causes electron flow, which is the definition of electricity.

INSULATORS

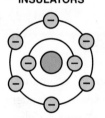

FIGURE 9–7 Insulators are elements with five to eight electrons in the outer orbit.

INSULATORS
Some materials hold their electrons very tightly; therefore, electrons do not move through them very well. These materials are called insulators. Insulators are materials with more than four electrons in their atom's outer orbit. Because they have more than four electrons in their outer orbit, it becomes easier for these materials to acquire (gain) electrons than to release electrons. ● SEE FIGURE 9–7.

Examples of insulators include:

- Rubber
- Plastic
- Nylon
- Porcelain
- Ceramic
- Fiberglass

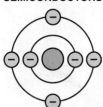

SEMICONDUCTORS

FIGURE 9–8 Semiconductor elements contain exactly four electrons in the outer orbit.

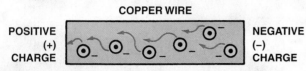

COPPER WIRE

POSITIVE (+) CHARGE

NEGATIVE (–) CHARGE

FIGURE 9–9 Electricity is the movement of electrons through a conductor.

SEMICONDUCTORS

Materials with exactly four electrons in their outer orbit are neither conductors nor insulators, but are called **semiconductors**. A semiconductor can be either an insulator or a conductor in different design applications. ● **SEE FIGURE 9–8**.

Examples of semiconductors include:

- Silicon
- Germanium
- Carbon

Semiconductors are used mostly in transistors, computers, and other electronic devices.

HOW ELECTRONS MOVE THROUGH A CONDUCTOR

CURRENT FLOW The following events occur if a source of power, such as a battery, is connected to the ends of a conductor—a positive charge (lack of electrons) is placed on one end of the conductor and a negative charge (excess of electrons) is placed on the opposite end of the conductor. For current to flow, there must be an imbalance of excess electrons at one end of the circuit and a deficiency of electrons at the opposite end. ● **SEE FIGURE 9–9**.

CONVENTIONAL THEORY VERSUS ELECTRON THEORY

- **Conventional theory**: It was once thought that electricity had only one charge and moved from positive to negative. This theory of the flow of electricity through a conductor is called the conventional theory of current flow. Most automotive applications use the conventional theory. ● **SEE FIGURE 9–10**.

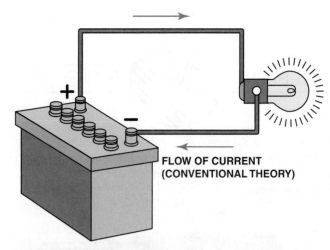

FLOW OF CURRENT (CONVENTIONAL THEORY)

FIGURE 9–10 Conventional theory states that current flows through a circuit from positive (+) to negative (–). Automotive electricity uses the conventional theory in all electrical diagrams and schematics.

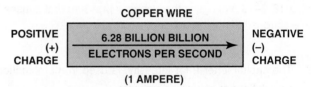

COPPER WIRE

POSITIVE (+) CHARGE

6.28 BILLION BILLION ELECTRONS PER SECOND

NEGATIVE (–) CHARGE

(1 AMPERE)

FIGURE 9–11 One ampere is the movement of 1 coulomb (6.28 billion billion electrons) past a point in 1 second.

- **Electron theory**: The discovery of the electron and its negative charge led to the electron theory, which states that there is electron flow from negative to positive.

UNITS OF ELECTRICITY

Electricity is measured using meters or other test equipment. The three fundamentals of electricity-related units include the ampere, volt, and ohm.

AMPERE The **ampere** is the unit used throughout the world to measure current flow. When 6.28 billion billion electrons (the name for this large number of electrons is a coulomb) move past a certain point in 1 second, this represents 1 ampere of current. ● **SEE FIGURE 9–11**.

The ampere is the electrical unit for the amount of electron flow, just as "gallons per minute" is the unit that can be used to measure the quantity of water flow. It is named for the French physicist Andrè Marie Ampére (1775–1836). The conventional abbreviations and measurement for amperes are as follows:

1. The ampere is the unit of measurement for the amount of current flow.

2. A and amps are acceptable abbreviations for amperes.

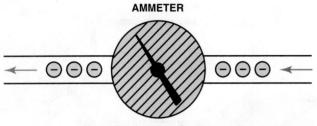

FIGURE 9-12 An ammeter is installed in the path of the electrons similar to a water meter used to measure the flow of water in gallons per minute. The ammeter displays current flow in amperes.

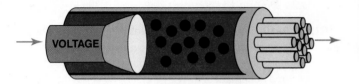

VOLTAGE IS PRESSURE

FIGURE 9-13 Voltage is the electrical pressure that causes the electrons to flow through a conductor.

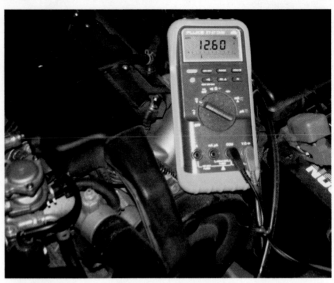

FIGURE 9-14 This digital multimeter set to read DC volts is being used to test the voltage of a vehicle battery. Most multimeters can also measure resistance (ohms) and current flow (amperes).

3. The capital letter I, for intensity, is used in mathematical calculations to represent amperes.

4. Amperes do the actual work in the circuit. It is the movement of the electrons through a light bulb or motor that actually makes the electrical device work. Without amperage through a device, it will not work at all.

5. Amperes are measured by an ammeter (not ampmeter). ● **SEE FIGURE 9-12**.

VOLTS The **volt** is the unit of measurement for electrical pressure. It is named for an Italian physicist, Alessandro Volta (1745–1827). The comparable unit using water pressure as an example would be pounds per square inch (PSI). It is possible to have very high pressures (volts) and low water flow (amperes). It is also possible to have high water flow (amperes) and low pressures (volts). Voltage is also called electrical potential, because if there is voltage present in a conductor, there is a potential (possibility) for current flow. ● **SEE FIGURE 9-13**.

The conventional abbreviations and measurement for voltage are as follows:

1. The volt is the unit of measurement for the amount of electrical pressure.

2. Electromotive force, abbreviated EMF, is another way of indicating voltage.

3. V is the generally accepted abbreviation for volts.

4. The symbol used in calculations is E, for electromotive force.

5. Volts are measured by a voltmeter. ● **SEE FIGURE 9-14**.

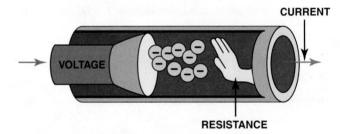

FIGURE 9-15 Resistance to the flow of electrons through a conductor is measured in ohms.

OHMS Resistance to the flow of current through a conductor is measured in units called **ohms**, named after the German physicist George Simon Ohm (1787–1854). The resistance to the flow of free electrons through a conductor results from the countless collisions the electrons cause within the atoms of the conductor. ● **SEE FIGURE 9-15**.

Resistance can be

▪ Desirable when it is part of how a circuit works, such as the resistance of a filament in a light bulb.

▪ Undesirable, such as corrosion in a connection restricting the amount of current flow in a circuit.

The conventional abbreviations and measurement for resistance are as follows:

1. The ohm is the unit of measurement for electrical resistance.

2. The symbol for ohms is Ω (Greek capital letter omega), the last letter of the Greek alphabet.

3. The symbol used in calculations is R, for resistance.

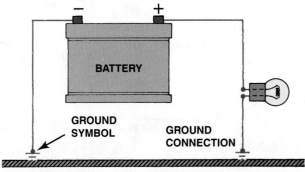

FIGURE 9–16 The return path back to the battery can be any electrical conductor, such as a copper wire or the metal frame or body of the vehicle.

4. Resistance is measured by an ohmmeter.

5. Resistance to electron flow depends on the material used.

ELECTRICAL CIRCUITS

DEFINITION A circuit is a complete path that electrons travel from a power source (such as a battery) through a load such as a light bulb and back to the power source. It is called a circuit because the current must start and finish at the same place (power source). For any electrical circuit to work at all, it must be continuous from the battery (power), through all the wires and components, and back to the battery (ground). A circuit that is continuous throughout is said to have continuity.

PARTS OF A COMPLETE CIRCUIT Every complete circuit contains the following parts:

1. A power source, such as a vehicle's battery.

2. Protection from harmful overloads (excessive current flow). (Fuses, circuit breakers, and fusible links are examples of electrical circuit protection devices.)

3. The power path for the current to flow through, from the power source to the resistance. (This path from a power source to the load—a light bulb in this example—is usually an insulated copper wire.)

4. The electrical load or resistance, which converts electrical energy into heat, light, or motion.

5. A return path (ground) for the electrical current from the load back to the power source so that there is a complete circuit. (This return, or ground, path is usually the metal body, frame, ground wires, and engine block of the vehicle.) ● SEE FIGURE 9–16.

6. Switches and controls that turn the circuit on and off. ● SEE FIGURE 9–17.

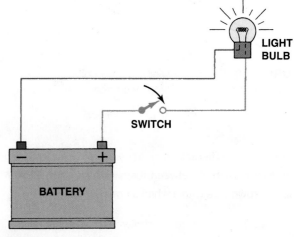

FIGURE 9–17 An electrical switch opens the circuit and no current flows. The switch could also be on the return (ground) path wire.

ELECTRICAL SCHEMATICS

TERMINOLOGY Automotive manufacturer's service information includes wiring schematics of every electrical circuit in a vehicle. A wiring **schematic**, sometimes called a *diagram*, shows electrical components and wiring using symbols and lines to represent components and wires. A typical wiring schematic may include all of the circuits combined, or they may be broken down to show individual circuits. All circuit schematics or diagrams include:

▪ Power-side wiring of the circuit

▪ All splices

▪ Connectors

▪ Wire size

▪ Wire color

▪ Trace color (if any)

▪ Circuit number

▪ Electrical components

▪ Ground return paths

▪ Fuses and switches

CIRCUIT INFORMATION Many wiring schematics include numbers and letters near components and wires that may confuse readers of the schematic. Most letters used near or on a wire identify the color or colors of the wire.

▪ The first color or color abbreviation is the color of the wire insulation.

▪ The second color (if mentioned) is the color of the stripe or tracer on the base color. ● SEE FIGURE 9–18.

FIGURE 9–18 The center wire is a solid color wire, meaning that the wire has no other identifying tracer or stripe color.

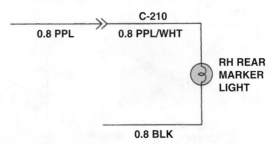

FIGURE 9–19 Typical section of a wiring diagram. Notice that the wire color changes at connection C210. The ".8" represents the metric wire size in square millimeters.

Wires with different color tracers are indicated by both colors with a slash (/) between them. For example, BRN/WHT means a brown wire with a white stripe or tracer.

WIRE SIZE Wire size is shown on all schematics. For example, ● **FIGURE 9–19** illustrates a rear side-marker bulb circuit diagram where ".8" indicates the metric wire gauge size in square millimeters (mm^2) and "PPL" indicates a solid purple wire.

The wire diagram also shows that the color of the wire changes at the number C210. This stands for "connector #210" and is used for reference purposes. The symbol for the connection can vary depending on the manufacturer. The color change from purple (PPL) to purple with a white tracer (PPL/WHT). The ground circuit is the ".8 BLK" wire.

● **SEE FIGURE 9–20**, which shows many of the electrical and electronic symbols that are used in wiring and circuit diagrams.

TYPES OF CIRCUIT FAULTS

Circuits can experience several different types of faults or problems, which often result in improper operation. The types of faults include opens, shorts, and high resistance.

OPEN CIRCUITS An **open circuit** is any circuit that is not complete, or that lacks continuity, such as a broken wire. ● **SEE FIGURE 9–21** on page 146.

Open circuits have the following features.

1. No current will flow through an open circuit.
2. An open circuit may be created by a break in the circuit or by a switch that opens (turns off) the circuit and prevents the flow of current.
3. In any circuit containing a power load and ground, an opening anywhere in the circuit will cause the circuit not to work.
4. A light switch in a home and the headlight switch in a vehicle are examples of devices that open a circuit to control its operation.

NOTE: A blown fuse opens the circuit to prevent damage to the components or wiring in the circuit in the event of an overload caused by a fault in the circuit.

SHORT-TO-VOLTAGE If a wire (conductor) or component is shorted to voltage, it is commonly referred to as being shorted. A **short-to-voltage** occurs when the power side of one circuit is electrically connected to the power side of another circuit. ● **SEE FIGURE 9–22** on page 146.

A short circuit has the following features.

1. It is a complete circuit in which the current usually bypasses some or all of the resistance in the circuit.
2. It involves the power side of the circuit.
3. It involves a copper-to-copper connection (two power side wires touching together).
4. It is also called a short-to-voltage.
5. It usually affects more than one circuit. In this case, if one circuit is electrically connected to another circuit, one of the circuits may operate when it is not supposed to because it is being supplied power from another circuit.
6. It may or may not blow a fuse. ● **SEE FIGURE 9–23** on page 146.

SHORT-TO-GROUND A **short-to-ground** is a type of short circuit that occurs when the current bypasses part of the normal circuit and flows directly to ground. A short-to-ground has the following features.

1. Because the ground return circuit is metal (vehicle frame, engine, or body), it is often identified as having current flowing from copper to steel.
2. A short-to-ground can occur at any place where a power path wire accidentally touches a return path wire or conductor. ● **SEE FIGURE 9–24** on page 146.
3. A defective component or circuit that is shorted to ground is commonly called grounded.
4. A short-to-ground almost always results in a blown fuse, damaged connectors, or melted wires.

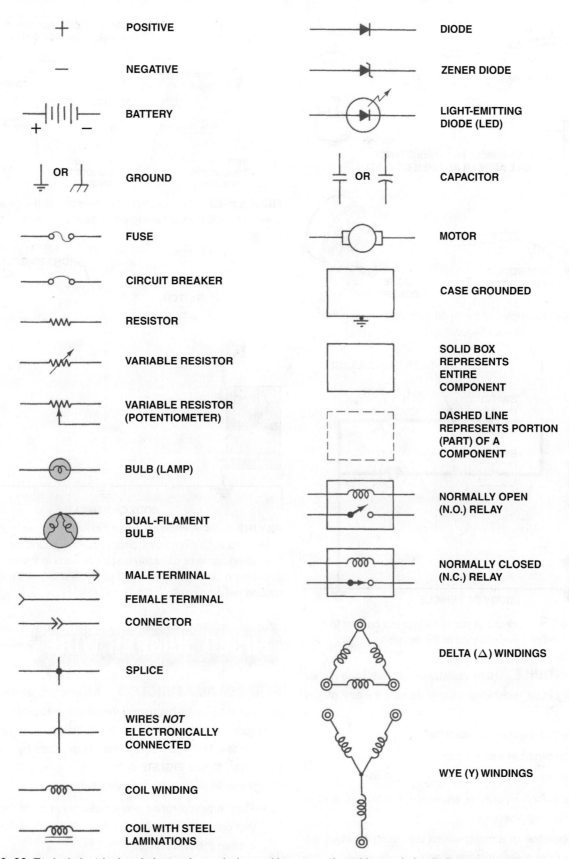

FIGURE 9–20 Typical electrical and electronic symbols used in automotive wiring and circuit diagrams.

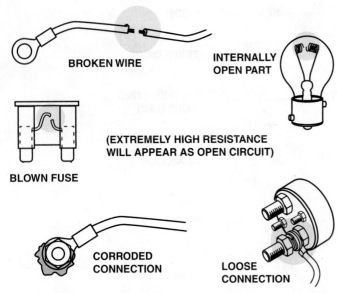

BROKEN WIRE INTERNALLY OPEN PART

(EXTREMELY HIGH RESISTANCE WILL APPEAR AS OPEN CIRCUIT)

BLOWN FUSE

CORRODED CONNECTION   LOOSE CONNECTION

FIGURE 9–21 Examples of common causes of open circuits. Some of these causes are often difficult to find.

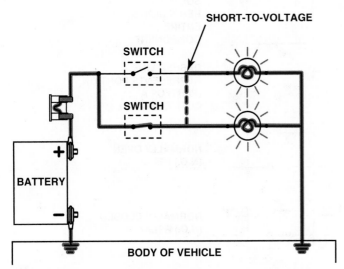

SHORT-TO-VOLTAGE

SWITCH

SWITCH

BATTERY

BODY OF VEHICLE

FIGURE 9–22 A short circuit permits electrical current to by-pass some or all of the resistance in the circuit.

HIGH RESISTANCE

High resistance is resistance higher than normal circuit resistance usually caused by any of the following:

- Corroded connections or sockets
- Loose terminals in a connector
- Loose ground connections

If there is high resistance anywhere in a circuit, it may cause the following problems.

1. Slow operation of a motor-driven unit, such as when the transfer case makes a range change
2. Dim lights
3. "Clicking" of relays or solenoids
4. No operation of a circuit or electrical component

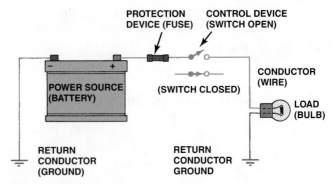

PROTECTION DEVICE (FUSE)   CONTROL DEVICE (SWITCH OPEN)

POWER SOURCE (BATTERY)

CONDUCTOR (WIRE)

(SWITCH CLOSED)

LOAD (BULB)

RETURN CONDUCTOR (GROUND)

RETURN CONDUCTOR GROUND

FIGURE 9–23 A fuse or circuit breaker opens the circuit to prevent possible overheating damage in the event of a short circuit.

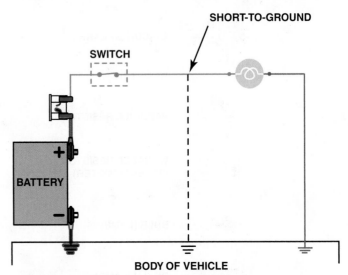

SHORT-TO-GROUND

SWITCH

BATTERY

BODY OF VEHICLE

FIGURE 9–24 A short-to-ground affects the power side of the circuit. Current flows directly to the ground return, bypassing some or all of the electrical loads in the circuit. There is no current in the circuit past the short. A short-to-ground will also cause the fuse to blow.

FUSED JUMPER WIRE

PURPOSE AND FUNCTION   A fused jumper wire is used to check a circuit by bypassing the switch or to provide a power or ground to a component. A fused jumper wire, also called a fused test lead, can be purchased or made by the service technician. ● **SEE FIGURE 9–25.**

It should include the following features:

- *Fuse*: A typical fused jumper wire has a blade-type fuse that can be easily replaced. A 10 ampere fuse (red color) is often the value used.
- *Alligator clip ends*: Alligator clips on the ends allow the fused jumper wire to be clipped to a ground or power source while the other end is attached to the power side or ground side of the unit being tested.

FIGURE 9–25 A technician-made fused jumper lead, which is equipped with a red 10 ampere fuse. This fused jumper wire uses terminals for testing circuits at a connector instead of alligator clips.

- *Good-quality insulated wire:* Most purchased jumper wire is about 14 gauge stranded copper wire with a flexible rubberized insulation to allow it to move easily even in cold weather.

CAUTION: Never use a fused jumper wire to bypass any resistance or load in the circuit. The increased current flow could damage the wiring and could blow the fuse on the jumper lead. Be very cautious when working on or around any computer circuit. Permanent damage to the computer or electronic module could result if power or ground goes to the wrong circuit.

TEST LIGHT

NON-POWERED TEST LIGHT
A 12-volt test light is one of the simplest testers that can be used to detect electricity. A test light is simply a light bulb with a probe and a ground wire attached. ● **SEE FIGURE 9–26**.

A test light is used to detect battery voltage potential at various test points. Battery voltage cannot be seen or felt, and can be detected only with test equipment. The ground clip is connected to a clean ground on either the negative terminal of the battery or a clean metal part of the body and the

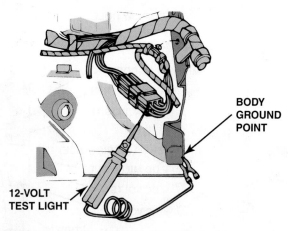

FIGURE 9–26 A 12-volt test light is attached to a good ground while probing for power.

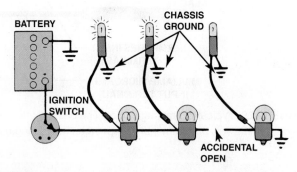

FIGURE 9–27 A test light can be used to locate an open in a circuit. Note that the test light is grounded at a different location than the circuit itself.

probe touched to terminals or components. If the test light comes on, this indicates that voltage is available. ● **SEE FIGURE 9–27**.

A purchased test light should be labeled as "12-volt test light." Do not purchase a test light designed for household current (110 or 220 volts), as it will not light with 12 to 14 volts.

USES OF A 12-VOLT TEST LIGHT
A 12-volt test light can be used to check the following:

- *Electrical power:* If the test light lights, then there is power available. It will not, however, indicate the voltage level or if there is enough current available to operate an electrical load. It only indicates that there is enough voltage and current to light the test light (about 0.25 A).

- *Grounds:* A test light can be used to check for grounds by attaching the clip of the test light to the positive terminal of the battery or any positive 12-volt electrical terminal. The tip of the test light can then be used to touch the ground wire. If there is a ground connection, the test light will light.

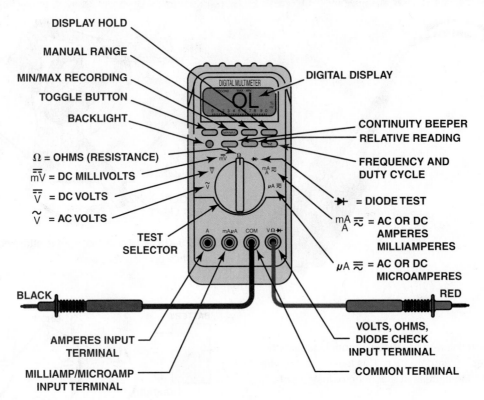

DISPLAY HOLD
MANUAL RANGE
MIN/MAX RECORDING
TOGGLE BUTTON
BACKLIGHT
Ω = OHMS (RESISTANCE)
$\overline{\overline{mV}}$ = DC MILLIVOLTS
$\overline{\overline{V}}$ = DC VOLTS
$\widetilde{V}$ = AC VOLTS
TEST SELECTOR

DIGITAL DISPLAY
CONTINUITY BEEPER
RELATIVE READING
FREQUENCY AND DUTY CYCLE
⊬ = DIODE TEST
$\overset{mA}{A} \overset{\sim}{=}$ = AC OR DC AMPERES MILLIAMPERES
$\mu A \overset{\sim}{=}$ = AC OR DC MICROAMPERES

A   mAμA   COM   VΩ⊬

BLACK
RED

AMPERES INPUT TERMINAL
MILLIAMP/MICROAMP INPUT TERMINAL
VOLTS, OHMS, DIODE CHECK INPUT TERMINAL
COMMON TERMINAL

FIGURE 9–28 Typical digital multimeter. The black meter lead always is placed in the COM terminal. The red meter test lead should be in the volt-ohm terminal except when measuring current in amperes.

DIGITAL METERS

TERMINOLOGY Digital multimeter (DMM) and digital volt-ohm-meter (DVOM) are terms commonly used to describe digital meters. ● **SEE FIGURE 9–28**.

The common abbreviations for the units that many meters can measure are often confusing. ● **SEE CHART 9–1** for the most commonly used symbols and their meanings.

MEASURING VOLTAGE A **voltmeter** measures the pressure or potential of electricity in units of volts. A voltmeter is connected to a circuit in parallel. Voltage can be measured by selecting either AC or DC volts.

- *DC volts (DCV).* This setting is the most common for automotive use. Use this setting to measure battery voltage and voltage to all lighting and accessory circuits.

- *AC volts (ACV).* This setting is used to check some computer sensors and to check for unwanted AC voltage from alternators.

SYMBOL	MEANING
AC	Alternating current or voltage
DC	Direct current or voltage
V	Volts
mV	Millivolts (1/1,000 volts)
A	Ampere (amps), current
mA	Milliampere (1/1,000 amps)
%	Percent (for duty cycle readings only)
Ω	Ohms, resistance
kΩ	Kilohm (1,000 ohms), resistance
MΩ	Megohm (1,000,000 ohms), resistance
Hz	Hertz (cycles per second), frequency
kHz	Kilohertz (1,000 cycles/sec.), frequency
Ms	Milliseconds (1/1,000 sec.) for pulse width measurements

CHART 9–1

Common symbols and abbreviations used on digital meters.

- *Range.* The range is automatically set for most meters but can be manually adjusted if needed. ● **SEE FIGURES 9–29 AND 9–30.**

FIGURE 9–29 Typical digital multimeter (DMM) set to read DC volts.

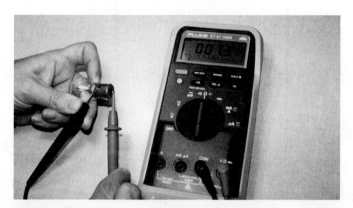

FIGURE 9–31 Using a digital multimeter set to read ohms (Ω) to test this light bulb. The meter reads the resistance of the filament.

MEASURING RESISTANCE An **ohmmeter** measures the resistance in ohms of a component or circuit section when no current is flowing through the circuit. An ohmmeter contains a battery (or other power source) and is connected in parallel with the component or wire being measured. Note the following facts about using an ohmmeter.

- Zero ohms on the scale means that there is no resistance between the test leads, thus indicating continuity or a continuous path for the current to flow in a closed circuit.
- Infinity means no connection, as in an open circuit.
- Ohmmeters have no required polarity even though red and black test leads are used for resistance measurement.

Different meters have different ways of indicating infinity resistance, or a reading higher than the scale allows. Examples of an over-limit display include the following:

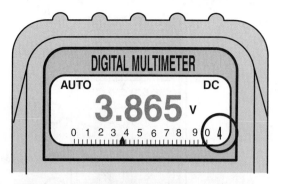

BECAUSE THE SIGNAL READING IS BELOW 4 VOLTS, THE METER AUTORANGES TO THE 4-VOLT SCALE. IN THE 4-VOLT SCALE, THIS METER PROVIDES THREE DECIMAL PLACES.

(a)

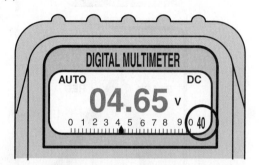

WHEN THE VOLTAGE EXCEEDED 4 VOLTS, THE METER AUTORANGES INTO THE 40-VOLT SCALE. THE DECIMAL POINT MOVES ONE PLACE TO THE RIGHT LEAVING ONLY TWO DECIMAL PLACES.

(b)

FIGURE 9–30 A typical autoranging digital multimeter automatically selects the proper scale to read the voltage being tested. The scale selected is usually displayed on the meter face. (a) Note that the display indicates "4," meaning that this range can read up to 4 volts. (b) The range is now set to the 40 volt scale, meaning that the meter can read up to 40 volts on the scale. Any reading above this level will cause the meter to reset to a higher scale. If not set on autoranging, the meter display would indicate OL if a reading exceeds the limit of the scale selected.

- OL, meaning over limit or overload
- Flashing or solid number 1
- Flashing or solid number 3 on the left side of the display

Check the meter instructions for the exact display used to indicate an open circuit or over-range reading. ● **SEE FIGURES 9–31 AND 9–32.**

To summarize, open and zero readings are as follows:

0.00 Ω = Zero resistance (component or circuit has continuity)

OL = An open circuit (no current flows) or the reading is higher than the scale selected.

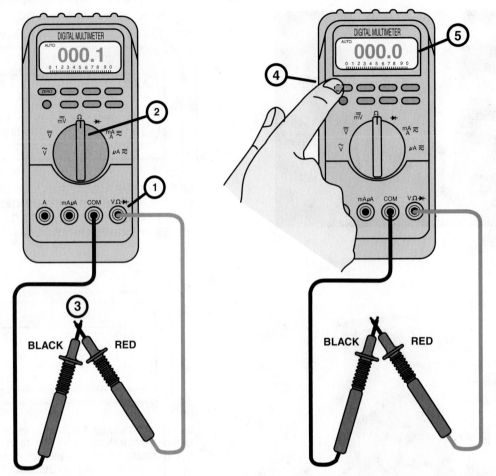

FIGURE 9–32 Many digital multimeters can have the display indicate zero to compensate for test lead resistance. (1) Connect leads in the V Ω and COM meter terminals. (2) Select the Ω scale. (3) Touch the two meter leads together. (4) Push the "zero" or "relative" button on the meter. (5) The meter display will now indicate zero ohms of resistance.

MEASURING AMPERES

An **ammeter** measures the flow of current through a complete circuit in units of amperes or milliamperes (1/1,000 of an ampere). The ammeter has to be installed in the circuit (in series) so that it can measure all the current flow in that circuit, just as a water flow meter would measure the amount of water flow (cubic feet per minute, for example). ● SEE FIGURE 9–33.

CAUTION: An ammeter must be installed in series with the circuit to measure the current flow in the circuit. If a meter set to read amperes is connected in parallel, such as across a battery, the meter or the leads may be destroyed, or the fuse will blow, by the current available across the battery. Some DMMs beep if the unit selection does not match the test lead connection on the meter. However, in a noisy shop, this beep sound may be inaudible.

Digital meters require that the meter leads be moved to the ammeter terminals. Most digital meters have an ampere scale that can accommodate a maximum of 10 amperes. See the Tech Tip "Fuse Your Meter Leads!"

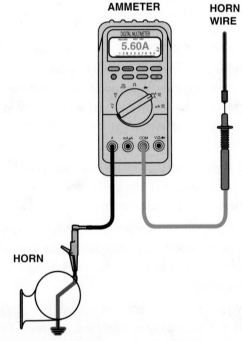

FIGURE 9–33 Measuring the current flow required by a horn requires that the ammeter be connected to the circuit in series and the horn button be depressed by an assistant.

Fuse Your Meter Leads!

Most digital meters include an ammeter capability. When reading amperes, the leads of the meter must be changed from volts or ohms (V or Ω) to amperes (A) or milliamperes (mA). A common problem may then occur the next time voltage is measured.

Although the technician may switch the selector to read volts, often the leads are not switched back to the volt or ohm position. Because the ammeter lead position results in zero ohms of resistance to current flow through the meter, the meter or the fuse inside the meter will be destroyed if the meter is connected to a battery. Many meter fuses are expensive and difficult to find. To avoid this problem, simply solder an inline 10 ampere blade-fuse holder into one meter lead. ● **SEE FIGURE 9–34.**

Do not think that this technique is for beginners only. Experienced technicians often in a hurry forget to switch the lead. A blade fuse is faster, easier, and less expensive to replace than a meter fuse or the meter itself. Also, if the soldering is done properly, the addition of an inline fuse holder and fuse does not increase the resistance of the meter leads. All meter leads have some resistance. If the meter is measuring very low resistance, touch the two leads together and read the resistance (usually no more than 0.2 ohm). Simply subtract the resistance of the leads from the resistance of the component being measured.

FIGURE 9–34 Note the blade-type fuse holder soldered in series with one of the meter leads. A 10 ampere fuse helps protect the internal meter fuse (if equipped) and the meter itself from damage that may result from excessive current flow if accidentally used incorrectly.

FIGURE 9–35 An inductive ammeter clamp is used with all starting and charging testers to measure the current flow through the battery cables.

FIGURE 9–36 A typical mini clamp-on-type digital multimeter. This meter is capable of measuring alternating current (AC) and direct current (DC) without requiring that the circuit be disconnected to install the meter in series. The jaws are simply placed over the wire and current flow through the circuit is displayed.

INDUCTIVE AMMETERS

OPERATION Inductive ammeters do not make physical contact with the circuit. Inductive ammeters have the advantage of being able to read much higher amperages than 10 amperes. A sensor is used to detect the strength of the magnetic field surrounding the wire carrying the current. The ammeter then uses the strength of the magnetic field to measure the electrical current. ● **SEE FIGURE 9–35.**

AC/DC CLAMP-ON DIGITAL MULTIMETERS An AC/DC clamp-on digital multimeter is a useful meter for automotive diagnostic work. ● **SEE FIGURE 9–36.**

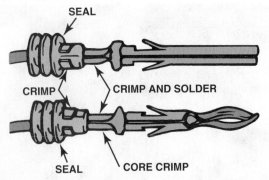

FIGURE 9–37 Some terminals have seals attached to help seal the electrical connections.

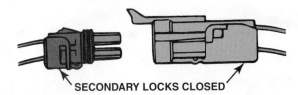

FIGURE 9–38 Separate a connector by opening the lock and pulling the two apart.

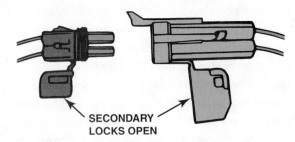

FIGURE 9–39 The secondary locks help retain the terminals in the connector.

The major advantage of the clamp-on-type meter is that there is no need to break the circuit to measure current (amperes). Simply clamp the jaws of the meter around the power lead(s) or ground lead(s) of the component being measured and read the display. Most clamp-on meters can also measure alternating current, which is helpful in the diagnosis of an alternator problem. Volts, ohms, frequency, and temperature can also be measured with the typical clamp-on DMM, but conventional meter leads should be used. The inductive clamp is used to measure only amperes.

THINK OF MONEY Digital meter displays can often be confusing. The display for a battery measured as 12 1/2 volts would be 12.50 V, just as $12.50 is 12 dollars and 50 cents. A 1/2 volt reading on a digital meter will be displayed as 0.50 V, just as $0.50 is half of a dollar. It is more confusing when low values are displayed. For example, if a voltage reading is 0.063 volt, an auto-ranging meter will display 63 millivolts (63 mV), or 63/1,000 of a volt, just like $63 of $1,000. (It takes 1,000 mV to equal 1 volt.) Think of millivolts as one-tenth of a cent, with 1 volt being $1.00. Therefore, 630 millivolts are equal to $0.63 of $1.00 (630 tenths of a cent, or 63 cents). To avoid confusion, try to manually range the meter to read base units (whole volts).

If the meter is ranged to base unit volts, 63 millivolts would be displayed as 0.063 or maybe just 0.06, depending on the display capabilities of the meter.

TERMINALS AND CONNECTORS

TERMINOLOGY A **terminal** is a metal fastener attached to the end of a wire, which makes the electrical connection. The term **connector** usually refers to the plastic portion that snaps or connects together, thereby making the mechanical connection. Wire terminal ends usually snap into and are held

by a connector. Male and female connectors can then be snapped together, thereby completing an electrical connection. Connectors exposed to the environment are also equipped with a weather-tight seal. ● SEE FIGURE 9–37.

SERVICING TERMINALS Terminals are retained in connectors by the use of a lock tang. Removing a terminal from a connector includes the following steps.

STEP 1 Release the connector position assurance (CPA), if equipped, that keeps the latch of the connector from releasing accidentally.

STEP 2 Separate the male and female connector by opening the lock. ● SEE FIGURE 9–38.

STEP 3 Release the secondary lock, if equipped. ● SEE FIGURE 9–39.

STEP 4 Using a pick, look for the slot in the plastic connector where the lock tang is located, depress the lock tang, and gently remove the terminal from the connector. ● SEE FIGURE 9–40.

WIRE REPAIR

SOLDERING Many manufacturers recommend that all wiring repairs be soldered. Solder is an alloy of tin and lead used to make a good electrical contact between two wires or connections in an electrical circuit. However, a flux must be used to help clean the area and to help make the solder flow. Therefore, solder is made with a resin (rosin) contained in the center, called *rosin-core solder*.

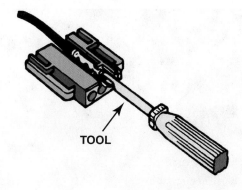

TOOL

RAISING RETAINING
FINGERS TO REMOVE
CONTACTS

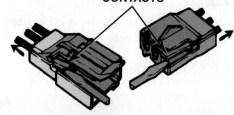

LOCKING WEDGE CONNECTOR

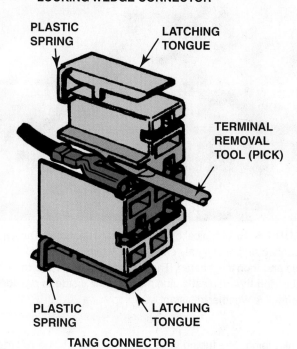

PLASTIC
SPRING

LATCHING
TONGUE

TERMINAL
REMOVAL
TOOL (PICK)

PLASTIC
SPRING

LATCHING
TONGUE

TANG CONNECTOR

FIGURE 9–40 Use a small removal tool, sometimes called a pick, to release terminals from the connector.

CAUTION: Never use acid-core solder to repair electrical wiring as the acid will cause corrosion. ● SEE FIGURE 9–41.

Solder is available with various percentages of tin and lead in the alloy. Ratios are used to identify these various types of solder, with the first number denoting the percentage of tin in the alloy and the second number giving the percentage of lead.

FIGURE 9–41 Always use rosin-core solder for electrical or electronic soldering. Also, use small-diameter solder for small soldering irons. Use large-diameter solder only for large-diameter (large-gauge) wire and higher-wattage soldering irons (guns).

The most commonly used solder is 50/50, which means that 50% of the solder is tin and the other 50% is lead. The percentages of each alloy primarily determine the melting point of the solder.

- 60/40 solder (60% tin/40% lead) melts at 361°F (183°C).
- 50/50 solder (50% tin/50% lead) melts at 421°F (216°C).
- 40/60 solder (40% tin/60% lead) melts at 460°F (238°C).

SOLDERING PROCEDURE Soldering a wiring splice includes the following steps.

STEP 1 While touching the soldering gun to the splice, apply solder to the junction of the gun and the wire.

STEP 2 The solder will start to flow. Do not move the soldering gun.

STEP 3 Just keep feeding more solder into the splice as it flows into and around the strands of the wire.

STEP 4 After the solder has flowed throughout the splice, remove the soldering gun and the solder from the splice and allow the solder to cool slowly.

The solder should have a shiny appearance. Dull-looking solder may be caused by not reaching a high enough temperature, which results in a cold solder joint. Reheating the splice and allowing it to cool often restores the shiny appearance.

CRIMPING TERMINALS Terminals can be crimped to create a good electrical connection if the proper type of crimping tool is used. Most vehicle manufacturers recommend

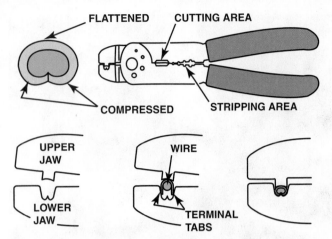

FIGURE 9–42 Notice that to create a good crimp, the open part of the terminal is placed in the jaws of the crimping tool toward the anvil or the W-shape part.

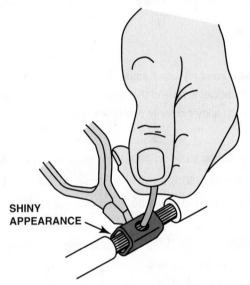

FIGURE 9–43 All hand-crimped splices or terminals should be soldered to be assured of a good electrical connection.

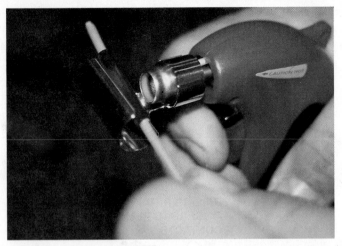

FIGURE 9–44 A butane torch especially designed for use on heat shrink applies heat without an open flame, which could cause damage.

FIGURE 9–45 A typical crimp-and-seal connector. This type of connector is first lightly crimped to retain the ends of the wires and then it is heated. The tubing shrinks around the wire splice, and thermoplastic glue melts on the inside to provide an effective weather-resistant seal.

that a W-shaped crimp be used to force the strands of the wire into a tight space. ● SEE FIGURE 9–42.

Most vehicle manufacturers also specify that all hand-crimped terminals or splices be soldered. ● SEE FIGURE 9–43.

HEAT SHRINK TUBING Heat shrink tubing is usually made from polyvinyl chloride (PVC) or polyolefin and shrinks to about half of its original diameter when heated; this is usually called a 2:1 shrink ratio. Heat shrink by itself does not provide protection against corrosion, because the ends of the tubing are not sealed against moisture. Chrysler Corporation recommends that all wire repairs that may be exposed to the elements be repaired and sealed using adhesive-lined heat shrink tubing. The tubing is usually made from flame-retardant flexible polyolefin with an internal layer of special thermoplastic adhesive. When heated, this tubing shrinks to one-third of its original diameter (3:1 shrink ratio) and the adhesive melts and seals the ends of the tubing. ● SEE FIGURE 9–44.

CRIMP-AND-SEAL CONNECTORS Several vehicle manufacturers recommend the use of crimp-and-seal connectors as the method for wire repair. **Crimp-and-seal connectors** contain a sealant and shrink tubing in one piece and are not simply butt connectors. ● SEE FIGURE 9–45.

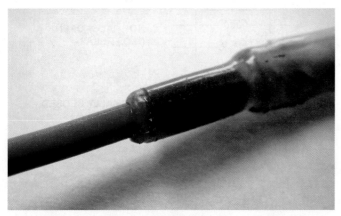

FIGURE 9–46 Heating the crimp-and-seal connector melts the glue and forms an effective seal against moisture.

The usual procedure specified for making a wire repair using a crimp-and-seal connector is as follows:

STEP 1 Strip the insulation from the ends of the wire (about 5/16 inch or 8 mm).

STEP 2 Select the proper size of crimp-and-seal connector for the gauge of wire being repaired. Insert the wires into the splice sleeve and crimp.

NOTE: Use only the specified crimping tool to help prevent the pliers from creating a hole in the cover.

STEP 3 Apply heat to the connector until the sleeve shrinks down around the wire and a small amount of sealant is observed around the ends of the sleeve, as shown in ● **FIGURE 9–46.**

RELAYS

DEFINITION   A **relay** is a magnetic switch that uses a movable armature to control a high-amperage circuit by using a low-amperage electrical switch.

TERMINAL IDENTIFICATION   Most automotive relays adhere to common terminal identification. The primary source for this common identification comes from the standards established by the International Standards Organization (ISO). Knowing this terminal information will help in the correct diagnosis and troubleshooting of any circuit containing a relay. ● **SEE FIGURES 9–47 AND 9–48.**

Relays are found in many circuits because they are capable of being controlled by computers, yet are able to

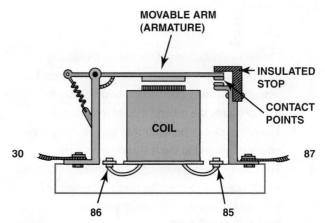

86 - POWER SIDE OF THE COIL
85 - GROUND SIDE OF THE COIL

(MOSTLY RELAY COILS HAVE BETWEEN 60–100 OHMS OF RESISTANCE)

30 - COMMON POWER FOR RELAY CONTACTS
87 - NORMALLY OPEN OUTPUT (N.O.)
87a - NORMALLY CLOSED OUTPUT (N.C.)

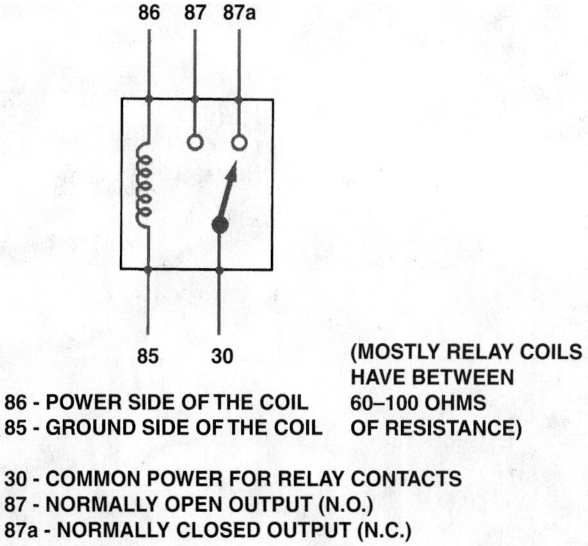

FIGURE 9–47 A relay uses a movable arm to complete a circuit whenever there is a power at terminal 86 and a ground at terminal 85. A typical relay only requires about 1/10 ampere through the relay coil. The movable arm then closes the contacts (#30 to #87) and can often handle 30 amperes or more.

FIGURE 9–48 A cross-sectional view of a typical four-terminal relay. Current flowing through the coil (terminals 86 and 85) causes the movable arm (called the armature) to be drawn toward the coil magnet. The contact points complete the electrical circuit connected to terminals 30 and 87.

handle enough current to power motors and accessories. Relays include the following components and terminals.

1. Coil (terminals 85 and 86)
   - A coil provides the magnetic pull to a movable armature (arm).
   - The resistance of most relay coils is usually between 60 ohms and 100 ohms.

FIGURE 9–49 A typical relay showing the schematic of the wiring in the relay.

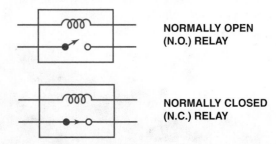

NORMALLY OPEN (N.O.) RELAY

NORMALLY CLOSED (N.C.) RELAY

FIGURE 9–50 On schematics, relays are shown in their normal, non energized position.

- The ISO identification of the coil terminals are 86 and 85. The terminal number 86 represents the power to the relay coil and the terminal labeled 85 represents the ground side of the relay coil.
- The relay coil can be controlled by supplying either power or ground to the relay coil winding.
- The coil winding represents the control circuit, which uses low current to control the higher current through the other terminals of the relay.
  ● SEE FIGURE 9–49.

2. Other terminals used to control the load current

- The higher amperage current flow through a relay flows through terminals 30 and 87, and often 87a.
- If there is power at terminal 85 and a ground at terminal 86 of the relay, a magnetic field is created in the coil winding, which draws the armature of the relay toward the coil. The armature, when energized electrically, connects terminals 30 and 87.

The maximum current through the relay is determined by the resistance of the circuit, and relays are designed to safely handle the designed current flow. ● SEE FIGURES 9–50 AND 9–51.

TECH TIP

Divide the Circuit in Half

When diagnosing any circuit that has a relay, start testing at the relay and divide the circuit in half.

- **High current portion**: Remove the relay and check that there are 12 volts at the terminal 30 socket. If there is, then the power side is okay. Use an ohmmeter and check between terminal 87 socket and ground. If the load circuit has continuity, there should be some resistance. If OL, the circuit is electrically open.

- **Control circuit (low current):** With the relay removed from the socket, check that there is 12 volts to terminal 86 with the ignition on and the control switch on. If not, check service information to see if power should be applied to terminal 86, then continue troubleshooting the switch power and related circuit.

- **Check the relay itself**: Use an ohmmeter and measure for continuity and resistance.

- Between terminals 85 and 86 (coil), there should be 60 ohms to 100 ohms. If not, replace the relay.

- Between terminals 30 and 87 (high-amperage switch controls), there should be continuity (low ohms) when there is power applied to terminal 85 and a ground applied to terminal 86 that operates the relay. If "OL" is displayed on the meter set to read ohms, the circuit is open, which requires that the reply be replaced.

- Between terminals 30 and 87a (if equipped), with the relay turned off, there should be low resistance (less than 5 ohms).

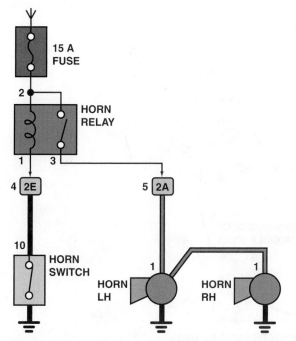

FIGURE 9–51 A typical horn circuit. Note that the relay contacts supply the heavy current to operate the horn when the horn switch simply completes a low-current circuit to ground, causing the relay contacts to close.

NEED FOR NETWORK Since the 1990s, vehicles have used modules to control the operation of most electrical components. A typical vehicle will have 10 or more modules and they communicate with each other over data lines or hard wiring, depending on the application. ● SEE FIGURE 9–52.

MODULES AND NODES Each module, also called a **node**, must communicate with other modules. For example, if the driver depresses the window-down switch, the power window switch sends a window-down message to the body control module. The body control module then sends the request to the driver's side window module. This module is responsible for actually performing the task by supplying power and ground to the window lift motor in the current polarity to cause the window to go down. The module also

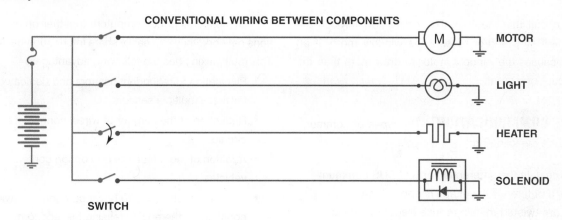

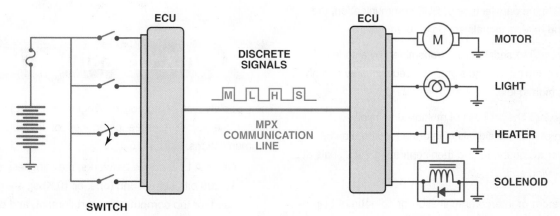

FIGURE 9–52 Module communications makes controlling multiple electrical devices and accessories easier by using simple low-current switches to signal another electronic control module (ECM), which does the actual switching of the current to the device.

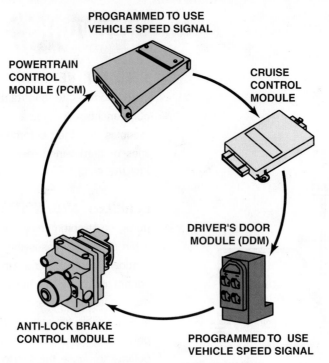

PROGRAMMED TO USE
VEHICLE SPEED SIGNAL

POWERTRAIN
CONTROL
MODULE (PCM)

CRUISE
CONTROL
MODULE

DRIVER'S DOOR
MODULE (DDM)

ANTI-LOCK BRAKE
CONTROL MODULE

PROGRAMMED TO USE
VEHICLE SPEED SIGNAL

FIGURE 9–53 A network allows all modules to communicate with other modules.

contains a circuit that monitors the current flow through the motor and will stop and/or reverse the window motor if an obstruction causes the window motor to draw more than the normal amount of current.

TYPES OF COMMUNICATION
The types of communications include the following:

- *Differential.* In the differential form of BUS communication, a difference in voltage is applied to two wires, which are twisted to help reduce electromagnetic interference (EMI). These transfer wires are called a twisted pair.

- *Parallel.* In the parallel type of BUS communication, the send and receive signals are on different wires.

- *Serial data.* The serial data is transmitted by a series of rapidly changing voltage signals pulsed from low to high or from high to low.

- *Multiplexing.* The process of multiplexing involves sending of multiple signals of information at the same time over a signal wire and then separating the signals at the receiving end.

This system of intercommunication of computers or processors is referred to as a network. ● **SEE FIGURE 9–53**.

By connecting the computers together on a communications network, they can easily share information back and forth. This multiplexing has the following advantages.

- Elimination of redundant sensors and dedicated wiring for these multiple sensors
- Reduction of the number of wires, connectors, and circuits
- Addition of more features and option content to new vehicles
- Weight reduction due to fewer components, wires, and connectors, thereby increasing fuel economy
- Changeable features with software upgrades versus component replacement

NETWORK CLASSIFICATIONS

The Society of Automotive Engineers (SAE) standards include the following three categories of in-vehicle network communications.

Class A Low-speed networks, meaning less than 10,000 bits per second (bps, or 10 Kbs), are generally used for trip computers, entertainment, and other convenience features.

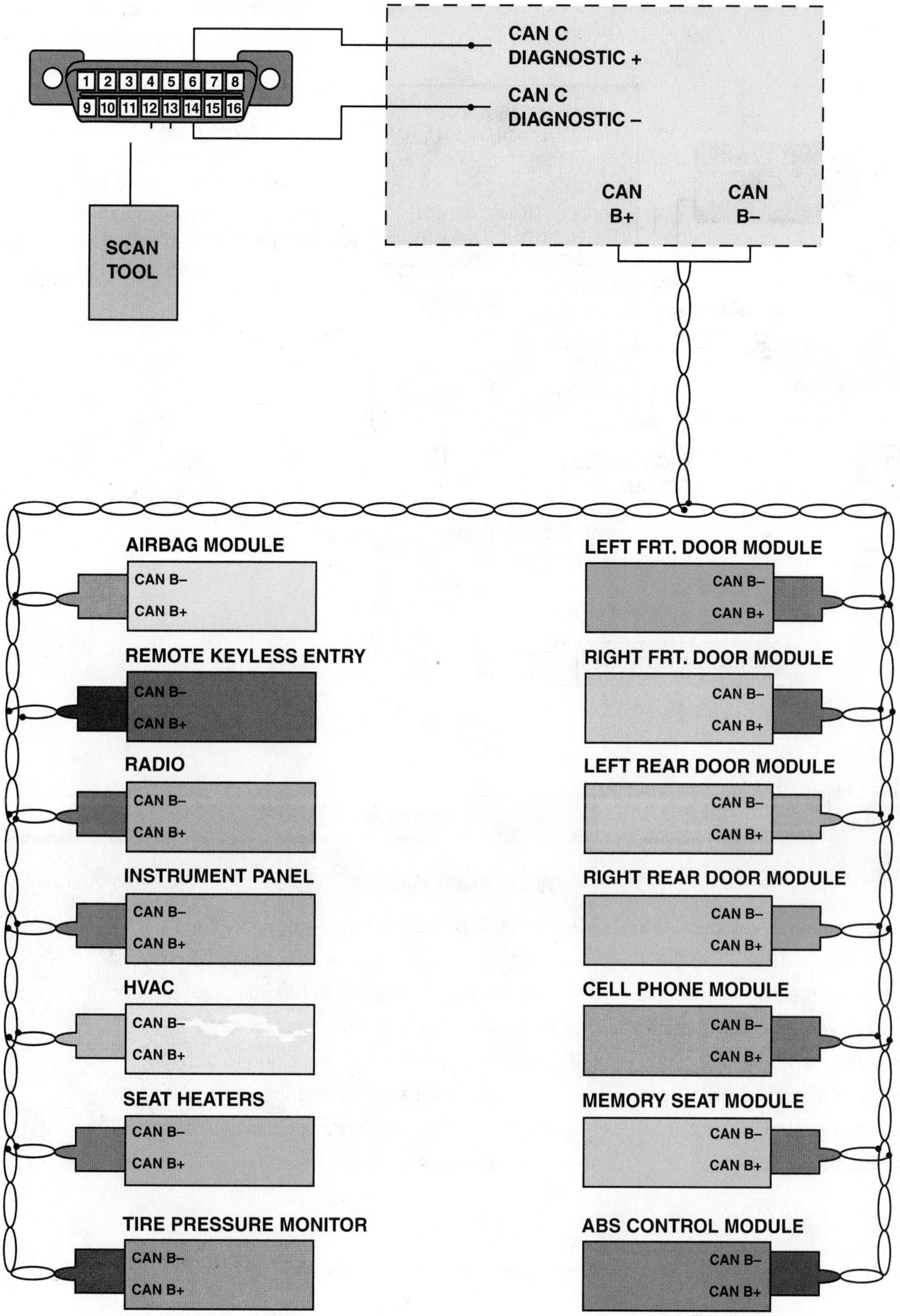

FIGURE 9–54 A typical BUS system showing module CAN communications and twisted pairs of wire.

Class B Medium-speed networks, meaning 10,000 bps to 125,000 bps (10 Kbs to 125 Kbs), are generally used for information transfer among modules, such as instrument clusters, temperature sensor data, and other general uses.

Class C High-speed networks, meaning 125,000 bps to 1,000,000 bps, are generally used for real-time powertrain and vehicle dynamic control. High-speed BUS communication systems now use a controller area network (CAN). ● **SEE FIGURE 9–54.**

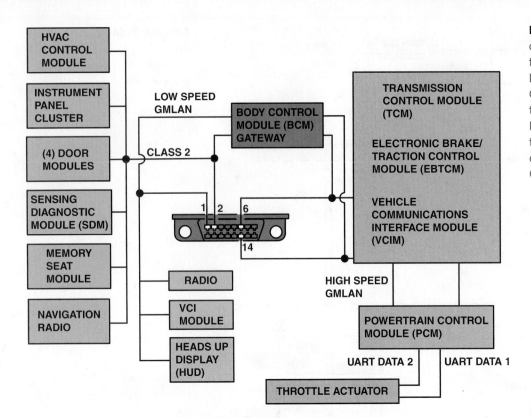

HVAC CONTROL MODULE

INSTRUMENT PANEL CLUSTER

(4) DOOR MODULES

SENSING DIAGNOSTIC MODULE (SDM)

MEMORY SEAT MODULE

NAVIGATION RADIO

LOW SPEED GMLAN

CLASS 2

BODY CONTROL MODULE (BCM) GATEWAY

RADIO

VCI MODULE

HEADS UP DISPLAY (HUD)

TRANSMISSION CONTROL MODULE (TCM)

ELECTRONIC BRAKE/ TRACTION CONTROL MODULE (EBTCM)

VEHICLE COMMUNICATIONS INTERFACE MODULE (VCIM)

HIGH SPEED GMLAN

POWERTRAIN CONTROL MODULE (PCM)

UART DATA 2   UART DATA 1

THROTTLE ACTUATOR

1 2   6

14

FIGURE 9–55 A schematic of a Chevrolet Equinox shows that the vehicle uses a GMLAN BUS (DLC pins 6 and 14), plus a Class 2 (pin 2). A scan tool can therefore communicate to the HVAC control module through the high-speed network. Pin 1 connects to the low-speed GMLAN network.

CONTROLLER AREA NETWORK

STANDARD Robert Bosch Corporation developed the CAN protocol, which was called CAN 1.2, in 1993. The CAN protocol was approved by the Environmental Protection Agency (EPA) for 2003 and newer vehicle diagnostics, and a legal requirement for all vehicles by 2008. The CAN diagnostic systems use pins 6 and 14 in the standard 16 pin OBD-II (J-1962) connector. Before CAN, the scan tool protocol had been manufacturer specific. ● **SEE FIGURE 9–55.**

? FREQUENTLY ASKED QUESTION

What Are U Codes?

The "U" diagnostic trouble codes were at first "undefined" but are now network-related codes. Use the network codes to help pinpoint the circuit or module that is not working correctly. Some powertrain-related faults are due to network communications errors and therefore can be detected by looking for "U" diagnostic trouble codes (DTCs).

SUMMARY

1. Electricity is the movement of electrons from one atom to another.

2. In order for current to flow in a circuit or wire, there must be an excess of electrons at one end and a deficiency of electrons at the other end.

3. Automotive electricity uses the conventional theory that electricity flows from positive to negative.

4. The ampere is the measure of the amount of current flow.

5. Voltage is the unit of electrical pressure.

6. The ohm is the unit of electrical resistance.

7. All complete electrical circuits have a power source (such as a battery), a circuit protection device (such as a fuse), a power-side wire or path, an electrical load, a ground return path, and a switch or a control device.

8. A short-to-voltage involves a copper-to-copper connection and usually affects more than one circuit.

9. A short-to-ground usually involves a power path conductor coming in contact with a return (ground) path conductor and usually causes the fuse to blow.

10. An open is a break in the circuit resulting in absolutely no current flow through the circuit.

11. Circuit testers include test lights and fused jumper leads.

12. Digital multimeter (DMM) and digital volt-ohm-meter (DVOM) are terms commonly used for electronic test meters.

13. Ammeters measure current and must be connected in series in the circuit.

14. Voltmeters measure voltage and are connected in parallel.

15. Ohmmeters measure resistance of a component and must be connected in parallel with the circuit or component disconnected from power.

16. A terminal is the metal end of a wire, whereas a connector is the plastic housing for the terminal.

17. All wire repair should use either soldering or a crimp-and-seal connector.

18. All switches and relays on a schematic are shown in their normal position either normally closed (N.C.) or normally open (N.O.).

19. A typical relay uses a small current through a coil (terminals 85 and 86) to operate the higher current part (terminals 30 and 87).

20. The use of a network for module communications reduces the number of wires and connections needed.

21. The SAE communication classifications for vehicle communications systems include Class A (low speed), Class B (medium speed), and Class C (high speed).

REVIEW QUESTIONS

1. What are ampere, volt, and ohm?

2. What is included in a complete electrical circuit?

3. Why must an ohmmeter be connected to a disconnected circuit or component?

4. List and identify the terminals of a typical ISO type relay.

5. Why is a communication network used?

CHAPTER QUIZ

1. An electrical conductor is an element with _____ electrons in its outer orbit.
   a. Less than 2
   b. Less than 4
   c. Exactly 4
   d. More than 4

2. Like charges _____.
   a. Attract each other
   b. Repel each other
   c. Neutralize each other
   d. Add

3. If an insulated wire gets rubbed through a part of the insulation and the wire conductor touches the steel body of a vehicle, the type of failure would be called a(n) _____.
   a. Short-to-voltage
   b. Short-to-ground
   c. Open
   d. Chassis ground

4. High resistance in an electrical circuit can cause _____.
   a. Dim lights
   b. Slow motor operation
   c. Clicking of relays or solenoids
   d. All of the above

5. If two power-side insulated wires were to melt together at the point where the copper conductors touched each other, the type of failure would be called a(n) _____.
   a. Short-to-voltage
   b. Short-to-ground
   c. Open
   d. Floating ground

6. When testing a relay using an ohmmeter, which two terminals should be touched to measure the coil resistance?
   a. 87 and 30
   b. 86 and 85
   c. 87a and 87
   d. 86 and 87

7. Technician A says that a good relay should measure between 60 ohms and 100 ohms across the coil terminals. Technician B says that OL should be displayed on an ohmmeter when touching terminals 30 and 87. Which technician is correct?
   a. Technician A only
   b. Technician B only
   c. Both Technicians A and B
   d. Neither Technician A nor B

8. If a wire repair, such as that made under the hood or under the vehicle, is exposed to the elements, which type of repair should be used?
   a. Wire nuts and electrical tape
   b. Solder and adhesive-lined heat shrink or crimp-and-seal connectors
   c. Butt connectors
   d. Rosin-core solder and electrical tape

9. A module is also known as a _____.
   a. BUS
   b. Node
   c. Terminator
   d. Resistor pack

10. A high-speed CAN BUS communicates with a scan tool through which terminal(s)?
    a. 6 and 14
    b. 2
    c. 7 and 15
    d. 4 and 16

chapter 10
COOLING SYSTEM OPERATION AND DIAGNOSIS

LEARNING OBJECTIVES

After studying this chapter, the reader should be able to:

1. Explain the purpose and function of the cooling system and cooling system operation.

2. Explain the purpose of thermostats, radiators, pressure caps, and water pumps.

3. Explain coolant flow in the engine and coolant recovery systems.

4. Explain the purpose of cooling fans and heater cores.

5. Describe cooling system testing and explain the purpose of the coolant temperature warning light.

6. Explain cooling system inspection and cooling system service.

KEY TERMS

Bar 169
Bleed holes 173
Bypass 165
Centrifugal pump 171
Coolant recovery system 170
Cooling fins 168
Core tubes 168
Impeller 171
Parallel flow system 172

Reverse cooling 171
Scroll 171
Series flow system 173
Series–parallel flow system 173
Silicone coupling 174
Steam slits 173
Surge tank 170
Thermostatic spring 174

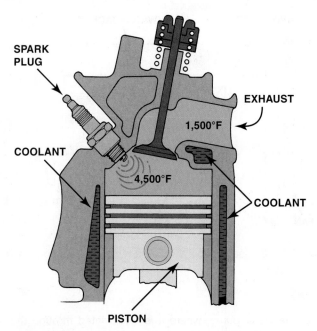

SPARK PLUG

EXHAUST

1,500°F

COOLANT

4,500°F

COOLANT

PISTON

FIGURE 10–1 Typical combustion and exhaust temperatures.

COOLING SYSTEM

PURPOSE AND FUNCTION Satisfactory cooling system operation depends on the design and operating conditions of the system. The design is based on heat output of the engine, radiator size, type of coolant, size of water pump (coolant pump), type of fan, thermostat, and system pressure. The cooling system must allow the engine to warm up to the required operating temperature as rapidly as possible and then maintain that temperature.

Peak combustion temperatures in the engine run from 4,000°F to 6,000°F (2,200°C to 3,300°C). The combustion temperatures will *average* between 1,200°F and 1,700°F (650°C and 925°C). Continued temperatures as high as this would weaken engine parts, so heat must be removed from the engine. The cooling system keeps the head and cylinder walls at a temperature that is within the range for maximum efficiency. The cooling system removes about one-third of the heat created in the engine. Another third escapes to the exhaust system. ● **SEE FIGURE 10–1.**

LOW-TEMPERATURE ENGINE PROBLEMS Engine operating temperatures must be above a minimum temperature for proper engine operation. If the coolant temperature does not reach the specified temperature as determined by the thermostat, then the following engine-related faults can occur.

TECH TIP

Overheating Can Be Expensive

A faulty cooling system seems to be a major cause of engine failure. Engine rebuilders often have nightmares about seeing their rebuilt engine placed back in service in a vehicle with a clogged radiator. Most engine technicians routinely replace the water pump and all hoses after an engine overhaul or repair. The radiator should also be checked for leaks and proper flow whenever the engine is repaired or replaced. Overheating is one of the most common causes of engine failure.

- A P0128 diagnostic trouble code (DTC) can be set. This code indicates "coolant temperature below thermostat regulating temperature," which is usually caused by a defective thermostat staying open or partially open.

- Moisture created during the combustion process can condense and flow into the oil. *For each gallon of fuel used, moisture equal to a gallon of water is produced.* The condensed moisture combines with unburned hydrocarbons and additives to form carbonic acid, sulfuric acid, nitric acid, hydrobromic acid, and hydrochloric acid.

To reduce cold engine problems and to help start engines in cold climates, most manufacturers offer block heaters as an option. These block heaters are plugged into household current (110 volts AC) and the heating element warms the coolant.

HIGH-TEMPERATURE ENGINE PROBLEMS Maximum temperature limits are required to protect the engine. Higher than normal temperatures can cause the following engine-related issues.

- High temperatures will oxidize the engine oil producing hard carbon and varnish. The varnish will cause the hydraulic valve lifter plungers to stick. Higher than normal temperatures will also cause the oil to become thinner (lower viscosity than normal). Thinned oil will also get into the combustion chamber by going past the piston rings and through valve guides to cause excessive oil consumption.

- The combustion process is very sensitive to temperature. High coolant temperatures raise the combustion temperatures to a point that may cause detonation (also called spark knock or ping) to occur.

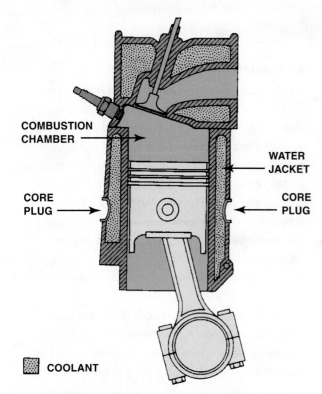

FIGURE 10–2 Coolant circulates through the water jackets in the engine block and cylinder head.

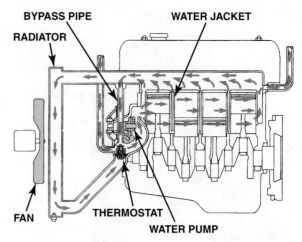

FIGURE 10–3 Coolant flow through a typical engine cooling system.

COOLING SYSTEM OPERATION

PURPOSE AND FUNCTION Coolant flows through the engine, where it picks up heat. It then flows to the radiator, where the heat is given up to the outside air. The coolant continually recirculates through the cooling system, as illustrated in ● **FIGURES 10–2 AND 10–3.**

COOLING SYSTEM OPERATION The temperature of the coolant rises as much as 15°F (8°C) as it goes through the engine and cools as it goes through the radiator. *The coolant flow rate may be as high as 1 gallon (4 liters) per minute for each horsepower the engine produces.*

Hot coolant comes out of the thermostat housing on the top of the engine on most engines. The engine coolant outlet is connected to the radiator by the upper radiator hose and clamps. The coolant in the radiator is cooled by air flowing through the radiator. As the coolant moves through the radiator, it cools. The cooler coolant leaves the radiator through an outlet at the lower radiator hose, and then flows to the inlet side of the water pump, where it is recirculated through the engine.

NOTE: Some newer engine designs such as Chrysler's 4.7 liter V-8 and General Motor's 4.8 liter, 5.3 liter, 5.7 liter, and 6.0 liter V-8s place the thermostat on the inlet side of the water pump. As the cooled coolant hits the thermostat, the thermostat closes until the coolant temperature again causes it to open. Placing the thermostat in the inlet side of the water pump therefore reduces the rapid temperature changes that could cause stress in the engine, especially if aluminum heads are used with a cast iron block.

Radiators are designed for the maximum rate of heat transfer using minimum space. Cooling airflow through the radiator is aided by a belt- or electric motor–driven cooling fan.

THERMOSTATS

PURPOSE AND FUNCTION There is a normal operating temperature range between low-temperature and high-temperature extremes. The thermostat controls the minimum normal temperature. The thermostat is a temperature-controlled valve placed at the engine coolant outlet on most engines.

THERMOSTAT OPERATION An encapsulated wax-based plastic pellet heat sensor is located on the engine side of the thermostatic valve. As the engine warms, heat swells the heat sensor. ● **SEE FIGURE 10–4.**

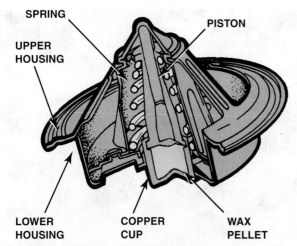

FIGURE 10–4 A cross section of a typical wax-actuated thermostat showing the position of the wax pellet and spring.

THERMOSTAT TEMPERATURE RATING	STARTS TO OPEN	FULLY OPEN
180°F	180°F	200°F
195°F	195°F	215°F

CHART 10–1

The temperature of the coolant depends on the rating of the thermostat.

A mechanical link, connected to the heat sensor, opens the thermostat valve. As the thermostat begins to open, it allows some coolant to flow to the radiator, where it is cooled. The remaining part of the coolant continues to flow through the bypass, thereby bypassing the thermostat and flowing back through the engine. ● **SEE FIGURE 10–5**.

The rated temperature of the thermostat indicates the temperature at which the thermostat starts to open. The thermostat is fully open at about 20°F higher than its opening temperature. ● **SEE CHART 10–1**.

If the radiator, water pump, and coolant passages are functioning correctly, the engine should always be operating within the opening and fully open temperature range of the thermostat. ● **SEE FIGURE 10–6**.

NOTE: A bypass around the closed thermostat allows a small part of the coolant to circulate within the engine during warm-up. It is a small passage that leads from the engine side of the thermostat to the inlet side of the water pump. It allows some coolant to bypass the

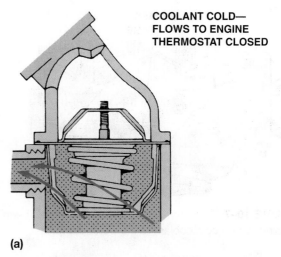

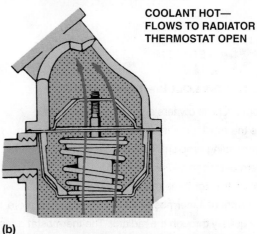

FIGURE 10–5 (a) When the engine is cold, the coolant flows through the bypass. (b) When the thermostat opens, the coolant can flow to the radiator.

FIGURE 10–6 A thermostat stuck in the open position caused the engine to operate too cold. If a thermostat is stuck closed, this can cause the engine to overheat.

thermostat even when the thermostat is open. The bypass may be cast or drilled into the engine and pump parts. ● SEE FIGURES 10–7 AND 10–8.

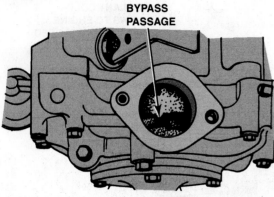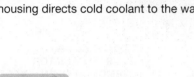

FIGURE 10–7 This internal bypass passage in the thermostat housing directs cold coolant to the water pump.

FIGURE 10–8 A cutaway of a small block Chevrolet V-8 showing the passage from the cylinder head through the front of the intake manifold to the thermostat.

The bypass aids in uniform engine warm-up. Its operation eliminates hot spots and prevents the building of excessive coolant pressure in the engine when the thermostat is closed.

THERMOSTAT TESTING   There are three basic methods used to check the operation of the thermostat.

1. **Hot water method.** If the thermostat is removed from the vehicle and is closed, insert a 0.015 inch (0.4 mm) feeler gauge in the opening so that the thermostat will hang on the feeler gauge. The thermostat should then be suspended by the feeler gauge in a container of water or coolant along with a thermometer. The container should be heated until the thermostat opens enough to release and fall from the feeler gauge. The temperature at which the thermostat falls is the opening temperature of the thermostat. If it is within 5°F (4°C) of the temperature stamped on the thermostat, the thermostat is satisfactory for use. If the temperature difference is greater, the thermostat should be replaced. ● **SEE FIGURE 10–9**.

2. **Infrared thermometer method.** An infrared thermometer (also called a pyrometer) can be used to measure the temperature of the coolant near the thermostat. The area on the engine side of the thermostat should be at the highest temperature that exists in the engine. A properly operating cooling system should cause the pyrometer to read as follows:

   ▪ As the engine warms, the temperature reaches near thermostat opening temperature.

TECH TIP

Do Not Take Out the Thermostat!

Some vehicle owners and technicians remove the thermostat in the cooling system to "cure" an overheating problem. In some cases, removing the thermostat can *cause* overheating rather than stop it. This is true for three reasons.

1. Without a thermostat the coolant can flow more quickly through the radiator. The thermostat adds some restriction to the coolant flow, and therefore keeps the coolant in the radiator longer. This also allows additional time for the heat transfer between the hot engine parts and the coolant. The presence of the thermostat thus ensures a greater reduction in the coolant temperature before it returns to the engine.

2. Heat transfer is greater with a greater difference between the coolant temperature and air temperature. Therefore, when coolant flow rate is increased (no thermostat), the temperature difference is reduced.

3. Without the restriction of the thermostat, much of the coolant flow often bypasses the radiator entirely and returns directly to the engine.

If overheating is a problem, removing the thermostat will usually not solve the problem. Remember, the thermostat controls the temperature of the engine coolant by opening at a certain temperature and closing when the temperature falls below the minimum rated temperature of the thermostat.

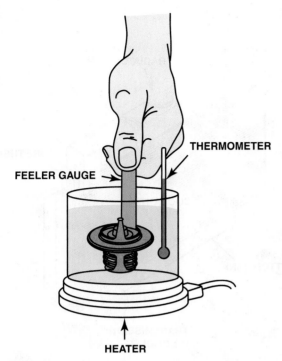

FIGURE 10–9 Checking the opening temperature of a thermostat.

- When the thermostat opens, coolant flows to the radiator.
- As the thermostat cycles, the temperature should range between the opening temperature of the thermostat and 20°F (11°C) above the opening temperature.

NOTE: If the temperature rises higher than 20°F (11°C) above the opening temperature of the thermostat, inspect the cooling system for a restriction or low coolant flow. A clogged radiator could also cause the excessive temperature rise.

3. **Scan tool method.** A scan tool can be used on many vehicles to read the actual temperature of the coolant as detected by the engine coolant temperature (ECT) sensor. Although the sensor or the wiring to and from the sensor may be defective, at least the scan tool can indicate what the computer "thinks" is the engine coolant temperature.

THERMOSTAT REPLACEMENT Two important things about a thermostat include:

1. An overheating engine *may* result from a faulty thermostat.
2. An engine that does not get warm enough *always* indicates a faulty thermostat.

FIGURE 10–10 Some thermostats are an integral part of the housing. This thermostat and radiator hose housing is serviced as an assembly. Some thermostats snap into the engine radiator fill tube underneath the pressure cap.

To replace the thermostat, coolant will have to be drained from the radiator drain petcock to lower the coolant level below the thermostat. It is not necessary to completely drain the system. The hose should be removed from the thermostat housing neck and then the housing removed to expose the thermostat. ● **SEE FIGURE 10–10.**

The gasket flanges of the engine and thermostat housing should be cleaned, and the gasket surface of the housing must be flat. The thermostat should be placed in the engine with the sensing pellet *toward* the engine. Make sure that the thermostat position is correct, and install the thermostat housing with a new gasket or O-ring.

CAUTION: Failure to set the thermostat into the recessed groove will cause the housing to become tilted when tightened. If this happens and the housing bolts are tightened, the housing will usually crack, creating a leak.

The upper hose should then be installed and the system refilled. Install the correct size of radiator hose clamp.

RADIATORS

TYPES The two types of radiator cores in common use in most vehicles are:

- Serpentine fin core
- Plate fin core

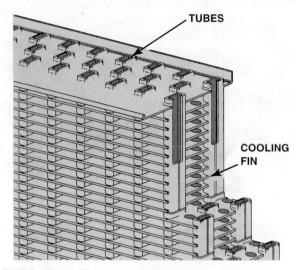

FIGURE 10–11 The tubes and fins of the radiator core.

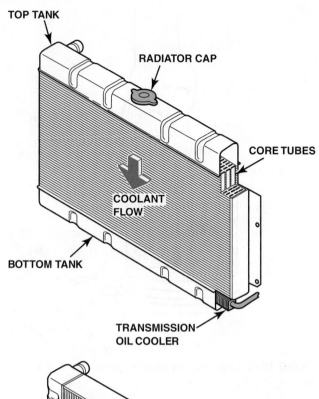

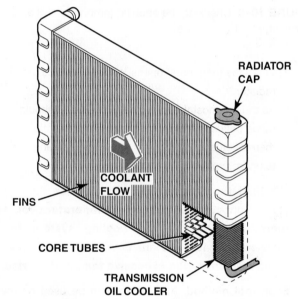

FIGURE 10–12 A radiator may be either a down-flow or a cross-flow type.

In each of these types, the coolant flows through oval-shaped **core tubes**. Heat is transferred through the tube wall and soldered joint to **cooling fins**. The fins are exposed to the air that flows through the radiator, which removes heat from the radiator and carries it away. ● **SEE FIGURES 10–11 AND 10–12.**

Older automobile radiators were made from yellow brass. Since the 1980s, most radiators have been made from aluminum with nylon-reinforced plastic side tanks. These materials are corrosion resistant, have good heat transferability, and are easily formed.

Core tubes are made from 0.0045 inch to 0.012 inch (0.1 mm to 0.3 mm) sheet brass or aluminum, using the thinnest possible materials for each application. The metal is rolled into round tubes and the joints are sealed with a locking seam.

The two basic designs of radiators include:

1. **Down-flow radiators.** This design was used mostly in older vehicles, where the coolant entered the radiator at the top and flowed downward, exiting the radiator at the bottom.

2. **Cross-flow radiators.** Most radiators use a cross-flow design, where the coolant flows from one side of the radiator to the opposite side.

HOW RADIATORS WORK The main limitation of heat transfer in a cooling system is in the transfer from the radiator to the air. Heat transfers from the water to the fins as much as seven times faster than heat transfers from the fins to the air, assuming equal surface exposure. The radiator must be capable of removing an amount of heat energy approximately equal to the heat energy of the power produced by the engine. *Each horsepower is equivalent to 42 BTUs (10,800 calories) per minute.* As the engine power is increased, the heat-removing requirement of the cooling system is also increased.

With a given frontal area, radiator capacity may be increased by increasing the core thickness, packing more material into the same volume, or both. The radiator capacity may also be increased by placing a shroud around the fan so that more air will be pulled through the radiator.

NOTE: The lower air dam in the front of the vehicle is used to help direct the air through the radiator. If this air dam is broken or missing, the engine may overheat, especially during highway driving due to the reduced airflow through the radiator.

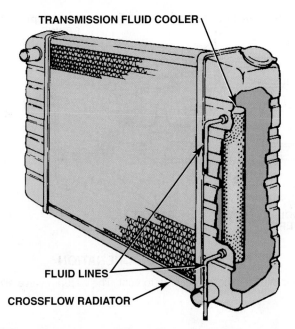

TRANSMISSION FLUID COOLER

FLUID LINES

CROSSFLOW RADIATOR

FIGURE 10–13 Many vehicles equipped with an automatic transmission use a transmission fluid cooler installed in one of the radiator tanks.

When a transmission oil cooler is used in the radiator, it is placed in the outlet tank, where the coolant has the lowest temperature. ● **SEE FIGURE 10–13**.

PRESSURE CAPS

OPERATION On most radiators the filler neck is fitted with a pressure cap. The cap has a spring-loaded valve that closes the cooling system vent. This causes cooling pressure to build up to the pressure setting of the cap. At this point, the valve will release the excess pressure to prevent system damage. Engine cooling systems are pressurized to raise the boiling temperature of the coolant.

- *The boiling temperature will increase by approximately 3°F (1.6°C) for each pound of increase in pressure.*
- At sea level, water will boil at 212°F (100°C). With a 15 PSI (100 kPa) pressure cap, water will boil at 257°F (125°C), which is a maximum operating temperature for an engine.

FUNCTIONS The specified coolant system temperature serves two functions.

1. It allows the engine to run at an efficient temperature, close to 200°F (93°C), with no danger of boiling the coolant.
2. The higher the coolant temperature, the more heat the cooling system can transfer. The heat transferred by the cooling system is proportional to the temperature

 TECH TIP

Working Better Under Pressure

A problem that sometimes occurs with a high-pressure cooling system involves the water pump. For the pump to function, the inlet side of the pump must have a lower pressure than its outlet side. If inlet pressure is lowered too much, the coolant at the pump inlet can boil, producing vapor. The pump will then spin the coolant vapors and not pump coolant. This condition is called *pump cavitation.* Therefore, a radiator cap could be the cause of an overheating problem. A pump will not pump enough coolant if not kept under the proper pressure for preventing vaporization of the coolant.

difference between the coolant and the outside air. This characteristic has led to the design of small, high-pressure radiators that are capable of handling large quantities of heat. For proper cooling, the system must have the right pressure cap correctly installed.

A vacuum valve is part of the pressure cap and is used to allow coolant to flow back into the radiator when the coolant cools down and contracts. ● **SEE FIGURE 10–14**.

NOTE: The proper operation of the pressure cap is especially important at high altitudes. The boiling point of water is lowered by about 1°F for every 550 ft increase in altitude. Therefore, in Denver, Colorado (altitude 5,280 ft), the boiling point of water is about 202°F, and at the top of Pike's Peak in Colorado (14,110 ft) water boils at 186°F.

METRIC RADIATOR CAPS According to the *SAE Handbook,* all radiator caps must indicate their nominal (normal) pressure rating. Most original equipment radiator caps are rated at about 14 PSI to 16 PSI (97 kPa to 110 kPa).

However, many vehicles manufactured in Japan or Europe use radiator pressure indicated in a unit called a **bar.** One bar is the pressure of the atmosphere at sea level, or about 14.7 PSI. The conversions in ● **CHART 10–2** can be used when replacing a radiator cap, to make certain it matches the pressure rating of the original.

NOTE: Many radiator repair shops use a 7 PSI (0.5 bar) radiator cap on a repaired radiator. A 7 PSI cap can still provide boil protection of 21°F (3°F × 7 PSI = 21°F) above the boiling point of the coolant. For example, if the boiling point of the antifreeze coolant is 223°F, then 21°F is added for the pressure cap, and boilover will not

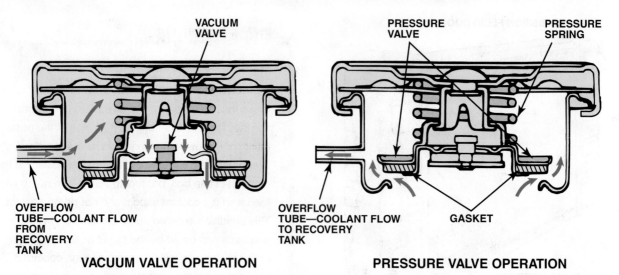

FIGURE 10–14 The pressure valve maintains the system pressure and allows excess pressure to vent. The vacuum valve allows coolant to return to the system from the recovery tank.

BAR OR ATMOSPHERES	POUNDS PER SQUARE INCH (PSI)
1.1	16
1.0	15
0.9	13
0.8	12
0.7	10
0.6	9
0.5	7

CHART 10–2

Comparison showing the metric pressure as shown on the top of the cap to pounds per square inch (PSI).

occur until about 244°F (223°F + 21°F = 244°F). Even though this lower pressure radiator cap provides some protection and will also help protect the radiator repair, the coolant can still boil *before* the "hot" dash warning light comes on and, therefore, should not be used. In addition, the lower pressure in the cooling system could cause cavitation to occur and damage the water pump. For best results, always follow the vehicle manufacturer's recommended radiator cap.

COOLANT RECOVERY SYSTEMS

PURPOSE AND FUNCTION Excess pressure usually forces some coolant from the system through an overflow. Most cooling systems connect the overflow to a plastic

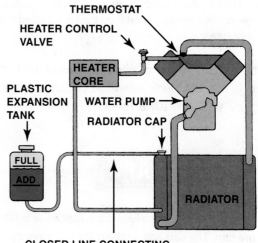

FIGURE 10–15 The level in the coolant recovery system raises and lowers with engine temperature.

reservoir to hold excess coolant while the system is hot. ● **SEE FIGURE 10–15**.

When the system cools, the pressure in the cooling system is reduced and a partial vacuum forms. This vacuum pulls the coolant from the plastic container back into the cooling system, keeping the system full. Because of this action, the system is called a **coolant recovery system**. A vacuum valve allows coolant to reenter the system as the system cools so that the radiator parts will not collapse under the partial vacuum.

SURGE TANK Some vehicles use a **surge tank**, which is located at the highest level of the cooling system and holds about 1 quart (1 liter) of coolant. A hose attaches to the bottom of the surge tank to the inlet side of the water pump. A smaller

REAL WORLD FIX

The Collapsed Radiator Hose Story

An automotive student asked the automotive instructor what brand of radiator hose is the best. Not knowing exactly what to say, the instructor asked if there was a problem with the brand of hose used. The student had tried three brands and all of them collapsed when the engine cooled. The instructor then explained that the vehicle needed a new pressure cap and not a new upper radiator hose. The student thought that because the lower hose did not collapse that the problem *had* to be a fault with the hose. The instructor then explained that the lower radiator hose has a spring inside to keep the lower hose from collapsing due to the lower pressure created at the inlet to the water pump. The radiator cap was replaced and the upper radiator hose did not collapse when the engine cooled.

FIGURE 10–16 Some vehicles use a surge tank, which is located at the highest level of the cooling system, with a radiator cap.

bleed hose attaches to the side of the surge tank to the highest point of the radiator. The bleed line allows some coolant circulation through the surge tank, and air in the system will rise below the radiator cap and be forced from the system if the pressure in the system exceeds the rating of the radiator cap. ● SEE FIGURE 10–16.

WATER PUMPS

OPERATION   The water pump (also called a coolant pump) is driven by one of two methods.

- Crankshaft belt
- Camshaft

Coolant recirculates from the radiator to the engine and back to the radiator. Low-temperature coolant leaves the radiator by the bottom outlet. It is pumped into the warm engine block, where it picks up some heat. From the block, the warm coolant flows to the hot cylinder head, where it picks up more heat.

NOTE: Some engines use reverse cooling. This means that the coolant flows from the radiator to the cylinder head(s) before flowing to the engine block.

Water pumps are not positive displacement pumps. The water pump is a **centrifugal pump** that can move a large volume of coolant without increasing the pressure of the coolant. The

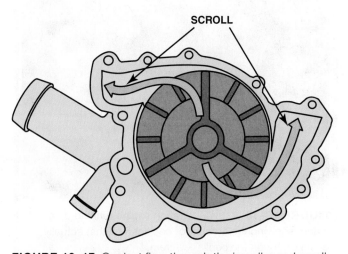

FIGURE 10–17 Coolant flow through the impeller and scroll of a coolant pump for a V-type engine.

pump pulls coolant in at the center of the **impeller.** Centrifugal force throws the coolant outward so that it is discharged at the impeller tips. ● SEE FIGURE 10–17.

As engine speeds increase, more heat is produced by the engine and more cooling capacity is required. The pump impeller speed increases as the engine speed increases to provide extra coolant flow at the very time it is needed.

Coolant leaving the pump impeller is fed through a **scroll.** The scroll is a smoothly curved passage that changes the fluid flow direction with minimum loss in velocity. The scroll is connected to the front of the engine so as to direct the coolant into the engine block. On V-type engines, two outlets are often used, one for each cylinder bank. Occasionally, diverters are necessary in the water pump scroll to equalize coolant flow between the cylinder banks of a V-type engine in order to equalize the cooling.

How Much Coolant Can a Water Pump Move?

A typical water pump can move a maximum of about 7,500 gallons (28,000 liters) of coolant per hour, or recirculate the coolant in the engine over 20 times per minute. This means that a water pump could be used to empty a typical private swimming pool in an hour! The slower the engine speed, the less power is consumed by the water pump. However, even at 35 mph (56 km/h), the typical water pump still moves about 2,000 gallons (7,500 liters) per hour or 0.5 gallon (2 liters) per second! ● **SEE FIGURE 10–18**.

FIGURE 10–18 A demonstration engine running on a stand, showing the amount of coolant flow that actually occurs through the cooling system.

FIGURE 10–19 This severely corroded water pump could not circulate enough coolant to keep the engine cool. As a result, the engine overheated and blew a head gasket.

WEEP HOLE

FIGURE 10–20 The bleed weep hole in the water pump allows coolant to leak out of the pump and not be forced into the bearing. If the bearing failed, more serious damage could result.

WATER PUMP SERVICE A worn impeller on a water pump can reduce the amount of coolant flow through the engine. ● **SEE FIGURE 10–19**.

If the seal of the water pump fails, coolant will leak out of the weep hole. The hole allows coolant to escape without getting trapped and forced into the water pump bearing assembly. ● **SEE FIGURE 10–20**.

If the bearing is defective, the pump will usually be noisy and will have to be replaced. Before replacing a water pump that has failed because of a loose or noisy bearing, check all of the following:

1. Drive belt tension
2. Bent fan
3. Fan for balance

If the water pump drive belt is too tight, excessive force may be exerted against the pump bearing. If the cooling fan is bent or out of balance, the resulting vibration can damage the water pump bearing. ● **SEE FIGURE 10–21**.

COOLANT FLOW IN THE ENGINE

TYPES OF SYSTEMS Coolant flows through the engine in one of the following ways.

- **Parallel flow system.** In the **parallel flow system**, coolant flows into the block under pressure and then

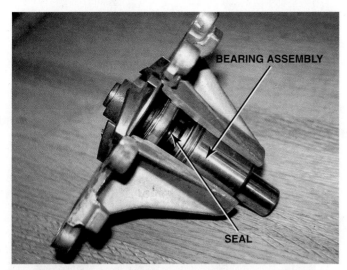

FIGURE 10–21 A cutaway of a typical water pump showing the long bearing assembly and the seal. The weep hole is located between the seal and the bearing. If the seal fails, then coolant flows out of the weep hole to prevent the coolant from damaging the bearing.

crosses the head gasket to the head through main coolant passages beside *each* cylinder.

- **Series flow system.** In the **series flow system,** the coolant flows around all the cylinders on each bank. All the coolant flows to the *rear* of the block, where large main coolant passages allow the coolant to flow across the head gasket. The coolant then enters the rear of the heads. In the heads, the coolant flows forward to a crossover passage on the intake manifold outlet at the *highest point* in the engine cooling passage. This is usually located at the front of the engine. The outlet is either on the heads or in the intake manifold.

- **Series–parallel flow system.** Some engines use a combination of these two coolant flow systems and call it a **series–parallel flow system.** Any steam that develops will go directly to the top of the radiator. In series flow systems, **bleed holes** or **steam slits** in the gasket, block, and head perform the function of letting out the steam.

COOLANT FLOW AND HEAD GASKET DESIGN Most V-type engines use cylinder heads that are interchangeable side to side, but not all engines. Therefore, based on the design of the cooling system and flow through the engine, it is very important to double check that the cylinder head is matched to the block and that the head gasket is installed correctly (end for end) so that all of the cooling passages are open to allow the proper flow of coolant through the system. ● **SEE FIGURE 10–22**.

TECH TIP

Release the Belt Tension Before Checking a Water Pump

The technician should release water pump belt tension before checking for water pump bearing looseness. To test a water pump bearing, it is normal to check the fan for movement; however, if the drive belt is tight, any looseness in the bearing will not be felt.

FIGURE 10–22 A Chevrolet V-8 block that shows the large coolant holes and the smaller gas vent or bleed holes that must match the head gasket when the engine is assembled.

COOLING FANS

ELECTRONICALLY CONTROLLED COOLING FAN Two types of electric cooling fans used on many engines include:

- One two-speed cooling fan

- Two cooling fans (one for normal cooling and one for high heat conditions)

The PCM commands low-speed fans on under the following conditions.

- Engine coolant temperature (ECT) exceeds approximately 223°F (106°C).

- A/C refrigerant pressure exceeds 190 PSI (1,310 kPa).

- After the vehicle is shut off, the engine coolant temperature at key-off is greater than 284°F (140°C) and system voltage is more than 12 volts. The fan(s) will stay on for approximately three minutes.

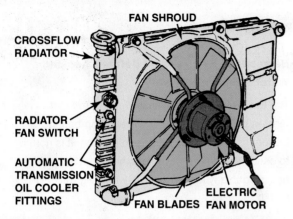

FAN SHROUD

CROSSFLOW RADIATOR

RADIATOR FAN SWITCH

AUTOMATIC TRANSMISSION OIL COOLER FITTINGS

FAN BLADES

ELECTRIC FAN MOTOR

FIGURE 10–23 A typical electric cooling fan assembly showing the radiator and related components.

☠ **WARNING**

Some electric cooling fans can come on after the engine is off without warning. Always keep hands and fingers away from the cooling fan blades unless the electrical connector has been disconnected to prevent the fan from coming on. Always follow all warnings and cautions.

The PCM commands the high-speed fan on under the following conditions.

- Engine coolant temperature (ECT) reaches 230°F (110°C).
- A/C refrigerant pressure exceeds 240 PSI (1,655 kPa).
- When certain diagnostic trouble codes (DTCs) are set.

To prevent a fan from cycling on and off excessively at idle, the fan may not turn off until the ignition switch is moved to the off position or the vehicle speed exceeds approximately 10 mph (16 km/h).

Many rear-wheel-drive vehicles and all transverse engines drive the fan with an electric motor. ● **SEE FIGURE 10–23.**

NOTE: Most electric cooling fans are computer controlled. To save energy, most cooling fans are turned off whenever the vehicle is traveling faster than 35 mph (55 km/h). The ram air caused by the vehicle speed is enough to keep the radiator cool. Of course, if the computer senses that the temperature is still too high, the computer will turn on the cooling fan, to "high," if possible, in an attempt to cool the engine to avoid severe engine damage.

THERMOSTATIC FANS On some rear-wheel-drive vehicles, a thermostatic cooling fan is driven by a belt from the crankshaft. It turns faster as the engine turns faster. Generally, the engine is required to produce more power at higher speeds. Therefore, the cooling system will also transfer more heat. Increased fan speed aids in the required cooling. Engine heat also becomes critical at low engine speeds in traffic where the vehicle moves slowly. The thermostatic fan is designed so that it uses little power at high engine speeds and minimizes noise. Two types of thermostatic fans include:

1. **Silicone coupling.** The **silicone coupling** fan drive is mounted between the drive pulley and the fan.

THERMOSTATIC SPRING

FIGURE 10–24 A typical engine-driven thermostatic spring cooling fan.

NOTE: When diagnosing an overheating problem, look carefully at the cooling fan. If silicone is leaking, then the fan may not be able to function correctly and should be replaced.

2. **Thermostatic spring.** A second type of thermal fan has a **thermostatic spring** added to the silicone coupling fan drive. The thermostatic spring operates a valve that allows the fan to freewheel when the radiator is cold. As the radiator warms to about 150°F (65°C), the air hitting the thermostatic spring will cause the spring to change its shape. The new shape of the spring opens a valve that allows the drive to operate like the silicone coupling drive. When the engine is very cold, the fan may operate at high speeds for a short time until the drive fluid warms slightly. The silicone fluid will then flow into a reservoir to let the fan speed drop to idle. ● **SEE FIGURE 10–24.**

Be Sure to Always Use a Fan Shroud

A fan shroud forces the fan to draw air through the radiator. If a fan shroud is not used, then air is drawn from around the fan and will reduce the airflow through the radiator. Many overheating problems are a result of not replacing the factory shroud after engine work or body repair work to the front of the vehicle.

The fan is designed to move enough air at the lowest fan speed to cool the engine when it is at its highest coolant temperature. The fan shroud is used to increase the cooling system efficiency.

HEATER CORES

PURPOSE AND FUNCTION Most of the heat absorbed from the engine by the cooling system is wasted. Some of this heat, however, is recovered by the vehicle heater. Heated coolant is passed through tubes in the small core of the heater. Air is passed across the heater fins and is then sent to the passenger compartment. In some vehicles, the heater and air conditioning work in series to maintain vehicle compartment temperature. ● **SEE FIGURE 10–25**.

HEATER PROBLEM DIAGNOSIS When the heater does not produce the desired amount of heat, many owners and technicians replace the thermostat before doing any other troubleshooting. It is true that a defective thermostat is the reason for the *engine* not to reach normal operating temperature, but there are many other causes besides a defective thermostat that can result in lack of heat from the heater. To determine the exact cause, follow this procedure.

STEP 1 After the engine has been operated, feel the upper radiator hose. If the engine is up to proper operating temperature, the upper radiator hose should be too hot to hold. The hose should also be pressurized.
    a. If the hose is not hot enough, replace the thermostat.
    b. If the hose is not pressurized, test or replace the radiator pressure cap if it will not hold the specified pressure.
    c. If okay, see step 2.

STEP 2 With the engine running, feel both heater hoses. (The heater should be set to the maximum heat position.)

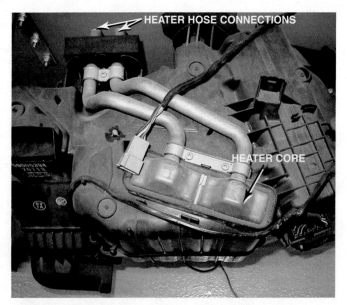

FIGURE 10–25 A typical heater core installed in a heating, ventilation, and air-conditioning (HVAC) housing assembly.

Both hoses should be too hot to hold. If both hoses are warm (not hot) or cool, check the heater control valve for proper operation (if equipped). If one hose is hot and the other (return) is just warm or cool, remove both hoses from the heater core or engine and flush the heater core with water from a garden hose.

STEP 3 If both heater hoses are hot and there is still a lack of heating concern, then the fault is most likely due to an airflow blend door malfunction. Check service information for the exact procedure to follow.

NOTE: Heat from the heater that "comes and goes" is most likely the result of low coolant level. Usually with the engine at idle, there is enough coolant flow through the heater. At higher engine speeds, however, the lack of coolant through the heads and block prevents sufficient flow through the heater.

COOLING SYSTEM TESTING

VISUAL INSPECTION Many cooling system faults can be found by performing a thorough visual inspection. Items that can be inspected visually include:

- Water pump drive belt for tension or faults
- Cooling fan for faults

FIGURE 10–26 A heavily corroded radiator from a vehicle that was overheating. A visual inspection discovered that the corrosion had eaten away many of the cooling fins, yet did not leak. This radiator was replaced and it solved the overheating problem.

FIGURE 10–27 Pressure testing the cooling system. A typical hand-operated pressure tester applies pressure equal to the radiator cap pressure. The pressure should hold; if it drops, this indicates a leak somewhere in the cooling system. An adapter is used to attach the pump to the cap to determine if the radiator can hold pressure, and release it when pressure rises above its maximum rated pressure setting.

- Heater and radiator hoses for condition and leaks
- Coolant overflow or surge tank coolant level
- Evidence of coolant loss
- Radiator condition ● SEE FIGURE 10–26.

PRESSURE TESTING

Pressure testing using a hand-operated pressure tester is a quick and easy cooling system test. The radiator cap is removed (engine cold!) and the tester is attached in the place of the radiator cap. By operating the plunger on the pump, the entire cooling system is pressurized. ● SEE FIGURE 10–27.

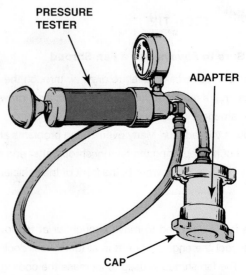

FIGURE 10–28 The pressure cap should be checked for proper operation using a pressure tester as part of the cooling system diagnosis.

CAUTION: Do not pump up the pressure beyond that specified by the vehicle manufacturer. Most systems should not be pressurized beyond 14 PSI (100 kPa). If a greater pressure is used, it may cause the water pump, radiator, heater core, or hoses to fail.

If the cooling system is free from leaks, the pressure should stay and not drop. If the pressure drops, look for evidence of leaks anywhere in the cooling system, including:

1. Heater hoses
2. Radiator hoses
3. Radiator
4. Heater core
5. Cylinder head
6. Core plugs in the side of the block or cylinder head

Pressure testing should be performed whenever there is a leak or suspected leak. The pressure tester can also be used to test the radiator cap. An adapter is used to connect the pressure tester to the radiator cap. Replace any cap that will not hold pressure. ● SEE FIGURE 10–28.

COOLANT DYE LEAK TESTING

One of the best methods to check for a coolant leak is to use a fluorescent dye in the coolant, one that is specifically designed for coolant. Operate the vehicle with the dye in the coolant until the engine reaches normal operating temperature. Use a black light to inspect all areas of the cooling system. When there is a leak, it will be easy to spot because the dye in the coolant will be seen as bright green. ● SEE FIGURE 10–29.

FIGURE 10–29 Use dye specifically made for coolant when checking for leaks using a black light.

FIGURE 10–30 When an engine overheats, often the coolant overflow container boils.

COOLANT TEMPERATURE WARNING LIGHT

PURPOSE AND FUNCTION　Most vehicles are equipped with a heat sensor for the engine operating temperature indicator light. If the warning light comes on during driving (or the temperature gauge goes into the red danger zone), then the coolant temperature is about 250°F to 258°F (120°C to 126°C), which is still *below* the boiling point of the coolant (assuming a properly operating pressure cap and system). ● **SEE FIGURE 10–30**.

PRECAUTIONS　If the coolant temperature warning light comes on, follow these steps.

STEP 1　Shut off the air conditioning and turn on the heater. The heater will help rid the engine of extra heat. Set the blower speed to high.

STEP 2　If possible, shut the engine off and let it cool. (This may take over an hour.)

STEP 3　Never remove the radiator cap when the engine is hot.

STEP 4　Do *not* continue to drive with the hot light on, or serious damage to your engine could result.

STEP 5　If the engine does not feel or smell hot, it is possible that the problem is a faulty hot light sensor or gauge. Continue to drive, but to be safe, stop occasionally and check for any evidence of overheating or coolant loss.

COMMON CAUSES OF OVERHEATING　Overheating can be caused by defects in the cooling system, such as the following:

1.　Low coolant level
2.　Plugged, dirty, or blocked radiator
3.　Defective fan clutch or electric fan
4.　Incorrect ignition timing (if adjustable)
5.　Low engine oil level
6.　Broken fan drive belt
7.　Defective radiator cap
8.　Dragging brakes
9.　Frozen coolant (in freezing weather)
10.　Defective thermostat
11.　Defective water pump (the impeller slipping on the shaft internally)
12.　Clogged cooling passages in the block or cylinder head(s)

COOLING SYSTEM INSPECTION

COOLANT LEVEL　The cooling system is one of the most maintenance-free systems in the engine. Normal maintenance involves an occasional check on the coolant level. It should also include a visual inspection for signs of coolant system leaks and for the condition of the coolant hoses and fan drive belts.

CAUTION: The coolant level should only be checked when the engine is cool. Removing the pressure cap from a hot engine will release the cooling system pressure while the coolant temperature is above its atmospheric

Highway Overheating

A vehicle owner complained of an overheating vehicle, but the problem occurred only while driving at highway speeds. The vehicle, equipped with a 4-cylinder engine, would run in a perfectly normal manner in city driving situations.

The technician flushed the cooling system and replaced the radiator cap and the water pump, thinking that restricted coolant flow was the cause of the problem. Further testing revealed coolant spray out of one cylinder when the engine was turned over by the starter with the spark plugs removed.

A new head gasket solved the problem. Obviously, the head gasket leak was not great enough to cause any problems until the engine speed and load created enough flow and heat to cause the coolant temperature to soar.

The technician also replaced the oxygen (O_2) sensor, because the IAT-type coolant contains phosphates and silicates that often contaminate the sensor. The deteriorated oxygen sensor could have contributed to the problem.

NUMBER OF RIBS USED	TENSION RANGE (LB.)
3	45–60
4	60–80
5	75–100
6	90–125
7	105–145

CHART 10–3

The number of ribs determines the tension range of the belt.

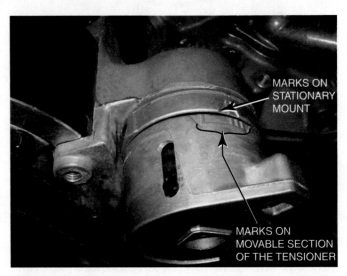

FIGURE 10–31 Typical marks on an accessory drive belt tensioner.

boiling temperature. When the cap is removed, the pressure will instantly drop to atmospheric pressure level, causing the coolant to boil immediately. Vapors from the boiling liquid will blow coolant from the system. Coolant will be lost, and someone may be injured or burned by the high-temperature coolant that is blown out of the filler opening.

ACCESSORY DRIVE BELT TENSION Drive belt condition and proper installation are important for the proper operation of the cooling system.

There are four ways vehicle manufacturers specify that the belt tension is within factory specifications.

1. **Belt tension gauge.** A belt tension gauge is needed to achieve the specified belt tension. Install the belt and operate the engine with all of the accessories turned on, to run in the belt for at least five minutes. Adjust the tension of the accessory drive belt to factory specifications or use ● **CHART 10–3** for an example of the proper tension based on the size of the belt. Replace any serpentine belt that has more than three cracks in any one rib that appears in a 3 inch span.

2. **Marks on the tensioner.** Many tensioners have marks that indicate the normal operating tension range for the accessory drive belt. Check service information for the location of the tensioner mark. ● **SEE FIGURE 10–31**.

3. **Torque wrench reading.** Some vehicle manufacturers specify that a beam-type torque wrench be used to determine the torque needed to rotate the tensioner. If the torque reading is below specifications, the tensioner must be replaced.

4. **Deflection.** Depress the belt between the two pulleys that are the farthest apart and the flex or deflection should be 1/2 inch.

COOLING SYSTEM SERVICE

FLUSHING COOLANT Flushing the cooling system includes the following steps.

STEP 1 Drain the system (dispose of the old coolant correctly).

STEP 2 Fill the system with clean water and flushing/cleaning chemical.

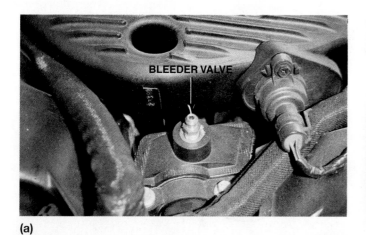

BLEEDER VALVE

(a)

(b)

FIGURE 10–32 (a) Many vehicle manufacturers recommend that the bleeder valve be opened whenever refilling the cooling system. (b) Chrysler recommends that a clear plastic hose (1/4 inch ID) be attached to the bleeder valve and directed into a suitable container to keep from spilling coolant onto the ground and on the engine and to allow the technician to observe the flow of coolant for any remaining air bubbles.

 TECH TIP

The Water Spray Trick

Lower-than-normal alternator output could be the result of a loose or slipping drive belt. All belts (V and serpentine multigroove) use an interference angle between the angle of the Vs of the belt and the angle of the Vs on the pulley. A belt wears this interference angle off the edges of the V of the belt. As a result, the belt may start to slip and make a squealing sound even if tensioned properly.

A common trick to determine if the noise is from the belt is to spray water from a squirt bottle at the belt with the engine running. If the noise stops, the belt is the cause of the noise. The water quickly evaporates and therefore, the water just finds the problem, but it not fix the problem.

STEP 3 Start the engine until it reaches operating temperature with the heater on.

STEP 4 Drain the system and fill with clean water.

STEP 5 Repeat until drain water runs clear (any remaining flush agent will upset pH).

STEP 6 Fill the system with 50/50 antifreeze/water mix or pre-mixed coolant.

STEP 7 Start the engine until it reaches operating temperature with the heater on.

STEP 8 Adjust coolant level as needed.

Bleeding the air out of the cooling system is important because air can prevent proper operation of the heater and can cause the engine to overheat. Use a clear hose attached to the bleeder valve and the other end in a "suitable" container. This prevents coolant from getting on the engine and gives the technician a visual clue as to the color of coolant. ● **SEE FIGURE 10–32.**

Check service information for specific bleeding procedures and location of the air bleeder fittings.

COOLANT EXCHANGE MACHINE Many coolant exchange machines are able to perform one or more of the following operations.

- Exchange old coolant with new coolant
- Flush the cooling system
- Pressure or vacuum check the cooling system for leaks

The use of a coolant exchange machine pulls a vacuum on the cooling system which helps eliminate air pockets from forming during coolant replacement. If an air pocket were to form, the following symptoms may occur.

1. **Lack of heat from the heater.** Air rises and can form in the heater core, which will prevent coolant from flowing.

2. **Overheating.** The engine can overheat due to the lack of proper coolant flow through the system.

Always follow the operating instructions for the coolant exchange machine being used. ● **SEE FIGURE 10–33.**

HOSE INSPECTION Coolant system hoses are critical to engine cooling. As the hoses get old, they become either

FIGURE 10–33 Using a coolant exchange machine helps eliminate the problem of air getting into the system which can cause overheating or lack of heat due to air pockets getting trapped in the system.

 **TECH TIP**

Always Replace the Pressure Cap

Replace the old radiator cap with a new cap with the same pressure rating. The cap can be located on the following:

1. Radiator
2. Coolant recovery reservoir
3. Upper radiator hose

WARNING: Never remove a pressure cap from a hot engine. When the pressure is removed from the system, the coolant will immediately boil and will expand upward, throwing scalding coolant in all directions. Hot coolant can cause serious burns.

soft or brittle and sometimes swell in diameter. Their condition depends on their material and on the engine service conditions. If a hose breaks while the engine is running, all coolant will be lost. A hose should be replaced any time it appears to be abnormal. ● **SEE FIGURE 10–34.**

NOTE: To make hose removal easier and to avoid possible damage to the radiator, use a utility knife and slit the hose lengthwise. Then simply peel the hose off.

The hose and hose clamp should be positioned so that the clamp is close to the bead on the neck. This is especially

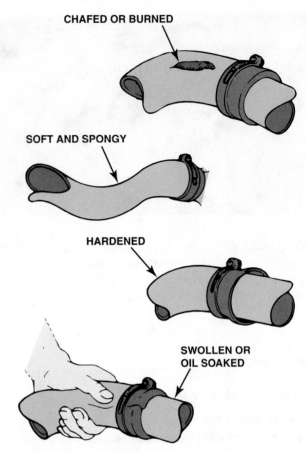

CHAFED OR BURNED

SOFT AND SPONGY

HARDENED

SWOLLEN OR OIL SOAKED

FIGURE 10–34 All cooling system hoses should be checked for wear or damage.

important on aluminum hose necks to avoid corrosion. When the hoses are in place and the drain petcock is closed, the cooling system can be refilled with the correct coolant mixture.

DISPOSING OF USED COOLANT Used coolant drained from vehicles should be disposed of according to state or local laws. Some communities permit draining into the sewer. Ethylene glycol will easily biodegrade. There could be problems with groundwater contamination, however, if coolant is spilled on open ground. Check with recycling companies authorized by local or state governments for the exact method recommended for disposal in your area.

CLEANING THE RADIATOR EXTERIOR Overheating can result from exterior and interior radiator plugging. External plugging is caused by dirt and insects. This type of plugging can be seen if you look straight through the radiator while a

TECH TIP

Always Use Heater Hoses Designed for Coolant

Many heater hoses are sizes that can also be used for other purposes such as oil lines. Always check and use hose that states it is designed for heater or cooling system use. ● **SEE FIGURE 10–35**.

FIGURE 10–35 The top 3/8 inch hose is designed for oil and similar liquids, whereas the 3/8 inch hose below is labeled "heater hose" and is designed for coolant.

TECH TIP

Quick and Easy Cooling System Problem Diagnosis

1. If overheating occurs in slow stop-and-go traffic, the usual cause is low airflow through the radiator. Check for airflow blockages or cooling fan malfunction.
2. If overheating occurs at highway speeds, the cause is usually a radiator or coolant circulation problem. Check for a restricted or clogged radiator.

light is held behind it. It is most likely to occur on off-road vehicles. The plugged exterior of the radiator core can usually be cleaned with water pressure from a hose. The water is aimed at the *engine side* of the radiator. The water should flow freely through the core at all locations. If this does not clean the core, the radiator should be removed for cleaning at a radiator shop.

RADIATOR REPLACEMENT

1 The removal of the radiator starts by removing the fan shroud.

2 The coolant overflow and windshield washer fluid reservoir assembly is removed.

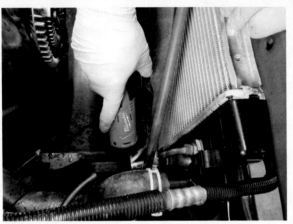

3 The radiator retaining fasteners being removed.

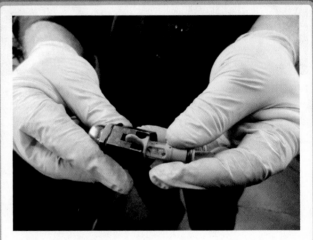

4 The radiator drain plug is removed using a special peacock removal tool.

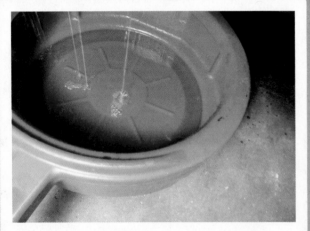

5 The coolant being drained into a suitable container.

6 The automatic transmission cooler lines are removed from the radiator.

7 The upper and lower radiator hoses are removed from the radiator.

8 To get the radiator out of the this vehicle, the radiator core support is being removed, then the radiator was lifted up and out.

9 The replacement radiator (left) was placed beside the old radiator and checked to see that it was the correct unit for the vehicle and that it matched the original.

10 The new radiator was installed and the hoses reattached using new radiator hose clamps.

11 A special fill funnel was connected in place of the radiator cap and the cooling system filled with the specified premixed coolant.

12 Air is escaping the system as the engine warmed up and the thermostat opened.

SUMMARY

1. The purpose and function of the cooling system is to maintain proper engine operating temperature.

2. The thermostat controls engine coolant temperature by opening at its rated opening temperature to allow coolant to flow through the radiator.

3. Coolant fans are designed to draw air through the radiator to aid in the heat transfer process, drawing the heat from the coolant and transferring it to the outside air through the radiator.

4. The cooling system should be tested for leaks using a hand-operated pressure pump.

5. Water pumps are usually engine driven and circulate coolant through the engine and the radiator when the thermostat opens.

6. Coolant flows through the radiator hoses to and from the engine and through heater hoses to send heated coolant to the heater core in the passenger compartment.

REVIEW QUESTIONS

1. What is normal operating coolant temperature?

2. Explain the flow of coolant through the engine and radiator.

3. Why is a cooling system pressurized?

4. What is the purpose of the coolant system bypass?

5. Describe how to perform a drain, flush, and refill procedure on a cooling system.

6. Explain the operation of a thermostatic cooling fan.

7. Describe how to diagnose a heater problem.

8. What are 10 common causes of overheating?

CHAPTER QUIZ

1. The upper radiator hose collapses when the engine cools. What is the most likely cause?
   a. Defective upper radiator hose
   b. Missing spring from the upper radiator hose, which is used to keep it from collapsing
   c. Defective thermostat
   d. Defective pressure cap

2. What can be done to prevent air from getting trapped in the cooling system when the coolant is replaced?
   a. Pour the coolant into the radiator slowly.
   b. Use a coolant exchange machine that draws a vacuum on the system.
   c. Open the air bleeder valves while adding coolant.
   d. Either b or c

3. Heat transfer is improved from the coolant to the air when the _____.
   a. Temperature difference is great
   b. Temperature difference is small
   c. Coolant is 95% antifreeze
   d. Both a and c

4. What type of pump is a typical water pump?
   a. Gear
   b. Centrifugal
   c. Rotor
   d. Vane

5. Water pumps _____.
   a. Work only at idle and low speeds and are disengaged at higher speeds
   b. Use engine oil as a lubricant and coolant
   c. Are driven by the engine crankshaft or camshaft
   d. Disengage during freezing weather to prevent radiator failure

6. What diagnostic trouble code (DTC) could be set if the thermostat is defective?
   a. P0300
   b. P0171
   c. P0440
   d. P0128

7. Which statement is *true* about thermostats?
   a. The temperature marked on the thermostat is the temperature at which the thermostat should be fully open.
   b. Thermostats often cause overheating.

c. The temperature marked on the thermostat is the temperature at which the thermostat should start to open.

d. Both a and b

8. What is commonly wrong when the heat from a heater "comes and goes"?

a. Cooling system is low on coolant

b. A coolant restriction

c. A worn water pump drive belt

d. Incorrect heater hoses

9. What helps prevent water pump cavitation?

a. Using the specified brand of heater hose

b. Using the specified pressure cap

c. Using the correct water pump

d. Use a higher output water pump

10. The normal operating temperature (coolant temperature) of an engine equipped with a 195°F thermostat is _____.

a. 175°F to 195°F   **c.** 195°F to 215°F

b. 185°F to 205°F   **d.** 175°F to 215°F

HEATING SYSTEM OPERATION AND DIAGNOSIS

LEARNING OBJECTIVES

After studying this chapter, the reader should be able to:

1. Prepare for the ASE Heating and Air Conditioning (A7) certification test content area "C" (Heating and Engine Cooling Systems Diagnosis and Repair).

2. Discuss the operation of heating systems.

3. Discuss the diagnosis of heating systems.

4. Explain the operation of electrically heated seats.

5. Explain the operation of heated and cooled seats.

6. Explain the operation of heated steering wheel.

KEY TERMS

Cellular 188	Outlet hose 188
Control valve 188	Peltier effect 190
Heater core 187	Thermoelectric device
Inlet hose 188	(TED) 190

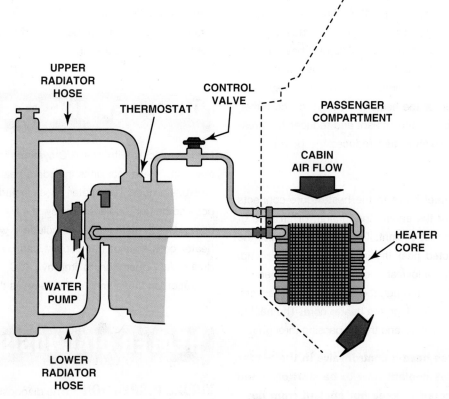

FIGURE 11–1 The main parts of a vehicle's heating system are the heater core, blower, heater hoses, and, in some cases, a heater control valve.

HEATING SYSTEM

PURPOSE AND FUNCTION   The heating system uses heat that would normally be wasted (removed by the radiator) to warm the interior of the vehicle. The heating system is made up of the heater core, hoses, engine and/or electric water pump, and, in some systems, a control valve as well as a blower motor to create the needed airflow into the passenger compartment. ● SEE FIGURE 11–1.

The Federal Motor Vehicle Safety Standard (FMVSS) 103 requires that every vehicle sold in the United States must be able to defrost or defog certain areas of the windshield in a specified amount of time. Most HVAC systems will default to defrost if there is a failure in the control part of the system. The defrost/defog system in most vehicles uses the heater and diverts the airflow to the base of the windshield.

HEATER CORE   The **heater core** is a heat exchanger much like the condenser, evaporator, and radiator. Heat transfers from the coolant, to the fins, and to the air passing through the core. As with other heat exchangers, there is a large area of fin-to-air contact to allow sufficient heat transfer and airflow. ● SEE FIGURE 11–3.

? **FREQUENTLY ASKED QUESTION**

What Are Side Window Defoggers?

Most vehicles direct airflow from the defroster discharge vents to the side windows to defog them. This helps the driver to see through the side window and observe the side mirror to improve safety. ● SEE FIGURE 11–2.

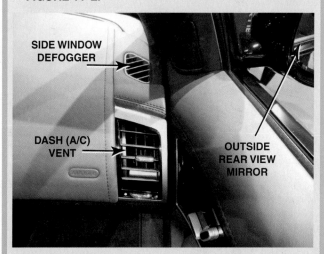

FIGURE 11–2 The side window defogger, also called a side window demister, directs air to the side window to clear the area so the side view mirror can be seen by the driver.

Most heater cores use a **cellular** form of construction that is somewhat like a plate-type evaporator. The tubes are made by joining two corrugated brass or aluminum plates, and the corrugated fins are attached between pairs of tubes. In most cores, the tanks at the ends of the core serve as manifolds to direct the flow back and forth through the core. Many systems use a smaller diameter for the heater inlet than for the outlet. This allows an easier exit of the coolant and reduces the pressure inside the core, which in turn reduces the possibility of leaks.

OPERATION   The **inlet hose** to the heater core connects to an outlet fitting near the engine thermostat, or an area of the engine with the hottest coolant. The **outlet hose** from the heater core is connected near the inlet of the water pump, which is the area with the lowest coolant pressure. When the engine runs, coolant flows through the engine's water jackets, past the thermostat, and through the heater core. The heated coolant warms the heater core and the air passing through it.

NOTE: Some vehicles have a control valve in the heater inlet hose that allows coolant flow to be shut off when MAX cooling is selected to keep hot coolant from flowing through the heater core. Most new vehicles do not use a control valve, and the temperature of the air to the passenger compartment is controlled by an air temperature blend door in the heater plenum.

FLOW RESTRICTORS   Some systems include a restrictor to slow the coolant velocity as it passes through the heater core. The restrictor can be part of the manifold fitting or the inlet heater hose assembly. The major purpose of the restrictor is to slow the flow rate in order to reduce noise and to allow for a better heat transfer to the fins and for a better heat transfer from the coolant to the air.

DUAL HEATING SYSTEMS

Larger vehicles with rear A/C systems include a heater in the rear unit. These rear units include a heater core and temperature-blend door. The heater hoses include a tee fitting in each hose so heated coolant can flow through either or both heater cores. Some manufacturers include a water valve in the rear heater core so that hot coolant can be kept out of the core during A/C operation to improve A/C efficiency. The heater operation on these units is the same as that for a front unit.

HEATER DIAGNOSIS

VISUAL INSPECTION   The diagnosis of a heater problem or concern should start with a visual inspection. The following items should be checked or tested:

1. **Coolant level and condition**—Low coolant level can cause a lack of heat from the heater. Low coolant level can also cause occasional loss of heat. The coolant should also be tested to make sure that it provides the needed freezing protection and pH.

2. **Water pump drive belt condition and proper tension**

   Drive belt condition and proper installation are important for the proper operation of the cooling system. There are four ways vehicle manufacturers specify that the belt tension is within factory specifications.

   - **Belt tension gauge.** A belt tension gauge is needed to achieve the specified belt tension. Install the belt and operate the engine with all of the accessories turned on, to run in the belt for at least five minutes. Adjust the tension of the accessory drive belt to factory

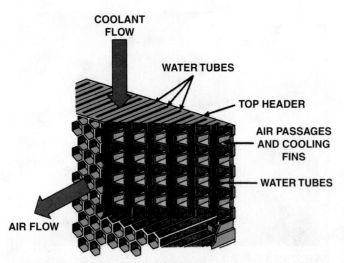

FIGURE 11–3 Heat is transferred from the hot coolant flowing through the water tubes to warm the air flowing through the fins of the core.

WARNING

Do not remove the radiator cap when the engine is hot. Allow the vehicle to sit several hours before removing the pressure cap to check the radiator coolant level.

Always Follow the Vehicle Manufacture's Recommended Procedure

The cooling system will not function correctly if air is not released (burped) from the system after a refill. On some vehicles the radiator cap is on the overflow bottle and is not the highest point. The manufacturer may have a very specific bleed procedure or the air will NEVER come out. If the system has had the coolant replaced and there is a complaint for lack of heat from the heater, then it is possible that air is trapped in the heater core.

FIGURE 11–4 A special wrench being used to remove the tension from the accessory drive belt so it can be removed.

specifications. Replace any serpentine belt that has more than three cracks in any one rib that appears in a 3 inch span.

- **Marks on the tensioner.** Many tensioners have marks that indicate the normal operating tension range for the accessory drive belt. Check service information for the location of the tensioner mark. ● **SEE FIGURE 11–4.**

- **Torque wrench reading.** Some vehicle manufacturers specify that a beam-type torque wrench be used to determine the torque needed to rotate the tensioner. If the torque reading is below specifications, the tensioner must be replaced.

- **Deflection.** Depress the belt between the two pulleys that are the farthest apart and the flex or deflection should be 1/2 inch.

NOTE: **The water pump itself can have a slipping or corroded impeller, which can cause a reduction in the amount of coolant that is circulated.**

3. **To check a radiator or condenser for possible clogged or restricted areas**—Carefully touch the outside of the unit with your hand. Any cool spots indicate that the radiator or condenser is clogged in that cool area.

4. **Check the temperature of the heater hoses**—Both should be hot to the touch. If the supply hose is hotter than the return hose, this indicates that the heater core could be partially clogged. Check that the control valve, if equipped, is open by checking to see that the temperature is the same on both sides of the valve.

5. **Check for proper airflow across the heater core**—If the airflow is blocked by leaves or debris, this can reduce the amount of heat being delivered to the passenger compartment. Check that the cabin filter is clean and not restricted.

 TECH TIP

Use a Belt Wear Gauge

Gates Rubber Company offers a free belt wear gauge that can be used to measure the depth of the curves in a serpentine belt. Wear cannot be seen but can result in a drive belt slipping, especially on belts used to drive AC compressors on hot days. ● **SEE FIGURE 11–5.**

GAUGE RESULTS ON A GOOD BELT   GAUGE RESULTS ON A WORN BELT

FIGURE 11–5 When the plastic tool is placed in to the grooves of a good belt (left), the gauge sits above the surface. When the gauge tool is placed in the grooves of a belt that is worn and requires replacement (right), the gauge is below the surface of the ribs of the belt.

6. **Pressure test the cooling system**—Pressure testing the cooling system insures that the system is leak-free and that the pressure cap is working as designed.

SCAN TOOL DIAGNOSIS   Using a factory or factory-level aftermarket scan tool, perform the following:

- Use a scan tool and check for any stored or pending diagnostic trouble codes, especially those that pertain to the HVAC controls.

Hot/Cold/Hot/Cold Heater Diagnosis

A common customer complaint is a lack of heat from the heater but only at idle, even though there seems to be plenty of heat when the engine is operating at highway speeds. This is a classic symptom of low coolant level. The heater core is usually mounted higher than the water jackets/passages in the engine and low coolant levels will allow circulation when idling, but will not allow heater operation at higher engine speeds. This is because the velocity of the coolant drops at idle, therefore putting air into the highest point (heater core) resulting in no heat at idle. The lower-than-normal coolant level in the radiator prevents enough flow to supply the heater core.

- Check that the coolant temperature as measured by the engine coolant temperature (ECT) sensor is correct, usually 180°F to 200°F (82°C to 93°C). Check service information for the specified coolant temperature for the vehicle being checked.
- Perform a bidirectional control of the blend door and blower motor speed, if possible, to confirm that these are operating correctly.

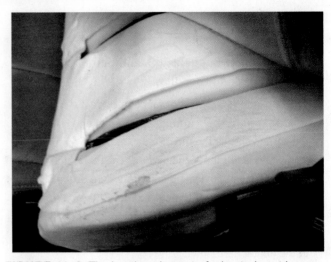

FIGURE 11–6 The heating element of a heated seat is a replaceable part, but service requires that the upholstery be removed. The yellow part is the seat foam material and the entire white cover is the replaceable heating element. This is then covered by the seat material.

DIAGNOSIS AND SERVICE After verifying that the heated seats are not functioning as designed, check that the switch is in the on position and that the temperature of the seat is below normal body temperature. Using service information, check for power and ground at the control module and to the heating element in the seat. Most vehicle manufacturers recommend replacing the entire heating element if it is defective. ● SEE FIGURE 11–6.

ELECTRICALLY HEATED SEATS

PARTS AND OPERATION Heated seats use electric heating elements in the seat bottom, as well as in the seat back in many vehicles. The heating element is designed to warm the seat and/or back of the seat to about 100°F (37°C) or close to normal body temperature (98.6°F). Many heated seats also include a high position or a variable temperature setting, so the temperature of the seats can therefore be as high as 110°F (44°C). A temperature sensor in the seat cushion is used to regulate the temperature. The sensor is a variable resistor that changes with temperature and is used as an input signal to a heated seat control module. The heated seat module uses the seat temperature input, as well as the input from the high–low (or variable) temperature control, to turn the current on or off to the heating element in the seat. Some vehicles are equipped with heated seats in both the rear and the front.

HEATED AND COOLED SEATS

PARTS AND OPERATION Most electrically heated and cooled seats use a **thermoelectric device (TED)** located under the seat cushion and seat back. The thermoelectric device consists of positive and negative connections between two ceramic plates. Each ceramic plate has copper fins to allow the transfer of heat to air passing over the device and directed into the seat cushion. The thermoelectric device uses the **Peltier effect**, named after the inventor, Jean C. A. Peltier, a French clockmaker. When electrical current flows through the module, one side is heated and the other side is cooled. Reversing the polarity of the current changes the side being heated. ● SEE FIGURE 11–7.

Most vehicles equipped with heated and cooled seats use two modules per seat, one for the seat cushion and one for the seat back. When the heated and cooled seats are turned on, air is forced through a filter and then through the thermoelectric

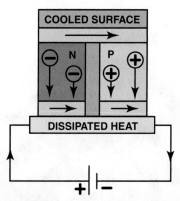

FIGURE 11–7 A Peltier effect device is capable of heating or cooling, depending on the polarity of the applied current.

modules. The air is then directed through passages in the foam of the seat cushion and seat back. Each thermoelectric device has a temperature sensor, called a thermistor. The control module uses sensors to determine the temperature of the fins in the thermoelectric device so the controller can maintain the set temperature.

DIAGNOSIS AND SERVICE   The first step in any diagnosis is to verify that the heated–cooled seat system is not functioning. Check the owner's manual or service information for the correct operating instructions and specified diagnostic procedures.

HEATED STEERING WHEEL

PARTS INVOLVED   A heated steering wheel usually consists of the following components.

- Steering wheel with a built-in heater in the rim
- Heated steering wheel control switch
- Heated steering wheel control module

OPERATION   When the steering wheel heater control switch is turned on, a signal is sent to the control module and electrical current flows through the heating element in the rim of the steering wheel. ● **SEE FIGURE 11–8.**

The system remains on until the ignition switch is turned off or the driver turns off the control switch. The temperature of the steering wheel is usually calibrated to stay at about 90°F (32°C), and it requires three to four minutes to reach that temperature depending on the outside temperature.

DIAGNOSIS AND SERVICE   Diagnosis of a heated steering wheel starts with verifying that it is not working as designed.

TECH TIP

Check the Seat Filter

Heated and cooled seats often use a filter to trap dirt and debris to help keep the air passages clean. If a customer complains of a slow heating or cooling of the seat, check the air filter and replace or clean as necessary. Check service information for the exact location of the seat filter and for instructions on how to remove and/or replace it.

FIGURE 11–8 The heated steering wheel is controlled by a switch on the steering wheel in this vehicle.

NOTE: Most heated steering wheels do not work if the temperature inside the vehicle is about 90°F (32°C) or higher.

If the heated steering wheel is not working, follow the service information testing procedures, which includes a check of the following:

1. Check the heated steering wheel control switch for proper operation. This is usually done by checking for voltage at both terminals of the switch. If voltage is available at only one of the two terminals of the switch and the switch has been turned on and off, an open (defective) switch is indicated.

2. Check for voltage and ground at the terminals leading to the heating element. If voltage is available at the heating element and the ground has less than 0.2 volt drop to a good chassis ground, the heating element is defective. The entire steering wheel has to be replaced if the element is defective. Always follow the vehicle manufacturer's recommended diagnosis and testing procedures.

1 The diagnosis of a lack of heat from the heater started by checking the temperature of the heater hoses. The return hose was colder than the inlet hose.

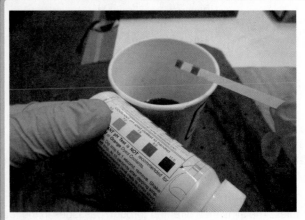

2 A test strip was used to check the coolant pH and freezing point. The coolant did not look fresh, but the test strip results were normal.

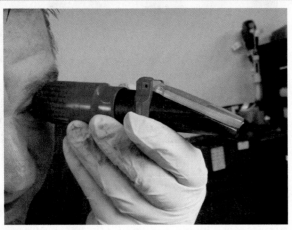

3 The refractometer test confirmed that the freezing protection was −32°F (−36°C).

4 The heater core was flushed and the coolant flow through the hoses seemed to be normal.

5 The heater core had to be removed and this required that the dash assembly be removed. Starting to remove the dash components to get access to the heater core.

6 The fasteners used to retain the dash to the bulkhead being removed.

7 The A/C system was evacuated because it was necessary to remove HVAC module which contained the evaporator.

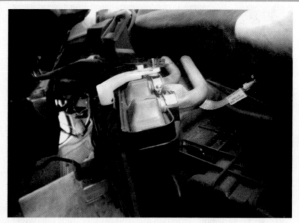

8 The dash was pulled back and the heater core became visible.

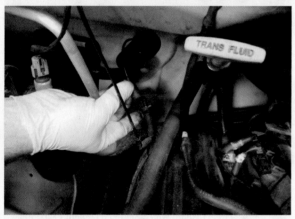

9 The vacuum connection for the HVAC vacuum actuators was disconnected from under the hood.

10 The AC hose connections to the evaporator were removed.

11 The heater core being removed from inside the vehicle.

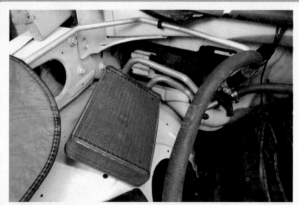

12 The heater core was removed from the inside of the vehicle and connected to the heater hoses and then the engine was started. The heater core felt hot across the entire surface.

CONTINUED ▶

LACK OF HEAT CONCERN DIAGNOSIS (CONTINUED)

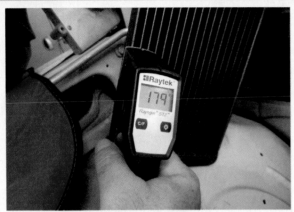

13 However, when an infrared temperature gun was used, the temperature measured about 20 degrees different depending on where it was measured.

14 The evaporator had signs that it was leaking as indicted by the oil seen on the surface. It was replaced at the same time as the heater core.

15 The replacement heater core was made of aluminum instead of brass like the original but it fit correctly.

16 Fresh coolant was added to a coolant exchange machine. Conventional green (IAT) coolant was used because it had been converted to this coolant during a previous service.

17 The coolant was replaced using the exchange machine, which also purged any air from the system. The heater worked great and was very hot and the vehicle owner was pleased.

18 The end cap was removed from the old heater core and connected to a water hose. Only about half of the tubes were flowing water indicating that this heater core did require replacement.

1. Hot coolant from the engine cooling system provides the heat for heater output.

2. The heater core resembles a small radiator, and it is connected to the engine by a pair of hoses.

3. Some vehicles use a coolant flow valve to control heater output temperature.

4. Heated seats can use either a resistance type heater located under the seat covering or a thermoelectric (TE) device.

5. Heater diagnosis includes verifying the problem, visual inspections and scan tool usage.

REVIEW QUESTIONS

1. What is the purpose and function of the heating system?

2. How does a thermoelectric (TE) device work?

3. What steps are included in performing a visual inspection of the heating system?

4. How can a scan tool be used to check the operation of the heater?

CHAPTER QUIZ

1. Heat is transferred from the hot coolant flowing through the _____ to warm the air flowing through the fins of the heater core.
   - a. Water tubes
   - b. Hoses
   - c. Radiator
   - d. Blower motor

2. The heater control valve, if used, shuts off the coolant flow to the heater core when what setting is selected?
   - a. Defrost
   - b. MAX cooling
   - c. Recirculation
   - d. Bi-level (both dash vents and floor vents)

3. The heating element is designed to warm the seat and/or back of the seat to about_____.
   - a. 50°F (10°C)
   - b. 70°F (21°C)
   - c. 90°F (32°C)
   - d. 100°F (38°C)

4. A typical vehicle heater works by_____.
   - a. Electrically controlled using a thermostat
   - b. Making the A/C system operate in reverse using the evaporator as the heater
   - c. Heat transfers from the coolant, to the fins, and to the air passing through the core.
   - d. Uses hot coolant from the engine to heat the evaporator

5. How does a thermoelectric device (TED) work?
   - a. Uses an electric current passed through coolant
   - b. A type of electric resistance heating
   - c. When electrical current flows through the module, one side is heated and the other side is cooled.
   - d. Using a temperature-controlled thermostat in the cooling system to control coolant temperature.

6. What is the purpose of a flow restrictor, if used?
   - a. Slow the coolant velocity as it passes through the heater core.
   - b. To reduce noise
   - c. Allow for a better heat transfer to the fins/air
   - d. All of the above

7. Coolant is hottest in which area?
   - a. Bottom of the radiator
   - b. Near the thermostat
   - c. At the overflow container
   - d. Near the outlet of the water pump

8. A seat filter is used with what type of system?
   - a. Most cabin heating systems
   - b. Heated and cooled seats
   - c. All heated seats
   - d. Heated steering wheels to keep the air around the driver free from dust and pollen

9. If the cooling system is low on coolant, what is a common symptom?
   - a. The cooling system will not supply any coolant to the heater core so there will be complaint for a lack of heat
   - b. Hot air comes from the heater at all times due to an overheated engine
   - c. Lack of heat from the heater, but only when the vehicle is at idle, yet plenty of heat when the engine is operating at highway speeds.
   - d. None of the above

10. The water pump drive belt should be checked for_____.
    - a. Proper tension
    - b. Condition
    - c. Wear using a gauge
    - d. All of the above

chapter 12

AUTOMATIC TEMPERATURE CONTROL SYSTEMS

LEARNING OBJECTIVES

After studying this chapter, the reader should be able to:

1. Discuss the purpose and function of automatic temperature control (ATC) systems.
2. Discuss the sensors used in ATC systems.
3. State the need for airflow control.
4. Discuss the purpose of automatic HVAC controls.
5. Discuss how to diagnose the electrical ATC system faults.
6. Explain the automatic climatic control diagnostic procedure.
7. Explain the types of actuators in ATC systems.

KEY TERMS

Ambient temperature sensor 197
Air management system 200
Automatic air-conditioning system 197
Automatic climatic control system 197
Automatic temperature control (ATC) system 197
Blend door 201
Compressor speed sensor 199
Discharge air temperature (DAT) sensor 198
Dual-position actuator 201
Dual-zone systems 203
Engine coolant temperature (ECT) sensor 199
Evaporator temperature (EVT) sensor 199

Infrared (IR) sensors 199
In-vehicle temperature sensor 198
Heating ventilation and air conditioning (HVAC) 197
Mode door 202
Negative temperature coefficient (NTC) 198
Outside air temperature (OAT) sensor 197
Pressure transducer 199
Relative humidity (RH) sensor 200
Smart motor 205
Smart control head 205
Sun load sensor 199
Temperature-blend door 202
Temperature door 201
Three-position actuator 202
Variable-position actuator 202

FIGURE 12–1 The automatic climatic control display is part of the navigation screen on this vehicle.

FIGURE 12–2 The outside air temperature sensor is mounted on the radiator core support in front of the A/C condenser on this vehicle.

AUTOMATIC TEMPERATURE CONTROL SYSTEM

PURPOSE AND FUNCTION The purpose and function of the **heating, ventilation, and air conditioning (HVAC)** system is to provide comfortable temperature and humidity levels inside the passenger compartment. Proper temperature control to enhance passenger comfort during heating should maintain air temperature at the foot level about 7°F to 14°F (4°C to 8°C) above the temperature around the upper body. This is accomplished by directing the heated airflow to the floor. During A/C operation, the upper body should be cooler, so the airflow is directed to the instrument panel registers. Most new HVAC systems use an electronic control head and some use electronic blower speed control, radiator fan, and control of compressor displacement.

OPERATION Automatic temperature control (ATC) **System** is also called **automatic climatic control system** or **automatic air-conditioning system**. With an automatic temperature control system (ATC), the driver can turn the automatic controls on or off and select the desired temperature. The ATC will adjust the following:

- Blower speed
- Temperature door
- Air inlet door

- Mode door to achieve the proper temperature
- Control the air-conditioning compressor operation.
  ● **SEE FIGURE 12–1.**

SENSORS

PURPOSE AND FUNCTION The purpose of using sensors is to provide information to the HVAC controller regarding the conditions outside as well as inside the vehicle. Sensors provide data about the following:

- Different conditions that can affect temperature conditions within the vehicle.
- Temperature setting at the control head.
- Operation of the A/C system.
- Operation of the engine.

Pressure and temperature sensors are used to determine the condition in the air-conditioning system so that the controller can

- Provide the most efficient use of energy.
- Provide a comfortable interior environment for the driver and passengers.
- Reduce the load on the engine and electrical system as much as possible to improve fuel economy.

OUTSIDE AIR TEMPERATURE SENSOR The **outside air temperature (OAT) sensor**, also called the **ambient temperature sensor**, measures outside air temperature and is often mounted at the radiator shroud or in the area behind the front grill. ● **SEE FIGURE 12–2.**

FIGURE 12–3 The outside air temperature in displayed on the navigation screen on this vehicle and uses the information from the outside air temperature sensor.

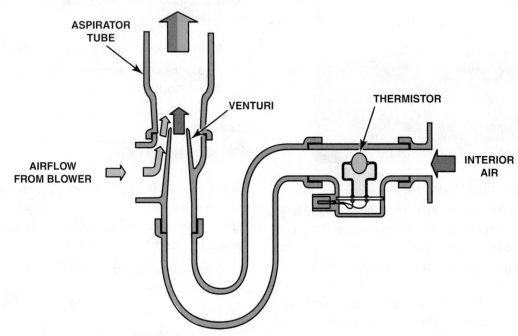

FIGURE 12–4 The airflow from the blower causes airflow to flow past the in-vehicle temperature sensor.

An ambient sensor is a thermistor that is mounted in the air stream passing through the front of the vehicle or the airflow entering the HVAC case.

- Most automotive thermistors are of the **negative temperature coefficient (NTC)** type; the resistance changes in an inverse or negative relationship with temperature.

- The resistance is low when the temperature is high.

- This sensor is used to determine the outside air temperature that is displayed on the dash. ● **SEE FIGURE 12–3.**

IN-VEHICLE TEMPERATURE SENSOR The **in-vehicle temperature sensor** is often mounted behind the instrument

panel, and a set of holes or a small grill allows air to pass by it. Air from the blower motor passes through the venturi of the aspirator and pulls in-vehicle air past the thermistor. This tube is called an aspirator tube and is connected to the blower housing. Blower operation produces airflow through the aspirator and past the sensor. ● **SEE FIGURE 12–4.**

DISCHARGE AIR TEMPERATURE SENSOR The **discharge air temperature (DAT)** sensor is used to measure the temperature of the air leaving the dash vents.

- This discharge air temperature can be used to determine the proper temperature position or control compressor output.

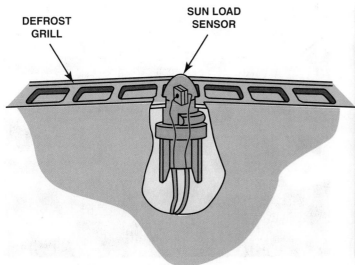

FIGURE 12–5 Sun load sensors are usually located at the top of the instrument panel.

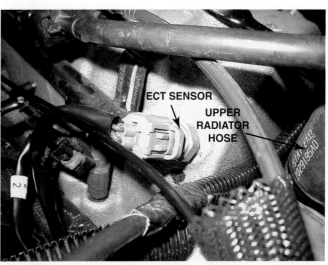

FIGURE 12–6 The engine coolant temperature (ECT) sensor is usually located near the engine thermostat so it can accurately measure the temperature of the coolant.

- This sensor reading is used by the controller, which compares the discharge temperature reading with the temperature set by the driver. The control module calculates the temperature difference and automatically adjusts the HVAC system to minimize this temperature difference.

EVAPORATOR TEMPERATURE SENSOR The **evaporator temperature (EVT) sensor** is used to measure the temperature of the air leaving the evaporator. Evaporator air temperature can be used to determine the proper temperature position or control compressor output. The long probe of this sensor passes between the evaporator fins. It provides an evaporator temperature input to the HVAC controller.

SUN LOAD SENSOR The **sun load sensor** (also called a *solar sensor*) is normally mounted on top of the instrument panel and is used to measure radiant heat load that might cause an increase of the in-vehicle temperature. Bright sunshine provides a signal to the Electronic Control Module (ECM) that things are going to get hotter. Sun load sensors are photodiodes that change their electrical conductivity based on the level of sunlight striking the sensor.

A typical sun load sensor uses a 5-volt operating voltage and produces an output signal voltage based on the intensity of the light.

- Dark = 0.3 volts
- Bright sunshine = 3.0 volts. ● **SEE FIGURE 12–5.**

INFRARED SENSORS **Infrared (IR) sensors** are mounted in the control head or overhead in the headliner. They monitor the surface temperature of the head and chest area of the

driver and passenger. The system will adjust the temperature and position of the airflow depending on the temperature they measure and the settings on the control head. The detector does not emit an infrared beam but instead measures the infrared rays that are emitted from the person's body.

COMPRESSOR SPEED SENSOR The air-conditioning (A/C) **compressor speed sensor**, also called a *lock* or *belt lock* sensor, is used so the ECM will know if the compressor is running, and by comparing the compressor and engine speed signals, the ECM can determine if the compressor clutch or drive belt is slipping excessively. It prevents a locked-up compressor from destroying the engine drive belt, which, in turn, can cause engine overheating or loss of power steering. If the ECM detects an excessive speed differential for more than a few seconds, it will turn the compressor off. The sensor can be either a magnetic type or a Hall-effect sensor. Check service information for details about the sensor for the vehicle being serviced.

ENGINE COOLANT TEMPERATURE SENSOR The **engine coolant temperature (ECT) sensor** is a thermistor and measures the temperature of the engine coolant and is usually located near the engine thermostat. The ECT sensor is used to keep the system from turning on the heater before the coolant is warmed up, which is often called *cold engine lockout*. ● **SEE FIGURE 12–6.**

PRESSURE TRANSDUCERS A **pressure transducer** can be used in the low- and/or high-pressure refrigerant line. The transducer converts the system pressure into an electrical

LOW SIDE PRESSURE	HIGH SIDE PRESSURE	CONDITION
25–35 PSI	170–200 PSI	Normal operation
Low	Low	Low refrigerant charge level
Low	High	Restriction in high-side line
High	High	System is overcharged
High	Low	Restriction in the low-side line

CHART 12–1

Sample refrigerant system pressures and possible causes as shown from the pressure sensors and displayed on a scan tool. Check service information for the exact procedures to follow if the pressures are not correct.

FIGURE 12–7 Some automatic HVAC system use the information from the factory navigation system to fine tune the interior temperature and airflow needs based on location and the direction of travel.

signal that allows the ECM to monitor pressure. The pressure signal can be used by the controller to:

- Cycle the compressor to prevent evaporator freeze-up.
- Change orifice tube size.
- Change the compressor displacement.
- Shut off the compressor or speedup cooling fan operation because of high pressures.
- Prevent compressor operation if the refrigerant level is low or empty.

The pressures of the refrigerant systems can be checked by looking at the scan tool scan data of a factory or factory-level scan tool. ● **SEE CHART 12–1** for some sample pressures and what they could indicate.

AIR QUALITY SENSORS Some systems use an *air quality sensor*, which detects hydrocarbons (HC) or ozone (O_3). HC can come from vehicle engine exhaust or decaying animal material and often produces offensive odors. Ozone is an irritant to the respiratory system. When the system detects an air quality issue, it automatically switches to using mostly inside air, about 80%, and reduces the amount of outside air entering the system to about 20% from the normal 80% level. This reduces the amount of outside air that is being brought into the passenger compartment until the system detects healthy outside air.

RELATIVE HUMIDITY SENSOR A few vehicles use a **relative humidity (RH) sensor** to determine the level of in-vehicle humidity. High RH increases the cooling load. A relative humidity sensor uses the capacitance change of a polymer thin film capacitor to detect the relative amount of moisture in the air. A dielectric polymer layer absorbs water molecules

through a thin metal electrode and causes capacitance change proportional to relative humidity. The thin polymer layer reacts very fast, usually in less than 5 seconds to 90% of the final value of relative humidity. The sensor responds to the full range from 0% to 100% relative humidity. The output of the sensor is sent to the HVAC controller, which uses the information to control the air inlet door and the air-conditioning compressor operation to achieve the desired level of humidity (20% to 40%) in the passenger compartment.

GPS SENSOR A few vehicles that are equipped with a global positioning system (GPS) for navigation will have a sun position strategy that tracks the angle of the sunlight entering the vehicle. Cooler in-vehicle temperatures are required if the vehicle is positioned so sunlight enters through the windshield or side windows. ● **SEE FIGURE 12–7.**

AIRFLOW CONTROL

NEED FOR AIRFLOW CONTROL The system that controls the airflow to the passenger compartment is called the **air management system** or *air distribution system*. Air flows into the housing (case) that contains the evaporator and heater core from two possible inlets.

1. **Outside air,** often called *fresh air*
2. **Inside air,** usually called *recirculation* (recirc)

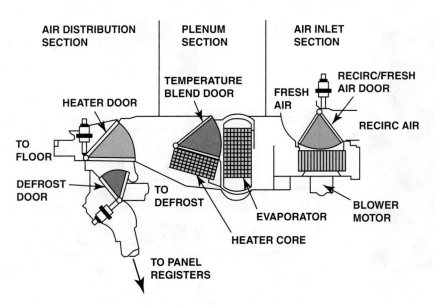

AIR DISTRIBUTION SECTION

PLENUM SECTION

AIR INLET SECTION

HEATER DOOR

TEMPERATURE BLEND DOOR

FRESH AIR

RECIRC/FRESH AIR DOOR

TO FLOOR

RECIRC AIR

DEFROST DOOR

TO DEFROST

EVAPORATOR

BLOWER MOTOR

HEATER CORE

TO PANEL REGISTERS

FIGURE 12–8 The three major portions of the A/C and heat system are air inlet, plenum, and air distribution. The shaded portions show the paths of the four control doors.

AIRFLOW CONTROL DOORS

From the case, the air can travel to one or more of three possible outlets. Airflow is usually controlled by three or more doors. Air flow inside the case can travel to one or more of three possible outlets.

The doors control:

- Air inlet to select outside or inside air inlet (often called the *recirculation* or *inlet* door)
- Temperature/blend to adjust air temperature (often just called the **blend door** or **temperature door**)
- Mode door to select air discharge location (direct air to the defrosters, the floor, or to the dash vents). ● **SEE FIGURE 12–8.**

A multispeed blower is included in this system to force air through the HVAC case when the vehicle is moving at low speeds or to increase the airflow at any speed.

CONTROLLING AIRFLOW

The amount or volume of HVAC air is controlled by blower speed. Higher speeds move more air. The inlet and outlet directions of the airflow and the discharge air temperature are controlled by swinging, sliding, or rotating doors. Most systems use a door (flap) that swings about 45° to 90°.

The duct system can be divided into three major sections:

1. *air inlet*
2. *plenum,* where the cold and hot air are mixed, and
3. *air distribution.*

Most doors are very simple and require little maintenance. A temperature-blend door is positioned at any place between the stops, wherever needed to produce the proper

air temperature. Reducing the HVAC assembly size usually reduces the weight. Several designs of doors include:

- *Sliding mode door* (also called a *rolling door*).
- Some of these door designs roll up, somewhat like a window shade, and unroll to block a passage.
- Another design uses a *rotary door*. This pan-shaped door has openings at the side and edge, and the door rotates about 100° to one of four different positions. Each position directs airflow to the desired outlet(s).

ACTUATORS

PURPOSE AND FUNCTION

HVAC actuators are electric or mechanical devices that move doors to provide the needed airflow at the correct time and location. Actuators include:

- Electric motors that operate the air/temperature doors, also called *flaps.*
- Feedback circuits that provide position information to the HVAC controller.

TYPES OF ACTUATORS

An actuator is a part that moves the vanes or valves. Actuators used in air-conditioning systems are either electric or vacuum operated and include three different types.

1. **Dual-Position Actuator.** A **dual-position actuator** is able to move either open or closed. An example of this type of actuator is the recirculation door, which can be either open or closed.

FIGURE 12–9 Three electric actuators can be easily seen on this demonstration unit. However, accessing these actuators in a vehicle can be difficult.

2. **Three-Position Actuator.** A **three-position actuator** is able to provide three air door positions, such as the bi-level door, which could allow defrost only, floor only, or a mixture of the two.

3. **Variable-Position Actuator.** A **variable-position actuator** is capable of positioning a valve in any position. All variable position actuators use a *feedback potentiometer*, which is used by the controller to detect the actual position of the door or valve. ● **SEE FIGURE 12–9.**

ELECTRIC ACTUATOR MOTORS Electric actuator motors are used to move air doors. Electric door actuators can be either continuous-position or two-position units (open or closed). Variable-position actuators can stop anywhere in their range and need a feedback circuit so the ECM will know their position. The temperature-blend door is operated by an electric servomotor (continuous-position actuator) that can move the door to any position called for to produce an air mix of the desired temperature. Some systems have the ability to count the actuator motor commutator segments so it is able to determine how far the motor revolves. A small current-flow reduction occurs as the space between the commutator bars passes under the brushes of a DC motor. This system needs no feedback circuit, but a calibration procedure must be performed if a motor or HVAC controller is replaced. Newer systems have an output from the ECM to each of the controlled actuators or outputs. ● **SEE FIGURE 12–10.**

■ **Temperature Control Actuators.** The heater core is placed downstream from the evaporator in the airflow so that air can be routed either through or around it and one

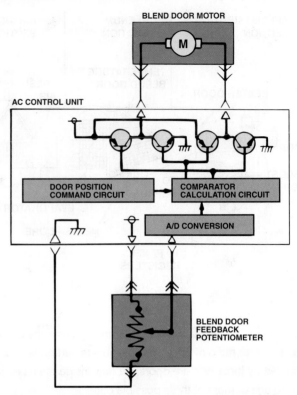

FIGURE 12–10 The feedback circuit signals the AC control unit with the blend door position.

or two doors are used to control this airflow. This door is usually called the **temperature-blend door**. Some other names that are used depending on the vehicle manufacturer include the following:

■ *air mix door*
■ *temperature door*
■ *blend door*
■ *diverter door*
■ *bypass door*

■ **Mode control actuators.** Some vehicles include ducts to transfer air to the rear seat area, and some vehicles include ducts to demist the vehicle's side windows with warm air. Airflow to these ducts is controlled by one or more **mode doors** controlled by the function lever or buttons. Mode doors are also called *function, floor-defrost,* or *panel-defrost* doors. Mode/function control sets the doors as follows:

■ **A/C:** in-dash registers with outside air inlet
■ **Max A/C:** in-dash registers with recirculation
■ **Heat:** floor level with outside air inlet
■ **Max Heat:** floor level with recirculation
■ **Bi-level:** both in-dash and floor discharge
■ **Defrost:** windshield registers

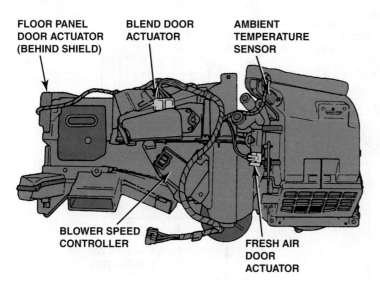

FLOOR PANEL
DOOR ACTUATOR
(BEHIND SHIELD)

BLEND DOOR
ACTUATOR

AMBIENT
TEMPERATURE
SENSOR

BLOWER SPEED
CONTROLLER

FRESH AIR
DOOR
ACTUATOR

FIGURE 12–11 A typical HVAC system showing some of the airflow door locations.

Many control heads also provide for in-between settings, which combine some of these operations. In many systems, a small amount of air is directed to the defroster ducts when in the heat mode, and while in defrost mode a small amount of air goes to the floor level.

- **Inlet Air control door actuators.** Air can enter the duct system from either the plenum chamber in front of the windshield (outside air) or return register (inside air). The return register is often positioned below the right end of the instrument panel. (The right and left sides of the vehicle are always described as seen by the driver.) The *inlet air control door* can also be called the

  - *fresh air door,*
  - *recirculation door, or*
  - *outside air door*

This door is normally positioned so it allows airflow from one source while it shuts off the other. It can be positioned to allow outside air to enter

- While shutting off the recirculation opening.
- To allow air to return or recirculate from inside the vehicle while shutting off outside (fresh) air.
- To allow a mix of outside air and return air.

In most vehicles, the door is set to the outside air position in all function lever positions except off, max heat, and max A/C. Max A/C and max heat settings position the door to recirculate in-vehicle air. ● **SEE FIGURE 12–11.**

DUAL-ZONE SYSTEMS In many vehicles, the HVAC system is capable of supplying discharge air of more than one temperature to different areas in the vehicle. This type of system is usually referred to as a **Dual-Zone System** and allows

the driver and front seat passenger to set their own desired temperature. Dual-zone systems contain two separately commanded temperature-blend doors. The temperature difference between the driver and front seat passenger can be up to 30°F (16°C), usually with settings between 60°F (16°C) minimum and 90°F (32°C) maximum. ● **SEE FIGURE 12–12.**

Tri-Zone and *Quad-Zone* systems are usually found in passenger vans, sport utility vehicles, and luxury cars, which allow the passengers in the rear of the vehicle to control the temperature at their location.

AUTOMATIC HVAC CONTROLS

OPERATION The HVAC control head or panel is mounted in the instrument cluster. The control head provides the switches and levers needed to control the different aspects of the heating and A/C system, which include:

- HVAC system on and off
- A/C on/off
- Outside or recirculated air
- A/C, defrost, or heating mode
- Temperature desired
- Blower speed

COMPRESSOR CONTROLS Most air-conditioning compressors use an electromagnetic clutch. A coil of wire inside the clutch creates a strong magnetic field that when activated connects the input shaft of the compressor to the drive pulley.

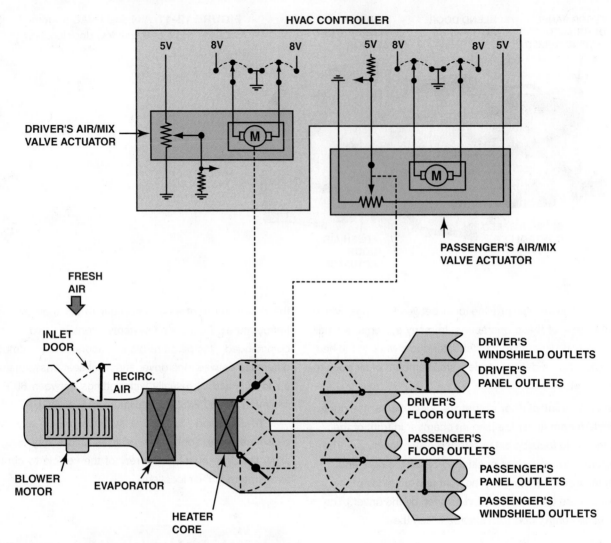

FIGURE 12–12 A dual-climate control system showing the airflow and how it splits.

Most electromagnetic coil assemblies have between 3 ohms and 4 ohms of resistance. According to Ohm's law, about 3 amperes to 4 amperes of current are required to energize the air-conditioning compressor clutch. All electrical circuits require the following to operate:

1. A voltage source

2. Protection (fuse)

3. Control (switch)

4. An electrical load (the air-conditioning compressor clutch)

5. A ground connection

All five of these must be working before current (amperes) can flow, causing the compressor clutch to engage. Some systems may connect one or more switches in series with the compressor clutch so that all have to be functioning before the compressor clutch can be engaged. A low- and high-pressure switch or sensor may also be an input to the PCM or HVAC controller for use in controlling the compressor.

- **Low-pressure switch:** This pressure switch is electrically closed only if there is 8 PSI to 24 PSI (55 kPa to 165 kPa) of refrigerant pressure. This amount of pressure means that the system is sufficiently charged to provide lubrication for the compressor.

- **High-pressure switch:** This pressure switch is located in the high-pressure side of the A/C system. If the pressure exceeds a certain level, typically 375 PSI (2,600 kPa), the pressure switch opens, thereby preventing possible damage to the air-conditioning system due to excessively high pressure.

- **A/C relay:** The relay supplies power to the compressor.

CONTROL MODULE The control module used for automatic climatic control systems can be referred by various terms depending on the exact make and model of vehicle. Some commonly used terms include the following:

- ECM (Electronic control module)
- BCM (Body control module)
- HVAC control module (often is built into the smart control head)
- HVAC controller or programmer

The control modules are programmed to open or close circuits to the actuators based on the values of the various sensors. Although it is unable to handle the electric current for devices such as the compressor clutch or blower motor, the control module can operate relays. These relays in turn control the electric devices. Units that use small current flows, such as a light-emitting diode (LED) or digital display, can operate directly from the control module.

An ECM is programmed with various strategies to suit the requirements of the particular vehicle. For example, when A/C is requested by the driver of a vehicle with a relatively small engine, the ECM will probably increase the engine idle RPM. On this same vehicle, the ECM will probably shut off the compressor clutch during wide-open throttle (WOT).

- On other vehicles, the ECM might shut off the compressor clutch at very high speeds to prevent the compressor from spinning too fast.
- In some cases, part of the A/C and heat operating strategy is built into the control head and are called **smart control heads**. In some cases, door operating strategy is built into the door operating motors, and these are called **smart motors**.
- Many control modules are programmed to run a test sequence, called *self-diagnosis*, at start-up (when the ignition key is turned on). If improper electrical values are found, the ECM indicates a failure often by blinking the A/C indicator light at the control head. Some ECMs also monitor the system during operation and indicate a failure or stop the compressor if there is a problem. One system, for example, notes the frequency of clutch cycling that indicates a low refrigerant charge level. If there are too many clutch cycles during a certain time period, the control module will shut off the compressor and set a diagnostic trouble code (DTC). ● **SEE FIGURE 12–13.**

? FREQUENTLY ASKED QUESTION

Why Is the Blower Speed So High?

This question is often asked by passengers when riding in a vehicle equipped with automatic climatic control. The controller does command a high blower speed if:

- The outside temperature is low and the engine coolant temperature is hot enough to provide heat. The high blower speed is used to warm the passenger compartment as quickly as possible then when the temperature has reached the preset level, then the blower speed is reduced to maintain the preset temperature.
- The outside temperature is hot and the air-conditioning compressor is working to provide cooling. The high speed blower is used to circulate air through the evaporator in an attempt to cool the passenger compartment as quickly as possible. Once the temperature reaches close to the preset temperature, the blower speed is reduced to keep the temperature steady.

CONTROLLING AIR TEMPERATURE Most HVAC systems are considered *reheat* systems in that the incoming air is chilled as it passes through the evaporator. The air is then heated as part or all of the flow passes through the heater core so it reaches the desired in-vehicle temperature. Chilling the incoming air is a good method of removing water vapor to reduce humidity, but it is not the most efficient method to get cool air. There is an increasing trend to use an electronically controlled variable displacement compressor with an air temperature sensor after the evaporator. Compressor displacement is adjusted to cool the evaporator just enough to cool the air to the desired temperature, which reduces the load on the compressor and improves fuel economy.

AIR FILTRATION

PURPOSE AND FUNCTION Many newer systems include an HVAC air filter, usually called a cabin filter, in the air distribution system. Cabin filters are located outside the air inlet and are serviced under the hood, or between blower and

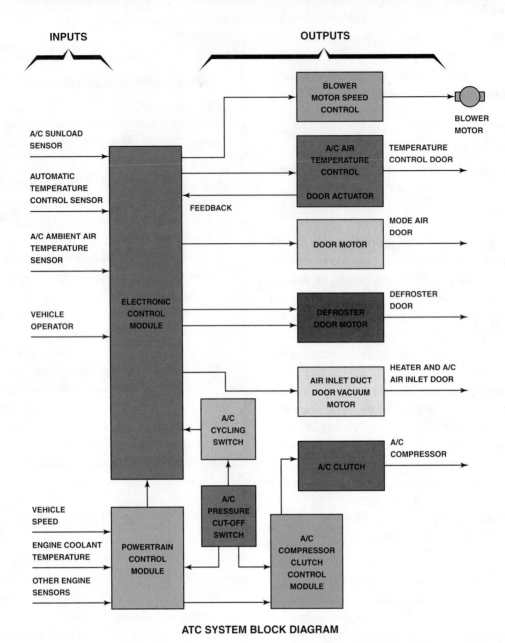

INPUTS

OUTPUTS

ATC SYSTEM BLOCK DIAGRAM

FIGURE 12–13 A block diagram showing the inputs to the electronic control assembly and the outputs; note that some of the outputs have feedback to the ECM.

evaporator which are serviced from under the dash. ● **SEE FIGURE 12–14.**

This filter can also be referred to as

- *interior filter*
- *ventilation filter*
- *micron filter*
- *particulate filter*
- *pollen filter*

The cabin filter removes small dust or pollen particles from the incoming airstream. These filters require periodic replacement and if they are not serviced properly, can cause an airflow reduction when they become plugged.

TYPES OF CABIN FILTERS There are two types of filter media.

1. **Particle filters.** Particle filters remove solid particles such as dust, soot, spores, and pollen using a special paper or nonwoven fleece material; they can trap particles that are about 3 microns or larger.

2. **Adsorption filters.** Adsorption filters remove noxious gases and odors using an activated charcoal media with the charcoal layer between layers of filter media.

These two filter types can be combined into a combination or two-stage filter. The filter media can have an electrostatic charge to make it more efficient.

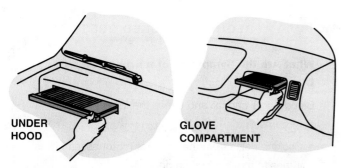

UNDER HOOD

GLOVE COMPARTMENT

FIGURE 12–14 A cabin filter can be accessed either through the glove compartment or under the hood on most vehicles.

 REAL WORLD FIX

Cabin Filter Fault

The owner of a 2008 Ford Escape complained that the air-conditioning system was not cooling the inside of the vehicle and there seemed to be no air-flow from the dash vents yet the blower motor could be heard running. A quick visual inspection of the cabin air with access under the hood showed that the cabin filter was almost completely blocked with paper, leaves, and debris. The vehicle had almost 80,000 miles on the odometer and the way it looked, the air filter had never been replaced. Most vehicle manufacturers recommend replacement of the cabin air filter about every three years or every 36,000 miles. Replacing the cabin air filter restored proper operation of the A/C system.

AUTOMATIC CLIMATIC CONTROL DIAGNOSIS

DIAGNOSTIC PROCEDURE If a fault occurs in the automatic climatic system, check service information for the specified procedure to follow for the vehicle being checked. Most vehicle service information includes the following steps:

STEP 1 Verify the customer concern. Check that the customer is operating the system correctly. For example, most automatic systems cannot detect when the defrosters are needed so most systems have a control that turns on the defroster(s).

STEP 2 Perform a thorough visual inspection of the heating and cooling system for any obvious faults.

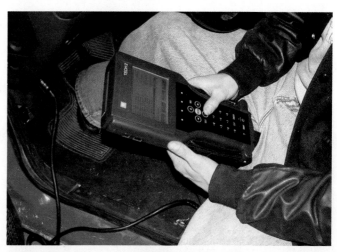

FIGURE 12–15 A TECH 2 scan tool is the factory scan tool used on General Motors vehicles.

STEP 3 Use a factory scan tool or a factory level aftermarket scan tool and check for diagnostic trouble codes (DTCs).

NOTE: Older systems can be accessed using the buttons on the control panel and then the diagnostic trouble codes and system data are displayed. Check service information for the exact procedures to follow for the vehicle being serviced.

STEP 4 If there are stored diagnostic trouble codes, follow service information instructions for diagnosing the system. ● **SEE CHART 12–2** for sample diagnostic trouble codes (DTCs).

STEP 5 If there are no stored diagnostic trouble codes, check scan tool data for possible fault areas in the system.

SCAN TOOL BIDIRECTIONAL CONTROL Scan tools are the most important tool for any diagnostic work on all vehicles. Scan tools can be divided into two basic groups:

1. **Factory scan tools.** These are the scan tools required by all dealers that sell and service a specific brand of vehicle. Examples of factory scan tools include:
   - **General Motors**—TECH 2. ● **SEE FIGURE 12–15.**
   - **Ford**—WDS (Worldwide Diagnostic System) and IDS (Integrated Diagnostic Software).
   - **Chrysler**—DRB-III, Star Scan or WiTECH
   - **Honda**—HDS or Master Tech
   - **Toyota**—Master Tech; Tech Stream

All factory scan tools are designed to provide bidirectional capability, which allows the service technician the opportunity to operate components using the scan tool, thereby confirming that the component is able to work when commanded.

ATC-RELATED DIAGNOSTIC TROUBLE CODES

BODY DIAGNOSTIC TROUBLE CODE (DTC)	DESCRIPTION
B0126	Right Panel Discharge Temperature Fault
B0130	Air Temperature/Mode Door Actuator Malfunction
B0131	Right Heater Discharge Temperature Fault
B0145	Auxiliary HAVC Actuator Circuit
B0159	Outside Air Temperature Sensor Circuit Range/Performance
B0160/B0162	Ambient Air Temperature Sensor Circuit
B0164	Passenger Compartment Temperature Sensor #1 (Single Sensor or LH) Circuit Range/Performance
B0169	In-Vehicle Temp Sensor Failure (passenger—not used)
B0174	Output Air Temperature Sensor #1 (Upper Single or LH) Circuit Range/Performance
B0179	Output Air Temperature Sensor #2 (Lower Single or LH) Circuit Range/Performance
B0183	Sun Load Sensor Circuit
B0184	Solar Load Sensor #1 Circuit Range (sun load)
B0188	Sun Load Sensor Circuit
B0189	Solar Load Sensor #2 Circuit Range (sun load)
B0229	HVAC Actuator Circuit
B0248	Mode Door Inoperative Error
B0249	Heater/Defrost/AC Door Range Error
B0263	HVAC Actuator Circuit
B0268	Air/Inlet Door Inoperative Error
B0269	Air Inlet Door Range Error
B0408	Temperature Control #1 (Main/Front) Circuit Malfunction
B0409	Air Mix Door #1 Range Error
B0414	Air Temperature/Mode Door Actuator Malfunction
B0418	HVAC Actuator Circuit
B0419	Air Mix Door #2 Range Error
B0423	Air Mix Door #2 Inoperative Error
B0424	Air Temperature/Mode Door Actuator Malfunction
B0428	Air Mix Door #3 Inoperative Error

CHART 12–2

Sample automatic climatic control diagnostic trouble codes.

 FREQUENTLY ASKED QUESTION

What Are the Symptoms of a Broken Blend Door?

Blend doors can fail and cause the following symptoms:

- Clicking noise from the actuator motor assembly as it tries to move a broken door.
- Outlet temperature can change from hot to cold or from cold to hot at any time especially when cornering because the broken door is being forced one way or the other due to the movement of the vehicle.
- A change in the temperature when the fan speed is changed. The air movement can move the broken blend door into another position which can change the vent temperature.

If any of these symptoms are occurring, then a replacement blend door is required.

ATC components that may be able to be controlled or checked using a scan tool include:

- Blower speed control (faster and slower to check operation)
- Command the position of airflow doors to check for proper operation and to check for proper airflow from the vents and ducts
- Values of all sensors
- Pressures of the refrigerant in the high and low sides of the systems

2. **Aftermarket scan tools.** These scan tools are designed to function on more than one brand of vehicle. Examples of aftermarket scan tools include:

- **Snap-on** (various models, including the Ethos, Modis, and Solus)
- **OTC** (various models, including Pegasus, Genisys, and Task Master). ● **SEE FIGURE 12–16.**
- **AutoEnginuity** and other programs that use a laptop or handheld computer for the display.

While many aftermarket scan tools can display most if not all of the parameters of the factory scan tool, there can be a difference when trying to troubleshoot some faults.

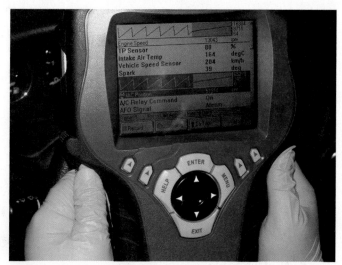

FIGURE 12–16 An OTC Genisys being used to troubleshoot a vehicle. This scan tool can be used on most makes and models of vehicles and is capable of diagnosing other computer systems in the vehicles such as the automatic temperature control system as well as the antilock braking system (ABS) and airbag systems.

SENSOR	TYPICAL VALUE
Inside air temperature sensor	−40°F to 120°F (−40°C to 49°C)
Ambient air temperature sensor	−40°F to 120°F (−40°C to 49°C)
Engine coolant temperature (ECT) sensor	40°F to 250°F (−40°C to 121°C)
Sun load Sensor	0.3 volts (dark) 3.0 volts (bright)
Evaporator temperature sensor	Usually 34°F to 44°F (1°C to 7°C)
Relative Humidity sensor	0% to100%

CHART 12–3

Typical sensors and values that may be displayed on a scan tool. Check service information for the exact specifications for the vehicle being serviced.

SCAN TOOL DATA Scan data related to the automatic climatic control system can be confusing. Typical data and their meaning are shown in ● **CHART 12–3.**

SUMMARY

1. Automatic temperature control (ATC) systems use sensors to detect the conditions both inside and outside the vehicle.

2. The sensors used include the following:
   - Sun load sensor
   - Evaporator temperature sensor
   - Ambient air temperature (outside air temperature) sensor
   - In-vehicle temperature sensor
   - Infrared Sensors
   - Engine coolant temperature (ECT) sensor

3. Pressure transducers detect the pressures in the refrigerant system.

4. Some systems use a compressor speed sensor to detect if the drive belt or compressor clutch is slipping.

5. The heater core is placed downstream from the evaporator in the airflow so that air can be routed either through or around it and one or two doors are used to control this airflow. This door is called the *temperature-blend door.*

6. In many vehicles, the HVAC system is capable of supplying discharge air of more than one temperature to different areas in the vehicle. This type of system is usually referred to as a *Dual-Zone Climate Control System.*

7. The diagnostic steps include:
   - Verify the customer concern
   - Perform a thorough vial inspection
   - Retrieve diagnostic trouble codes (DTCs)
   - Check the data as displayed on a scan tool to determine what sensors or actuators are at fault

REVIEW QUESTIONS

1. What sensors are used in a typical automatic temperature control (ATC) system?

2. What are the three airflow sections in a typical HVAC system?

3. Why is a feedback potentiometer used on an electric actuator?

4. What is the purpose of the aspirator tube in the in-vehicle temperature sensor section?

1. What is the purpose of a compressor speed sensor?
   a. To allow the ECM to control compressor speed
   b. So the ECM can control high-side pressure
   c. So the ECM can control low-side pressure
   d. To let the ECM know if the compressor is turning

2. Which sensor is also called the ambient air temperature sensor?
   a. Outside air temperature (OAT)
   b. In vehicle temperature
   c. Discharge air temperature
   d. Evaporator outlet temperature

3. What is the most common type of sun load sensor?
   a. Potentiometer
   b. Negative temperature coefficient (NTC) thermistor
   c. Photodiode
   d. Positive temperature coefficient (PTC) thermistor

4. An actuator can be capable of how many position(s)?
   a. Two
   b. Three
   c. Variable
   d. All of the above

5. Some cabin filters contain _____ to absorb odors.
   a. Perfume
   b. Activated charcoal
   c. Paper filter material
   d. Synthetic fibers

6. Which sensor might use an aspirator tube?
   a. In vehicle temperature
   b. Outside air temperature (OAT)
   c. Discharge air temperature
   d. Evaporator outlet temperature

7. Technician A says that some cabin filters are accessible behind the glove compartment. Technician B says that some cabin filters are accessible from under the hood. Which technician is correct?
   a. Technician A only
   b. Technician B only
   c. Both technicians A and B
   d. Neither technician A nor B

8. Automatic temperature control (ATC) diagnosis includes _____.
   a. Verify customer concern
   b. Perform a visual inspection
   c. Check for stored diagnostic trouble codes
   d. All of the above

9. The control module used for automatic climatic control systems is called _____.
   a. ECM
   b. BCM
   c. HVAC control module
   d. Any of the above depending on the make and model of vehicle

10. A feedback potentiometer is used to _____.
    a. Provide feedback to the driver as to where the controls are set
    b. Provide feedback to the controller as to the location of a door or valve
    c. Give temperature information about the outside air temperature to the dash display
    d. Any of the above depending on the exact make and model of vehicle

chapter 13
HYBRID AND ELECTRIC VEHICLE HVAC SYSTEMS

LEARNING OBJECTIVES

After studying this chapter, the reader will be able to:

1. Prepare for the ASE Heating and Air Conditioning (A7) certification test content area "A" (A/C System Service, Diagnosis and Repair).

2. Explain the basic operation of the air-conditioning system used in hybrid electric vehicles.

3. Discuss the types of compressors used in a hybrid electric vehicle.

4. Explain the components and modes of operation of a coolant heat storage system.

5. Describe the parts and operation of cabin heating systems.

6. Explain the effect of heat on the electrical/electronic systems of a hybrid electric vehicle.

KEY TERMS

Coolant heat storage system 215

PTC heater 219

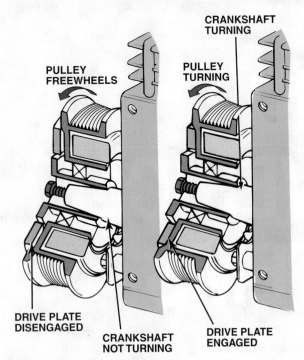

FIGURE 13-1 The A/C compressor clutch allows the compressor to engage and disengage as necessary while the ICE continues to run.

HYBRID VEHICLE AIR-CONDITIONING SYSTEMS

BASIC OPERATION The fundamental purpose of any air-conditioning system is to absorb heat in one location and then dissipate (move) that heat to another location. Control of the air-conditioning system is the operation of the compressor, as well as the airflow across the evaporator and condenser. The types of compressors used in hybrid electric vehicles include:

- Belt-driven by the internal combustion engine (ICE) accessory drive. The belt drive often uses an electrically operated clutch, which allows the compressor pulley to disconnect from the compressor and stop refrigerant flow in the system while the ICE continues to run. ●SEE FIGURE 13-1.

- Dual compressor where a large section of it is driven by the internal combustion engine and another smaller section driven by a high-voltage electric motor to provide cooling during idle/stop (start/stop) operation.

- Electric-motor powered compressor used in all electric vehicles and many hybrid electric vehicles.

In most situations, fresh air is brought in from outside the vehicle and then is heated or cooled before being sent to the appropriate vents. It is also possible to draw air from the passenger compartment itself, when the system is placed in the recirculation mode.

The fresh air coming into the vehicle is sometimes sent through a cabin filter first, in order to remove particulate matter and prevent clogging of the evaporator. All the incoming air must pass through the A/C evaporator core after leaving the blower motor. ●SEE FIGURE 13-2.

In defrost mode, the A/C compressor is activated and the evaporator core is cooled to the point where any humidity in the air will condense on the evaporator and then be drained outside the vehicle. When in defrost mode, the air leaving the A/C evaporator core can be sent through the heater core to raise its temperature. This warm air is sent to the defrost outlets on the driver's and the passenger side of the windshield.

The temperature of the air is controlled by the position of the air blend door, as it either directs varying amounts of air over the heater core or bypasses it completely. On most systems, when the controls are in the heat position (mode), the A/C compressor is turned off and the evaporator operates at ambient temperature. This means that any temperature change of the incoming air is now controlled only by the blend door as it directs the air across the heater core. The heater core is part of the ICE cooling system, and hot coolant is circulated through it by the water pump. ●SEE FIGURE 13-3.

When the system is placed in the *A/C mode,* the A/C compressor is engaged and the blower motor circulates air over the evaporator.

- The cool, dehumidified air is then sent to the blend door, where the air can bypass the heater core completely when maximum cooling effect is required.

- If warmer air is desirable, its temperature can be increased by changing the position of the blend door so that some of the air passes through the heater core on its way to the distribution ducts.

- The final air temperature is achieved by blending the heated air from the heater core with the unheated air.

HYBRID ELECTRIC VEHICLE COMPRESSORS

CONVENTIONAL COMPRESSORS Many hybrid vehicles use an electrically driven compressor, which allows compressor and A/C operation with the engine at idle-stop. Hybrids using belt-driven compressors use a 12-volt electromagnetic clutch,

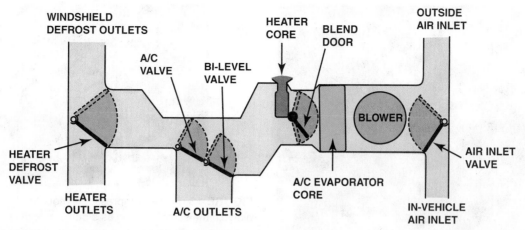

FIGURE 13–2 A basic air distribution system. Air can enter the system from outside the vehicle, or from the passenger compartment while in the recirculation mode.

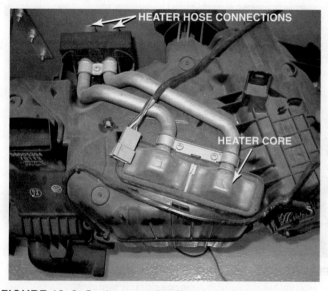

FIGURE 13–3 Coolant can circulate through the heater core when the thermostat is closed.

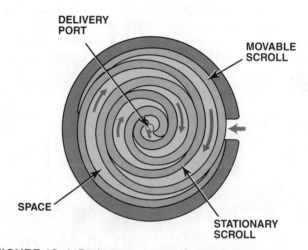

FIGURE 13–4 Basic components of a scroll compressor. Note the "pockets" of refrigerant that occupy the spaces labeled with red arrows.

similar to non-hybrid vehicles. When this type is used on a hybrid electric vehicle, the idle stop (start/stop) function is disabled so that cooling can continue when the vehicle is stopped. The most commonly used compressor design in hybrid electric vehicles is the scroll compressor. ● SEE FIGURE 13–4.

DUAL COMPRESSORS
A few hybrid vehicles use a dual compressor that is belt- (85%) and electrically (15%) driven. The electrically driven portion of a Honda hybrid electric vehicle compressor operates at more than 150 volts (depending on the vehicle), 3-phase AC and provides cooling during idle stop.

- One part is a 4.6 cu. inch (75 cc) belt-driven compressor that will stop when the engine stops
- The other part is a smaller 0.9 cu. inch (15 cc) electric compressor that runs during idle-auto-stop to keep the A/C operating.

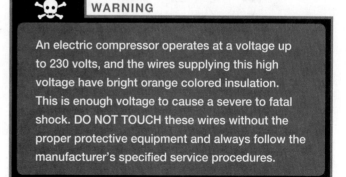

☠ WARNING

An electric compressor operates at a voltage up to 230 volts, and the wires supplying this high voltage have bright orange colored insulation. This is enough voltage to cause a severe to fatal shock. DO NOT TOUCH these wires without the proper protective equipment and always follow the manufacturer's specified service procedures.

Some hybrid vehicles use an A/C system much like other vehicles, but run the engine constantly when the A/C is turned on. Many hybrid vehicles use an electrically driven compressor that allows compressor and A/C operation with the engine at idle stop. ● SEE FIGURES 13–5 AND 13–6.

FIGURE 13–5 Hybrid electric vehicle A/C compressor. Note that this unit is primarily belt driven but has a high-voltage electric motor built in to allow A/C system operation during idle stop. The orange cable indicates that the wires carry high voltage. Always follow the safety warning precautions as specified by the vehicle manufacturer.

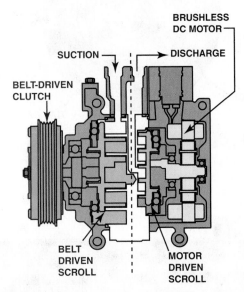

FIGURE 13–6 This hybrid vehicle A/C compressor uses two scrolls with one being belt driven (left) and the other driven by a brushless DC motor (right).

ELECTRIC COMPRESSORS
Electric vehicles do not have an internal combustion engine, and hybrid vehicles do not always run the engine continuously during vehicle operation. An electric compressor operates from the high-voltage (HV) battery pack and can therefore provide cooling under all conditions if the vehicle is moving or has stopped. An electric compressor combines a scroll compressor with a DC electric motor. ● SEE FIGURE 13–7.

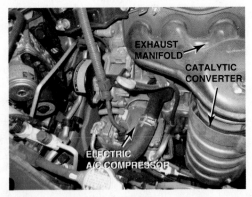

FIGURE 13–7 The compressor is mounted to the engine block in the same location as a conventional engine-driven compressor. This mounting helps reduce noise and vibration.

FIGURE 13–8 Specific A/C compressor oil designed for use in Honda hybrid vehicle air-conditioning systems.

The electric motor is cycled on and off to produce the desired cooling. This unit can be mounted at any convenient place on the vehicle since it does not need to be connected to an engine.

Hybrid vehicles use an internal combustion engine (ICE) to charge the HV battery pack, and is also used to power the vehicle when needed. Most hybrid vehicles shut the ICE off when the vehicle is stopped.

REFRIGERANT OIL Hybrid vehicle A/C systems that use electric-driven compressors must use POE (polyol ester) oil, unlike all other compressors. PAG (polyalkylene glycol) oil, which is used in non-hybrid vehicles, is slightly conductive and can cause deterioration of the insulation on the windings of the compressor motor. This can cause the compressor to become electrically conductive, which can result in electrical leakage. This leakage can potentially be hazardous during future service. ● SEE FIGURE 13–8.

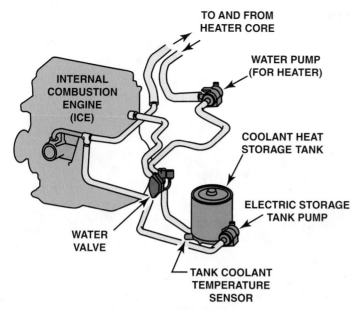

FIGURE 13–9 Toyota's coolant heat storage system. Note that the electric storage tank pump is located behind the coolant storage tank.

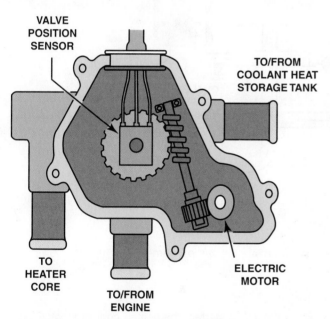

FIGURE 13–11 The valve position sensor in the water valve provides feedback to the ECM concerning the position of the water valve.

COOLANT HEAT STORAGE SYSTEM

PRIUS-2004–2009 In order to meet ever-increasing emissions standards, engineers strive to limit the impact that cold starts have on emissions and drivability. One approach is to use a **coolant heat storage system** where heated coolant

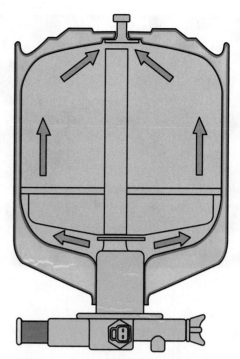

FIGURE 13–10 A vacuum exists between the inner and outer casing of the coolant heat storage tank. The outlet temperature sensor and the drain plug are located in the manifold at the bottom of the tank.

is stored during normal vehicle operation and is then used to warm the engine intake ports prior to a cold start. Toyota uses this system in the second-generation Prius (2004–2009).

COMPONENTS The heated coolant storage system is part of the ICE cooling system, but adds the major components described on the following page. ● SEE FIGURE 13–9.

The coolant heat storage tank is built very similar to a Thermos® bottle. The tank is built with an inner and outer casing, and a vacuum is formed between them. This is done to prevent heat transfer from the inner casing. Approximately 3 quarts (liters) of coolant are stored inside the inner casing, and the coolant can be kept warm for up to three days. There is a standpipe that extends inside of the inner casing, so coolant must rise in order to exit the tank through the standpipe. ● SEE FIGURE 13–10.

A water valve is used to direct the coolant flow between the coolant storage tank, the ICE, and the vehicle's heater core. The water valve is controlled by the ECM and consists of an electric motor, drive gears, a rotary valve, and a valve position sensor. ● SEE FIGURE 13–11.

The storage tank pump is used to move coolant through the heat storage tank at times when the ICE is shut off. This pump is located on the side of the heated coolant storage tank and is plumbed in series with the tank inlet. ● SEE FIGURE 13–12.

FIGURE 13–12 The storage tank and pump assembly as removed from underneath the vehicle. This pump is energized when coolant must be moved through the tank but the ICE is shut off.

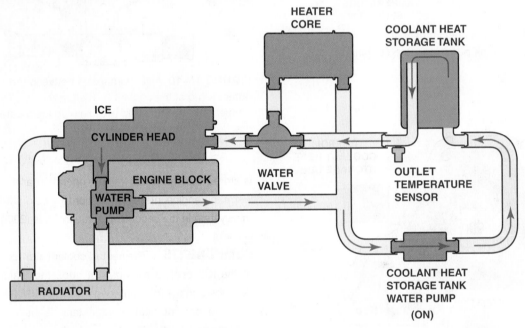

HEATER
CORE

COOLANT HEAT
STORAGE TANK

ICE

CYLINDER HEAD

ENGINE BLOCK

WATER
PUMP

WATER
VALVE

OUTLET
TEMPERATURE
SENSOR

RADIATOR

COOLANT HEAT
STORAGE TANK
WATER PUMP
(ON)

FIGURE 13–13 During preheat mode, the ICE remains off while the coolant heat storage pump is turned on. The water valve directs hot coolant from the storage tank to the ICE cylinder head.

MODES OF OPERATION

The coolant heat storage system has four modes of operation. These include:

1. Preheat
2. Engine warm-up
3. Storage during driving
4. Storage during ignition off

The preheat mode is enabled prior to the starting of the ICE. The ECM turns on the electric storage tank pump and directs the water valve to send hot coolant from the storage tank into the cylinder head. This allows for easier starting and minimizes emissions during a cold start. ● SEE FIGURE 13–13.

Once the ICE is started, the heated coolant storage system enters the engine warm-up mode. The storage water pump is turned off and the water valve directs coolant from the ICE into the heater core, bypassing the heated coolant storage tank. This feature provides warm air for the passenger compartment until the ICE reaches operating temperature. ● SEE FIGURE 13–14.

Once the ICE has reached operating temperature, the water valve is moved to allow coolant from the ICE to flow into both the heater core and the coolant heat storage tank. This process replaces the cold coolant in the storage tank with heated coolant, and is known as storage operation (driving).

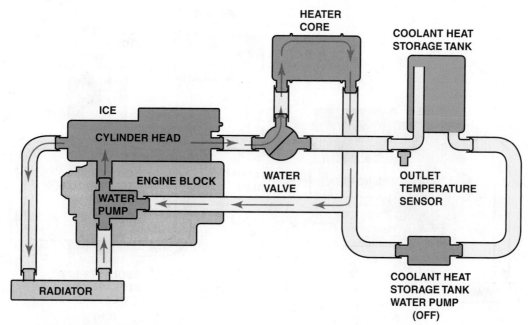

FIGURE 13–14 Coolant bypasses the coolant heat storage tank during engine warm-up mode.

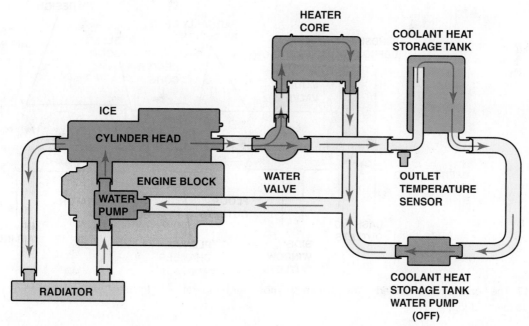

FIGURE 13–15 The coolant heat storage tank is filled with hot coolant when the ICE reaches operating temperature. This coolant is then used to warm the engine before the next cold start.

The heated coolant storage water pump remains off and coolant is moved through the system using only the ICE mechanical water pump. ● **SEE FIGURE 13–15**.

Once the tank is filled with hot coolant, the water valve moves back to the engine warm-up position. This directs coolant from the ICE into the heater core, and

bypasses the heated coolant storage tank. If the ICE is shut off while the heated coolant storage tank is being filled, the water valve stays in the storage position and the storage tank pump is turned on to finish filling the tank. This phase is known as storage operation (ignition off). ● **SEE FIGURE 13–16**.

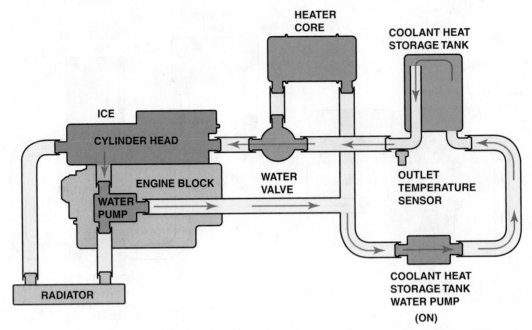

FIGURE 13–16 Storage operation (ignition off) mode. This takes place if the ICE is shut off while the coolant tank is being filled.

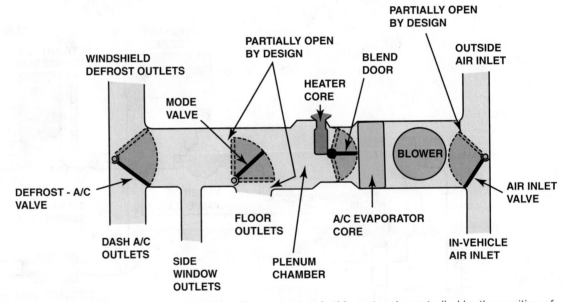

FIGURE 13–17 The heater core is located in the plenum chamber. Air temperature in this system is controlled by the position of the air mix valve (blend door).

CABIN HEATING SYSTEMS

PARTS AND OPERATION Heater cores are built similar to radiators, but are much smaller and often have the inlet and outlet pipes located at the same end of the assembly. The heater core is located in the passenger compartment, inside the plenum chamber (air distribution box) for the vehicle's heater and air-conditioning components. ● **SEE FIGURE 13–17.**

Air entering the plenum chamber must first pass through the A/C evaporator core, and then is directed either through or around the heater core by the blend door (*air mix valve*). The temperature of the air can be adjusted by changing the position of the blend door and the percentage of air that is sent through the heater core. Once the air leaves the heater core, it is blended with any air that has bypassed it and then is sent to its destination through a series of mode doors. These direct the air to specific areas of the vehicle, depending on the mode that is

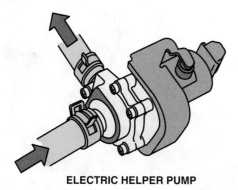

ELECTRIC HELPER PUMP

FIGURE 13–18 The electric helper pump is turned on whenever cabin heating is requested and the ICE is in idle stop mode. The pump is plumbed in series with the hoses running to the vehicle heater core.

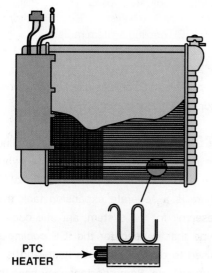

FIGURE 13–19 PTC heaters can be located on the heater core itself to help boost heat to the passenger compartment when coolant temperature is low.

selected at the time. For instance, the defrost mode will require that the air be directed toward the windshield outlets. In the heat mode, however, the air can be sent to the instrument panel outlets and/or the floor vents depending on make and model.

ENGINE-OFF HEATER OPERATION Some vehicles, including some hybrid and non-hybrids, have a feature that allows the heater to keep operating when the engine is turned off. In cold climates, this keeps the vehicle warm during start/stop operation. The main component is an electric pump, called an *auxiliary water pump*, along with a bypass valve. ● **SEE FIGURE 13–18.**

When the heater is on and the engine is off, the bypass valve closes, and the pump operates to maintain a hot coolant flow through the heater core. When the heater is on with the engine running, the pump is shut off, and the bypass valve is open to allow normal heater operation.

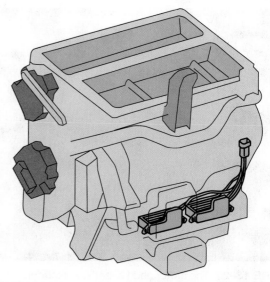

FIGURE 13–20 Two PTC heaters are located in the footwell air ducts in the Toyota Prius. These are energized when the coolant temperature is low and MAX HOT is requested in the FOOT or FOOT/DEF modes.

PTC HEATERS Another approach used to heat the interior on a hybrid electric vehicle is to use **PTC heaters** built into the heater core itself. Positive temperature coefficient (PTC) refers to the tendency of a conductor to increase its electrical resistance as its temperature increases. PTC heaters convert electrical energy into heat, and this is used to boost heat to the passenger compartment. ● **SEE FIGURE 13–19.**

PTC heaters can also be located in the air ducts in the form of a honeycomb-shaped grid. Air that is leaving the plenum chamber passes through these heaters before it enters the passenger compartment. The Toyota Prius uses PTC heaters located in the heater core, as well as the footwell air ducts. The A/C electronic control unit turns on the PTC heaters when the coolant temperature is low and MAX HOT is requested. ● **SEE FIGURE 13–20.**

HEV ELECTRIC MOTOR AND CONTROL SYSTEM COOLING

NEED FOR COOLING Hybrid electric vehicles are unique in that they have electric motors and electronic controls that are not found in vehicles with conventional drivetrains. These components are designed to operate under heavy load with high current and voltage demands, so they tend to generate excessive heat during vehicle operation. Special auxiliary

FIGURE 13–21 The motor and HV battery electronics on Honda hybrid vehicles are air cooled. Note the cooling fins for the modules.

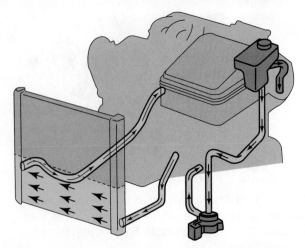

FIGURE 13–22 The electric motors and the motor controls are cooled using a separate cooling system. This Toyota Hybrid Synergy Drive (HSD) system uses a radiator that is integral with the ICE cooling system radiator.

? FREQUENTLY ASKED QUESTION

Why Isn't the ICE Cooling System Used to Cool HEV Motors and Motor Controls?

Most internal combustion engine (ICE) cooling systems operate at over 200°F (93°C) and use a thermostat to control the cooling system temperature. For maximum efficiency, it is important that the engine operate as close to this temperature at all times. Electric motors and the motor controls, however, tend to operate more efficiently at lower temperatures. The engine cooling system runs too hot to allow these components to operate at peak efficiency, so a separate low-temperature system is often used.

Many hybrid electric vehicles use a liquid cooling system for their motors and motor controls.

SYSTEM CONSTRUCTION The liquid cooling systems used for the motors and motor controls on hybrid electric vehicles have much in common with conventional ICE cooling systems. There is a separate expansion tank that acts as a coolant reservoir for the system, and the coolant is often the same type that is used for the ICE cooling system. A radiator is used to dissipate excess heat, and is located at the front of the vehicle. Some designs may have the radiator incorporated into the ICE radiator, or it may be separate.
● SEE FIGURE 13–22.

A low-voltage electric water pump is used to circulate the coolant, and it is often configured to run whenever the vehicle is in operation. The coolant is circulated through the various components in the system, which could include the following:

- Electric motor-generator(s)

- DC–DC converter

- Inverter

- Transmission oil cooler

- Other high-load control modules and the high-voltage batteries in some cases, although these often have their own separate system to warm and cool the battery pack

A thermostat is not used in these systems. In some HEV systems, the electric pump will circulate coolant whenever the

cooling systems are incorporated into hybrid electric vehicles to prevent overheating of these critical components.

EFFECTS OF HEAT ON THE ELECTRICAL/ ELECTRONIC SYSTEM Electronic components operate more efficiently as their temperature decreases, and can suffer permanent damage if overheated. All hybrid electric vehicles have cooling systems for their motors and motor controls, and some utilize air cooling to remove excess heat from these components. ● SEE FIGURE 13–21.

FIGURE 13–23 This Prius transaxle has cooling passages for both of the motor-generators. Note the coolant pipes (two on each assembly) on the lower left of this photograph.

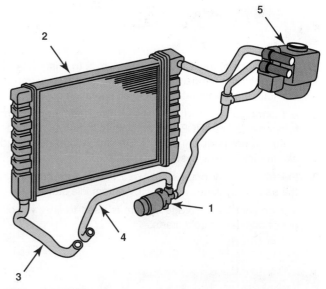

FIGURE 13–24 The motor electronics cooling system in a Ford Escape Hybrid. The electric pump (1) circulates coolant through the eCVT and the DC–DC converter and dissipates the excess heat at the radiator (2). The eCVT connects to hoses (3) and (4), and the DC–DC converter is connected to the hoses beside the coolant reservoir bottle (5).

FREQUENTLY ASKED QUESTION

What Coolant Is Used in a Motor/Electronics Cooling System?

Most hybrid electric vehicle manufacturers specify that the same coolant used in the vehicle's ICE (engine) be used for cooling the motors and electronics. For instance, Toyota specifies that its Super Long Life Coolant be used in the second generation Prius ICE cooling system as well as the inverter cooling system.

key is on. In other systems, peak temperature is controlled by turning on the pump, and then the fan, at progressively higher speeds as the coolant temperature rises. Toyota hybrid transaxles have cooling passages located near both of the electric motor-generators and these are part of the inverter cooling system. Coolant hoses connect to fittings on the transmission case, and direct coolant in and out of each of the motor-generator assemblies. ● **SEE FIGURE 13–23.**

The Ford Escape Hybrid has a motor electronic (M/E) cooling system that is similar to the inverter cooling system used in the Toyota Prius. Coolant is circulated by an electric pump through the DC–DC converter and the heat exchange unit mounted on top of the hybrid transaxle called the electronic

continuously variable transmission (eCVT). The power electronics for the hybrid drive system is located on top of the transaxle, and the coolant circulated through this unit also removes heat from the transmission fluid used for cooling the electric motors. ● **SEE FIGURE 13–24.**

SERVICE PROCEDURES

Most hybrid electric vehicle HVAC-related service procedures are the same as a conventional vehicle except for the following precautions:

- If recovering the refrigerant, use a hybrid-specific refrigerant recovery, recycling, and recharge (RRR) machine.
- If removing a compressor that is powered by high voltage and has orange cables running to it, disable the HV system by removing the high-voltage disconnect (service) plug before work is begun.
- Always follow the vehicle specific service procedures.
- Read, understand, and follow all safety notices and precautions.

SUMMARY

1. The purpose of the ICE cooling system is to bring the ICE up to optimum temperature as quickly as possible and to maintain that temperature under all operating conditions.

2. A thermostat is used to maintain the optimum coolant temperature in the ICE cooling system, however, thermostats are not normally used in EV- and hybrid-dedicated electronics cooling systems.

3. Electric auxiliary pumps are used to circulate coolant in the heating system when an HEV enters idle stop mode.

4. The coolant heat storage system is used to limit vehicle emissions during cold starts.

5. Most HEVs use scroll compressors in their air-conditioning systems.

6. Some HEVs use A/C compressors with electric drive or a combination belt-electric drive mechanism.

7. PTC heaters are used to provide supplemental heat in HEV heating systems.

8. Most hybrid electric vehicle manufacturers specify that the same coolant used in the vehicle's ICE (engine) be used for cooling the motors and electronics.

REVIEW QUESTIONS

1. How does a coolant heat storage system work?

2. Why is an HEV motor/electronics cooling system separate from that of the ICE?

3. What is the function of a PTC heater, and why is it used in an HEV heating system?

CHAPTER QUIZ

1. A coolant heat storage tank can keep coolant warm for a maximum of _____ day(s).
   a. One
   b. Two
   c. Three
   d. Four

2. The coolant heat storage system is being discussed. Technician A says that the water valve is driven by an electric motor. Technician B says that the storage tank has its own electric water pump. Which technician is correct?
   a. Technician A only
   b. Technician B only
   c. Both Technicians A and B
   d. Neither Technician A nor B

3. Technician A says that PTC heaters can be built into a conventional heater core assembly. Technician B says that a PTC heater's electrical resistance will decrease as its temperature increases. Which technician is correct?
   a. Technician A only
   b. Technician B only
   c. Both Technicians A and B
   d. Neither Technician A nor B

4. All of the following statements about hybrid electric vehicle A/C compressors are true, *except* _____.
   a. Most are reciprocating piston designs
   b. Some use a belt drive along with an electric motor
   c. Some use only an electric motor without a belt drive
   d. Nonconductive refrigeration oil must be used with A/C compressors utilizing an electric drive motor

5. What is the color of the plastic conduit used over high-voltage wiring to an electric A/C compressor?
   a. Blue
   b. Orange
   c. Yellow
   d. Red

6. In a dual compressor that uses both an ICE powered part and an electrical-power part, what percentage of the capacity is electrically powered?
   a. 85%
   b. 55%
   c. 35%
   d. 15%

7. Electrically powered A/C compressors should use what type of refrigerant oil?
   a. PAO
   b. PAG
   c. POE
   d. Polyalkylene glycol

8. What is used to help keep the passenger compartment warm during idle-stop (start-stop) operation?
   a. A larger than normal heater core
   b. An auxiliary electric water pump
   c. Operating the A/C in reverse to provide heating instead of cooling
   d. A larger than usual water jackets in the ICE

9. In most hybrid electric vehicles, the air entering the plenum chamber passes through the_____.
   a. Heater core
   b. Cabin filter
   c. Evaporator
   d. Recirculation door

10. What coolant is used in a motor/electronics cooling system?
    a. Special electrically insulted coolant
    b. DEX-COOL
    c. The same coolant that is used in the ICE cooling system
    d. Either a or c depending on the vehicle

chapter 14

REFRIGERANT RECOVERY, RECYCLING, AND RECHARGING

LEARNING OBJECTIVES

After studying this chapter, the reader should be able to:

1. Prepare for the ASE Heating and Air Conditioning (A7) certification test content area "A" (A/C System Service, Diagnosis and Repair).

2. Explain the steps involved in the service and repair of A/C systems.

3. Discuss the procedure for identifying refrigerants in an A/C system.

4. Explain the procedure for refrigerant recovery in A/C systems.

5. Explain the procedure for recycling refrigerant in A/C systems.

6. Discuss the purpose of flushing an A/C system.

7. Explain the procedure for evacuating an A/C system.

8. Discuss the procedure for recharging an A/C system.

9. Explain how to retrofit a R-12 system to a R-134a system.

10. Explain the purpose of sealants and stop leaks.

KEY TERMS

Black death 231
Conversion fitting 240
Cubic feet per minute (cfm) 235
Evacuation 235
Flushing 231
Identifier 225
Micron 235

Noncondensable gases (NCG) 226
Recovery 224
Recycling 224
Retrofitting 239
Refrigerant recovery, recycling, and recharging (RRR) 225
Slugging 239

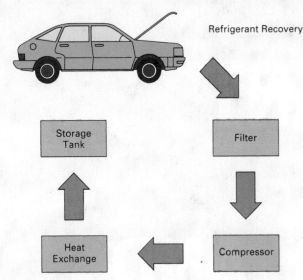

Refrigerant Recovery

FIGURE 14–1 A recovery unit removes refrigerant vapor from the vehicle. Then it filters the refrigerant before compressing it so it condenses and can be stored as a liquid in the storage tank.

CLEAN AIR ACT

SECTION 609 The U.S. Clean Air Act has placed a group of requirements on A/C service. These requirements can be viewed at www.epa.gov/ozone/title6/609

Section 609 of the Act gives EPA the power to enforce the following requirements:

- Preventing the release or venting of CFC-12 or HFC-134a.
- Technicians are required to use approved equipment to recover and recycle CFC-12 and HFC 134a.
- Technicians who repair or service CFC-12 and HFC-134a systems must be trained and certified by an EPA-approved organization. Visit www.ase.com or www.macsw.org for details on how to become a certified air-conditioning technician.
- Service shops must maintain records of refrigerant transfer and technician certification.
- Service shops must certify to EPA that they have and are properly using approved refrigerant recovery equipment.
- The sales of small cans of CFC-12 (R-12) can be made only to certified technicians.
- CFC-12 equipment can be permanently converted to HFC-134a, but must meet SAE standard J2210.

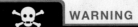

WARNING

There is a possibility of injury from refrigerant contact. Goggles or a face shield should be worn to keep liquid refrigerant from getting in the eyes, and gloves should be worn to protect the hands and avoid breathing refrigerant vapors.

- CFC-12 systems can be retrofitted to use a SNAP refrigerant.
- EPA can assess civil penalties and fines for violations of these requirements.

REQUIREMENTS A major part of the Clean Air Act requires recycling of R-12 and R-134a instead of releasing/venting the refrigerant to the atmosphere, which is banned by Section 609. This makes economic sense. At one time, new (also called virgin) R-12 was inexpensive, well under $1.00 per pound. When R-12 was inexpensive, it was standard practice to simply vent the contents of a system to the atmosphere when service was needed. Also, many people kept adding R-12 to a system rather than going through the trouble and expense of repairing a leak. This was called *topping off a system*. It is socially irresponsible not to repair any fixable leaks. Small containers of R-12 are no longer available to do-it-yourselfers.

A/C SERVICE OPERATIONS

Air conditioning service usually begins by identifying what refrigerant or other chemicals may be in the system and the recovery of whatever refrigerant is left in the system. ● SEE **FIGURE 14–1**.

Recovery means that all refrigerant is removed from a system so it can be stored in a container in liquid form. This refrigerant will be recycled into the same or another A/C system.

Recycling is the process of removing moisture (water), oil, and noncondensable gases (air) from the recovered R-12 or R-134a so it meets the standards of new refrigerant. Recycled refrigerant should be at least 98% pure. R-134a can also be recovered and recycled, but separate equipment, dedicated to R-134a, is required. Recycled R-12 or R-134a can be used in the same way as new refrigerant.

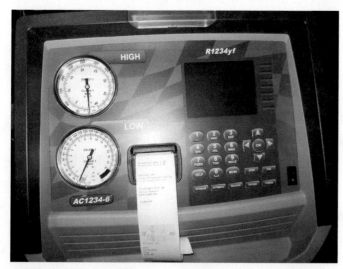

FIGURE 14–2 An RRR machine designed for use with systems that use R-1234yf. The machine used must match the refrigerant used in the vehicle.

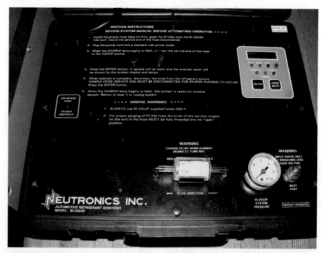

FIGURE 14–3 A typical refrigerant identification machine. The readout indicates what kind of refrigerant is in the system. If a blend or some other contaminated refrigerant is discovered, it should be recovered and stored in a separate container to keep it from contaminating fresh refrigerant.

FREQUENTLY ASKED QUESTION

What Is an AC Virus?

Recovering an A/C system which is contaminated by a substance such as R-22 or a hydrocarbon into the recovery container that is half full of R-134a will ruin the R-134a in the container. If the container is then used to service another vehicle, the contaminated refrigerant will contaminate the other system(s) as well. Many compare a system with contaminated refrigerant to a virus that can sometimes spread from person to person at a very rapid rate.

SAE RRR MACHINE STANDARDS **Refrigerant recovery, recycling, and recharging (RRR)**, equipment must be certified to meet SAE J2788, which has more stringent requirements starting in 2006 over the previous SAE J2210 standard (1991–2005). Under the old SAE J2210 standard, recovery efficiency and charge accuracy were never requirements. Some features of the SAE 2788 units include:

- The new SAE J-2788 standard requires that all R-134a service equipment manufactured after January 1, 2008 must recover 95% of the refrigerant and recharge to within an accuracy of 1/2 ounce.

- The old J2210 standard claimed to be accurate to only within 0.88 oz (which is a 3% error on a system that holds 2 pounds of refrigerant or a 7% error on a system that holds 14 oz).

- Machines compliant with standard SAE 2788 will remove more of the old refrigerant during the recovery process and provide more accurate refrigerant measurement during charging.

- Recovery equipment is available as a single unit or in combination with a recycling unit. Recovery-only units are simpler and less expensive than equipment that handle both recovery and recycling. ● **SEE FIGURE 14–2**.

SERVICE AND REPAIR OF A/C SYSTEMS

STEPS INVOLVED The service and repair of heating and A/C systems consists of the following steps:

- Identifying the refrigerant in a system using an **identifier**. ● **SEE FIGURE 14–3**.

- Recovery and disposal of contaminated refrigerant.

- Evacuation of the system.

- Repair of the system as needed, including the replacement of system components.

- Maintaining proper oil level when components are serviced.

- Checking the oil level in a compressor or system.

Several important facts when servicing an A/C system include the following:

- A/C systems are designed to operate using a specific amount of a particular refrigerant.
- A/C systems are designed to operate using a specific amount of particular refrigerant oil.
- Adding any other chemical into a system can create a chemical problem that can cause system damage or failure. Most original equipment manufacturer (OEM) and aftermarket suppliers consider any chemical other than the refrigerant and oil to be a foreign material.

REFRIGERANT CONTAMINATION At one time, contaminated refrigerant was rare, and the majority of the problems were caused by air from improper service procedures. Today, there are a variety of sealants, blends, hydrocarbons, and other refrigerants, along with recycled refrigerants available to both repair facilities and do-it-your (DIY) consumers that make the potential for contamination a much greater problem. The A/C industry defines refrigerant as:

- 98% and better is considered pure.
- Less than 97% pure is contaminated.
- Between 97% and 98% is questionable

Purity standards (SAE J1991 and J2099 and ARI 700-88) permit a small amount of contamination with new (virgin) and recycled refrigerant.

NONCONDENSABLE GASES (NCG) Any refrigerant that contains **noncondensable gases (NCG)**, usually air, or with 2% or greater of another material (foreign refrigerant), is considered contaminated. If the contamination is greater than 5%, problems such as excessive high-side pressures and incorrect clutch cycling rate result. Other unseen problems of oil breakdown, seal deterioration, or compressor wear can also occur. NCG contamination can be reduced by recycling the refrigerant, purging the air out, or diluting the contaminated refrigerant with pure refrigerant. Contamination from a foreign refrigerant requires that the refrigerant be sent off for reclaiming or disposal.

SEALANT CONTAMINATION HVAC technicians believe that contamination is caused by chemicals that are intended to seal refrigerant leaks. There are two general types of sealants:

- A chemical that promotes swelling of rubber O-rings and seals
- An epoxy/epoxy-like, one- or two-part, moisture-cure polymer

TECH TIP

Always Check for Sealant

It is possible for an A/C system to contain a sealant, and this sealant can damage a refrigerant identifier and/or a service unit when that refrigerant in the system is recovered. It is highly recommended to test for a sealant before starting any other refrigerant service. The only sure way to completely remove a sealant from a system is to replace every component that contains refrigerant.

A simple and relatively inexpensive sealant identifier is Quick Detect made by Neutronics. Recovering refrigerant that contains a sealant might cause damage to the recovery unit. There have been cases where sealant has cured inside the machine, causing loss of the machine or expensive repairs.

REFRIGERANT IDENTIFICATION

TYPES OF IDENTIFIERS To determine what the correct refrigerant is for the system being serviced, inspect the service fittings and the refrigerant label. There are two types of refrigerant identifiers.

1. A *go-no-go identifier* (accuracy to about 90% or better), indicates the purity of the refrigerant with lights that indicate pass or fail.

2. A *diagnostic identifier* (accuracy to 98% or better), displays the percentage by weight of R-12, R-134a, R-22, hydrocarbons, and air (displayed as NCG). If the contaminant is air, the refrigerant can be safely recovered and recycled for reuse. If the contaminant is another refrigerant or a hydrocarbon, then a special recovery procedure is required and the recovered mixture needs to be sent off for disposal or recycling. Recycling machines cannot remove a foreign refrigerant, only air, water, oil, or particulates. Newer identifiers include a printer port, so hard-copy readout can be printed for the customer's use. ● **SEE FIGURE 14–4.**

STEPS TO IDENTIFY THE REFRIGERANT To identify the refrigerant in a system, perform the following steps:

STEP 1 The first step on all identifiers is CALIBRATION, because most units do not allow it to be connected to

FIGURE 14–4 A typical printout showing that the system has 100% R-1234yf refrigerant in the system.

the low side line until the identifier shows what to do on the display.

STEP 2 With the engine and the system shut off, connect the identifier to the low-side service port using the correct hose assembly for the system's refrigerant type.

STEP 3 Check the filter on the identifier for the incoming gas because it will show a color change when it needs to be changed.

STEP 4 Allow a gas sample to enter the unit. Some units include a warning device to make sure liquid refrigerant does not enter it. Many units include a warning device to indicate a flammable refrigerant.

STEP 5 Read the display to determine the nature of the refrigerant. Some units allow printing of the results at that time. If the refrigerant is good or is contaminated with air, it can be safely recovered and recycled.

STEP 6 When the analysis is complete, some units display instructions to disconnect the sampling hose and then bleed out the gas that was sampled. If the hose is not disconnected when prompted, the identifier can bleed all of the refrigerant from the system.

REFRIGERANT RECOVERY

EQUIPMENT NEEDED Most recovery units are made as part of the service equipment and contain two service hoses (a low and high side) that are connected to the system service ports and low- and high-side pressure gauges. For R134a systems, confirm that the service connector knurled knob is turned fully

 **TECH TIP**

Check New Refrigerant to Be Sure

Some shops are using the diagnostic-style identifier as a quality-control check of new refrigerant they purchase. Badly contaminated new (virgin) refrigerant is also being found, some of which is manufactured and being imported illegally. Contaminated refrigerant should not be charged into a system. An identifier cannot identify a blend directly, but can identify the refrigerants contained in the blend.

counterclockwise. Then slide the quick connect collar up the hose and press the fitting onto the system service fitting and release the collar. It should "snap into place" and not be able to be removed. Slowly tighten the knurled knob until fully opened.

- Remove the caps (blue for the low side and red for the high side) from the service fittings and connect the A/C manifold gauge.
- The connector has a sliding collar and a knurled knob. Slide the collar up the hose, press the fitting onto the orifice and release the collar, and then hand-tighten the knurled knob.

NOTE: Some recovery units are connected to the center hose (yellow hose) of a manifold gauge set and are used for adding refrigerant or evacuating the system.

Blends or contaminated mixtures should be recovered using a different, separate machine. The hoses should be equipped with shutoff valves within 12 inches of the ends and have end fittings to match the refrigerant used.

A wise technician is careful to check the service history of the vehicle. Many refuse to service a vehicle if there is a chance that it contains contaminated refrigerant. Recovery units contain the following:

- An oil separator
- A compressor-like pump
- A condenser-like heat exchanger

RECOVERY OPERATION Recovery units draw refrigerant vapor out of a system and convert it into liquid for storage. Recovery units weigh the amount of refrigerant that is recovered, which tells the technician if all refrigerant from a fully charged system has been recovered or whether the system was fully charged. Oil removed and separated during

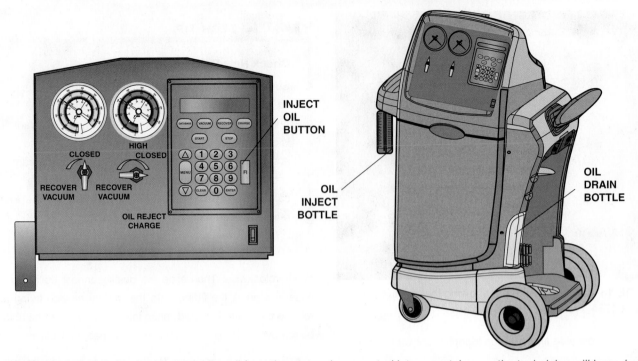

FIGURE 14–5 During the recovery process, oil from the system is separated into a container so the technician will know how much oil was removed.

the recovery process is usually drained into a measuring cup and noted so that this amount of new oil can be replaced in the system as it is recharged. Oil recovery also gives an indication of the oil volume in the system. If no oil is recovered, then the system was likely low on oil. If an excessive amount of oil is recovered, the system probably had too much oil.

Some refrigerant in a system is absorbed in the oil and does not leave the oil immediately when a system is emptied. This trapped refrigerant *out-gases* or boils out of the oil later, after the pressure has been removed. Recovery units shut off automatically after the main refrigerant charge has been removed and the system drops into a slight vacuum. To completely remove the refrigerant, run the normal recovery procedure and then recheck the pressure after a 5-minute wait. If the pressure has increased, restart the recovery process.

STORAGE CONTAINER CERTIFICATION The storage container for recovered refrigerant must be approved by the Department of Transportation (DOT) and carry the letters *DOT* and the certification numbers. The tank must also include the date for tank retesting. Recovery tanks must be inspected and certified to be in good condition every 5 years. Some rules to follow for refrigerant recovery storage tanks include:

- Do not reuse disposable cylinders.
- Make sure that the recovery cylinder is labeled for the refrigerant being recovered.

- Make sure the *tank certification* is in order and the cylinder retest date has not expired.
- Inspect the cylinder for damage and do not fill if damaged.

STEPS TO RECOVER REFRIGERANT To recover the refrigerant from a system, usually include the following steps:

STEP 1 Identify the refrigerant in the system.

STEP 2 Make sure the hoses have the proper shutoff valves and are compatible with the refrigerant in the system.

STEP 3 Connect the recovery unit to the system or to the center hose of the manifold gauge set, following the directions of the manufacturer.

STEP 4 Open the required valves and turn the machine on to start the recovery process, following the directions of the machine's manufacturer.

STEP 5 Continue the recovery until the machine shuts off or the pressure reading has dropped into a vacuum.

STEP 6 Verify completion of recovery by shutting off all valves and watching the system pressure. If pressure rises above 0 PSI within 5 minutes, repeat steps 4 and 5 to recover the remaining refrigerant.

STEP 7 Drain, measure, and record the amount of oil removed from the system with the refrigerant and dispose of properly. This amount of new oil should be added during the recharging process. ● **SEE FIGURE 14–5.**

The system can now be repaired. Present standards and good work habits require that recovered refrigerant be recycled before reuse, even if it is to be returned to the system from which it was recovered.

SMALL CANS

At one time, refrigerants were commonly sold in small cans that contained 12 oz or 15 oz of refrigerant. Refrigerant is available in larger containers, usually 30 pound, and larger, and these are commonly used by service shops. Small cans are commonly used by untrained do-it-yourself (DIY) vehicle owners.

There are concerns that DIY service often results in the wasting or release of a substantial amount of unused refrigerant for several reasons:

- A tendency to not repair refrigerant leaks and instead just add additional refrigerant to the leaking system.

- Partially charged systems are topped off, so they probably end up over- or undercharged.

- A small can may not have the correct amount of refrigerant for the system, so charging is often stopped before the can is empty.

- The remaining refrigerant in the can will probably leak out over time.

RECOVERING CONTAMINATED REFRIGERANT

Special procedures should be followed to remove a contaminated or a blend refrigerant from a system. Do not use an R-12 or R-134a recovery machine to remove a contaminated or a blend refrigerant. One alternative is to convert an older R12 machine and gauge set to recover refrigerant blends, but this equipment should be used only for blends from that point on unless it is decontaminated after each use. If the mixture contains more than 4% hydrocarbon, it should be considered explosive, and this mixture should not be recovered using an electric-powered machine. Air-powered recovery machines are available and can be safely used for explosive mixtures.

Hydrocarbon refrigerants, blends, and unknown mixtures should be recovered into containers clearly labeled "CONTAMINATED REFRIGERANT." The proper color for these containers is gray with a yellow top. Recovery of contaminated refrigerant using a recovery machine is essentially the same as recovering uncontaminated refrigerant except that the contaminated material must be sent off for disposal or off-site recycling.

QUALITY STANDARDS

Most recycling units pump the recovered refrigerant through a very fine filter to remove foreign particles, past a desiccant to remove water, and through an oil separator to remove any excess oil. Air is removed by venting it, using the noncondensable purge, from the top of the liquid refrigerant. Recycled refrigerant must meet the same purity standards as new (virgin) refrigerant including:

- Less than 15 ppm moisture
- Less than 4000 ppm oil
- Less than 330 ppm air

Some machines have a sight glass equipped with a moisture indicator so that the operator can tell when the moisture has been removed.

SAE 2788 recovery units are designed to stop operation if a filter or desiccant change is needed. Some units can perform the recycling process in a single pass from the storage container through the cleaning process and back to the storage container. These machines often complete the recycling process while the system is being evacuated. Others require several passes, and the recovery process continues to circulate the refrigerant as long as necessary. ● SEE FIGURE 14–6.

The recycling machine is dedicated to a particular type of refrigerant, and a recycled blend can only be recharged back into the vehicle it came from or another vehicle from the same fleet.

PROCEDURE FOR RECYCLING

To recycle a refrigerant, perform the following steps:

STEP 1 Open the valves or perform the programming steps required by the machine manufacturer and turn on the machine.

STEP 2 The machine operates until excess foreign particles and water have been removed or for a programmed length of time and then shuts off. Check the moisture indicator to ensure that the refrigerant is dry. If the machine does not shut off in the proper amount of time, its internal filters or desiccant probably require service. ● SEE FIGURE 14–7.

NOTE: Sometimes all of the air will not be removed in one recycling pass. Repeat the recycling as needed to remove all of the excess air.

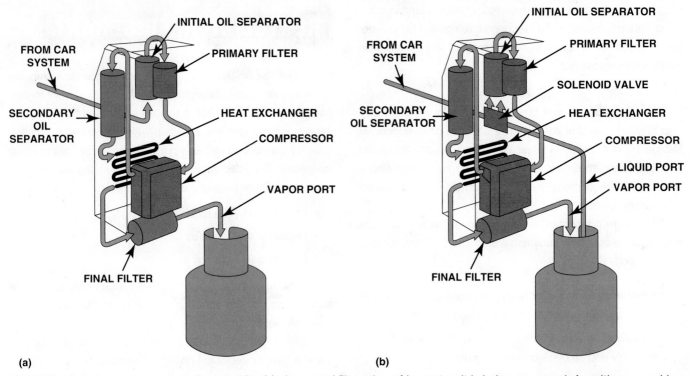

FIGURE 14–6 A single-pass recycling machine (a) cleans and filters the refrigerant as it is being recovered. A multipass machine (b) recovers the refrigerant in one operation and then cycles the refrigerant through filters and separators in another operation.

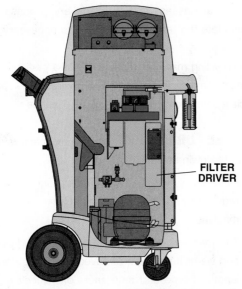

FIGURE 14–7 Recycling machines have a filter and desiccant that must be replaced after a certain amount of use.

AIR CONTAMINATION CHECKS After recovery is completed, check for excess air in the refrigerant can be done by looking at the *pressure–temperature (PT)* relationship. This is best done after the temperature of the refrigerant has stabilized to the level it was at the start of the workday.

To check the PT relationship, perform the following steps:

STEP 1 Keep the storage container at a temperature above 65°F (21°C) and away from direct sunlight for 12 hours.

STEP 2 Read the pressure in the container using a calibrated pressure gauge with 1 PSI increments.

STEP 3 Read the temperature of the air next to the container.

STEP 4 Compare the pressure and temperature readings in ● **SEE CHART 14–1.**

TEST RESULTS

- If the pressure for a particular temperature is less than that given in the table, the refrigerant does not contain an excess amount of air and is considered uncontaminated.

- If the pressure is greater than that given in the table, slowly vent or purge gas from the top of the container (red valve) until the pressure drops below that given in the table.

- If the pressure does not drop, the refrigerant must be recycled or sent off for disposal or recovery.

- Some recycling machines can purge air from the system during recycling using either a manual or an automatic process. If recycling is attempted with contaminated refrigerants or some blends, the entire mix can be

TEMPERATURE °F	PRESSURE (PSIG) R-12	PRESSURE (PSIG) R-134a
65	74	69
66	75	70
67	76	71
68	78	73
69	79	74
70	80	76
71	82	77
72	83	79
73	84	80
74	86	82
75	87	83
76	88	84
77	90	85
78	92	88
79	94	90
80	96	91
81	98	93
82	99	95
83	100	96
84	101	98
85	102	100
86	103	102
87	105	103
88	107	105
89	108	107
90	110	109
91	111	111
92	113	113
93	115	115
94	116	117
95	118	118
96	120	120
97	122	122
98	124	125
99	125	127
100	127	129
101	129	131
102	130	133
103	132	135
104	134	137
105	136	139
106	138	142
107	140	144
108	142	146
109	144	149
110	146	151

CHART 14–1

Pressure/temperature chart used to determine if there is air trapped in the refrigerant container.

TECH TIP

Watch Out for "Black Death"

Debris from a failed compressor is often a fine, black material called *goo* or **black death** by many technicians. This mixture of small particles of aluminum and Teflon from the piston rings of the compressor, mixed with overheated refrigerant oil, will be trapped between the compressor discharge port and the orifice tube. It is very difficult to flush this out, especially from the condenser.

discharged as the machine attempts to purge air. With refrigerant that is severely contaminated with air, it is thought that some of the excess air is contained in the liquid, not just sitting on top of it, making it much more difficult to purge. If this is the case, make a partial air purge and then let the PT relationship stabilize over a period of time and recheck.

FLUSHING AN A/C SYSTEM

PURPOSE **Flushing** is using a liquid or a gas to clean the inside passages of an air-conditioning system. When a compressor fails, it usually sends solid compressor particles into the high and possibly the low sides, which can plug the condenser passages and orifice tube. It is always a good practice to check the orifice tube or TXV filter screen for debris when there is a compressor failure and to flush the system, install a filter, or both before completing the job.

Flushing is done by pumping a liquid material through the passages in a reverse or normal flow direction. A gas, such as shop air or nitrogen, is not really effective in removing solid material. Flushing agents can be a commercial flushing solution, liquid refrigerant, or very lightweight ester oil. However, ester oil has very little or no solvent action, and remaining ester oil might be difficult to remove from the system.

NOTE: Manufacturers may not warranty a replacement compressor if the accumulator and orifice tube or receiver–drier is not also replaced.

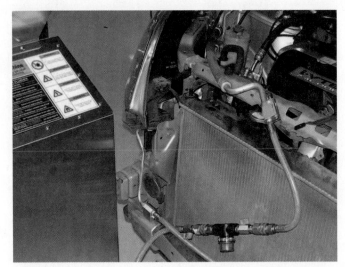

FIGURE 14–8 Portions of an A/C system can be flushed to remove debris and excess oil. Adapters are used to connect a flushing unit, which pumps the flushing material through the components. Most flushing machines are fully automated, meaning that it will vacuum, flush, recover, recycle, vacuum, and purge the cleaning solvent all automatically.

CAUTIONS AND PRECAUTIONS   No flushing operation will remove 100% of metal debris from a failed compressor. The very small metal particles can be stopped only by a filter.

- A compressor cannot be flushed.
- An accumulator or receiver–drier is not flushed and is simply replaced.
- If the evaporator is flushed, it is simply done to remove excessive refrigerant oil that may be trapped in the system during previous service.
- Most experts believe that the OT or TXV screen will filter out larger debris.
- Most flushing is done on the high side, from the compressor connection of the discharge line to the OT or receiver–drier fitting of the liquid line, or vice versa.
  ● **SEE FIGURE 14–8**.

Approved flush solvents for A/C systems are based on HFC refrigerants that have a fairly high boiling point such as Genesolv SF, which has a boiling point of 59°F (15°C). Technicians using flushing chemicals have a professional responsibility to:

- Obtain, read, and understand the MSDS (SDS) for that chemical.
- Learn how that chemical works and how it should be used.
- Determine if that chemical will do no harm to the system and the materials like gaskets and seals.

The Coffee Filter Trick

Some technicians place a paper coffee filter to catch the debris in the flush material going to the catch container. This allows them to inspect the material being flushed from the system and to determine the effectiveness of the flushing process.

- Determine how to remove that chemical from the system and how to properly recycle or dispose of it.

If the flush is needed only to remove oil, a low-pressure, low-flow method can be used to fill the component so the solvent can dissolve the oil. Some recovery–recycling machines can be fitted with a flushing kit that allows them to pump liquid refrigerant into one line and recover that refrigerant from the other line.

If the flush is needed to remove solid debris or chemical sealants, there must be enough flow velocity to break the material loose and carry it out of the component. Better flush machines will pulsate the flow to increase the cleaning power.

When the flush is completed, the chemical should be removed from the system by blowing nitrogen or clean, dry air through the system, and the chemical should be recycled or properly disposed of. The nitrogen/air should be blown through the system for 20 minutes to 30 minutes to evaporate the remaining solvent.

CAUTION: It is very difficult or impossible to flush a modern flat-tube condenser with its multiple, small passages without a flushing machine that can supply a strong, pulsating solvent flow. One or more of the small passages can be plugged so the flush material will pass through any open passages.

REPLACING COMPONENTS

GENERAL GUIDELINES   After all refrigerant has been removed from the system, repairs can be accomplished. For example, the evaporator can be removed from the vehicle and replaced. Seal all openings of the system during service to

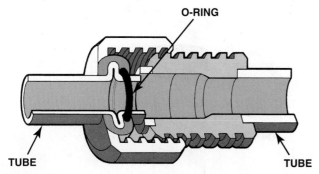

FIGURE 14–9 O-rings are usually made of neoprene rubber or highly saturated nitriles (HSN) to withstand high temperatures and flexing. O-rings should be changed during a retrofit procedure.

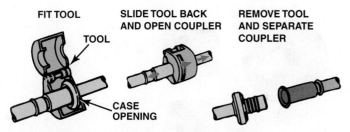

FIT TOOL   SLIDE TOOL BACK AND OPEN COUPLER   REMOVE TOOL AND SEPARATE COUPLER

TOOL

CASE OPENING

FIGURE 14–11 A special tool is needed to remove and install this spring-lock coupling.

prevent moisture and contaminants from entering. If the system has been opened to the atmosphere for a length of time (over 24 hours), most experts recommend replacing the drier to help prevent the possibility of damaging moisture being trapped in the system. After all repairs are completed, the system should then be evacuated.

NOTE: Be sure to follow all instructions regarding the amount of oil that needs to be added to the system if components have been replaced.

O-RINGS

The O-ring seal is part of a fitting that holds the ends of two refrigerant lines or hoses together inside a connector. ● **SEE FIGURE 14–9.**

The O-ring forms the seal between the lines or hoses and the connector. The O-rings usually are made of highly saturated nitriles (HSN) or neoprene rubber and remain flexible over a wide range of temperatures. The O-ring must be lubricated with clean refrigerant oil before assembly to ensure a good seal. ● **SEE FIGURES 14–10 AND 14–11.**

TIGHTENING CONNECTIONS

All threaded connections should be started by hand to avoid cross-threading. Two wrenches, one on each threaded fitting, should be used to loosen or tighten O-ring fittings. Using two wrenches is often called using "double-wrenches" or a "backup wrench" and is specified to be used by most vehicle manufacturers.

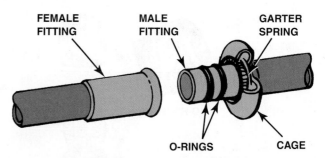

FEMALE FITTING   MALE FITTING   GARTER SPRING

O-RINGS   CAGE

FIGURE 14–10 A typical spring-lock coupling.

SERVICE FITTINGS AND CAPS

Each type of refrigerant has its own unique service fitting. This prevents accidental use of the wrong service equipment and/or the introduction of the wrong refrigerant. Service valves are found almost anywhere on the system. They may be located on the receiver–drier, accumulator, compressor, muffler, or in the lines themselves. All service valves should have plastic coverings called *service caps*. ● **SEE FIGURE 14–12.**

Along with preventing dirt from entering the system, service valve caps have O-rings which become the primary seal if a valve leaks.

Always reattach the caps after any service has been performed, and replace them if missing. Another built-in precaution is the refrigerant cut-off valve, which keeps the refrigerant in the service hose instead of allowing it to vent to the atmosphere.

SCHRADER VALVES

A Schrader valve is similar to a tire valve. Internal pressure holds Schrader valves closed. There is also a small spring to keep the valve seated if the internal pressure becomes insufficient. When the service connection is made, the depressor in the end of the service hose or service coupling pushes on a small pin inside the valve which opens the valve. The valve opens only when the service line connection is nearly complete, preventing contamination of the system or the unnecessary release of refrigerant. Many experts recommend that the Schrader valves be replaced whenever the system is open after recovery of refrigerant. ● **SEE FIGURE 14–13.**

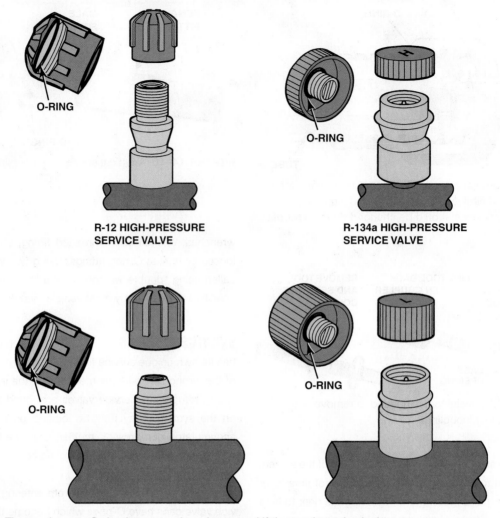

O-RING

R-12 HIGH-PRESSURE
SERVICE VALVE

O-RING

R-134a HIGH-PRESSURE
SERVICE VALVE

O-RING

O-RING

FIGURE 14–12 The service cap O-ring becomes the primary seal if the service valve leaks.

IN-LINE FILTER

PURPOSE AND FUNCTION If a compressor fails, debris in the form of metal particles often travels downstream through the condenser and is trapped in the receiver–drier or orifice tube, where it can cause plugging. Some compressor failures send debris into the suction line. The technician can install an in-line filter in either the high side or low side to trap any debris still in the system to protect the new compressor. They are available with connections to fit different line sizes. Some filters include a new orifice tube. ● **SEE FIGURE 14–14**.

INSTALLING AN IN-LINE FILTER To install an in-line filter, perform the following steps:

STEP 1 Recover the refrigerant from the system.

STEP 2 Select the location for the filter. The flexibility of hose allows a great deal of freedom. With metal tubing, locate a straight section of tubing slightly longer than the filter's connections.

STEP 3 Evacuate and recharge the system after installation of the filter.

NOTE: Most aftermarket air-conditioning filters have a directional arrow that indicates refrigerant flow direction.

REFRIGERANT OIL

ADDING OIL When it is determined that additional oil must be added, several types of low cost injectors can be used to push oil into a charged or empty system. The proper amount of

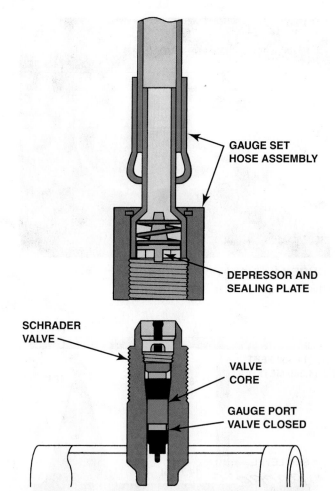

FIGURE 14–13 A depressor pin on the gauge set opens the Schrader valve when the connection is almost completely tightened. This prevents accidental refrigerant discharge.

oil can be kept in a system by adding oil to replace the amount of oil removed when a component is replaced. This is usually only a small amount. Compressor replacement requires a slightly larger amount. ● SEE FIGURE 14–15.

EVACUATING A SYSTEM

PURPOSE OF EVACUATING THE SYSTEM After a system has been repaired, all of the air and moisture that might have entered must be removed. **Evacuation** means that a vacuum will be applied to the system to remove the air and to vaporize any moisture that may be in the system. Although water boils at 212°F (100°C) at sea level, it can boil at much lower temperatures when the pressure is reduced. In other

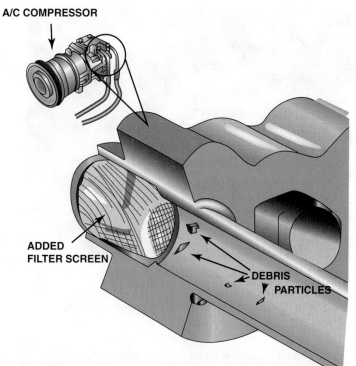

FIGURE 14–14 A typical aftermarket filter is installed in the suction line at the entrance to the compressor that is designed to catch any debris that could harm the compressor.

words, if a vacuum is applied to the air-conditioning system, the low pressure will cause any trapped moisture in the system to vaporize (boil). This water vapor is then removed from the system through the vacuum pump and released into the atmosphere. It is important to evacuate the system to at least 29 inch Hg of vacuum for at least 45 minutes to be assured that all of the moisture has been removed. For best results, the vacuum should be higher than 29.2 inch Hg. The higher the vacuum and the longer that it is allowed to evacuate, the better.

MICRON RATING Vacuum pumps are rated by both **cubic feet per minute (cfm)** and **micron** ratings.

- The cfm rating is the volume it can pump.
- The micron rating is how deep a vacuum the pump can pull.

An automotive A/C system requires about a 1.2-cfm to 1.5-cfm rating, whereas a larger system used in a bus or truck needs about a 5-cfm to 6-cfm vacuum pump. Using a vacuum pump that is too small requires a much longer evacuation time, which causes excess wear on the vacuum pump.

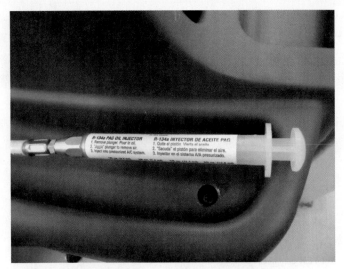

FIGURE 14–15 A variety of oil injectors are available for purchase. Some can be used while the system is under a vacuum, and some can force oil into a charged system.

- A perfect vacuum is 29.92 inch Hg, or 0 microns (a micron is equal to one-millionth of a meter).
- A good vacuum pump will pull a system down to under 500 microns (29.90 inch Hg). This high vacuum drops the boiling point of water to around 0°F (–18°C). ● SEE FIGURE 14–16.

VACUUM PUMP SERVICE A vacuum pump must be maintained with the proper oil level and periodic oil changes to ensure proper operation. If service is neglected, it will not pump to its design capabilities. Some modern electronic units flash a warning if the oil has not been changed at the proper interval (about 10 hours).

New refrigerant service machines are equipped with oilless vacuum pumps. These units eliminate the need to service the vacuum pump. To run without lubricating oil, the pump uses two high-temperature plastic pistons operating in anodized aluminum cylinders with a Teflon-type cup seal. The piston and connecting rod are one piece. The crankshaft and connecting rod bearings use a lubricated and sealed ball bearing.

EVACUATION TIME It is accepted practice to evacuate an automotive system for at least 45 minutes. Vacuum readings are affected by altitude and the drop in atmospheric pressure that occurs.

- At 1,000 feet (305 m) above sea level, a complete vacuum is 28.92 inch Hg, about 1 inch Hg less than at sea level.

FIGURE 14–16 An air-conditioning vacuum gauge that reads in microns.

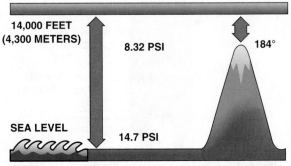

FIGURE 14–17 At sea level, water boils at 212°F (100°C), whereas at the top of Pike's Peak, at 14,000 feet, water boils at 184°F (84°C) because the atmospheric pressure is reduced from 14.7 PSI to just 8.32 PSI.

- This pressure will decrease at a rate of about 1 inch Hg per 1,000-foot elevation increase. ● SEE FIGURE 14–17.

EVACUATION PROCEDURE To evacuate a system using a manifold gauge set and portable vacuum pump, perform the following steps:

STEP 1 Connect the manifold service hoses to the system service ports if necessary but these are normally still connected from the recovery process. There should be no or very little pressure in the system.

STEP 2 Open both manifold valves completely (and the vacuum pump valve if there is one) and start the vacuum pump. An air discharge should be noticed

What Is a Micron?

A typical vacuum gauge reads in inches of Mercury (inch Hg) and the recommended vacuum level needed to remove moisture from the system is a vacuum of 29.2 inch Hg. or lower. However, many experts recommend using a vacuum gauge that measures the amount of air remaining in the system rather than just the vacuum.

- A micron is one millionth of a meter and there are about 760,000 microns of air at atmospheric pressure.
- The lower the pressure, the lower the number of microns of air.
- A vacuum reading of 29.72 inch Hg. is about 5,000 microns.
- Many experts recommend that the micron level be 500 or less for best results.

This is particularly important when evacuating a dual-climate control system where two evaporators are used and there are long lengths of refrigerant lines. ● SEE CHART 14–2.

TEMPERATURE F°/C°	INCH HG	MICRONS*	PRESSURE (PSI)
212/100	0.00	759,068	14.7
205/96	5.00	536,000	12.3
194/90	9.81	525,526	10.2
176/80	16.0	355,092	6.9
158/70	20.8	233,680	4.5
140/60	24.1	149,352	2.9
122/50	26.4	92,456	1.8
104/40	27.9	55,118	1.1
86/30	28.8	31,750	0.6
80/27	29.0	25,400	0.5
76/24	29.1	22,860	0.4
72/22	29.2	20,320	0.4
69/21	29.3	17,780	0.3
64/18	29.4	15,240	0.3
59/15	29.5	12,700	0.2
53/12	29.6	10,160	0.2
45/7	29.7	7,620	0.1
32/0	29.8	4,572	0.1
21/−6	29.9	2,540	0.1
6/−14	29.9	1,270	0.1
−24/−31	30.0	254	0.0
−35/−37	30.0	127	0.0

*The remaining pressure in the system in microns.

CHART 14–2

Boiling temperature of water at converted pressures.

FIGURE 14–18 The timer was set on this RRR machine to 60 minutes so the technician can be doing other service work while the AC system was being evacuated.

from the vacuum pump as well and a drop in gauge pressures. ● SEE FIGURE 14–18.

STEP 3 Check the gauge pressures periodically. After about 5 minutes, the pressure should be lower than 20 inch Hg. A leak is usually the cause if the pressure has not dropped this low. Confirm a leak by closing all valves, shutting off the vacuum pump, and watching the pressure. If it steadily increases, there is a leak that must be located and repaired before continuing.

NOTE: Some vehicles with rear A/C use an electric solenoid valve to block flow through the rear unit when it is turned off. This solenoid should be activated so it will open and allow a more complete evacuation of the system.

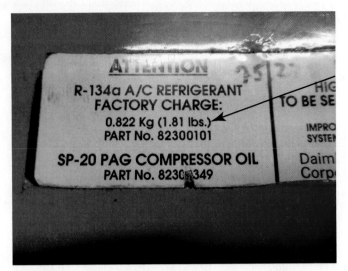

FIGURE 14–19 The underhood decal states that this vehicle requires 1.81 pounds (0.822 Kg) of R-134a refrigerant.

STEP 4 Continue evacuating until 500 microns is reached or for the desired length of time, close all valves, shut off the vacuum pump, and note the low-side pressure.

STEP 5 After 5 minutes, recheck the low-side pressure. If the vacuum is held steady, the system is good and ready to be recharged. If the low-side pressure increases, a possible leak is indicated.

When using an A/C service unit, evacuation is often simply a matter of flipping a switch, assuming the service hoses are still connected from the recovery operation. Most recent machines use electric solenoids to control the flow inside the machine, and starting the evacuation process opens the solenoids needed for this process. Some also include a microprocessor that can be programmed to run the vacuum pump for the desired length of time. Some older charging stations are purely mechanical and on these units, the proper valves must be opened as the vacuum pump is started.

RECHARGING THE SYSTEM

PROCEDURES After the system has been evacuated, it can be recharged with the correct amount of new or recycled refrigerant. Charge level is system specific, and as the volume of HVAC systems has been downsized, the amount of refrigerant has become critical. The charge level is normally found on a specification decal fastened to some location under the hood and includes both the type and volume of refrigerant used. The decal is attached to the compressor on some older systems. If the decal is missing or illegible, charge specifications are also

🔧 **TECH TIP**

Check the Scale for Accuracy

Most charging scales can be calibrated to ensure accuracy. If a known amount of weight is placed on the scale, the weight indicator should show the correct amount of charge. If a test weight is not available use:

- 9 pennies weigh 1 ounce
- 27 pennies weigh 3 ounces

given in service information from the vehicle manufacturer or aftermarket A/C component suppliers. ● SEE FIGURE 14–19.

RECOMMENDED CHARGING PROCEDURE The best method to charge a system is to start with an empty system and charge the specific amount of refrigerant as measured by accurate scales. Most shops use larger refrigerant containers, in the 30-lb size, so the amount to be charged into the system must be measured. The most commonly used A/C service machines use charging cylinders and electronic scales. These can be either individual portable units or parts of a charging station.

Current service units use electronic scales that can be programmed for the desired charge level. The refrigerant container is placed on the scale, and a hose is used to connect its valve to the scale. The operator then programs in the charge volume desired and starts the charge process. When the proper amount of refrigerant has left the container, an electric solenoid in the unit shuts off the refrigerant flow. These units can also be operated manually, with the operator holding down a button or switch until the desired amount of refrigerant has left the container. ● SEE FIGURE 14–20.

Moving the refrigerant into the system requires that the charging container pressure be greater than the system pressure. Because the process begins with the system in a vacuum, the first portion goes rather quickly, but the first 1/2 lb or so fills the internal volume and starts generating pressure. As refrigerant boils and leaves the container, it cools the remaining refrigerant and causes a pressure drop. Many charging stations include heaters, which are similar to an electric blanket, to raise the internal pressure of the refrigerant container to help force refrigerant into the system. When heaters are used, the system does not need to be operated. The pressure difference can also be increased by starting the A/C system so the low-side pressure drops and then charging only into the low side.

FIGURE 14–20 The calibrated scale on the RRR machine displayed the exact amount of refrigerant that was specified was added to the system (1.81 lb.).

With the system running, caution should be exercised if charging liquid into it to avoid **slugging** the compressor, which is allowing liquid refrigerant to enter a running compressor which can cause severe damage.

- If the container is upright, gas will exit.
- If the container is upside down, liquid will exit.

To charge a system using a charging station, perform the following steps:

STEP 1 Enter the specified amount of refrigerant into the charging scale or into the charging cylinder unit. This charge process begins with the system still under a vacuum, with the manifold valves closed.

STEP 2 Follow the machine instructions for the unit being used.

STEP 3 When the charge volume has entered the system, close the necessary valves.

STEP 4 Start the A/C system, let it run until the pressures stabilize, and note system pressures.

RETROFITTING R-134a INTO AN R-12 SYSTEM

PURPOSE **Retrofitting** is the changing of a system from one refrigerant to another and is normally a repair-driven operation and not done until absolutely necessary. All experts agree that if a system was designed for R-12, then R-12 should

be used in it when it requires service, even though some systems cool better after changing to R-134a.

SECTION 609, EPA RETROFIT REQUIREMENTS For a proper retrofit, this section of the Clean Air Act requires:

- The technician must be Section 609 certified.
- Recover the original refrigerant using EPA-approved equipment.
- Replace service fittings to match new refrigerant.
- Install new label to cover the old one.
- Ensure that the system has barrier hoses.
- Ensure that the system has a high-pressure shutoff switch.

REFRIGERANT CHOICE FOR RETROFIT Any EPA SNAP-approved refrigerant can be used to replace R-12. All of them require a similar retrofit procedure. Some of the points to consider when choosing the refrigerant include the following:

- It must be EPA approved and have unique service fittings and label.
- R-134a is the refrigerant used in every new vehicle and is EPA SNAP-approved refrigerant.
- Unique service, recovery, and charging equipment are required for each refrigerant. Most shops have R-12 and R-134a equipment.
- Most major compressor manufacturers and builders will not warranty a compressor that failed if a blend refrigerant was used in it.
- Blends are outlawed in some areas, including at least one Canadian province.

All vehicle manufacturers, the Mobile Air Conditioning Society (MACS), and most service shops prefer using R-134a for retrofits. It is relatively inexpensive, used in all new vehicles (so the service equipment is fairly common), readily available, and, because it is a single-compound refrigerant, can be recycled in service shops.

RECOMMENDED GUIDELINES When retrofitting, at least 99% of the R-12 must be removed from the system and as much of the mineral oil as practical. A recovery unit removes the R-12 vapor and some of the oil and measures the amount of refrigerant and oil removed. Complete R-12 removal can be difficult because of the amount absorbed by any remaining oil.

FIGURE 14–21 When a system is retrofitted from R-12 (CFC-12) to R-134a (HFC-134a), the proper service fittings have to be used to help assure that cross-contamination does not occur.

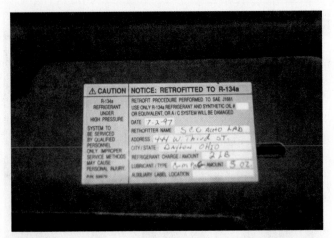

FIGURE 14–22 An underhood sticker is also installed indicating that the system was retrofitted to HFC-134a and when it was done and by whom.

- Oil removal also helps remove R-12 from the system. Oil removal is more difficult because it must be drained out, flushed out, or pulled out with the R-12. Complete draining of some components requires removal of the component, which greatly increases the labor costs. Any remaining mineral oil will probably gel and settle at the bottom of the accumulator or evaporator.

- R-134a is lighter than R-12, so a system should be charged to about 80% to 90% the amount of the R-12 capacity. Some aftermarket sources have made R-134a retrofit charge capacities available. To figure the new charge level, simply multiply the R-12 charge level by 0.8. For example, if the R-12 charge is 2 pound (32 oz), 32 × 0.8 = 27 oz. General Motors guidelines for retrofitting its vehicles recommend multiplying the R-12 charge level by 0.9 and subtracting 0.25 pound (4 oz). Using this procedure, 32 × 0.9 = 29 − 4 = 25, slightly less than the 27 oz (80% level).

RETROFIT KITS Both vehicle and aftermarket manufacturers produce kits that include the parts needed to convert particular systems. Vehicle manufacturer kits are for Type I retrofit, and most aftermarket sources provide Type II kits. Depending on the particular make and model, a kit can include the following:

- A sticker to identify that it is an R-134a system, along with the charge level. ● **SEE FIGURE 14–21**

- R-134a-type service fittings to be permanently installed over the existing service fittings

- Replacement hoses with the R-134a service fittings

- Replacement O-rings

- Ester or PAG oil

- Replacement receiver–drier or accumulator with XH-7 or XH-9 desiccant

- Replacement system switches calibrated for R-134a pressures

- Replacement TXV or OT calibrated for R-134a pressures

- High-pressure cutoff switch

The R-12 service fittings must either be converted to R-134a service fittings or permanently capped to make them unusable. Normally, they are converted using a **conversion fitting**. A conversion fitting is threaded over the R-12 fitting, using the same Schrader valve, and a thread-lock adhesive locks it in place. It is a good practice to replace the old Schrader valves with ones that are compatible with R-134a. ● **SEE FIGURE 14–22.**

TECH TIP

Orifice Tube Size

When retrofitting an OT system, it is a good practice to replace the orifice tube with one that is about 0.010 inch (0.026 mm) smaller than the one used in the R-12 system. R-134a is lighter than R-12, and the R-12 orifice tube will allow too much R-134a to flow. This can drop high-side pressure and increase low-side pressure.

RETROFIT PROCEDURE To retrofit a system, perform the following steps:

STEP 1 Visually inspect the system to ensure good condition, install a gauge set, and operate the system to bring it up to operating temperatures. Check for proper operation and note any needed repairs. Record the high-side pressure for later comparison.

STEP 2 Recover the R-12 from the system and remove as much oil-dissolved R-12 as possible.

STEP 3 Make any repairs to the system to cure problems that were found in step 1.

STEP 4 If the compressor failed, remove the failed compressor, flush the system and/or install a high-side filter, and install the replacement compressor along with a new accumulator or receiver–drier.

STEP 5 Check the system to determine whether a high-pressure relief valve is used. If it has one, a high-pressure cutoff switch must be installed to stop the compressor before pressure relief valve release pressures occur. The switch is installed so it senses high-side pressure and is wired into the clutch circuit or relay so it can interrupt clutch operation.

STEP 6 If directed, replace the receiver–drier or accumulator.

STEP 7 Replace any line-fitting O-rings on connections that were disturbed, or as directed.

STEP 8 Replace any switches and valves as directed.

STEP 9 Add the proper type and amount of oil—ester or PAG—into the compressor oil fill port or suction port. If the accumulator or receiver–driver is replaced, pour part of the oil into the inlet port.

STEP 10 Install the R-134a service fittings. Any old Schrader valves that remain in service should be replaced with new R-134a valves.

STEP 11 Fill out and install the identifying decal to properly identify the system. The old label must be rendered unreadable.

STEP 12 Connect a vacuum pump to the system and pull a minimum vacuum of 29 inch Hg (500 microns) for at least 30 minutes to evacuate the system.

STEP 13 Recharge the system using R-134a. Charge the system with 80% to 90% of the specified amount of R-12.

STEP 14 Operate the system and check for proper operation, paying careful attention to the high-side pressure.

STEP 15 Test for leaks.

SEALANTS AND STOP LEAKS

PURPOSE Sealants and stop leaks are included in many do-it-yourself (DIY) automotive air conditioning charging products and are designed to plug or stop small refrigerant leaks. Most HVAC technicians dislike stop leaks as they are considered an inadequate or temporary repair method, and the best repair is to actually fix the leak.

SEALANT CONCERNS Sealants and stop leaks will not always be successful in stopping leaks and may damage the A/C system. Stop leaks also have a reputation of plugging up small orifices that might reduce the proper flow of refrigerant or oil. There is also a question of whether the stop leak material will contaminate the rather delicate chemical balance within an A/C system. In spite of these misgivings, sealants have become popular with do-it-yourselfers.

TYPES There are two types of sealants:

1. *Type I* is a rubber "conditioner," often called a "seal swell." It contains a hydrocarbon or alcohol that softens rubber that has hardened and causes it to swell. Type I sealants are generally low cost and will cause little harm and are often available combined in a small can of refrigerant.

REFRIGERANT RECOVERY, RECYCLING, AND RECHARGING   **241**

FIGURE 14–23 Use A/C stop leak with caution.

Other sealants are single- or two-part chemicals that are moisture-activated and remain fluid until in contact with moisture.

2. *Type II* is a stop-leak chemical that hardens when it contacts moisture as it escapes, which results in sealing the leak. Type II sealants have hardened and caused plugging inside a system and service machines. The sealant is purchased as a kit that includes the sealant with a valve and short adapter hose. The absence of moisture inside the A/C system along with the heat and pressure prevent the sealant from hardening inside the system. ● **SEE FIGURE 14–23**.

CAUTION: Refrigerant service machines have experienced problems of lines plugging up and solenoids sticking after recovering refrigerant from systems containing sealants. One compressor manufacturer will not warranty compressors if sealant residue is found in them.

SUMMARY

1. The first refrigerant service operation is to identify the refrigerant in the system and check to make sure that it does not contain a sealant.

2. Evacuation is the process of removing the refrigerant form the system and storing it for reuse.

3. Recharging is the process of charging the system with the specified amount of refrigerant.

4. Sealants should be detected before a system is evacuated to protect the recovery machine from damage and to prevent the sealant from being added to the refrigerant in the RRR machine.

5. Retrofitting is the process of changing the refrigerant from one refrigerant to another, usually from R-12 to R-134a.

6. The refrigerant is recovered from a system so that service operations can be performed.

7. Recycling removes foreign particles, water, and air from refrigerant.

REVIEW QUESTIONS

1. What does the EPA Section 609 act affect?

2. What is considered to be a noncondensable gas (NCG)?

3. What are the steps to recover refrigerant?

4. What are the criteria for recycled refrigerant?

5. Why do A/C experts recommend using a micron meter to measure the vacuum in the system?

6. What are the steps required to be performed when retrofitting an R-12 system to R-134a?

CHAPTER QUIZ

1. Section 609 of the Act gives EPA the power to enforce _____.
   a. Preventing the release or venting of CFC-12 or HFC-134a
   b. Technicians are required to use approved equipment to recover and recycle CFC-12 and HFC 134a
   c. Technicians who repair or service CFC-12 and HFC-134a systems must be trained and certified by an EPA-approved organization
   d. All of the above

2. What is the SAE specification number of an RRR machine that meets the 2006 and newer standards?
   a. J-2788   c. J-1930
   b. J-2210   d. J-0560

3. The storage container for recovered refrigerant must be approved by_____.
   a. EPA   c. DOT
   b. OSHA   d. MSDS

4. Why should service technicians check a system for the presence of sealant before recovering the refrigerant?
   a. It can harm the recovery machine.
   b. It can contaminate the refrigerant that is stored in the recovery container.
   c. It can damage a refrigerant identifier.
   d. All of the above.

5. Present standards and good work habits require that recovered refrigerant be_____.
   a. Sent out to be discarded at an EPA-certified facility
   b. Recycled
   c. Sent back to the manufacturer
   d. Kept for 90 days

6. A container of R-134a tested at a pressure of 115 PSI at an ambient temperature of 75°F. This means _____.
   a. This is normal pressure for R-134a at that temperature
   b. That there is R-12 in the container
   c. Air is in the refrigerant
   d. That there is sealant in the container

7. What component cannot be flushed?
   a. The compressor
   b. The condenser
   c. The receiver–drier
   d. None of the above can be flushed

8. What is called "black death"?
   a. Dried refrigerant
   b. Teflon from the compressor piston rings
   c. Sealant
   d. Desiccant

9. When retrofitting a system from R-12 to R-134a, what is required to be done?
   a. Install a label
   b. Convert the fittings
   c. Replace the receiver–drier
   d. All of the above

10. Most experts recommend that the system be drawn down to how many microns?
    a. 500 or lower
    b. 10,000 or higher
    c. 243
    d. 127

chapter 15

A/C SYSTEM DIAGNOSIS AND REPAIR

LEARNING OBJECTIVES

After studying this chapter, the reader should be able to:

1. Prepare for the ASE Heating and Air Conditioning (A7) certification test content area "A" (A/C System Service, Diagnosis, and Repair).

2. Describe the eight-step diagnostic procedure for an A/C system.

3. Explain how to perform a visual inspection of an A/C system.

4. Discuss how to perform an A/C performance test.

5. Describe how to determine the root cause of the problem in an A/C system.

KEY TERMS

After-blow module 253	Groundout 255
Body control module (BCM) 249	Technical service bulletin (TSB) 249
Diagnostic trouble codes (DTC) 248	Visual inspection 246
Electronic evaporator dryer (EED) 253	

THE DIAGNOSTIC PROCEDURE

STEPS INVOLVED When diagnosing a heating and air-conditioning system problem, most vehicle manufacturers recommend that the following steps be performed.

STEP 1 **Verify the Customer Complaint (concern).** Some times the customer does not understand how the system is supposed to work or does not explain the fault clearly. Verifying the fault also means that the technician can verify that the problem has been corrected after the service procedure has been performed.

STEP 2 **Perform a Thorough Visual Inspection.** Heating and air-conditioning problems are often found by looking carefully at all of the components, checking for obvious faults or damage due to an accident or road debris.

STEP 3 **Check for Diagnostic Trouble Codes (DTCs).** Many heating and air-conditioning systems use sensors and actuators, which are computer-controlled and will set diagnostic trouble codes in the event of component failure.

STEP 4 **Check for Related Technical Service Bulletins (TSBs).** If there has been a technical service bulletin (TSB) released to solve a known problem, it saves a lot of time to know what to do rather than spend a lot of time trying to find and correct a customer concern.

STEP 5 **Perform an A/C Performance Test.** An A/C performance test is used to determine how well the system is able to remove heat from inside the vehicle and move it to the outside of the vehicle.

STEP 6 **Determine the Root Cause.** Perform pressure and temperature measurements to help determine the root cause of the customer concern.

STEP 7 **Repair the System.** Replace or repair the components that are defective or are no longer working as designed and recharge the system according to factory specifications.

STEP 8 **Verify the Repair.** Drive the vehicle under similar conditions that caused the customer to complain and verify that the concern has been corrected.

STEP 1 VERIFY THE CUSTOMER CONCERN

UNDERSTAND THE EXACT FAULT The customer concern needs to be addressed and if possible, when the problem occurs if the problem is intermittent, identify when it occurs. Sometimes the A/C system is functioning normally for the conditions which could include any of the following:

- Higher than normal outside air (ambient) temperature
- High humidity level
- A new vehicle that is larger or has more glass area than the customer's previous vehicle
- A new vehicle that is black or dark in color compared their previous vehicle that was a lighter color such as white or silver. A light-colored vehicle reflects light and the heat from the sun instead of being absorbed as with a dark-colored vehicle.

Other needed information include the following:

1. What recent service work was performed on the vehicle? (Previous repairs could have somehow affected the HVAC system).

2. Has the vehicle been in storage? (Animals like to build nests in HVAC ducts and this would affect A/C operation and airflow.)

 TECH TIP

"Evaporator Dandruff"

Many evaporators have a chemical coating to prevent bacterial growth that can cause bad odors. The coating can flake off and can sometimes be seen as dust specks on the top of the dash where it flows out of the defroster ducts and lands on the dash. This is commonly called "evaporator dandruff." The only fix for this condition is to replace the evaporator but because this usually involves the removal of the entire dash assembly, most vehicle owners simply ignore the dust on the dash.

What Does "short cycling" Mean?

If the system is low on refrigerant, it will short cycle, or rapidly cycle on and off. This is the result of the compressor pulling the refrigerant out of the low side quickly to open either the cycling switch or the low-pressure switch. With the compressor off, the flow into the evaporator raises the pressure enough to reclose the switch and restart the compressor. With a normal charge, the low-side pressure should be 15 PSI to 35 PSI and the clutch should be on for 45 seconds to 90 seconds and be off for only about 15 seconds to 30 seconds.

3. Has the vehicle been involved in a collision? (Hidden damage could cause faults in the HVAC system yet may not be visible from the outside).

4. Has the A/C system been serviced before? (This may indicate that the system has sealant or other impurities in the system).

5. The service adviser or shop owner should ask the customer to state their concern in their own words such as:

   ▪ "Does not seem to cool as fast as last year"

   ▪ " Airflow through the driver's side vent appears to be blocked"

   ▪ "The fan noise is high but I can't feel much cool air coming from the vents"

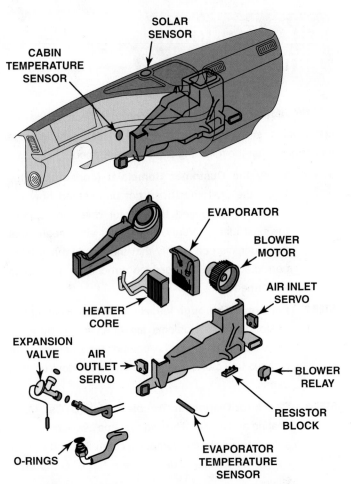

FIGURE 15–1 A visual inspection checks all of the visible, underhood components for possible wear or damage. The underdash components are checked for noise and proper airflow.

STEP 2 VISUAL INSPECTIONS

UNDERHOOD CHECKS Most vehicle manufacturers specify that the first step after the customer concern has been verified is that a **visual inspection** be performed. A visual inspection of the underhood items includes the following:

1. Check the condition of the A/C compressor drive belt.

2. Check the tension of the A/C compressor drive belt and the automatic tensioner.

3. Inspect the refrigerant hoses and lines for signs of oily residue and damage. Oil residue with caked-on dirt indicates a probable leak. Check that each of the A/C service ports is capped.

4. While checking the hoses and lines, determine if the system uses a thermal expansion valve system (TXV) or an orifice tube (OT) system and if a variable displacement compressor is used. The compressor shape and model number are used for identification.

5. Check that the compressor mounting bolts are tight.

6. Check to make sure that the air gap of the A/C compressor clutch is correct.

7. Check the electrical wires to the clutch, blower motor, and any A/C switches for good, tight connections, and possible damage. ●**SEE FIGURE 15–1.**

8. Check the condition of any vacuum hoses between the intake manifold and bulkhead, if equipped.

9. Check the faces of the condenser and radiator core for restriction to airflow caused by debris and clean as needed.

Broken Condenser Line?—Check the Engine Mounts!

Most air-conditioning systems use aluminum and flexible rubber lines between the compressor and the condenser. Because the compressor is mounted on and driven by the engine and the condenser is mounted to the body, these lines can break if the engine mounts are defective. The rubber hoses attached between the aluminum fittings of the compressor and condenser are designed to absorb normal engine movement. Worn engine mounts would allow the engine to move too much. Aluminum lines cannot be flexed without crushing and breaking. Therefore, the wise technician will carefully inspect and replace any and all worn engine mounts if a broken aluminum condenser line is discovered to prevent a premature failure of a replacement condenser.

IN-VEHICLE CHECKS
With the engine off, the in-vehicle checks include:

1. Operate the blower switch through its various speeds while listening to the fan and motor for unusual noises. Note that some systems do not have blower operation unless the heat or A/C controls are on or unless the engine is running.

2. Move the temperature lever of mechanically operated doors to both ends of its travel. It should move smoothly and stop before making contact at the ends. An early or late stop indicates that adjustment is needed.

ENGINE RUNNING CHECKS
With the engine running, the underhood checks include:

1. Make sure the compressor clutch is engaged and the compressor is running. Listen for any signs of improper compressor operation.

2. Turn off the A/C clutch to make sure it releases smoothly. With the clutch released, listen for proper clutch bearing operation.

3. Feel the temperature of the A/C lines and hoses. Be cautious on the high side because the lines should be warm to hot, with the temperature increasing. All the lines on the low side should be cool to cold, with the temperature getting colder. ● **SEE FIGURE 15–2.**

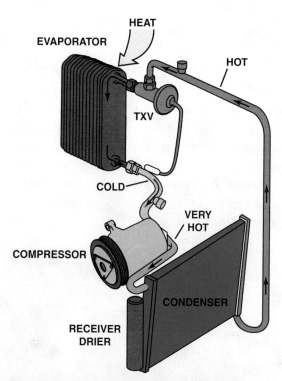

FIGURE 15–2 When a system is operating properly, the suction line to the compressor should be cool, and the discharge line should be hot to very hot. The liquid lines should also be hot.

Listen for the Thunk

On some vehicles, a "thunk" noise occurs as the temperature door contacts the stop. In an area with cold winters, it may "thunk" at the full heat stop. If in an area with hot summers, it may "thunk" at the full cool stop.

4. Feel the temperature of the heater hoses. If the engine is at operating temperature, both hoses should feel hot. Expect a temperature difference on heater systems with a coolant flow control valve.

5. Check the engine cooling fan operation (if running). The fan should be turning smoothly, with good airflow.

6. Check the evaporator drain. After a few minutes of operation on a humid day there should be a small puddle of water under the evaporator area and drops of water coming from the drain. With some vehicles, the drain is routed through a frame member. Check the service information for the location of the drain.

NOTE: In areas with very low humidity, water may not drain out.

Water on the Carpet? Check the Evaporator Water Drain

If the evaporator water drip tube becomes clogged with mud, leaves, or debris, water will build up inside the evaporator housing and spill out onto the carpet on the passenger side. Customers often think that the windshield or door seals are leaking. Most evaporator water drains are not visible unless the vehicle is hoisted. ● **SEE FIGURE 15–3.**

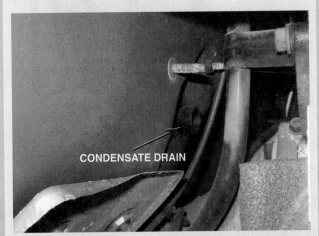

FIGURE 15–3 Check the condensate drain to be sure it is open if there is water on the carpet on the passenger side.

7. With the engine still running, check inside the vehicle for overall operation. By now the A/C system should be delivering cool to cold air from the instrument panel registers. Refer to performance check for actual expected temperatures. Moving the temperature control should cause a temperature change. Changing the function control to heat should move the air discharge to floor level.

STEP 3 CHECK DIAGNOSTIC TROUBLE CODES

Check for any stored **diagnostic trouble codes (DTCs)**. While most HVAC-related trouble codes will be "B", "C" or "U" codes, there are some that are Powertrain-related P-codes including:

- P0645 A/C Clutch Relay Control Circuit
- P0646 A/C Clutch Relay Control Circuit Low

Look for DTCs in "Body" and "Chassis"

Whenever diagnosing a customer concern with the HVAC system, check for diagnostic trouble codes (DTCs) under chassis and body systems and do not just look under engines. Therefore, a global or generic scan tool that can read only "P" codes is not suitable for diagnosing an HVAC system. Engine or emission control-type codes are "P" codes, whereas module communications are "U" codes. These are most often found when looking for DTCs under chassis or body systems. Chassis related codes are labeled "C" and body system-related codes are labeled "B" codes and these can cause an HVAC issue if they affect a sensor that is used by the system. ● **SEE FIGURE 15–4.**

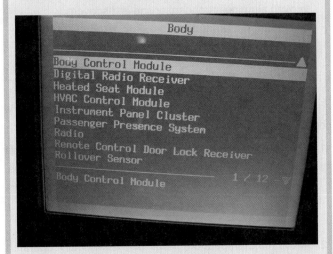

FIGURE 15–4 Under "Body" on most scan tools, select "HVAC Control Module" for access to the HVAC-related data and diagnostic trouble codes.

- P0647 A/C Clutch Relay Control Circuit High
- P0691 Fan 1 Control Circuit Low
- P0692 Fan 1 Control Circuit High
- P0693 Fan 2 Control Circuit Low
- P0694 Fan 2 Control Circuit High

These P codes can be read using global (generic) scan tools that are available at low cost. However, to get access to the codes set for most of the HVAC-related faults requires the use of a factory scan tool or an enhanced factory-level aftermarket scan tool.

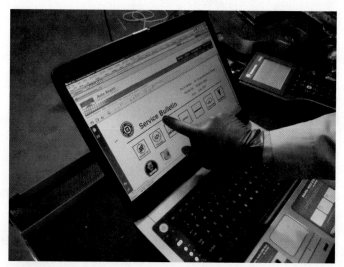

FIGURE 15–5 After checking for stored diagnostic trouble codes (DTCs), the wise technician checks service information for any technical service bulletins that may relate to the vehicle being serviced.

FIGURE 15–6 A temperature and humidity gauge is a useful tool for air-conditioning work. The higher the relative humidity, the more difficult it is for the air-conditioning system to lower the temperature inside the vehicle.

Many HVAC systems are controlled by the **body control module (BCM)**. The air conditioning-related diagnostic trouble codes are usually found under "Body" or "Chassis" and if set, will NOT light the "check engine" warning light. The check engine light is called the *malfunction indicator light (MIL)* and is commanded on if there is a fault that can affect emissions. Because HVAC-related faults often do not affect emissions, a DTC will be stored and may light another warning lamp or a message on the dash, such as the "A/C on" lamp will flash to indicate that a fault has been detected with the HVAC system.

STEP 4 CHECK FOR TECHNICAL SERVICE BULLETINS

Technical service bulletins (TSBs) are issued by vehicle and aftermarket manufacturers to inform technicians of a situation or technical problem and give the corrective steps and a list of parts needed to solve the problem. Any diagnostic trouble codes should be retrieved before looking at the technical service bulletins because many bulletins include what DTCs may or may not be present. TSBs are often released by new vehicle manufacturers to dealership service departments. ● SEE FIGURE 15–5.

While some of these TSBs concern minor problems covering few vehicles, many contain very helpful solutions to hard-to-find problems that cover many vehicles. TSBs can also be purchased through aftermarket companies that are licensed and available on a Web site. Visit the National Automotive Service Task Force (NASTF) Web site (www.NASTF.org) for a list of the Web addresses for all vehicle manufacturers' sites where the full text of TSBs can be purchased directly. Factory TSBs can often save the technician many hours of troubleshooting.

STEP 5 PERFORM A/C PERFORMANCE TEST

PROCEDURE An A/C performance test is used to determine if the system is capable of performing as designed. Most A/C performance tests include the following steps:

STEP 1   Install pressure gauges to the service ports.

STEP 2   Start the engine, set the parking brake, and raise the idle to 2000 RPM.

STEP 3   Measure ambient temperature 3 inches (80 mm) in front of the condenser and measure the humidity. ● SEE FIGURE 15–6.

STEP 4   Place a thermometer in the air conditioner center vent.

STEP 5   Set the air conditioner for maximum cooling.

STEP 6   Open the doors and set the blower speed to high, which applies the maximum load on the system.

LOW SIDE	HIGH SIDE	CONDITION (POSSIBLE CAUSE)
25 PSI–35 PSI	170 PSI–200 PSI	Normal
Low	Low	Low refrigerant charge level
Low	High	Restriction in high-side line
High	High	System is over-charged. Expansion valve stuck open
High	Low	Restriction in the low-side line

CHART 15–1

Pressure gauge readings and possible causes.

AMBIENT AIR TEMPERATURE	HUMIDITY	LOW-SIDE PRESSURE (PSI)	HIGH-SIDE PRESSURE (PSI)
70°F/21°C	Low	25–30	140–190
	High	28–35	165–220
80°F/27°C	Low	26–33	150–200
	High	30–36	190–260
90°F/32°C	Low	31–37	170–220
	High	37–45	210–290
100°F/38°C	Low	35–44	195–245
	High	38–48	230–320
110°F/43°C	Low	40–50	235–285
	High	42–52	260–350

CHART 15–2

The average R-134a pressure–temperature readings during a performance test. The high-side pressure of R-12 systems will be lower at higher temperatures.

STEP 7 Allow the system to operate for another five minutes before recording the gauge readings.

- Check the sight glass (if equipped). Clear? Bubbles? Foam?
- Check the A/C lines for frosting:
  - Low-Side Lines: Frosted (indicates low refrigerant level and should be corrected before continuing the test).
  - High-Side Lines: Frosted (indicates a restriction where the frost begins and should be corrected before continuing the test).

SYSTEM TEST RESULTS Wait several minutes to allow the system to reach maximum output and observe the thermometer.

- If 35°F to 45°F (2°C to 7°C) or 30°F (15°C) cooler than the outside air temperature, the system is functioning normally.
- If over 45°F (7°C) or over 30°F (15°C) warmer than the outside air temperature, continue with pressure gauge testing.

If pressures are okay and the sight glass is clear, but vent temperature is high, check for a blend door or heater control valve problem, or look for a possible system oil overcharge. If pressures vary from specifications, perform further tests to locate the problem. ●SEE CHART 15–1.

STEP 6 DETERMINE THE ROOT CAUSE

TEMPERATURE AND PRESSURE MEASUREMENTS

Temperature and pressure are directly related in A/C systems. As the ambient temperature increases, the high-side pressure must also increase to have a heat transfer at the condenser. The temperature of the vapor must be higher than the ambient temperature to allow enough heat to be removed for condensation. Also, higher ambient temperatures, and high humidity, usually mean a higher heat load on the evaporator. This means a larger quantity of heat has to be removed at the condenser.

- The **high-side pressure** is directly related to the amount of heat that needs to be removed, and the heat transfer at the condenser.
- **Low-side pressure** indicates the boiling point of the temperature of the evaporator. If the pressure is too high, the boiling point of the refrigerant and temperature of the evaporator are too high. Low-side pressure that is too low indicates the evaporator is too cold and may ice, or that there is not enough boiling refrigerant in the evaporator to remove an adequate amount of heat. ●SEE CHART 15–2.

Insufficient heat transfer at the condenser is usually the cause of high side pressure that is too high. The number one cause of poor heat transfer is lack of airflow across the condenser.

TECH TIP

The Paper Test

To determine if there is adequate airflow through a condenser, many technicians place a sheet of paper or a dollar bill in front of the condenser when the cooling fans are operating. With the engine running at idle speed, the bill should stick to the condenser.

FIGURE 15–8 Both low- and high-side pressures higher than normal indicate that the system is overcharged with refrigerant.

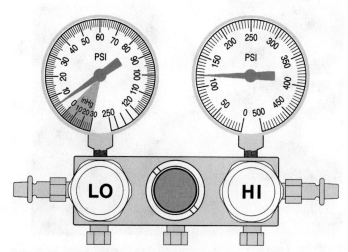

FIGURE 15–7 When both low- and high-side pressures are low, the system is undercharged with refrigerant.

The vehicle is dependent upon portable fans to move enough air when testing in the shop. It may be necessary to drive the vehicle at 30 MPH (48 km/h) to get the ram air necessary to determine if lack of airflow is the reason for the poor heat transfer.

Another cause of excessive high-side pressure is contamination with a different refrigerant. Mixing R-12 and R-134a raises the condensing pressure of the mixture. If the system is contaminated with R22, the pressures can become extremely high. At 150°F, the pressure of R-12 is 235 PSI (1,620 kPa), R-134a is 263 PSI (1,813 kPa), and R-22 is 381 PSI (2,627 kPa). This is an important reason to use a refrigerant identifier. ● **SEE FIGURES 15–7** through **15–9.**

TEMPERATURE DIFFERENCES ACROSS COMPONENTS

Test for heat transfer at the evaporator and the condenser.

- **Temperature change across the evaporator**—The temperature difference between the inlet and outlet of the evaporator should be same or within 5° (−5° to +5°). If

FIGURE 15–9 Lack of proper airflow across the condenser is usually the cause of high low side and higher high side pressures.

the temperature at the evaporator outlet is more than 6° different than the inlet temperature, then the system is overcharged.

- **Temperature change across the condenser**—The temperature difference between the inlet and outlet of the condenser should be 20°F to 50°F (10°C to 30°C).

  - If the temperature difference is higher than 50°, then the system is undercharged or has a restriction.
  - If the temperature difference is less than 19°, then the system is overcharged.

LEAK DETECTION If the A/C system is low on a charge of refrigerant, the sources of the leak should be found and

The Clogged Orifice Tube Test

A clogged orifice tube is a common air-conditioning system failure. When the orifice tube becomes clogged, it blocks the flow of refrigerant through the evaporator, which causes a reduced cooling of the passenger compartment. To check for a possible restriction in the system, follow these easy steps:

STEP 1 Connect the A/C pressure gauge to both low and high-side pressure fittings.

STEP 2 Operate the A/C system for 5 minutes to 10 minutes.

STEP 3 Shut off the A/C system and watch the pressure gauges. If the pressures do not equalize quickly, then there is a restriction in the system. Normal time needed to equalize is often 15 seconds to 30 seconds, depending on the amount of refrigerant.
● **SEE FIGURES 15–10 AND 15–11.**

NOTE: To locate a restriction anywhere in the system, feel along the system lines. The restriction exists at the point of greatest temperature difference. "Frosting" is a good indication of a restriction.

FIGURE 15–10 A clogged orifice tube.

FIGURE 15–11 A partially restricted orifice tube should be replaced if discovered during service.

corrected. Look for oily areas that are formed when refrigerant leaks and some refrigerant oil is lost. It is this oil that indicates a refrigerant leak. The two preferred methods of leak detection available include:

- **Electronic leak detector.** Many of these units can detect both CFC-12 and HFC-134a. The detector will sound a tone if a leak is detected.

- **Dye in the refrigerant.** A dye is added to some refrigerant to help the technician visually spot a leak in the refrigerant system. This method works well except for leaks in the evaporator, which are usually not visible.
● **SEE FIGURE 15–12.**

ADDRESSING SYSTEM ODORS
Some systems develop a musty, moldy smell, which is not really a fault of the system. Some sources classify these odors into two types:

- "Dirty socks/gym locker" odor, which has an organic cause

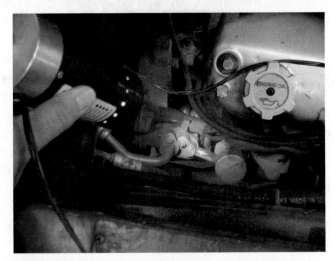

FIGURE 15–12 A black light being used to look for refrigerant leaks after a fluorescent dye was injected into or added to the system.

- "Refrigerator, cement, or dusty room" odor, which is caused by chemicals

The Touch, Feel Test

A quick-and-easy test to check the state of charge of an orifice tube system is to use one hand and touch the evaporator side of the orifice tube. Touch your other hand to the inlet to the accumulator. The following conditions can be determined by noticing the temperature of these two locations. ● SEE FIGURE 15–13.

- **Normal operation**—both temperatures about the same
- **Undercharged condition**—accumulator temperature higher (warmer) than the orifice tube temperature

Just remember: High pressure means that the temperature of the component or line will also be high (hot). Low pressure means that the temperature of the component or line will also be low (cold). For example, the inlet to the compressor (low pressure) should always be cool, whereas the outlet of the compressor (high pressure) should always be hot.

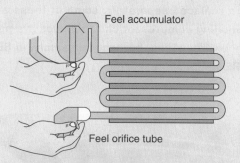

Feel accumulator

Feel orifice tube

FIGURE 15–13 If the system is fully charged, the outlet temperature of the line leaving the evaporator should be about the same as the temperature of the line entering the evaporator after the expansion valve or orifice tube. In a fully to slightly undercharged orifice tube system, the bottom of the accumulator is as cold as the line just downstream from the orifice tube. A warmer accumulator indicates an undercharge.

Leak-Testing the Evaporator

A quick-and-easy test to check whether the evaporator is leaking refrigerant is to remove the blower motor resistor pack. The blower motor resistor pack is almost always located directly "downstream" and near the blower motor. Removing the blower motor resistor pack gives access to the area near the evaporator. Inserting the probe of a leak detector into this open area allows the detector to test the air close to the evaporator and bend the detector hose to check the LOWER part of the evaporator box, because refrigerant will fall to the lower point. If the vehicle does not use a blower motor resistor or if it is difficult to access, hoist the vehicle and insert the sniffer probe in the condensate tube.

CAUTION: This is not recommended if the system has been run recently. If water is drawn into the electronic leak detector, it will be destroyed. If checking at the condensate line, make sure that the tube is dry and that there is no condensation ready to drip out of the tube.

surface of the evaporator warms up, and this warm, wet area becomes an ideal environment for fungus and bacteria growth. A coating is applied to many evaporators to speed up water runoff, which helps dry the evaporator and reduce bacterial growth. Airborne bacteria also collect on this surface, and if the surface stays moist, these bacteria will live and grow, creating the unpleasant smell. Then when the air conditioning or blower motor is turned on, that smell blows through the vehicle.

Several companies market chemicals, essentially fungicides, to kill the bacterial growth, or detergents to clean the evaporator core. Some of these chemicals and a procedure to use them have been approved by vehicle manufacturers. These chemicals are sprayed into the ductwork or onto the evaporator fins. ● SEE FIGURE 15–14.

Some manufacturers install an **electronic evaporator dryer (EED)**, also called an **after-blow module**. In some vehicles, the A/C control module is programmed to operate the blower for a drying cycle after the car is shut off. This device turns on the blower (with the ignition switched off for 30 minutes to 50 minutes) and lets it run long enough to dry off

The organic odor problem is most common in areas with high relative humidity, and it is caused by mildew-type fungus growth on the evaporator and in the evaporator plenum. Modern evaporators have more fins that are closer together, and they tend to trap more moisture and bacterial growth. The cool surface of the evaporator collects moisture as it dehumidifies the air, and most of this moisture runs out the bottom of the case. After a vehicle is shut off, the moist

Hot/Cold Sides

A complaint of uneven air discharge temperature from the instrument panel registers (cold on one side and warm on the other) can be caused by a low charge level. This will cause some parts of the evaporator to be cold while others are warm. It is possible for the air from the cold side to flow to a single register.

(a)

(b)

FIGURE 15–14 (a) A spray can of mold and mildew eliminator available at local parts stores and used on the evaporator before installing it into the vehicle is good insurance against HVAC-related odors. (b) Spraying the clear liquid mold and mildew eliminator onto the surface of the replacement evaporator prior to installation.

The Radio "POP" Trick

Most air-conditioning compressor clutch circuits contain a diode that is used to suppress the high-voltage spike that is generated whenever the compressor clutch coil is disengaged (turned off). If this diode were to fail, a high voltage (up to 400 volts) could damage sensitive electronic components in the vehicle including the electronic air-conditioning compressor clutch control unit (if so equipped). Another thing that can occur is that the radio will often turn off and then back on whenever the electronics inside the radio detect a high-voltage spike. This can create a "pop" in the radio that is very intermittent because it only occurs when the air-conditioning compressor clutch cycles off. To check this diode, simply tune the radio to a weak AM station near 1400 Hz and cycle the air-conditioning compressor on and off. If a "pop" is heard from the radio speaker(s), then the diode is defective and must be replaced.

NOTE: While some A/C compressor diodes can be replaced separately, some of these air-conditioning compressor clutch diodes are part of an entire wiring harness assembly. ● SEE FIGURE 15–15.

FIGURE 15–15 A diode connected to both terminals of the air-conditioning compressor clutch used to reduce the high-voltage spike that results when a coil (compressor clutch coil) is de-energized.

the evaporator after the vehicle has been shut off. One system waits 10 minutes, runs the blower on high for 10 seconds, shuts down for another 10 minutes, and then repeats the 10-second operation and 10-minute pause for 10 cycles. The object is to blow the moist air out of the evaporator without discharging the battery. EED modules are available for vehicles with either ground or B+ side blower switch systems.

ADDRESSING NOISE ISSUES

The A/C system is the potential source for several noise problems, and the compressor and clutch are the main culprits.

- A moaning or growling noise is a relatively low-frequency noise caused by something moving slowly.
- A whine or squeal is a high-pitch and high-frequency noise produced by something moving rapidly.

Another problem can be **groundout**, in which a vibrating metal A/C line contacts another surface (flat surfaces produce the most noise). Groundout problems also occur when the exhaust pipes make metal-to-metal contact with the vehicle body.

STEP 7 REPAIR THE SYSTEM

PURPOSE OF ANY REPAIR The purpose of any repair is to restore the system to like-new condition. Typical repairs include the replacement of components such as the accumulator, compressor, evaporator, condenser, and refrigerant lines/hoses.

TYPICAL REPAIRS Many repairs require the proper identification, recovery, evacuation, and charging of the refrigerant. After the repairs, the system should function and operate as designed and the repair should be performed according to established industry and vehicle manufacturer's recommendations. All safety precautions should be adhered to and the refrigerant handled according to federal and local laws.

STEP 8 VERIFY THE REPAIR

OPERATE THE SYSTEM After the repairs or service procedures have been performed, verify that the system is working as designed. If needed, drive the vehicle under the same conditions that it was when the customer concern was corrected to verify the repair. Document the work order and return the vehicle to the customer in clean condition.

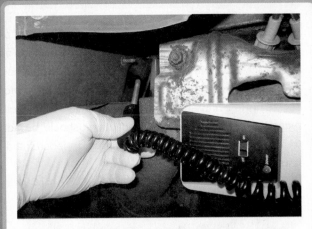

1 The lack of cooling was diagnosed using a leak detector which showed the evaporator was leaking when tested at the condensate drain.

2 The recovery process was started by connecting an RRR machine to the high-side fitting.

3 The low-side fitting was connected and the recovery was begun.

4 Very little refrigerant was left in the system (0.1 pound) but it was recovered.

5 The lines to the accumulator were removed.

6 The lines to the evaporator were disconnected using a quick connect tool to release the fitting.

7 The retaining nuts were removed that held the HVAC case to the bulkhead from under the hood. In one case, the entire stud came out instead of just the nut.

8 Before going into the passenger compartment, the negative battery cable was disconnected from the battery.

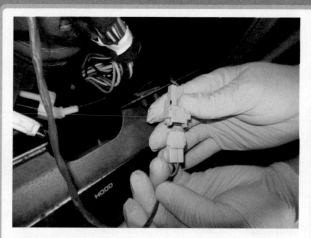

9 The dash assembly is being removed and this process includes disconnecting the airbag wiring connectors.

10 The driver/passenger side of the dash is removed to gain access to the additional fasteners.

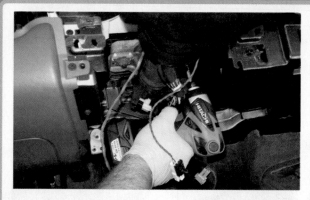

11 The two retaining fasteners that hold the steering column to the dash are removed and the steering column lowered into the seat, which is protected using a fender cover.

12 The entire dash assembly is being gently removed.

CONTINUED ▶

LACK OF COOLING DIAGNOSIS AND REPAIR (CONTINUED)

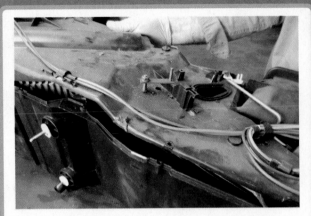

13 The HVAC case is being disassembled after being removed from the vehicle.

14 The evaporator is removed and it shows signs of leaking. The root cause of the lack of cooling has been found.

15 The heater core was also removed and replaced at the same time as insurance against possible future leaks from this unit.

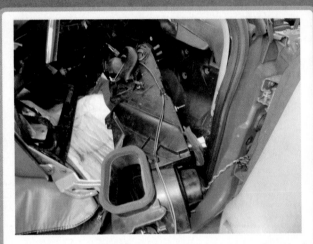

16 The reassembled HVAC case is now being installed back into the vehicle.

17 A new accumulator is installed.

18 The system was evacuated and charged to the specified amount and the pressure gauge and temperature reading indicated that the system was restored to like-new performance.

1. When diagnosing a heating and air-conditioning system problem, most vehicle manufacturers recommend that the following steps be performed.

    STEP 1   Verify the Customer Complaint (concern).

    STEP 2   Perform a Thorough Visual Inspection.

    STEP 3   Check for Diagnostic Trouble Codes (DTCs).

    STEP 4   Check for Related Technical Service Bulletins (TSBs).

    STEP 5   Perform an A/C Performance Test.

    STEP 6   Determine the Root Cause.

    STEP 7   Repair the System.

    STEP 8   Verify the Repair.

2. Sometimes the A/C system is functioning normally for the conditions which could include any of the following:

    - Higher than normal outside air (ambient) temperature
    - High humidity level

REVIEW QUESTIONS

1. What are the steps that a technician should follow when diagnosing and repairing an air-conditioning-related problem?

2. What should be checked as part of a visual inspection?

3. Why should the diagnostic trouble codes be checked before checking for technical service bulletins?

4. What does the temperature difference across the condenser and evaporator tell the technician?

5. How can leaks in the refrigeration system be detected?

CHAPTER QUIZ

1. When should the service technician check for technical service bulletins?
    a. As soon as the work order is received with the customer complaint shown.
    b. Before performing a visual inspection.
    c. After checking for any stored diagnostic trouble codes.
    d. After making the repair.

2. Clear water is seen dripping from beneath the vehicle on the passenger side. This means_____.
    a. Normal operation
    b. Possible clogged evaporator
    c. Possible restricted condenser
    d. Receiver–drier is at the end of its normal life

3. What should the technician use when checking for diagnostic trouble codes?
    a. Any global (generic) scan tool that can read body and/or chassis codes.
    b. Any enhanced scan tool that can read body and/or chassis codes.
    c. Only a factory scan tool can be used.
    d. A paper clip because it is needed to read codes.

4. What could be wrong if the A/C compressor clutch cycles on and off rapidly?
    a. Defective A/C compressor
    b. Defective A/C compressor clutch
    c. Low of refrigerant charge
    d. Shorted compressor clutch diode

5. The low-side pressure is low and the high-side pressure is higher than normal. What is the most likely cause?
    a. Low refrigerant charge level.
    b. System is overcharged. Expansion valve stuck open.
    c. Restriction in the low-side line.
    d. Restriction in high-side line.

6. The temperature difference between the inlet and outlet of the condenser should be _____.
    a. Equal
    b. 10°F to 30°F
    c. 20°F to 50°F
    d. Greater than 60°

7. Most A/C performance tests include_____.
    a. Start the engine, set the parking brake, and raise the idle to 2000 RPM
    b. Measure ambient temperature 3 inches (80 mm) in front of the condenser and measure the humidity
    c. Open the doors and set the blower speed to high, which applies the maximum load on the system
    d. All of the above

8. Several different methods of leak detection are available including_____.
    a. Visual inspection looking for refrigerant oil stains
    b. Dye
    c. Using a leak detector
    d. Any of the above

9. A "pop" is heard from the radio speaker(s) when the system is operating with the air conditioning on. What is the most likely cause?
   a. Normal operation
   b. A defective compressor clutch diode
   c. A restricted evaporator
   d. A worn A/C compressor

10. A musty, moldy smell in the air-conditioning system is usually due to _____.
   a. Mildew-type fungus growth
   b. A restricted evaporator
   c. A clogged condenser
   d. A weak or defective AC compressor

SAMPLE A7 ASE CERTIFICATION-TYPE TEST WITH ANSWERS

HEATING AND AIR CONDITIONING (A7)	NUMBER OF ASE CERTIFICATION TEST QUESTIONS 50
A. A/C System Service, Diagnosis, and Repair	17
B. Refrigeration System Component Diagnosis and Repair	10
1. Compressor and Clutch (5)	
2. Evaporator, Condenser, and Related Components (5)	
C. Heating and Engine Cooling Systems Diagnosis and Repair	4
D. Operating Systems and Related Controls Diagnosis and Repair	19
1. Electrical (10)	
2. Vacuum/Mechanical (2)	
3. Automatic and Semi- Automatic Heating, Ventilating, and A/C Systems (7)	

A. AIR-CONDITIONING SYSTEM DIAGNOSIS AND REPAIR QUESTIONS

1. Both high-side and low-side pressures are low with the engine running and the selector set to the air-conditioning position. Technician A says that the system is undercharged. Technician B says the cooling fan could be inoperative. Which technician is correct?
    a. Technician A only
    b. Technician B only
    c. Both Technicians A and B
    d. Neither Technician A nor B

2. Which component is located in the low pressure side of the refrigeration system?
    a. Accumulator
    b. TXV
    c. Orifice tube
    d. Receiver-drier

3. A lack of cooling is being diagnosed. A technician discovers that the high-pressure line is hot to the touch on both sides of the orifice tube. Technician A says that is normal operation for an orifice tube system. Technician B says that the orifice tube may be clogged. Which technician is correct?

    a. Technician A only
    b. Technician B only
    c. Both Technicians A and B
    d. Neither Technician A nor B

4. Frost is observed on the line between the condenser and the receiver–drier. Technician A says that this is normal if the air conditioning were being operated on a hot and humid day. Technician B says that a restriction in the line or at the outlet of the condenser could be the cause. Which technician is correct?
    a. Technician A only
    b. Technician B only
    c. Both Technicians A and B
    d. Neither Technician A nor B

5. The owner of a vehicle equipped with an orifice tube-type air-conditioning system complains that the inside of the vehicle does not cool properly. The air-conditioning compressor clutch rapidly cycles on and off whenever the air conditioning is on. Technician A says that the system is likely low on refrigerant. Technician B says that the most likely cause is an electrical short in the wiring to the air-conditioning compressor clutch. Which technician is correct?
    a. Technician A only
    b. Technician B only

c. Both Technicians A and B
d. Neither Technician A nor B

6. A customer states that the vehicle does not cool as well as it should. Technician A says that the system could be low on refrigerant charge. Technician B says that if the electric radiator cooling fan is not functioning, this can cause a lack of cooling inside the vehicle. Which technician is correct?
   a. Technician A only
   b. Technician B only
   c. Both Technicians A and B
   d. Neither Technician A nor B

7. An automotive air-conditioning system is being tested for a lack-of-cooling complaint. Both high and low side pressures are higher than normal. Technician A says that the system is low on charge. Technician B says that the system is overcharged. Which technician is correct?
   a. Technician A only
   b. Technician B only
   c. Both Technicians A and B
   d. Neither Technician A nor B

8. The high-side pressure is higher than normal. Technician A says that the compressor may be defective. Technician B says that the condenser may be clogged with leaves or other debris blocking the airflow. Which technician is correct?
   a. Technician A only
   b. Technician B only
   c. Both Technicians A and B
   d. Neither Technician A nor B

9. A customer complained of a clear liquid leaking from underneath the vehicle on the passenger side after driving for a short time with the air conditioning on. The problem occurs only when the air conditioner is operating. Technician A says that the evaporator may be leaking. Technician B says that this may be normal condensed water formed on the cold evaporator coil. Which technician is correct?
   a. Technician A only
   b. Technician B only
   c. Both Technicians A and B
   d. Neither Technician A nor B

10. Both the low and the high pressures are within normal ranges, yet the inside of the vehicle is not cooling. Technician A says that a partially clogged orifice tube could be the cause. Technician B says that too much refrigerant oil in the system could be the cause. Which technician is correct?
    a. Technician A only
    b. Technician B only
    c. Both Technicians A and B
    d. Neither Technician A nor B

11. A technician is observing the pressure gauges when the engine is turned off and notices that the high-side and low-side pressures do not equalize quickly as they should. Technician A says that the orifice tube may be clogged. Technician B says that the desiccant may be saturated with moisture. Which technician is correct?

a. Technician A only
b. Technician B only
c. Both Technicians A and B
d. Neither Technician A nor B

12. A customer states that the carpet on the floor on the passenger side is wet and noticed this when the air conditioning was first being used in the spring during damp weather. Which is the most likely cause?
    a. Evaporator refrigerant leak
    b. Clogged evaporator case drain
    c. Saturated desiccant in the drier
    d. Clogged screen in the accumulator

13. What two items must be installed or replaced when retrofitting a CFC-12 system to an HFC-134a system?
    a. Fitting adaptors and a label
    b. Compressor and O-rings
    c. Label and the condenser
    d. Fitting adaptors and the evaporator

14. An air-conditioning performance test is being performed. All of the following should be done except:
    a. Turn blower to high speed
    b. Open the doors
    c. Set the controls for maximum cooling
    d. Place a thermometer in the inside air inlet door

15. Two technicians are discussing refrigerant oil. Technician A says that PAG oil comes in more than one viscosity and that using the wrong thickness of oil could cause damage to the compressor. Technician B says that refrigerant oil must be kept in a sealed container. Which technician is correct?
    a. Technician A only
    b. Technician B only
    c. Both Technicians A and B
    d. Neither Technician A nor B

16. A vehicle is being checked for a lack of cooling concern about two months after another shop had replaced the compressor. Technician A says that debris from the old compressor could have clogged the orifice tube. Technician B says that the system could be low on charge due to a leak in the system. Which technician is correct?
    a. Technician A only
    b. Technician B only
    c. Both Technicians A and B
    d. Neither Technician A nor B

17. On an older vehicle, the air flows from the heater (floor) and defroster (windshield) ducts all of the time regardless of the position of the heater/air-conditioning mode control. Which is the most likely cause?
    a. A disconnected vacuum hose from the intake manifold
    b. A defective heater/air-conditioning mode control unit
    c. Air-conditioning system is discharged
    d. A stuck blend door

B. REFRIGERATION SYSTEM COMPONENT DIAGNOSIS AND REPAIR QUESTIONS

18. Technician A says that all HFC-134a systems use the same refrigerant oil. Technician B says that refrigerant oil, regardless of type, must be kept in a sealed container to

keep it from absorbing moisture from the air. Which technician is correct?

a. Technician A only
b. Technician B only
c. Both Technicians A and B
d. Neither Technician A nor B

19. A front-wheel-drive vehicle has a broken condenser line. What other vehicle component may also be defective that could have caused the condenser line to break?

a. A shock absorber
b. An engine mount
c. A cooling fan
d. An air-conditioning compressor drive belt

20. Technician A says that the air-conditioning compressor should operate when the controls are set to the heat position. Technician B says the air-conditioning compressor should operate when the controls are set to the defrost position. Which technician is correct?

a. Technician A only
b. Technician B only
c. Both Technicians A and B
d. Neither Technician A nor B

21. The air-conditioning compressor clutch does not engage when the air-conditioning mode is selected and the engine is running. Technician A says that the system may be low on refrigerant charge. Technician B says the low-pressure switch may be electrically open. Which technician is correct?

a. Technician A only
b. Technician B only
c. Both Technicians A and B
d. Neither Technician A nor B

22. An air-conditioning compressor is noisy whenever the clutch is engaged. Technician A says that the drive belt may be defective. Technician B says the compressor may be defective. Which technician is correct?

a. Technician A only
b. Technician B only
c. Both Technicians A and B
d. Neither Technician A nor B

23. Technician A says that some refrigerant oil should be added to a replacement condenser to make sure that the system has the correct amount of oil. Technician B says that a specified viscosity of oil must be used to ensure proper lubrication of the compressor. Which technician is correct?

a. Technician A only
b. Technician B only
c. Both Technicians A and B
d. Neither Technician A nor B

24. Technician A says that the old refrigerant oil can be mixed with and disposed of with used engine oil. Technician B says that refrigerant oil should be added to a new condenser if being replaced. Which technician is correct?

a. Technician A only
b. Technician B only
c. Both Technicians A and B
d. Neither Technician A nor B

25. Technician A says that if an evaporator has been replaced, 2 or 3 ounces of refrigerant oil should be added to the system. Technician B says that the old evaporator should be drained and the oil measured to determine how much

oil to add when installing the replacement evaporator. Which technician is correct?

a. Technician A only
b. Technician B only
c. Both Technicians A and B
d. Neither Technician A nor B

26. A noisy compressor is being discussed. Technician A says that the air-conditioning system could be low on lubricating oil. Technician B says that the system could be overcharged. Which technician is correct?

a. Technician A only
b. Technician B only
c. Both Technicians A and B
d. Neither Technician A nor B

27. Both pressure gauge needles are oscillating rapidly. Which component is the most likely cause?

a. The compressor (reed valves)
b. The orifice tube (clogged)
c. The expansion valve (stuck closed)
d. The drier (desiccant bag is saturated with moisture)

C. HEATING AND ENGINE COOLING SYSTEMS DIAGNOSIS AND REPAIR QUESTIONS

28. A service technician is replacing a water (coolant) pump. Technician A says that used coolant should be properly disposed of or kept for recycling. Technician B says that the used coolant should be reused to refill the cooling system after the repair is completed. Which technician is correct?

a. Technician A only
b. Technician B only
c. Both Technicians A and B
d. Neither Technician A nor B

29. A customer complained of lack of heat from the heater. A check of the cooling system shows that the upper radiator hose is not getting hot. Technician A says that the thermostat may be defective (stuck open). Technician B says that the cause could be a defective (always engaged) thermostat cooling fan. Which technician is correct?

a. Technician A only
b. Technician B only
c. Both Technicians A and B
d. Neither Technician A nor B

30. A lack of heat from the heater is being diagnosed. Which is the most likely cause?

a. A partially clogged radiator
b. Hoses reversed on the heater core
c. A partially clogged heater core
d. A defective water pump

31. The temperature gauge approaches the red part of the temperature gauge (260°F or 127°C) if driven at slow speeds but does not overheat if driven at highway speeds. What is the most likely cause?

a. Low coolant level
b. Incorrect antifreeze/water mixture
c. Defective water (coolant) pump
d. Inoperative cooling fan

32. A "pop" is heard from the radio speakers occasionally when the defroster or air conditioning is selected. Technician A says that the compressor clutch clamping diode may be blown. Technician B says that the air-conditioning compressor clutch may have a poor electrical ground connection. Which technician is correct?
    a. Technician A only
    b. Technician B only
    c. Both Technicians A and B
    d. Neither Technician A nor B

33. A reduced amount of airflow from the air-conditioning vents is being discussed. Technician A says that the evaporator could be clogged as a result of a small refrigerant leak causing oil to trap and hold dirt. Technician B says that the blower motor ground connection could have excessive voltage drop. Which technician is correct?
    a. Technician A only
    b. Technician B only
    c. Both Technicians A and B
    d. Neither Technician A nor B

34. Technician A says that an electrical open in the low-pressure switch can prevent the compressor from working. Technician B says that the compressor may not operate at low outside temperatures depending on the pressure sensed by the low-pressure switch. Which technician is correct?
    a. Technician A only
    b. Technician B only
    c. Both Technicians A and B
    d. Neither Technician A nor B

35. Technician A says that the voltage to the air-conditioning compressor may be turned off when some vehicles are accelerating rapidly. Technician B says that a fault in the power steering pressure switch could prevent the air-conditioning compressor from operating. Which technician is correct?
    a. Technician A only
    b. Technician B only
    c. Both Technicians A and B
    d. Neither Technician A nor B

36. An automatic air-conditioning system is being diagnosed for cooler than the set temperature. Technician A says that a blocked inside air temperature sensor could be the cause. Technician B says that a blocked sun load sensor could be the cause. Which technician is correct?
    a. Technician A only
    b. Technician B only
    c. Both Technicians A and B
    d. Neither Technician A nor B

37. A blower motor is drawing more than the specified current. Technician A says that the blower motor ground connection could be corroded. Technician B says that the blower relay is shorted. Which technician is correct?
    a. Technician A only
    b. Technician B only
    c. Both Technicians A and B
    d. Neither Technician A nor B

38. The A/C compressor clutch does not engage. Technician A says that an open high pressure cutout switch could be the problem. Technician B says a blown compressor clutch diode could be the cause. Which technician is correct?
    a. Technician A only
    b. Technician B only
    c. Both Technicians A and B
    d. Neither Technician A nor B

39. A vehicle equipped with automatic climate control was involved in a minor front-end collision. Afterward the system stopped cooling. What is the most likely cause?
    a. Reduced airflow through the radiator
    b. Air trapped in the refrigerant system
    c. A defective blower motor resistor
    d. A broken ambient air temperature sensor

40. In the dual climate control system, the temperatures for the driver and passenger are regulated by controlling which components or system?
    a. Airflow through the evaporator and heater core
    b. Air-conditioning pressures to the left and right side evaporator
    c. Amount of coolant flowing through the heater core
    d. Airflow from the outside to the left (driver's) side and right (passenger's) side

41. What is used to control the A/C compressor clutch operation?
    a. High and low side pressure switches
    b. Orifice tube
    c. TXV
    d. Receiver-drier

E. REFRIGERANT RECOVERY, RECYCLING, AND HANDLING

42. The technician can test for trapped air (noncondensable gases) inside the refrigerant container by _____.
    a. Checking the outside of the container for frost
    b. Checking the pressure versus temperature of the container
    c. Weighing the container
    d. Sending the container to a special laboratory for analysis

43. Technician A says that the refrigerant oil removed during reclaiming should be measured. Technician B says that refrigerant oil can be disposed of with regular engine oil. Which technician is correct?
    a. Technician A only
    b. Technician B only
    c. Both Technicians A and B
    d. Neither Technician A nor B

44. Refrigerant should be identified _____.
    a. After recovery, but before recycling
    b. Before recovery
    c. Before charging the system
    d. After charging the system, but before releasing the vehicle to the customer

45. To be sure that all of the moisture in an air-conditioning system has been boiled and removed, a vacuum of at least _____ in. Hg should be drawn on the system for at least _____ minutes.
- **a.** 28, 45
- **b.** 29, 60
- **c.** 30, 90
- **d.** 30, 120

46. After the refrigerant has been recovered and recycled, where should it be kept for long-term storage?
- **a.** In an EPA approved container
- **b.** In the recovery machine storage unit
- **c.** In the recycling machine storage unit
- **d.** In a DOT approved container

47. What should the technician do before recovering refrigerant from a vehicle?
- **a.** Test it using a refrigerant identifier and a sealant identifier
- **b.** Connect pressure gauges and check the high- and low-side pressures
- **c.** Tighten the Schrader valves to be sure they are properly sealed
- **d.** Start the engine and allow the air-conditioning system to work for several minutes

48. A technician discovers that 20% of the refrigerant in a vehicle is unknown. What service operation should the service technician perform?

- **a.** Recover and recycle the refrigerant as normal
- **b.** Recover the refrigerant into a container labeled unknown refrigerant
- **c.** Cycle the compressor clutch until the unknown refrigerant is purged from the system
- **d.** Recover the refrigerant and remove the noncondensable gases

49. A technician checked the pressure on a 30 lb. container of R-134a at 80°F (27°C) and the pressure was 101 PSI (700 kPa) (see chart on page on 231). Technician A says that the tank should be vented until the pressure is reduced if the identifier detected noncondensable gases (air) in the refrigerant. Technician B says that additional refrigerant should be added to lower the pressure. Which technician is correct?
- **a.** Technician A only
- **b.** Technician B only
- **c.** Both Technicians A and B
- **d.** Neither Technician A nor B

50. An orifice tube-type air-conditioning system is being serviced with HFC-134a (R-134a). Which SAE standard recovery, recycling, and recharging machine should be used?
- **a.** J1770
- **b.** J2210
- **c.** J2788
- **d.** J2851

ANSWERS

1.	a	**14.**	d	**27.**	a	**40.**	a
2.	a	**15.**	c	**28.**	a	**41.**	a
3.	d	**16.**	c	**29.**	a	**42.**	b
4.	b	**17.**	a	**30.**	c	**43.**	a
5.	a	**18.**	b	**31.**	d	**44.**	b
6.	c	**19.**	b	**32.**	a	**45.**	a
7.	b	**20.**	b	**33.**	c	**46.**	d
8.	b	**21.**	c	**34.**	c	**47.**	a
9.	b	**22.**	c	**35.**	c	**48.**	b
10.	b	**23.**	c	**36.**	a	**49.**	a
11.	a	**24.**	b	**37.**	d	**50.**	c
12.	b	**25.**	a	**38.**	a		
13.	a	**26.**	c	**39.**	d		

2013 NATEF CORRELATION CHART

MLR—Maintenance & Light Repair
AST—Automobile Service Technology (Includes MLR)
MAST—Master Auto Service Technology (Includes MLR and AST)

HEATING AND AIR CONDITIONING (A7)

TASK	PRIORITY	MLR	AST	MAST	TEXT PAGE #	TASK PAGE #
A. GENERAL: A/C SYSTEM DIAGNOSIS AND REPAIR						
1. Identify and interpret heating and air conditioning problems; determine necessary action.	P-1		✔	✔	245	16; 26
2. Research applicable vehicle and service information fluid type, vehicle service history, service precautions, and technical service bulletins.	P-1	✔	✔	✔	249	1; 19
3. Performance test A/C system; identify problems.	P-1		✔	✔	249	26
4. Identify abnormal operating noises in the A/C system; determine necessary action.	P-2		✔	✔	255	27
5. Identify refrigerant type; select and connect proper gauge set; record temperature and pressure readings.	P-1		✔	✔	250	28
6. Leak test A/C system; determine necessary action.	P-1		✔	✔	252	29
7. Inspect condition of refrigerant oil removed from A/C system; determine necessary action.	P-2		✔	✔	228	7
8. Determine recommended oil and oil capacity for system application.	P-1		✔	✔	121–122; 234–235	7
9. Using a scan tool, observe and record related HVAC data and trouble codes.	P-3		✔	✔	248	20
B. REFRIGERATION SYSTEM COMPONENT DIAGNOSIS AND REPAIR						
1. Inspect and replace A/C compressor drive belts, pulleys, and tensioners; determine necessary action.	P-1	✔	✔	✔	88	37
2. Inspect, test, service, or replace A/C compressor clutch components and/or assembly; check compressor clutch air gap; adjust as needed.	P-2	✔	✔	✔	86–87	6
3. Remove, inspect, and reinstall A/C compressor and mountings; determine recommended oil quantity.	P-2				89–91	6
4. Identify hybrid vehicle A/C system electrical circuits and service/safety precautions.	P-2	✔	✔	✔	214	21; 22
5. Determine need for an additional A/C system filter; perform necessary action.	P-3		✔	✔	234	30

TASK	PRIORITY	MLR	AST	MAST	TEXT PAGE #	TASK PAGE #
6. Remove and inspect A/C system mufflers, hoses, lines, fittings, O-rings, seals, and service valves; perform necessary action.	P-2		✔	✔	255	6
7. Inspect A/C condenser for airflow restrictions; perform necessary action.	P-1	✔	✔	✔	246; 250	9
8. Remove, inspect, and reinstall receiver/drier or accumulator/drier; determine recommended oil quantity.	P-2		✔	✔	122	10
9. Remove, inspect, and install expansion valve or orifice (expansion) tube.	P-1		✔	✔	252	11
10. Inspect evaporator housing water drain; perform necessary action.	P-1		✔	✔	247–248	34
11. Diagnose A/C system conditions that cause the protection devices (pressure, thermal, and PCM) to interrupt system operation; determine necessary action.	P-2			✔	207–209	31
12. Determine procedure to remove and reinstall evaporator; determine required oil quantity.	P-2		✔	✔	256–258	35
13. Remove, inspect, and reinstall condenser; determine required oil quantity.	P-2			✔	121–122	36

C. HEATING, VENTILATION, AND ENGINE COOLING SYSTEMS DIAGNOSIS AND REPAIR

TASK	PRIORITY	MLR	AST	MAST	TEXT PAGE #	TASK PAGE #
1. Inspect engine cooling and heater systems hoses; perform necessary action.	P-1	✔	✔	✔	166–167; 175–181; 188–190	15
2. Inspect and test heater control valve(s); perform necessary action.	P-2		✔	✔	188	16
3. Diagnose temperature control problems in the heater/ventilation system; determine PCM to interrupt system operation; determine necessary action.	P-2			✔	207–209	17
4. Determine procedure to remove, inspect, and reinstall heater core.	P-2		✔	✔	192–194	17; 35

D. OPERATING SYSTEMS AND RELATED CONTROLS DIAGNOSIS AND REPAIR

TASK	PRIORITY	MLR	AST	MAST	TEXT PAGE #	TASK PAGE #
1. Inspect and test A/C-heater blower motors, resistors, switches, relays, wiring, and protection devices; perform necessary action.	P-1		✔	✔	136	12; 14
2. Diagnose A/C compressor clutch control systems; determine necessary action.	P-2		✔	✔	203–204	5
3. Diagnose malfunctions in the vacuum, mechanical, and electrical components and controls of the heating, ventilation, and A/C (HVAC) system; determine necessary action.	P-2		✔	✔	132–133	13; 32
4. Inspect and test A/C-heater control panel assembly; determine necessary action.	P-3		✔	✔	132–135	13
5. Inspect and test A/C-heater control cables, motors, and linkages; perform necessary action.	P-3		✔	✔	132	13
6. Inspect A/C-heater ducts, doors, hoses, cabin filters, and outlets; perform necessary action.	P-1	✔	✔	✔	201	18
7. Identify the source of A/C system odors.	P-1	✔	✔	✔	252–254	33
8. Check operation of automatic or semiautomatic heating, ventilation, and air-conditioning (HVAC) control systems; determine necessary action.	P-2		✔	✔	207–209	20

TASK	PRIORITY	MLR	AST	MAST	TEXT PAGE #	TASK PAGE #
E. REFRIGERANT RECOVERY, RECYCLING, AND HANDLING						
1. Perform correct use and maintenance of refrigerant handling equipment according to equipment manufacturer's standards.	P-1		✔	✔	227–228	8; 23
2. Identify and recover A/C system refrigerant.	P-1		✔	✔	227–228	23
3. Recycle, label, and store refrigerant.	P-1		✔	✔	229	24
4. Evacuate and charge A/C system; add refrigerant oil as required.	P-1		✔	✔	235–239	25

GLOSSARY

Aboveground storage tank (AGST) A type of oil storage.

Absolute humidity The measurement of the weight of the water vapor in a given volume of air.

After-blow module An electrical control that will run the HVAC blower after the vehicle has been shut off. Its purpose is to dry the evaporator fins.

Air doors The doors inside of the HVAC case that direct the airflow to the proper location.

Air inlet The door that controls the source of air entering the A/C and heating unit.

Air management system The system that controls the airflow to the passenger compartment.

Ambient temperature sensor A sensor that measures the temperature of outside air entering the vehicle.

Ammeter An electrical test instrument used to measure amperes (unit of the amount of current flow).

Ampere The measurement for the amount of current flow in an electric circuit.

Asbestosis A health condition where asbestos causes scar tissue to form in the lungs, causing shortness of breath.

Automatic air-conditioning system A system that uses sensors and actuators to maintain a preset temperature inside a vehicle.

Automatic climatic control system See automatic temperature control system.

Automatic temperature control (ATC) system A system that uses sensors and actuators to maintain a preset temperature inside a vehicle.

Bar A pressure that is equal to atmospheric pressure.

Barrier hose A hose with a nonpermeable inner liner.

BCI Battery Council International.

Bench grinder An electric motor with a grinding stone and/or wire brush attached at both ends of the armature and mounted on a bench.

Black death A term referring to the black, gooey mess resulting from a catastrophic compressor failure.

Bleed holes In series flow systems, bleed holes or steam slits in the gasket, block, and head perform the function of letting out the steam.

Blend door An air mix valve located in the air distribution box of a HVAC system. The blend door blends air from the A/C evaporator with warm air from the heater core to deliver air at the desired temperature at the outlet ducts.

Body control module (BCM) Many HVAC systems are controlled by the body control module (BCM).

Bolts A threaded fastener that is used to hold two parts together with a nut on the other end of the threaded end. If installed into a threaded hole, then a bolt is often called a cap screw.

Breaker bar A handle used to rotate a socket; also called a flex handle.

British thermal unit (BTU) A measurement of heat quantity; the amount of heat needed to increase the temperature of 1 lb. of water 1°F.

Bump cap A hat that is made of plastic and is hard enough to protect the head from bumps.

Bypass A bypass around the closed thermostat allows a small part of the coolant to circulate within the engine during warm-up.

CAA Clean Air Act. Federal legislation passed in 1970 that established national air quality standards.

Cabin filter A filter in the HVAC system to remove small particles, like dust and pollen, and odors from the air.

Calibration codes Codes used on many powertrain control modules.

Calorie A measurement of heat quantity; the amount of heat required to increase the temperature of 1 g of water 1°C.

Campaign A recall where vehicle owners are contacted to return a vehicle to a dealer for corrective action.

Captive O-ring Captive O-rings use a larger-diameter cross section than standard O-rings placed positively in a shallow groove.

Casting number An identification code cast into an engine block or other large cast part of a vehicle.

Cellular Most heater cores use a cellular form of construction that is somewhat like a plate-type evaporator. The tubes are made by joining two corrugated brass or aluminum plates, and the corrugated fins are attached between pairs of tubes.

Centrifugal pump A type of pump used for water pumps where a large volume of liquid can be moved using a rotating impeller without building pressure.

CFR Code of Federal Regulations.

Cheater bar A pipe or other object used to lengthen the handle of a ratchet or breaker bar. Not recommended to be used as the extra force can cause the socket or ratchet to break.

Chisels A sharpened tool used with a hammer to separate two pieces of an assembly.

Clean Air Act A government action in 1990 to improve air quality.

Comfort zone The temperature range where humans feel comfortable, usually between 68°F and 78°F (20°C and 26°C).

Compressor The component in an A/C system that compresses refrigerant vapor and causes that vapor to move through the system.

Compressor speed sensor The air conditioning (A/C) compressor speed sensor, also called a lock or belt lock sensor, is used so the ECM will know if the compressor is running, and by comparing the compressor and engine speed signals, the ECM can determine if the compressor clutch or drive belt is slipping excessively.

Condenser The component in an A/C system in which heat is removed and vapor is changed to liquid.

Conductors A material that conducts electricity and heat. A metal that contains fewer than four electrons in its atom's outer shell.

Connector The plastic part of a wiring connector where metal electrical terminals plug in.

Control valve Some vehicles have a control valve in the heater inlet hose that allows coolant flow to be shut off when MAX cooling is selected to keep hot coolant from flowing through the heater core.

Conventional theory The theory that electricity flows from positive (+) to negative (−).

Conversion fitting A fitting installed over an R-12 service fitting to allow use of an alternate refrigerant.

Cooling fins Heat is transferred through the tube wall and soldered joint to cooling fins of the radiator.

Cooling load The removal of heat to provide a comfortable environment.

Coolant heat storage system A system used on the second generation Toyota Prius that stores hot coolant in order to warm the ICE prior to a cold start.

Coolant recovery system When the system cools, the pressure in the cooling system is reduced and a partial vacuum forms. This pulls the coolant from the plastic container back into the cooling system, keeping the system full.

Core tubes   Oval shaped tubes where coolant flows through a radiator.

Crimp-and-seal connectors   A type of electrical connector that has glue inside which provides a weather-proof seal after it is heated.

Cubic feet per minute (cfm)   The cfm rating is the volume a vacuum pump can pump.

Damper drive   A compressor-drive pulley with dampers/cushions to remove pulsations and no clutch.

Diagnostic trouble code (DTC)   An alphanumeric or numeric sequence indicating a fault in a vehicle operating system. Each sequence corresponds to a specific malfunction.

Digital multimeter (DMM)   A digital multimeter is capable of measuring electrical current, resistance, and voltage.

Digital volt-ohm-meter (DVOM)   A digital multimeter is capable of measuring electrical current, resistance, and voltage.

Discharge air temperature (DAT) Sensor   A temperature sensor located at the outlet of the evaporator.

Discharge line   The line that connects the compressor discharge port to the condenser.

Discharge stroke   The compressor piston movement that pumps refrigerant out of the cylinder.

Drive plate   The drive plate is attached to the compressor shaft. The drive plate is also called an armature or disc, and the pulley is also called a rotor.

Drive sizes   The size in fractions of an inch of the square drive for sockets.

Dual-position actuator   An actuator used in a heating ventilation and air conditioning (HVAC) system that has two positions.

Dual-zone   Dual-zone air distribution allows the driver and passenger to select different temperature settings. The temperature choices can be as much as 30°F (16°C) different.

Dual-zone system   An HVAC case design that allows an air-flow temperature difference between the driver and passenger.

Electricity   The movement of free electrons from one atom to another.

Electronic evaporator dryer (EED)   *See* After-blow module.

Electron theory   The theory that electricity flows from negative (–) to positive (+).

Engine coolant temperature (ECT) sensor   A device to monitor engine coolant temperature and convert it into an electrical signal.

Environmental Protection Agency (EPA)   A governmental agency that regulates gases that can affect our environment.

EPA   Environmental Protection Agency.

Evacuation   To pump a vacuum into an A/C system to remove contaminated refrigerant and water.

Evaporative cooling   The process of cooling a surface using the evaporation of water.

Evaporator   The component in an A/C system in which heat is absorbed and liquid is changed to a vapor.

Evaporator temperature (EVT) sensor   A sensor used in automatic temperature control systems used to measure the temperature of the evaporator.

Extensions   A socket wrench tool used between a ratchet or breaker bar and a socket.

Eye wash station   A water fountain designed to rinse the eyes with a large volume of water.

Files   A metal smoothing tool.

Fire blanket   A fire-proof wool blanket used to cover a person who is on fire and smother the fire.

Fire extinguisher classes   The types of fires that a fire extinguisher is designed to handle is referred to as fire class.

Flooded   A term that refers to overcharging a system so that liquid refrigerant fills an area.

Flushing   To clean a system by pumping a liquid through it.

GAWR   Gross axle weight rating. A rating of the load capacity of a vehicle and included on placards on the vehicle and in the owner's manual.

Global warming   The increase in average temperature for planet Earth.

Global warming potential (GWP)   The amount that refrigerants are expected to affect the temperature of planet Earth.

Grade   The tensile strength rating of a bolt.

Greenhouse effect   A layer of gases that traps heat at the Earth's surface and lower atmosphere, and it is increasing the temperature of our living area.

Greenhouse gases (GHG)   Gases that will affect the temperature of planet Earth if they escape into the atmosphere.

Groundout   Groundout is a vibrating metal A/C line that contacts another surface which produces noise.

GVWR   Gross vehicle weight rating. The total weight of the vehicle including the maximum cargo.

H-block   The H-block design is a type of TXV that uses four passages and controls the refrigerant flow using opposing pressures.

Hacksaws   A saw that uses a replaceable blade and is used to cut a variety of materials depending on the type of blade used.

Hammers   A hand tool used to deliver a force to a concentrated place.

Hazardous waste materials   Chemicals or components that are no longer needed and that can be a danger to people or the environment.

Heat   A form of energy that raises temperature.

Heater core   The component in a heater system that transfers heat from the coolant to the air.

Heating load   The term used when added heat is needed.

Heating, ventilation, and air conditioning (HVAC)   The term used to describe the heating and air-conditioning system in a vehicle.

Helper pump   An electric water pump used to circulate coolant through a hybrid electric vehicle's heater core when the ICE is in idle stop mode.

HEPA vacuum   High efficiency particulate air filter.

HEV   Hybrid electric vehicle.

High resistance   A circuit with loose or dirty connections that has more resistance than normal.

High side   Part of the A/C system that has high pressure and contains liquid refrigerant.

Hygroscopic   The ability to readily take in and retain moisture.

Identifier   A tester used to determine what the correct refrigerant is for the system being service.

Impeller   In a water pump, coolant enters at the center of the impeller. Centrifugal force throws the coolant outward so that it is discharged at the impeller tips.

Infrared (IR) sensors   A type of sensor used in many automatic air-conditioning systems that are used to detect the temperature of the passenger areas.

Inlet hose   The inlet hose to the heater core connects to an outlet fitting near the engine thermostat, or an area of the engine with the hottest coolant.

Inline filters   A filter that can be installed into a refrigerant line that is designed to trap foreign particles.

Inside air   The air for the HVAC that is drawn from inside the passenger compartment. Also called recirculation.

Insulators A material that does not readily conduct electricity and heat. A nonmetal material that contains more than four electrons in its atom's outer shell.

In-vehicle temperature sensor A thermistor used to measure the temperature of the interior of a vehicle and used in automatic air-conditioning systems.

Latent heat Heat that causes a change in state without a change in temperature.

LED Light-emitting diode. A high-efficiency light source that uses very little electricity and produces very little heat.

Lip seal A type of seal used on A/C compressors. The lip of the seal is made from Teflon and rides against a perfectly smooth portion of the drive shaft.

Liquid line The line that connects the condenser outlet to the receiver–drier inlet or orifice tube and the receiver–drier outlet to the TXV.

Low side Part of the A/C system that has low pressure and contains refrigerant vapor.

Mechanical refrigeration A cooling process that involves pumping a chemical with a very low boiling point through a series of heat exchangers.

Mercury A heavy metal.

Metric bolts Bolts manufactured and sized in the metric system of measurement.

Micron A measurement for deep vacuum, A micron is one millionth of a meter 25,400 microns = 1' Hg.

Mode door A flap valve that moves to divert airflow to the floor, instrument panel, or windshield outlets.

MSDS Material safety data sheets.

Muffler A device that quiets compressor pumping sounds.

Negative temperature coefficient (NTC) A material that decreases in resistance as the temperature increases.

Node A module and computer that is part of a communications network.

Noncondensable gases (NCG) Gases, such as air in an A/C system, that do not readily change to a liquid state as the refrigerant does.

Nuts A female threaded fastener to be used with a bolt or stud.

Ohmmeter An electrical test instrument used to measure resistance in a circuit (in ohms).

Ohm The unit of electrical resistance.

Open circuit An electrical circuit fault caused by a break in the circuit.

Orifice tube (OT) The component in some A/C systems that provides a restriction to meter the refrigerant flow into the evaporator. It causes a pressure buildup in the high side and a pressure drop in the evaporator and low side.

OSHA Occupational Safety and Health Administration. OSHA is the main federal agency responsible for enforcement of workplace safety and health legislation.

Outlet hose The outlet hose from the heater core is connected near the inlet of the water pump, which is the area with the lowest coolant pressure. When the engine runs, coolant flows through the engine's water jackets, past the thermostat, and through the heater core.

Outside air Air that enters the HVAC system from the outside.

Outside air temperature (OAT) sensor The outside air temperature (OAT) sensor, also called the ambient temperature sensor, measures outside air temperature and is often mounted at the radiator shroud or in the area behind the front grill.

Overcharge Too much refrigerant in a system.

Ozone A chemical link between three oxygen atoms (O_3).

Ozone depletion potential (ODP) The amount of effect that certain chemicals have on the ozone layer.

Parallel flow System The flow pattern through a condenser that allows refrigerant flow through more than one path.

Peltier effect A French scientist Peltier found that electrons moving through a solid can carry heat from one side of the material to the other side.

Pinch weld seam A strong section under a vehicle where two body panels are welded together.

Pitch The pitch of a threaded fastener refers to the number of threads per inch.

Plenum The chamber in the A/C and heat unit in which the cool and warm air are blended for the desired temperature.

Pliers A hand tool with two moveable jaws.

PPE Personal protective equipment, which can include gloves, safety glasses, and other items.

Pressure sensor A sensor in a refrigerant line that lets the control module measure the system pressure.

Pressure switch A switch in a refrigerant line that is designed to open or close a certain pressure.

Pressure transducer A pressure transducer can be used in the low- and/or high-pressure refrigerant line. The transducer converts the system pressure into an electrical signal that allows the ECM to monitor pressure.

PTC heater PTC heaters convert electrical energy into heat, and this is used to boost heat to the passenger compartment.

Punches A hand tool designed to be used with a hammer to drive out pins.

Ratchet A handle used to rotate a socket, which is reversible and allows the socket to be rotated in one direction and then free movement in the opposite direction of rotation.

RCRA Resource Conservation and Recovery Act.

Recall A notification to the owner of a vehicle that a safety issue needs to be corrected.

Receiver–drier The component in some A/C systems that contains the desiccant and provides a place to store liquid refrigerant. It is found in the high side.

Recirculation Airflow into the A/C and heat system from the passenger compartment.

Recovery The act of removing refrigerant from a system so that it can be recycled for reuse.

Recycling The act of using portable equipment to clean debris, oil, water, and noncondensable gases from refrigerant so it can be reused in a system.

Reed valves Flexible metal valves that control the refrigerant flow in and out of a compressor's cylinders.

Refrigerant recovery, recycling, and recharging (RRR) A machine used to recover refrigerant from a vehicle and then clean it for later use and recharge a system.

Refrigeration cycle The flow of a refrigerant through the system.

Relative humidity (RH) The amount of water vapor contained in air relative to the maximum amount it can contain at a given temperature.

Relative humidity (RH) sensor A few vehicles use a relative humidity (RH) sensor to determine the level of in-vehicle humidity. High RH increases the cooling load. A relative humidity sensor uses the capacitance change of a polymer thin film capacitor to detect the relative amount of moisture in the air.

Relay An electromagnetic switch.

Reverse cooling A type of cooling system where the coolant flows from the radiator to the cylinder head(s) before flowing to the engine block.

Right-to-know laws Laws that state that employees have a right to know when the materials they use at work are hazardous.

Schematic A wiring schematic, sometimes called a diagram, shows electrical components and wiring using symbols and lines to represent components and wires.

Screwdrivers A hand tool designed to remove or insert screws.

Scroll A smoothly curved passage that changes the fluid flow direction with minimum loss in velocity.

Scroll compressor A compressor design that uses two meshed scrolls to pump refrigerant.

Seal cartridge A compressor shaft seal that keeps refrigerant from leaking.

Seal seat A gasket or rubber O-ring is used so that the seal seat makes a gas-tight seal at the housing, and the seat has an extremely smooth sealing face.

Section 609 Section 609 is a portion of the Clean Air Act that places certain requirements on the mobile vehicle air conditioning (MVAC) service field.

Semiconductor A material that is neither a conductor nor an insulator; has exactly four electrons in the atom's outer shell.

Series flow system In the series flow system, the coolant flows around all the cylinders on each bank. All the coolant flows to the rear of the block, where large main coolant passages allow the coolant to flow across the head gasket.

Series–parallel flow system Some engines use a combination of these two coolant flow systems and call it a series–parallel flow system.

Short-to-ground A short circuit in which the current bypasses some or all the resistance of the circuit and flows to ground. Because ground is usually steel in automotive electricity, a short-to-ground (grounded) is a "copper-to-steel" connection.

Short-to-voltage A circuit in which current flows, but bypasses some or all the resistance in the circuit. A connection that results in a "copper-to-copper" connection.

Sight glass A window in the liquid line or receiver–drier that allows observation of refrigerant flow used in older R-12 systems.

Significant New Alternatives Policy (SNAP) An EPA process for determining acceptable replacement refrigerants for R-12.

Silicone coupling The silicone coupling fan drive is mounted between the drive pulley and the fan.

Slugging Charging liquid into a compressor which can cause severe damage.

Smart control head HVAC control heads that have the ability to process data.

Smart motor HVAC door motors that have the ability to process data.

Snips A hand tool designed to cut sheet metal.

Socket A tool that fits over the head of a bolt or nut and is rotated by a ratchet or breaker bar.

Socket adapter An adapter that allows the use of one size of driver (ratchet or breaker bar) to rotate another drive size of socket.

Solvent A liquid that is used to dissolve and rinse foreign materials from a system.

Spontaneous combustion A process in which a chemical reaction can generate enough heat to start a fire.

SST Special service tools.

Starved An evaporator that has a low pressure, but a temperature that is too warm is called "starved," which means that not enough refrigerant is entering to produce the desired cooling effect.

Steam slits In series flow systems, bleed holes or steam slits in the gasket, block, and head perform the function of letting out the steam.

Stratosphere The earth's upper atmosphere. Most of the earth's ozone is located in the stratosphere.

Stud A short rod with threads on both ends.

Sub-cooling Liquid that is cooled below the point of condensation; the decrease in temperature of the liquid leaving the condenser.

Suction line The line that connects the evaporator outlet to the compressor suction port.

Suction stroke The compressor piston movement that draws refrigerant into the cylinder.

Sun load sensor A sensor that detects the amount of sunlight and radiant heat entering the vehicle.

Superheat Vapor that is heated above the boiling point; the increase in temperature of the evaporator outlet above the inlet.

Surge tank A reservoir mounted at the highest point in the cooling system.

Technical service bulletins (TSBs) Special papers that describe certain repair operations for specific vehicles.

Temperature Temperature is the measure of the level of energy. Temperature is measured in degrees.

Temperature-blend door A door in the A/C and heat system that mixes cold and hot air to get the desired temperature.

Temperature door The door used to adjust air temperature. Also called the blend door.

Tensile strength The maximum stress used under tension (lengthwise force) without causing failure.

Terminal The metal end of a wire which fits into a plastic connector and is the electrical connection part of a junction.

Thermal expansion valve (TXV) The component in some A/C systems that meters the refrigerant flow into the evaporator. It causes a pressure buildup in the high side and a pressure drop in the evaporator and low side.

Thermistor A device used in electrical circuits that changes resistance relative to temperature.

Thermoelectric device (TED) An electrical unit that can produce heat or cold depending on the polarity of the applied current. Used in heated and cooled seats and cup holders.

Thermostatic spring The thermostatic spring operates a valve that allows the fan to freewheel when the radiator is cold. As the radiator warms to about 150°F (65°C), the air hitting the thermostatic spring will cause the spring to change its shape. The new shape of the spring opens a valve that allows the drive to operate like the silicone coupling drive.

Three-position actuator A three-position actuator is able to provide three air door positions, such as the bi-level door, which could allow defrost only, floor only, or a mixture of the two.

Total Environmental Warming Impact (TEWI) The Total Environmental Warming Impact (TEWI) index rates the impact of various refrigerants along with the energy required to perform the cooling operation.

Transducer A device used to change an incoming signal of one type to an outgoing signal of another type.

Trouble light A light used for close viewing of dark areas. Also called a *work light*.

TSB Bulletins issued by vehicle manufacturers to address how to correct known faults or issues.

UNC Unified national coarse.

Undercharge A system that is low on refrigerant.

Underground storage tank (UST) Underground storage tank.

UNF Unified national fine.

Universal joint A joint in a steering or drive shaft that allows torque to be transmitted at an angle.

Used oil Any petroleum-based or synthetic oil that has been used.

Vacuum actuator A device used to move air control doors.

Vane compressor   Vane compressor has vanes that contact the rotor housing at each end, and they slide to make a seal at each end as the rotor turns.

Variable-position actuator   A variable-position actuator is capable of positioning a valve in any position. All variable position actuators use a feedback potentiometer, which is used by the controller to detect the actual position of the door or valve.

VECI   Vehicle emission control information. This sticker is located under the hood on all vehicles and includes emission-related information that is important to the service technician.

VIN   Vehicle identification number. The alphanumeric number identifying vehicle type, assembly plant, powertrain.

Visual inspection   An inspection process using sight, feel, and sound to locate possible problems.

Voltmeter   An electrical test instrument used to measure volts (unit of electrical pressure). A voltmeter is connected in parallel with the unit or circuit being tested.

Volts   The unit of measurement for electrical pressure.

Washers   Flat or shaped pieces of round metal with a hole in the center used between a nut and a part or casting.

WHMIS   Workplace Hazardous Materials Information Systems.

Wrenches   A hand tool used to grasp and rotate a threaded fastener.

INDEX

Note: The letter 'f' following locators refers to figures.